2.5B
EFFECTIVE
MANAGEMENT

First edition June 1988
Second edition July 1989
Revised third edition May 1990

ISBN 0 86277 411 X (previous edition 0 86277 245 1)

A CIP catalogue record for this book is available from the British Library

Published by BPP Publishing Ltd
Aldine House
Aldine Place
142-144 Uxbridge Road
London W12 8AW

We are grateful to the Chartered Association of Certified Accountants and the Chartered Institute of Management Accountants for permission to reproduce past examination questions. The suggested solutions have been prepared by BPP Publishing Ltd. We also wish to express our gratitude to United Biscuits plc for permission to make reference to their corporate Ethics and Operating Principles.

DACOSTA PRINT
111 SALUSBURY ROAD
LONDON NW6 6RG
01-969 1111

©

BPP Publishing Limited

1990

CONTENTS

CONTENTS

PREFACE

In 1988 a substantial review of all its examination syllabuses by the ACCA led to a new syllabus being examinable from June 1989. In March 1990, however, the Association took the opportunity to revise the 2.5B syllabus once again, and also to change its name to *Effective Management*. The main effect of this revision is that there is now more emphasis on *management* as opposed to *organisation; that is, on the manager's exercise of discretion and responsibility*. The sections on management information systems have also been removed. It is examinable for the first time at the June 1991 examination (the international perspective being examinable only from June 1992).

As the leading publisher of ACCA texts, BPP welcomes the opportunity provided by the revised 1990 syllabus. Back in 1988 we brought out a completely new range of ACCA texts and kits, the aim being to provide the freshest and most comprehensive study aids available for ACCA students, and they were all updated in 1989. Now in 1990 we have substantially revised and updated our 2.5B text to reflect the 1990 syllabus alterations examinable from June 1991. So as ever you can be assured that your BPP Study Text is comprehensive, on-target and up-to-date - to meet *your* study needs.

You will find an expanded 'Study Guide' version of the new 1990 syllabus issued by the Association reproduced on pages (vi) and (vii).

BPP Publishing Ltd
May 1990

Objectives of the syllabus

The objectives of the syllabus are to ensure students:

- develop a broad awareness and understanding of concepts and theories and their practical application to the structure, functions and operation of business, commercial and public sector organisations, and of their interaction with national and international environments;

- develop a broad awareness and understanding of selected principles, practices and skills associated with the effective management of business and commercial enterprises, and public sector organisations;

- develop appropriate personal, communication and presentation skills to enhance their ability to use and apply within the work context the principles, practices and skills contained in this syllabus. Students should recognise (i) the need for information to be presented in a logical, coherent and consistent manner; and (ii) the importance of communicating effectively to others the implications of alternative policies and courses of action available to the organisation.

This paper is designed to ensure that students as accountants are familiar with the principles and practices associated with effective management, as these will enable them to participate fully in the planning, implementation and control of the policies and operations of the organisation. Students must also be aware of the importance of the relationship, in the running of the organisation, of the accounting and finance function (as studied in other papers) with other functional areas.

Format and standard of the examination paper

From December 1991 students will be required to answer four out of six questions. The first question will be compulsory, will be based upon a case study and will carry 28 marks. Students will be asked to answer this mini-case study in the form of a report to management. They will then choose three from the remaining five questions on the paper. Each of these questions will carry 24 marks. Within the maximum marks available for each question, marks will be awarded for written format and presentation.

Transitional arrangements for the June 1991 exam are that 5 out of 7 non-compulsory questions must be answered, one of which will be a report and two of which will be mini-case studies.

The standard of the examination paper will be comparable to that required in the second year of a three year UK honours degree course. Students will be expected to have an understanding of the content of all Level 1 papers. Students who have received exemption from any of these papers should read the relevant study guide(s) to ensure they are familiar with the coverage and approach required.

Students who select this option are advised to study it in conjunction with paper 2.6 Decision Making Techniques and prior to studying paper 2.7 Management Information Systems. The communication and presentation skills covered in this syllabus will also be of value to students when preparing for the remaining papers at Level 2 and Level 3.

SECTION 1 BUSINESS ORGANISATION

Knowledge level

Types of business organisation:

B

- private and public sector;
- co-operatives.

STUDY GUIDE

Formal organisation and structure: F

- scalar chain, hierarchy;
- span of control;
- line, staff and functional organisation;
- organisation by geographic area, function, product, brand or customer;
- centralisation, decentralisation;
- divisionalisation.

Small business management: B

- financing the small business;
- risk and the problems facing the small business.

SECTION 2 BUSINESS FUNCTIONS

Marketing: B

- the marketing concept and the marketing objective of the business;
- managing the relationship with clients/customers.

Research and development; the development of new products and services.   B

Production and operations management; Just In Time techniques.   B

Control and management of quality: B

- techniques of quality control and quality assurance;
- Quality Circles;
- concepts of Total Quality Management.

Purchasing and materials management.   B

SECTION 3 PRINCIPLES OF MANAGEMENT

Styles of management and motivation, and their conceptual/theoretical basis: F

- Theory X/authoritarian types;
- Theory Y/consultative - participative types;
- Theory Z (Ouchi).

Delegation, authority and responsibility.   F

Communication process: F

- communication methods (verbal and written), communication networks;
- barriers to communication;
- the role of interviews, meetings, committees; chairing and minuting, conferences.

Monitoring and controlling performance: F

- plans, standards, measurement criteria;
- feedback, comparison and control loops.

Boundary management: B

-   environmental, legal, customer and other constraints on the exercise of
    managerial authority;
-   stakeholder analysis;
-   social responsibility.

SECTION 4 MANAGEMENT SKILLS AND FUNCTIONS

Knowledge level

Business planning and strategic management.   B

Co-ordination and integration of tasks, workflows, functions and structures.   B

Leadership.   B

Organisational culture and style.   B

Role of innovation and intrapreneurship/entrepreneurship in business development
and growth.   B

The pursuit of "excellence" (Peters and Waterman etc).   B

Personnel management: F

-   recruitment and selection;
-   staff appraisal;
-   training and management development;
-   developing teamwork;
-   manpower planning;
-   employment termination and dismissal.

Personal skills of written communication and report writing, and other relevant
written presentational skills.   F

The management of professionally qualified staff.   F

The international perspective: thinking globally and managing locally.   B

FOREWORD

Note: the knowledge levels

Each topic in the study guide has been allocated a knowledge level. Three have been used:

I *Introductory*. Basic understanding of principles, concepts, theories and techniques.

B *Broad*. Application of principles, concepts, theories and techniques in the solution of straightforward problems.

F *Full*. Identification and solution of more complex problems through the selection and application of principles, concepts, theories and techniques.

> The knowledge level can change as the importance of a particular topic changes. Topics and their amended knowledge levels will be published in the *Students' Newsletter*.

Format of the exam paper

In the June 1991 examination you are required to answer 5 questions out of 7 set (all worth 20 marks). One question on the paper will require an answer in the form of a report. Two will be contextual questions, like a mini case study. Advice on how to tackle case-study questions is given below.

In December 1991 a new format will come into operation. One compulsory case study, to be answered in report form, is worth 28 marks. There will then be a choice of 3 out of five questions, worth 24 marks each. Marks will be awarded for presentation quality and written format.

Past examination papers

Apart from the syllabus and study guide, and any Exam Notes and articles that appear in the *'Newsletter'*, guidance on the kind of question that may appear in the examination can be gained from papers set under previous syllabuses. As you look at the following review, however, you should bear in mind that the revised 1990 syllabus:

- does not contain industrial relations and informal organisation, nor the detailed behavioural aspects and quantitative techniques that were in the pre-1988 syllabus

- gives a more practical and managerial emphasis by 'pruning' of the pre-1988 'Nature of undertakings' and 'People in undertakings' sections

- adds topics to the pre-1988 syllabus including:
  - small business management
  - entrepreneurship and business development
  - teamwork
  - the Japanese experience

} differences from the pre-1988 syllabus

FOREWORD

- does not contain management information systems

- gives a more practical and managerial emphasis by pruning the 1988 'Approaches to Management and Motivation' section

- adds topics to the 1988 syllabus including:
  - organisation by brand or customer
  - research and development management, operations management, quality control and purchasing management
  - chairing and minuting of meetings
  - stakeholder analysis
  - organisational culture and style, excellence
  - personal communication skills
  - the international perspective on management (not examinable until June 1992)

> differences from the 1988 syllabus

Note that in the analysis below, topics marked by an asterisk (*) are no longer included in the 1990 revised 2.5B *Effective Management* syllabus.

December 1989

1 The co-operative enterprise
2 Centralisation and decentralisation
3 The marketing concept and financial services
4 Theory Z
5 Barriers to communication; written and oral media
6 Principles of control
7 Improvement of training and competence

June 1989

1 Sole traders and partnerships
2 Types of production; quality control
3 Human Relations and Sociotechnical Systems*
4 Stakeholders and the constraints on managerial discretion
5 Staff appraisal
6 Management of professionally qualified staff
7 Strategic analysis, choice and implementation

December 1988

1 Role and function of chairman and directors*
2 Application of systems theory to organisation and management*
3 Objectives and stages of recruitment and selection
4 Planning, organising, directing, controlling
5 Role and purpose of MIS*; cost/benefit of computerisation*
6 Functional, line and staff authority
7 Role and function of PR department

FOREWORD

June 1988

1 Contribution of F W Taylor*
2 Line, staff and function in the accounting function
3 Principles of control systems
4 Role of R and D; management problems
5 Case study: integration of activities, introduction of teamwork
6 Information inputs for corporate appraisal, corporate planning, strategic management
7 Role of trade unions in employer/employee relations*

December 1987

1 Contingency approach*
2 Importance, advantages and disadvantages of committees
3 Feasibility study and market investigation: computerised MIS*
4 Quality circles
5 Corporate planning
6 Analysis and improvement of group motivation
7 Product life cycle and product development

June 1987

1 Brief notes on:
   (a) human relations school*
   (b) small business proprietorship
   (c) principles of delegation
2 Theories X, Y, Z
3 CPA and PERT*
4 Difficulties facing nationalised and semi-state enterprises
5 Co-ordination and integration
6 Quality control
7 Problems implementing computer-based MIS*

December 1986

1 Brief notes on:
   (a) main systems of production
   (b) databases and their applications*
   (c) consumerism
2 Main features of the systems approach
3 Line, staff and functional authority
4 The organisational purpose of divisionalisation
5 The marketing concept and other business orientations
6 Unitary and pluralistic attitudes towards industrial relations*
7 Barriers to communication

June 1986

1 Brief notes on:
   (a) theory Z
   (b) co-operative enterprises
   (c) the manager's choice between written and oral communication
2 Comparison of private sector with public sector enterprises

FOREWORD

How to use this study text

This text is structured according to the 1990 revised 2.5(B) syllabus. You will find that the section and chapter titles correspond closely with the topics set out in the study guide.

Each chapter opens with a list of topics covered, and a brief statement of study objectives.

At the conclusion of each chapter, there is a set of short questions which are a test of knowledge to be completed after the text has been studied. Answers should be checked against the paragraph references provided after each question. Some of the questions are longer exam-type problems, and are accompanied by brief points for discussion.

At the back of the text there is a bank of illustrative questions of examination standard. To obtain maximum benefit, these should be attempted as far as possible under examination conditions. Suggested solutions are provided.

Looking things up in the text

On page (iii) of this text you will find a contents list giving chapter titles and their page numbers.

At the beginning of each section of the text, there is a further indication of the contents and objectives of the section. A more detailed list of the topics dealt with in the chapters is given at the start of each one.

Finally, a detailed index at the back of the text enables you to refer easily to specific syllabus topics and other points.

Examination technique

Never forget that *Effective Management* is essentially a very practical subject where general knowledge and basic common sense need to be allied with a sound grasp of the principles involved. Remember also that this is a paper where the examiner is not merely seeking to test your theoretical knowledge of the underlying theory, but is also testing your ability to identify and solve problems and to communicate clearly.

The examiner's report on the December 1989 examination (set under the 1988 syllabus) pinpointed a number of ways in which students could do better justice to their knowledge:

● answer the question as set;
● plan and structure answers;
● illustrate answers with diagrams, examples from a local context and personal experience;
● prepare for the examination properly, particularly by studying the *entire* syllabus;
● answer all questions required by the rubric and all parts of each question attempted;
● 'set the scene' to an answer by making initial definitions or introductions;
● use common sense and think before writing;
● do not make unjustified generalisations;
● be familiar with the subject's 'jargon'.

FOREWORD

You have to answer 4 questions in three hours: this means that it will be essential for you to plan your timing and your answers carefully. Planning involves:

- reading quickly through the question to get the general feel of it;
- going through the question more slowly a second time, jotting down in note form what you see as being the main points on which you will need to elaborate;
- numbering the points in your answer plan so as to get them into a logical sequence.

Use your notes as a *checklist* to ensure that you haven't forgotten any important points, and to judge how far you have got in your answer as you keep an eye on the clock.

Finally, *read the question carefully, answer the question set* and *don't forget to state the obvious*.

Answering case study questions

Question 1 of the *Effective Management* paper is a 28-mark compulsory case study. Students frequently have difficulty in answering this type of question because:

(a) it does not simply require a *description* of a topic;
(b) it requires knowledge and understanding of the *application* of an idea to a particular situation or problem;
(c) it often involves more than one topic and an understanding of the *relationship* of several topics within a given problem.

Case studies test your ability to apply your knowledge in a practical way. They also test your appproach to problem solving. The examiner wishes to see you have benefited by your studies in applying a logical and systematic analysis to a problem; that you are aware of the *range* of causes and possible solutions to any given problem; and that you would be certain you had *identified* the causes of the problem before selecting any solution. The systematic approach to problem solving involves several stages in a carefully ordered sequence.

1 Define the problem.
2 Identify the factors likely to be causing the problem.
3 Collect and analyse the relevant facts.
4 Identify the range of alternative courses of action likely to solve the problem.
5 Examine the consequences of taking each action.
6 Select and implement the best course of action.
7 Follow up to ensure your actions have solved the problem.

Approach to case study questions

First of all   Read the case slowly and carefully. Ensure you have identified all the people, actions and issues involved in the case.

Be sure you know precisely what the question directs you to do in relation to the case: for example

    (a)   What is going wrong?
           What is your analysis of the situation?
    (b)   How would you help...?
           What other approaches could be tried?

Be sure you know the difference between these directions, but note that they frequently occur together, in which case your answer must cover *both* parts of the question.

Then   Re-read the case and make an *answer plan* relating the question to the factors you see in the case.

Step 1   Start your answer with a clear definition of the problem. Ensure you have identified the problem and not simply its symptoms.

Step 2   Identify and list the factors likely to be causing the problem. (There will often be 4-6 possible causes, so don't be satisfied with identifying a single cause).

Step 3   Demonstrate in your discussion how you would collect the relevant facts *before* attempting to solve the problem, eg check the records, interview appropriate staff. Analyse the facts and identify the actual cause(s) of the problem.

Step 4   Show, by writing down a list, that you are aware of the range of possible courses of action and the consequences of each.

Step 5   Demonstrate in your answer that you would only select the appropriate course of action *after* analysing the relevant facts and information. Refer to any constraints which would affect your selection, eg limited resources and time, company rules and policies.

Step 6   Show how you would implement your plan of action, eg counselling staff concerned, making arrangements for transfers, training and job changes.

Step 7   Always show how you would follow up or check back to ensure your actions have in fact solved the problem.

It is useful to remember that your *answer* should contain *seven steps* starting with a definition of the problem and finishing with the checks to ensure you have solved the problem. The two initial steps of reading and re-reading, and constructing the answer plan are also very important.

Practice in case study questions

Read the following case very carefully. Follow the problem-solving approach outlined in the previous section and prepare an answer in 45 minutes. When you have completed your answer compare this with the illustrative answer given on the next page. Identify any gaps or steps you left out. Re-examine the case to discover any clues or evidence you ignored in analysing the case. Ensure you understand *why* the factors identified might be causes of this particular problem.

The following exchanges were overheard in an office of an organisation:

Manager: I asked for this report on Friday - what delayed you?

Supervisor: I was trying to clear up the end-of-quarter returns.

Manager: But it's already the fourth of the month.

Supervisor: Yes, but I had two clerks away on holiday at the same time.

Manager: How did that happen?

Supervisor: Well they asked me separately - a few weeks apart - and I hadn't realised what the consequences would be.

Manager: I'm afraid it is not good enough. I am constantly having to complain about work which is produced at the last moment - or later. It is often badly prepared and faulty. What are you going to do about it?

Supervisor: I don't know. I never have the time to think ahead.

How would you help this supervisor?

Illustrative answer

Step 1   We should note on reading the case:

The problem   (a)   the supervisor is late with his reports and they are often badly prepared;
(b)   he has failed to anticipate and plan for the effects of two staff being on holiday;
(c)   these situations are not rare occurences since the manager is 'constantly' complaining;
(d)   the manager does not appear to have any plan himself to correct this situation;
(e)   the supervisor appears to be hard-working but is this enough for effective management?

Step 2
Causes   The question directs us to show *how* we would help this particular supervisor. To do this rationally we must define what the problem is and be sure we know what its causes are. Possible causes might include:

(a)   inability of the supervisor;
(b)   lack of proper procedures (eg holiday indent forms) to help the supervisor;
(c)   overwork of the supervisor;
(d)   poor help and advice from the manager.

Step 3
Analysis   Information needs to be gathered on the qualifications and training of the supervisor, the extent and effectiveness of formal procedures in the organisations, the amount of work loaded onto the supervisor and the training of the manager. This appears to be problem of a failure to *plan*. The problem might be aggravated by:

(a)   inability of the supervisor to *delegate*; and
(b)   the failure of his manager to provide help.

The likely factors actually causing the problem would include the following:

(a)   the supervisor does not know how to plan or does not see the need for planning;
(b)   the supervisor is overworked or fails to delegate and therefore has not got the time to plan and organise;
(c)   the supervisor may have been badly selected and does not possess the qualities of effective management;
(d)   the manager has given no coaching to help him overcome his difficulties;
(e)   the manager does not give enough information or time to allow his subordinate to plan.

Step 4
Courses of action

The appropriate help would depend on a complete analysis of the facts related to this problem which could only be made after interviewing both the manager and the supervisor, checking the records for evidence of the kinds of mistakes and their effects on the performance of the supervisor's section, with careful distinction between facts and opinions.

The nature of the help given to solve this problem would depend on causes disclosed by the evidence but could include the following:

- The *manager* should be counselled:
  (a) to ensure his subordinates understand their jobs and their wider significance on performance;
  (b) to provide the resources and information necessary for effective planning;
  (c) to provide feed-back on their performance and be prepared to coach, train or counsel to ensure they plan effectively;
  (d) to provide example by his own approach to planning and reward those who follow his example.

- The *subordinate* should be counselled:

  (a) so that he sees the need for planning and delegation within the wider framework of effective management of his section;
  (b) so that he accepts the need for further training in planning if this is considered necessary;
  (c) to accept the help of his manager and to follow his example and discuss with his own subordinates the appropriate approaches to delegation.

Steps 5 and 6
Select and implement course of action

The best course of action might be a combination of these alternatives. The actions must be combined into a plan which is adequately discussed and communicated to both people to ensure they know their part in the plan. The extent to which the supervisor can be retrained depends on how able he is and how much time is still available. If the problem is seen as really pressing it may be better to replace the supervisor with a better skilled one.

Step 7
Follow up

Allow a suitable amount of time for the plan to take effect. Follow up. Has the problem been solved? It might be necessary to consider:

(a) further training and counselling;
(b) transfer of the subordinate to other duties;
(c) dismissal in the unlikely case of wilful dereliction of duties.

SECTION 1

BUSINESS ORGANISATION

Topics covered in this section

- Chapter 1:   Types of business organisation

- Chapter 2:   Formal organisation structure

- Chapter 3:   Small business management

Objectives of this section

This section of the study text is designed to cover the first part of the 2.5B syllabus, and to describe the context in which the practice of management takes place. It sets out the particular characteristics, opportunities and problems of different types and sizes of business organisation, and the features of formal organisation structure.

Chapter 1

TYPES OF BUSINESS ORGANISATION

Topics covered in this chapter

- Why organisations exist
- Types of business organisation
- Private enterprises
  - o Sole traders
  - o Partnerships
  - o Private limited companies and public limited companies
  - o Holding companies
- Public sector organisations
- Other types of institution
  - o Trade unions and trade associations
  - o Co-operatives
- Reasons for organisations

Purpose of this chapter

To take an introductory look at the nature of business organisation and its various forms.

- **Why organisations exist**

1. The *Effective Management* syllabus is concerned with the nature, structure and functioning of organisations, and the principles on which they should (or might) be managed. Organisations pervade our lives and every individual is a member of many organisations whether large or small, formal or informal, or existing for social, economic, religious, political, military, governmental or educational purposes.

2. The principles of organisation and management extend not only to businesses and commercial enterprises, but also to nationalised industries, national government, local government, co-operative societies, trade unions, social clubs, political groups and parties, churches, the armed forces, hospitals, the police, the fire service, schools, colleges and universities, prisons, trade associations, charitable institutions and many other groups and bodies.

3. ‘Organisation’ (or ‘organising’) in a management context means defining the tasks that must be completed to achieve corporate aims and then grouping the work into logical areas and allocating authority and responsibility to carry out those tasks.

4. In general terms, organisations exist because they can achieve results which individuals cannot achieve alone. By grouping together, individuals overcome limitations imposed by both the physical environment and also their own biological limitations. Chester Barnard (1956) described the situation of a man trying to move a stone which was too large for him:

   (a) the stone was too big for the man (environmental limitation) and
   (b) the man was too small for the stone (biological limitation).

   By forming an organisation with another man, it was possible to move the stone with the combined efforts of the two men together.

5. Barnard further suggested that the limitations on man's accomplishments are determined by the effectiveness of his organisation.

Reasons for organisations

6. In greater detail, the reasons for organisations may be described as follows:

   (a) *social reasons:* to meet an individual's need for companionship;

   (b) to *enlarge abilities:* organisations increase productive ability because they make possible both:
   (i) specialisation; and
   (ii) exchange.

   The potential benefits of specialisation were recognised by Adam Smith in his famous book *The wealth of nations* (1776). Specialisation permeates our modern industrial and commercial society. (It has been suggested that increased specialisation tends to reduce job satisfaction - Shepard 1970);

   (c) to *accumulate knowledge* (for subsequent re-use and further learning);

   (d) to *save time:* organisations make it possible for objectives to be reached in a shorter time. (Reduction in the time required to reach an objective may result in some organisation inefficiency. For example, a company may spend £1 million on a crash programme to develop and launch a new product. The crash programme might be both costly and inefficient, but the time saved might be justified in terms of getting into the market ahead of competitors with rival product development.)

7. Organisations can have a synergistic effect. Synergy is explained, briefly, as the principle that $2 + 2 = 5$. In other words, by bringing together two separate and individual 'units of resource' the output of the units combined will exceed the joint output of the separated units so that:
   (a) before their combination, $2 + 2 = 4$; and
   (b) after their combination, $2 + 2 = 5$.

   Thus if A can grow 1,000 units of a product on his land, and B can grow 800 units on his land, by combining their resources (perhaps to buy some modern farming equipment and to organise their work more efficiently) they might succeed in growing, say, 2,100 units of the product.

1: TYPES OF BUSINESS ORGANISATION

● **Types of business organisation**

8. Business organisations may be of various types, which differ from each other according to:

> ● the ownership of capital invested;
> ● the amount of capital invested;
> ● the control of the enterprise's conduct;
> ● the accountability of its controllers;
> ● the division of profits; and
> ● the objects of the enterprise.

9. *The ownership of capital invested*. The owners of capital might be:

(a) shareholders. Shareholders in turn might be private individuals, companies or other organisations. Some of these shareholding organisations might be 'institutional investors' such as pension funds, insurance companies and unit trusts which specialise in holding the shares and loan stock of other organisations;

(b) providers of debt capital and other depositors of funds. Many organisations rely on borrowing for much of their capital. Debentures and other forms of loan capital feature in the balance sheets of companies, and banks lend much money to other businesses. Some organisations rely almost entirely on deposits from other people to conduct their operations: examples are banks, building societies and pension funds;

(c) the government. Government agencies and public corporations, indeed national and local government itself, are financed by public money.

10. *The amount of capital invested*. Organisations range from those with very small amounts of capital to the very large.

11. *The control of the enterprise's conduct*. Most business organisations are controlled by a board of directors or a similar management board. However, directors might be part-time or full-time, and they might or might not have an 'equity' (ownership) interest in the organisation. In large business organisations, much authority is delegated by the board of directors to career managers.

12. *The accountability of its controllers*. The controllers of a business organisation must be accountable to its owners. The owners might be the directors themselves, other shareholders or a government department. In the case of government business organisations there might also be accountability to a 'watchdog' committee and, in the end, to the electorate.

13. *The division of profits*. Some business organisations retain most of their profits for re-investment in the business, whereas others pay out most of their profits (as dividends or profit shares) to their owners. In some cases, a part of the profits might be paid to the organisation's employees as part of an incentive/reward scheme.

14. *The objects of the enterprise*. Every business organisation has its own objects. These are discussed later.

15.

> A common method of classifying business units is to divide them into:
>
> - private enterprises;
> - non-profit-making units - charities, educational institutions, professional bodies;
> - public sector organisations, comprising national and local government, public corporations and nationalised industries.

16. This method of classifying units is basically according to ownership.

(a) Private enterprises are owned and operated by certain clearly identified individuals who are also entitled to the rewards of the undertaking.

(b) Non-profit-making groups exist to confer benefits or promote objectives which may or may not involve commercial activities. Surpluses, if any, are merely incidental and may be shared between the membership or used to further the aims of the society.

(c) In the case of public sector organisations, the enterprise is publicly owned and operated, possibly on a commercial basis, but with the intention of supplying goods (or, more often, services) for the benefit of the whole community. The initial legislation setting up a public corporation or nationalised industry might require profitability to be an objective 'taking one year with another' - that is, in the long run.

17. Another common method of categorising business units is to make a distinction between manufacturing and service organisations. In countries of the Western world, employment in service organisations is increasing whereas employment in manufacturing has declined. In the UK, most manufacturing organisations are private enterprises, and public sector organisations typically provide services.

- **Private enterprises**

18. Private enterprises include:

(a) sole traders;
(b) partnerships;
(c) limited partnerships;
(d) private limited companies;
(e) public limited companies; and
(f) holding companies (which are themselves private or public limited companies).

Sole traders

19. A sole trader is a person who runs a business on his own account, contributing the capital to start the enterprise, running it with or without employees, and earning the profits or standing the loss of the venture.

    His business is a separate accounting entity - accounts are prepared for the business as an entity - but the business does not have its own 'legal personality.' Anyone making a legal contract with a sole trader does so with the trader as an individual, and does not make a contract with the trader's business.

20. Sole traders are found mainly in the retail trades (eg corner shops, local newsagencies), small scale service industries (eg garages, plumbers, office cleaning), and small manufacturing and craft industries (eg furniture making, bespoke tailoring and pottery).

21. The advantages of being a sole trader are:

    (a) no formal procedures are required to set up in business (except that for certain classes of business a licence must be obtained, eg retailing wines and spirits, operating a taxicab);

    (b) independence and self-accountability - a sole trader is under no obligation to consult others about the business decisions he takes and has no need to reveal the state of the business to anyone (except the tax authorities each year);

    (c) personal supervision of the business by the sole trader should ensure its effective operation. Decision-making will be speedier than if it involved reference to others. Close personal contact between the proprietor and clients/customers may enable the organisation to adapt to the environment;

    (d) the sole trader gains all the profits from his efforts, which can be a powerful motivator, and satisfying to the individual whose ability/energy results in reward.

22. The disadvantages of being a sole trader include:

    (a) the proprietor's 'unlimited liability' which means that he is personally liable to the full extent of his private assets for the debts of his business. If the business gets into debt, a sole trader will stand to lose his personal wealth (eg private house) if the debts are called in. This means that a sole tradership can have serious financial risks associated with it for the trader;

    (b) expansion of the business is usually only possible by ploughing back the profits of the business as further capital, although loans may be available from banks or personal contacts;

    (c) the business has a high dependence on the individual which can mean long working hours and difficulties during sickness or holidays;

    (d) the death of the proprietor may make it necessary to sell the business in order to pay the resulting tax liabilities. In any case, there may be a problem of succession: family members may not *wish* to continue the business;

(e) the individual may only have one skill. A sole trader may be, say, a good technical engineer or craftsman but may lack the skills to market effectively or maintain accounting records to control his business effectively;

(f) disadvantages associated with small size: the risks and problems of small business management are discussed in a later chapter, but include lack of diversification, absence of economies of scale, problems of raising finance etc.

Partnerships

23. A partnership is a particularly suitable form of business organisation for professional people. Indeed solicitors and doctors are only allowed to operate as sole traders or partnerships (although the Companies Act 1989 now allows firms of auditors to become incorporated). It is also suitable for many other small-scale enterprises similar to those operated by sole traders, where there are two or more 'joint' owners.

24. The reasons for taking a partner or partners include:

(a) increased capital, permitting more rapid expansion. Two or more partners can provide more finance than a single trader;

(b) the spread of the financial and operating responsibilities;

(c) the contribution of wider experience and skills to the firm, eg a technical man can combine with a marketing man;

(d) the continuing privacy of the affairs of the business, so that partners are under no obligation to show their accounts to anyone (except the tax authorities).

25. The disadvantages of a partnership are that:
(a) the partners still have unlimited liability for the debts of the business;
(b) the independence of the individual is lost as each partner must consult the others and consider their views every time a decision of any consequence is made.

Limited partnerships

26. The Limited Partnership Act 1907 permits a partnership between an active partner and one or more 'sleeping' partners. The sleeping partner contributes funds to the business and can receive a share of profits; he does not take any part in the conduct of the business of the management of the firm. In this case, the principle of limited liability applies to the sleeping partner who is liable only to the extent of the capital he has contributed to the business.

Private limited companies and public limited companies

27. These two types of business unit are closely connected since they are controlled by the Companies Act 1985. The Companies Act requires public limited companies to include 'Public Limited Co' or 'plc' in their names. Private limited companies must include 'Limited' or 'Ltd' in their names. Private limited companies are normally smaller enterprises whereas public companies can vary from quite a modest size up to multi-million pound international companies.

> The main difference between them concerns ownership and transferability of shares.
>
> - *Private* companies are often, but not always, owned by a small number of shareholders, whereas *public* companies are (usually, but not always) owned by a wider section of the investing public.
>
> - Shares in *public* companies are usually traded on an official stock market whereas shares in *private* companies cannot be traded on these markets. Shares in private companies are only transferable with the consent of the shareholders, which helps to explain why ownership is often confined to members of a family or a group of associates.

28. The reasons for forming a limited company, either private or public, are mainly to obtain sufficient capital (rarely can one person find enough for a large undertaking) and to obtain the benefits of *limited liability*. The two are interrelated, since if people know their liability is limited to the amount of capital they wish to invest then they are probably prepared to risk that amount in business; if they could be called upon to subscribe additional amounts or be responsible for a company's debts they might not invest anything. Hence limited liability companies are a means of bringing capital and enterprise together.

29. A company is formed by the promoters signing a memorandum of association setting out the objectives of the company and giving details such as its name, location and share capital, together with the articles of association which regulate the internal affairs of the company.

    The company is then registered by the Registrar of Companies who issues a Certificate of Incorporation.

    The Certificate of Incorporation bestows on the company a separate legal personality. It can therefore do all the legal things that are available to an ordinary person, eg it can own property, employ people and be involved in legal action.

30. The separate legal personality of the company, and the limited liability of its shareholders, are two important characteristics that distinguish companies from sole traders or partnerships.

31. Before a company can begin trading it must obtain the capital it requires. In a private company this will largely be contributed by the promoters or founders. As regards a public company, it will be obtained from the public either directly or indirectly through institutional investors such as insurance companies, pension funds, etc.

32. Many companies start in a small way, often as family businesses which operate as private companies, then grow to the point where they become public companies and can invite the public to subscribe for shares. The new capital thus made available enables the firm to expand its activities and achieve the advantages of large scale operation.

33. The company has a separate identity from the shareholders, and it is not managed or run by them. It is controlled by the directors and management but the shareholders or members may elect a new board of directors at the annual general meeting if they wish to do so. The shareholders' main function is the provision of capital and taking the risk that the company will succeed or fail. In return they receive their share of the profits as dividends. If the company fails, they stand to make a loss, but only to the extent of the capital which they have subscribed – this is the full extent of their limited liability.

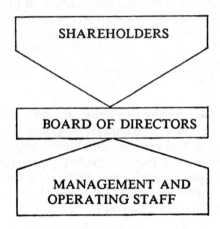

The board of directors controls management and staff, and is accountable to the shareholders, but it has responsibilities towards both groups – owners and employees alike.

1. Shareholders may consist of large institutional investors, such as insurance companies and pension funds, or private individuals. Many companies encourage their staff to invest in the company; for example, when British Telecom was floated on the stock exchange in 1984 employees were encouraged to acquire shares and preference was given to them when shares were allocated to the many applicants for them. Companies are likely to have one or more large shareholders owning a significant proportion of the total 'equity', say 5% or more.

2. Directors are often shareholders. 'Directors' can be divided into executive directors, who participate in the daily operations of the organisation, and non-executive directors, who are invited to join in an advisory capacity, usually to bring their particular skills or experience to the discussions of the board.

3. Operational management usually consists of career managers who are recruited to operate the business, and are accountable to the board. They too will often be shareholders.

Holding companies

34. Broadly speaking, a company has control of another company when it holds more then 50% of its voting shares. It is then said to be a *holding* company.

The company whose shares are owned by the holding company is called a *subsidiary*.

A holding company and its subsidiary or several subsidiaries form a *group* of companies.

35. There are several distinguishing features about holding and subsidiary companies as business organisations.

    (a) They provide an organisation structure for a large business with widespread interests. Putting all the operations of a business into a single company might be too cumbersome.

    (b) A holding company can control a range of business activities of various subsidiary companies, without owning 100% of the equity of the subsidiaries.

    (c) They provide a business structure that makes easier either:

        (i) growth through the acquisition of other companies, or
        (ii) 'rationalisation' through selling off parts of the business - selling off the shares of a subsidiary company to someone else.

36. A holding company can acquire other companies by purchasing their shares for cash, but a feature of growth through acquisition is that a holding company might buy the shares of another company by offering its own shares in exchange. For example, holding company X might purchase subsidiary company Y by offering its own shares (shares in company X) in exchange for the shares of Y. Former shareholders of company Y would then become shareholders of company X.

37. Acquiring companies in this way removes the need for cash to buy them, and many groups of companies in the past have expanded in this way. There are different strategies for expansion:

    (a) *Horizontal integration* occurs when one company buys up a competitor in the same line of business, in order to gain a bigger share of the market; for instance, a multiple chain store organisation might buy a sole trader's shop, or the store of a rival company, in order to open up a new retail outlet in a different town.

    (b) *Vertical integration* occurs when a company buys another business with the intention of operating more stages in the provision of a particular product or service. For example, in the cotton textile industry the stages of a product's manufacture and development are supply of the raw materials, carding, spinning, weaving, bleaching, dyeing, finishing and printing, wholesaling and retail selling to the final consumer. A company engaged in vertical integration would be extending the activities into another stage of the product, additional to the stages it is already engaged in.

        (i) Backwards vertical integration occurs when a company extends its activities back towards the supply of raw materials, with the intention of being able to control the supply. For example, an oil refinery company might expand by integrating backwards to acquire oil tankers or oil production fields.

        (ii) Forward vertical integration occurs when a company extends its activities forwards towards the final consumer. For example, an oil refinery company might integrate forwards to acquire delivery vehicles for oil products (eg a petrol tanker fleet) and petrol filling stations.

> Oil companies such as Shell, BP and Esso are examples of multinational companies that have achieved vertical integration through every stage of their product's development, from exploration to the sale of the end product to the consumer, and they have used a 'group' structure of holding company and subsidiary companies in achieving integration.

(c) *Diversification* occurs when a company takes over other companies operating in a completely different line of business. For example, a tobacco manufacturing company might diversify into other industries, such as insurance or the hotel business. Diversification is a way of spreading risks and seizing whatever profitable business opportunities that have arisen - it is useful for companies in an industry with an uncertain future (eg cigarette companies) but other large holding companies such as Hanson Trust 'specialise' in diversification (acquiring and selling off subsidiaries to make profits).

● **Public sector organisations**

38. About two thirds of the UK economy and a larger part of commerce is conducted by private enterprise firms of one kind or another. The remainder of the activities of the economy are conducted by publicly owned enterprises. Public enterprises might be run as government departments (eg the armed forces and police services), as nationalised industries (eg the Post Office) or as boards with an ultimate responsibility to the Minister of State (eg British Rail, British Coal).

39. Some activities, like the armed services, police, customs, coastguards etc, are clearly the sort of institutions which the State itself should control. Other activities have tended, in the past, to be performed by the State or local authorities because they are non-profit-making and as such are unlikely to be attractive to commercial operations, except on possibly a small scale at prices only payable by a small sector of the community. Therefore education, health and social services and hospitals are operated (at present) as publicly provided amenities for the benefit of all citizens.

40. Certain goods and services are by their nature monopolies, such as gas, electricity, water supply and some forms of transport. These natural monopolies have in the past been run in the UK by nationalised institutions, or by municipal authorities, for economic, political or social reasons. In the 1980s the reasons have become less persuasive and heretofore public enterprises, such as British Telecom, British Gas and the water boards are now private corporations. You should be aware of the fact that not every country operates in the same way. In the United States, for example, electricity and telephone services have been private enterprise corporations for a long time.

41. There are other industries such as coal, steel, aircraft-operation and ship-building that are not natural monopolies, but in which nationalisation was a result of a range of more complex factors, mainly political, ideological and social. In the UK most of these are being returned to the private sector, such as British Airways, British Steel and the shipyards.

Again, however, you should note that in France and Italy car manufacturers are still state-controlled, and so the nationalisation of non-monopoly industries was not unique to the UK.

Advantages and disadvantages of public enterprises

42. Arguments in favour of public enterprises are as follows.

   (a) They can provide necessary facilities which are non-profit-making. British Rail presently provides services which are uneconomic but are a social necessity.

   (b) In many cases the large-scale operations involved enable greater use to be made of economies of scale. Clearly the Central Electricity Generating Board's supply grid is technically and operationally more efficient than the host of small power stations that existed before nationalisation. Even so, privatisation will not necessarily alter this advantage since it is ownership and not organisational structure which is changed.

   (c) The necessary capital can be provided by rates and taxes, or by borrowing which can be backed by government guarantees. However, this is a questionable argument since any large efficient organisation will have little difficulty in raising capital. It is currently being demonstrated, for example, that construction of a Channel Tunnel does not have to be government-financed.

43. Arguments against public enterprises are as follows.

   (a) Inefficiency and waste may be encouraged since losses are borne by ratepayers and taxpayers.

   (b) Politicians and councillors may not be familiar with the operation of the business and yet their political pressures and/or indecision may influence adversely the decision-making process.

   (c) There can be conflict between economy of operation and adequacy of service. The public will demand as perfect a service as possible but will not wish to bear the cost involved. This can also apply to private operations, but in the case of public enterprises many people believe that these services should be subsidised by the local authority or the State.

   (d) Because public enterprises are publicly accountable this can lead to an excessive degree of caution on the part of the managers, who can slow down innovation for fear of being blamed or criticised.

General points about public enterprises

44. *Municipal undertakings* such as bus services, swimming baths, theatres and civic centres are usually run by a manager for each undertaking, who is responsible to an appropriate sub-committee of the council (although increasingly such undertakings are being transferred to private ownership and management).

   Capital for the undertaking is usually provided by loans against the security of the rates. The undertaking is expected to recover operating costs, and to service and repay capital during the lifetime of the assets it finances.

   The general public can make complaints or suggestions about the undertaking to local councillors, who can take up the matter in the council.

45. *A nationalised industry* is formed by an Act of Parliament setting up a board to run the industry as a business undertaking. Each industry is organised and controlled according to its Act of Parliament, which aims to suit the particular industry. Therefore, organisation and control differ between industries, but there are some general features in common.

    (a) The industries are set up to operate as commercial businesses without day-to-day parliamentary control of their activities.

    (b) The business is expected to break even or be economically self-sufficient taking one year with another.

    This means that a loss in one year should be recouped in subsequent years. Self-sufficiency has not always been achieved in each industry and Parliament has been forced to write off the losses to the Exchequer.

    (c) Control of the industries by Parliament is achieved in three main ways:
    (i) annual publication of accounts which are scrutinised by the Public Accounts Committee;
    (ii) if required, the industry's affairs can be debated in Parliament;
    (iii) the appointment of a minister to take general control of policy, while leaving day-to-day management and control of administration to the industry's chairman and board.

    (d) A consumers' council is set up for most of the nationalised industries. Each council represents the consumer and can raise questions about the service and its charges.

46. Unlike private enterprise industry, there are no shareholders able to vote a nationalised industry's board out of control. However, the Minister may remove the senior officials and in extreme cases may obtain removal of the chairman, although this would probably be done by not renewing his contract when it expires.

Local authorities

47. In the UK, local authorities' expenditure represents a large proportion (over 10%) of Gross National Product. This spending is currently met by local taxes (the poll tax and the Uniform Business Rate), by government grants such as housing subsidy and rent rebate grants, and by fee-paying services and council house rents. The remaining portion of local government expenditure is funded by borrowing (and some interest receipts). The two most important sources of income are government grants and local taxes.

48. Local authority departments can be considered 'business organisations' because of the operations they must fund, including:
    (a) education;
    (b) social services;
    (c) highways;
    (d) parks;
    (e) town planning;
    (f) refuse collection;
    (g) libraries;
    (h) housing; and
    (i) youth services.

● **Other types of institution**

49. Some business organisations are non-profit-making clubs and societies. They are formed for many different purposes but generally to confer upon their members certain facilities, eg recreation and sports clubs, social clubs, etc or to protect and promote their interests, eg trade unions and employers' organisations, etc. However, an institution may be formed for a commercial activity, eg co-operative societies and building societies.

50. Clubs, societies, trade unions and associations often make profits and these are the result of activities such as running bars and dining rooms, discount trading, insurance and sickness benefits, holiday and savings clubs, etc. These are not profits in the normal commercial meaning of the word, but merely represent overpayments by the members for the services that they have received. Therefore they are usually called 'surpluses'. The division and application of the surpluses depends on the organisation and its aims and objectives. In some cases they are divided amongst the members.

    For example, in *co-operative societies* surpluses are distributed by way of dividends, and in working men's and other clubs bar surpluses are divided by giving 'checks' (again in relation to purchases in some cases, but normally equally divided among membership). The 'checks' can then be used over the bar for free drinks. In other societies and organisations the surpluses are allied to meeting the expenses of running the organisation and furthering its objectives, eg trade unions and trade associations.

51. Among the larger groups of organisations in the non-profit sector are trade unions, trade associations, co-operative societies and building societies. These will be described briefly in the following paragraphs and can be taken as representative of the larger units within this sector.

Trade unions

52. Trade unions are organised associations of working people in a trade, occupation or industry (or several trades or industries) formed for protection and promotion of their common interests, mainly the regulation and negotiation of pay and conditions.

    There are four main types of trade union:

    (a) *craft or occupational unions:* mainly catering for skilled workers, such as printers, engineers, building trade craftsmen - eg the Amalgamated Union of Engineering Workers;

    (b) *general workers' unions:* mainly semi-skilled and unskilled workers across the full range of industry; eg, the Transport and General Workers Union and the General and Municipal Workers Union (each has over one million members);

    (c) *industrial unions:* covering many of the workers of all grades and occupations within a single industry, eg the National Union of Railwaymen and the National Union of Mineworkers;

    (d) *white collar unions:* a growing sector of trade unionism covering technical, professional, supervisory and managerial staffs (unions such as the National Association of Local Government Officers, National Union of Teachers, Association of Supervisory, Technical and Managerial Staffs). Since 1945 white collar unions have been the main growth area in trade union membership.

53. The roles, objectives and responsibilities of trade unions vary slightly from union to union but their broad policies are similar and most are co-ordinated by the Trades Union Congress.

54. A trade union's purpose and activities are centred around the requirements of its members. Its first objective is to promote their interests and improve their pay and conditions of employment, and to represent them in negotiations with employers and government. Most unions also provide personal services to members, such as representing and advising in cases involving grievances, discipline, accidents, dismissal and redundancy.

55. Most trade unions have other and wider social objectives and feel that they have responsibilities for promoting what they consider to be a more equitable society. They therefore have subsidiary political objectives and seek to influence governments on matters such as employment and the welfare of workers.

Trade associations

56. Trade associations have a role similar to that of trade unions insofar as they protect and promote the interests of members, but their membership and aims are very different. They represent the employers - the 'management side' of the business - and promote and protect their business interests.

57. In the larger industries there are often several trade associations connected with the different aspects of one broad industry grouping. The trade associations in these industries tend to be of two types:

● organisations representing employers; and
● organisations representing particular products or services.

58. The main function of the employer organisations is to negotiate terms and conditions of employment for the industry with the appropriate trade unions. There is usually only one employer organisation to an industry, although it may be subdivided into regional associations. For example, in the engineering industry there is the Engineering Employers Federation which deals with matters on a national scale, and the constituent engineering employers' associations which deal with regional, district and local issues.

Co-operative societies

59. The first successful 'co-op' was founded in 1844 by Rochdale textile workers to buy foodstuffs at wholesale prices and sell them to members at market prices, with the profits or surpluses divided among members in proportion to the value of their purchases.

60. Most of the principles of co-operative trading adopted by the Rochdale pioneers are today recognised throughout the world. They include:
    (a) open membership;
    (b) democratic control (one member, one vote);
    (c) distribution of the surplus in proportion to purchases;
    (d) political and religious neutrality;
    (e) cash trading:
    (f) promotion of education.

61. A major example of a co-operative in the UK is the co-operative retail store network. In addition there is the Co-operative Wholesale Society. This society supplies the retail societies like any ordinary wholesaler, but also runs the factories, farms, dairies, bakeries and transport services. The retail societies join the wholesale society in exactly the same way as the ordinary members join the retail societies.

62. In addition to general retailing the co-operative method of trading is applied to other business areas; particularly to farming and agriculture, where farmers buy feedstuffs, seeds, implements and vehicles on a co-operative basis.

Building societies

63. Building societies are mainly found in Britain and the USA. They are organisations which obtain funds from members (share account holders) and other depositors. The society's members use the society as a method of saving money, and earning interest on their savings/investment. The society then uses the funds invested to lend money for mortgages to house buyers, against the security of the freehold or leasehold of the house. In many cases, individuals who are members of a building society and who keep savings with the society also obtain a mortgage from the society to buy their home - so many investors are also borrowers.

64. Building societies in the UK are attempting to be more competitive with high street banks since legislation in the mid-1980s (the Building Societies Act 1986) gave them greater freedom. They now offer, among other things, current accounts, unsecured loans, insurance services and credit cards alongside their traditional core business of mortgage loans.

1: TYPES OF BUSINESS ORGANISATION

QUIZ

1. What are the different types of business undertaking found in the UK?

   - See paras 18, 44, 45, 49.

2. What aspects of organisation can be used to describe the differences between types of organisation?

   - See para 8-14.

3. What are the advantages of sole-tradership?

   - See para 21.

4. What are the main differences between private and public limited companies?

   - See para 27.

5. What are the disadvantages of public enterprise?

   - See para 43.

6. How are local authorities funded in the UK and what sorts of service do they provide?

   - See paras 47-48

7. What trading principles are adopted by co-operative societies? How do they distribute surpluses?

   - See paras 60, 50

Chapter 2

FORMAL ORGANISATION STRUCTURE

Topics covered in this chapter

- Efficient organisation structure
- Formal organisations
- Scalar chain
- Span of control
  - o Tall and flat organisations
- Line, staff and function
  - o The classical approach
  - o Implications for organisational design
  - o Finding a balance of influence
- Departmentation
- Centralisation and decentralisation
- Divisionalisation
- Matrix organisation

Purpose of this chapter

To outline the ways in which the tasks of organisation may be structured, and to describe common approaches to formal authority relationships.

● Efficient organisation structure

1. A formal organisation may be defined (Etzioni) as a social unit deliberately constructed to seek specific goals. It is characterised by:
   (a) planned divisions of responsibility;
   (b) power centres which control its efforts;
   (c) substitution of personnel;
   (d) the ability to combine its personnel in different ways.

2. Formal organisations have an explicit hierarchy in a well-defined structure; job specifications and communication channels are also well-defined.

3. An informal organisation, in contrast, is loosely structured, flexible and spontaneous. Membership is gained consciously or unconsciously and it is often difficult to determine the time when a person becomes a member. An example of an informal organisation is a group of managers who regularly go together for lunch to a local restaurant.

4. With every formal organisation there exists, to a greater or lesser extent, a complex informal organisation. The formal organisation is a structure of relationships and ideas; informal organisation, in practice, modifies this formal structure (Blau and Scott 1962).

The management task of organisation

5. Management has authority over the activities of an organisation. It can structure the work of the organisation and the jobs done within it to suit its requirements. The organisation structure it rules over will be inefficient or efficient. If it is inefficient it is management's duty to improve it.

6. The symptoms of a poor and inefficient organisation structure may be listed as:

    (a) the growth of many levels of management. An excessive number of management levels must inevitably involve the creation of much unnecessary work and reporting relationships. This can only result in inefficiency;

    (b) 'frictional' or 'unprofitable' overheads - these are 'co-ordinators, expeditors or assistants' who have no clear job responsibility of their own, but are supposed to help their superior do his job;

    (c) the need for special co-ordinating measures, such as appointing liaison officers, or co-ordination committees, or holding numerous co-ordination meetings;

    (d) the tendency to 'go through channels' rather than go directly to the person with the needed information or ideas. 'It greatly aggravates the tendency of functional organisation to make people think more of their function than of the business';

    (e) a lop-sided management age structure.

7. | Efficient organisation structure does not necessarily ensure good and effective management, but with a bad or inefficient organisation structure, good performance is impossible, no matter how able management might be. 'The right organisation structure is a necessary foundation; without it the best performance in all other areas of management will be ineffectual and frustrated'. (Drucker). |

● Formal organisations

8. The first responsibility of the manager as organiser is to divide the work and provide a means of co-ordination. There are two schools of thought on how this should be done. Most companies adhere to the classical approach, which entails considering the work first, and the personalities second. The work is divided into jobs, and people are then appointed to do the work of each job.

9.   There are, however, a few avant-garde organisations that follow the teachings of the behaviour-alist school and consider that motivation of the people comes before division of the work in the apparently-most-logical way. Volvo's experiments with groups working in the automobile industry is probably the best known of the large organisations attempting to follow the behaviouralist theories. In this approach, employees are consulted about how a work process should be organised, and the organisation is then established in accordance with their preferences.

10.   We have already briefly defined the concept of 'organisation'. This initial definition can now be developed by referring to the writings of Louis A Allen whose books *Management and Organisation* and *The Management Profession* discuss organisation principles. He tells us that 'organisation' is a mechanism or structure that enables living things to work effectively together. The basic elements of organisation are *division of labour*, a *source of authority* and *relationships*. This is true of all forms of organisation.

> Management organisation, in these terms, means first identifying the work that must be accomplished to attain objectives, then grouping that work into logically related and balanced positions. Next, responsibility and authority are defined and delegated. As a final step, relationships are established between positions and units to facilitate harmonious teamwork.
>
> 'One of the facts of life for organisations is that as they grow, they become more formalised... Just as growth sets up pressures for delegation, so it is also accompanied by formalisation' (John Child).

● **Scalar chain**

11.   The 'scalar chain' or 'chain of command' is the term used to describe the organisation's management hierarchy, that is the chain of superiors from lowest to highest rank. Formal communication runs up and down the lines of authority, eg E to D to C to B to A in the diagram below.

Note, however, that if communication between different branches of the chain is necessary (eg D to H) the use of a 'gang plank' of horizontal communication saves time and is likely to be more accurate, so long as superiors know that such communication is taking place.

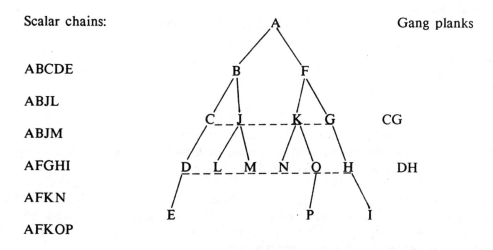

Scalar chains:

ABCDE

ABJL

ABJM

AFGHI

AFKN

AFKOP

Gang planks

CG

DH

2.1 Scalar chains

12. Henri Fayol criticised government departments for making insufficient use of the *gang plank*. By this, he means that the subordinates refer too many problems up the scalar chain to their boss because the problem involves a person in another section or department. Instead, the subordinate could contact the other person directly and ask for a joint solution to the problem. In the diagram here, if C has a problem with affects G, instead of referring it up to B (who might then refer it to A) C could cross the 'gang plank' - communicate horizontally - with G. The problem might then be solved jointly by C and G, provided that B and F are aware that this is happening.

13. One important problem for efficient and effective management is establishing the most suitable *number of links* in the chains of command for the organisation concerned.

    (a) Townsend *('Up the Organisation')* estimated that the addition of each extra level of management into the hierarchy, adding one more link in the chain of command, reduces the effectiveness of communication within the organisation by about 25%.

    Peter Drucker cites the Roman Catholic Church as a classic example of an organisation with a short chain of command. From Pope down to parish priest there is only one intermediary layer of management, the Bishops, so that a papal edict comes down to parish priests in just one step.

    (b) In the years before World War II, the average churchgoer or factory hand was poorly educated and dependent on orders from above to know what to do. In such an environment it is relatively easy for a superior to give instructions and use a dictatorial manner, perhaps with coercion and threats, to win obedience.

    The post-war years brought drastic changes: organisations are bigger and more complex, and employees are both better educated and also more protected from coercion by managers. Getting employees to do what is required of them is not easy in a diverse, complex business environment, where greater controls are necessary to protect investments. As a consequence, more managers have been introduced into organisations and chains of command have grown longer.

14. There might be a tendency for chains of command within a single organisation to get longer as the organisation grows older. The length of the chains of command is a function of:

    - the size of the organisation;
    - the type and complexity of the products it makes or services it provides;
    - the diversity of its products and services;
    - its geographical spread;
    - the number and complexity of controls required; and
    - the type of people it employs.

15. No rules have been (or can be) laid down for how chains of command should be structured, but a general observation is that chains of command should be kept as short as possible, consistent with sound management, and the factors listed above.

    (a) Management structure should be organised for *business performance* - converting all the business activities into 'drive'. Managers should fulfil valuable operational needs in a simple environment, and organisations should avoid a red-tape bureaucracy working on a mountain of paper or in a maze of procedures.

(b) Management structure should be organised so as *to direct the organisation's efforts away from bad performance*. Bad news should be communicated quickly so that problems can be rectified. Long chains of command create a tendency towards bad performance, such as in situations where trade unions can react to events much more quickly than a cumbersome slow-moving management.

(c) *Short chains of command* help managers to develop. Rosemary Stewart cited examples from nationalised industries as typical illustrations. Prior to nationalisation of the electricity industry, a power station manager reported to his managing director and saw him regularly: this direct and frequent contact gave the power station manager valuable insights into management problems and thinking 'at the top' which helped his own development as a manager.

(d) The chain of command and management structure should enable the organisation to *train tomorrow's managers*. Drucker has cited cases of well-known companies with as many as twelve links in the chain of command. Such a long chain makes promotion from the bottom to the top virtually impossible. To add to the problem, specialisation of skills in some management jobs (for example accountancy management) removes flexibility of appointments and restricts promotion prospects.

   (i) As a consequence, many large companies turn divisions into 'independent' subsidiary and sub-subsidiary companies, to ensure that its bright young managers with potential to rise to senior positions are given a more direct experience of running an organisation (albeit a subsidiary) from an early stage in their career. Within their subsidiary, the chain of command is short, and general management experience more easily gained.

   (ii) If large companies do not split their operations between subsidiary companies in this way, they will run the risk of losing their brightest management talents because managers will be frustrated by delays waiting from promotion, and will instead move to smaller companies to gain their experience and make their mark more quickly.

> In conclusion, chains of command should:
>
> - reflect the business organisation, its environment, products, employees, diversity, spread and controls;
> - be as short as possible consistent with efficiency and effectiveness;
> - be short enough to provide a training ground for developing managers.

● Span of control

16. The 'span-of-control' or 'span-of-management' refers to the number of subordinates working to the superior official. In other words, if a manager has five subordinates, the span of control is 5.

Various writers of the classical school, such as Fayol, Graicunas and Urwick, argued that the managerial span of control should be limited to between 3 and 6. Their arguments were based on the twin beliefs that:

(a) there should be tight managerial control from the top of the organisation; and
(b) there are physical and mental limitations to any single manager's ability to control people and activities.

17. To ensure effective control, the number of subordinates and tasks over which a manager has supervisory responsibilities should therefore be restricted to what is physically and mentally possible. A narrow span of control offers:

    (a) tight control and close supervision; better co-ordination of subordinates' activities;
    (b) time to think and plan; managers are not burdened with too many day to day problems;
    (c) reduced delegation; a manager can do more of his work himself;
    (d) better communication with subordinates, who are sufficiently small in number to allow this to occur.

18. The French writer V A Graicunas (1937) devised a formula to show how the number of possible relationships between members of an organisation increases geometrically in proportion to the number of members:

    $$N = (2^{n-1} + (n-1))$$

    Where N is the total number of possible relationships and n is the number of subordinates.

    The greater the number of subordinates becomes, the supervisor finds himself managing a mushrooming number of organisational relationships (where $n = 1$, $N = 1$, and where $n = 7$, $N = 490$). This exploding complexity of larger and larger units must impose some limitations on the capabilities of management - the span of control is limited by the number of inter-relationships that one person can manage.

19. Urwick suggested a slightly different approach, in response to a report by James Worthy in 1950 that the policy of the American Sears Roebuck company was to have as wide a span of control as possible between stores managers and their subordinates, who were merchandising managers. A wide span of control forced stores managers to delegate authority, and the consequences, Worthy claimed, were improved morale and greater efficiency of merchandising management.

    Urwick's counter-argument was that a wide span of control had been possible in this example of the Sears Roebuck company because the work of the merchandising managers did not interlock, therefore the need for co-ordination and integration was not present. This reduced the burdens of supervision and made a wider span of control feasible. Urwick concluded that the maximum management span of control should be 6, when the work of subordinates interlocks.

20. A wide span of control offers:
    - greater decision-making authority for subordinates;
    - fewer supervisory costs; and
    - less control, but perhaps greater motivation though job satisfaction.

Tall and flat organisations

21. The span of control concept has implications for the 'shape' of an organisation. A tall organisation is one which, in relation to its size, has a large number of management hierarchies, whereas a flat organisation is one which, in relation to its size, has a smaller number of hierarchical levels. A tall organisation implies a narrow span of control, and a flat organisation implies a wide span of control.

22. Some classical theorists accepted that a **tall organisation structure is inefficient**, because:

    (a) it increases overhead costs;

    (b) it creates extra communication problems, since top management is more remote from the 'actual work' done at the bottom end of the organisation, and information tends to get distorted or blocked on its way up or down through the organisation hierarchy;

    (c) management responsibilities tend to overlap and become confused as the size of the management structure gets larger. Different sections or departments may seek authority over the same 'territory' of operations, and superiors may find it difficult to delegate sufficient authority to satisfy subordinates;

    (d) the same work passes through too many hands;

    (e) planning is more difficult because it must be organised at more levels in the organisation.

    Behavioural theorists add that tall structures impose rigid supervision and control and therefore block initiative and ruin the motivation of subordinates.

23. Nevertheless, not all researchers favour flat organisation structures, and it can be argued that if work is organised on the basis of small groups or project teams (therefore narrow spans of control and a tall organisation structure) group members would be able to plan their work in an orderly manner, encourage participation by all group members in decision-making and monitor the consequences of their decisions better, so that their performance will be more efficient than the work of groups in a flat structure with a wide span of control. D Vander Weyer (*'Management and People in Banking'*, edited by Livy) suggested that in the case of large banking organisations 'it is virtually impossible for so complex an organisation as an international bank to work with less than five or six executive levels, and the writer's own bank (Barclays) has six'.

24. There is a trade-off between the span of control and the tallness/flatness of an organisation. The span of control should not be too wide, but neither should an organisation be too tall.

Tall organisations	
Reasons in favour	*Reasons against*
1. Keeps span of control narrow.	1. A wide span of control means that more authority will be delegated to subordinates. Greater discretion leads to job enrichment and motivation.
2. A large number of career/promotion steps are provided in the hierarchical ladder. More frequent promotions possible.	2. With many rungs in the hierarchical ladder, the *real* increases in authority between one rung and another might not seem obvious to managers.
	3. Tall organisations are more expensive in management overheads costs.
	4. Tall organisations tend to suffer from worse communications.

Span of control: conclusions

25. It is reasonable to accept the view that there is a limit to a supervisor's capabilities and that the span of control should be limited. However, the span of control is now thought to be dependent on several factors.

26. The nature of the manager's work load is likely to influence the span of control he or she can deal with efficiently.

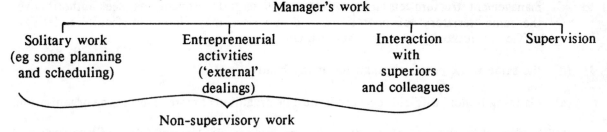

The greater the proportion of non-supervisory work in a manager's work load,
(a) the narrower the span of control should be; or
(b) the greater the delegation of authority to subordinates should be.

27. Other factors influencing the width of the span of control are:
    (a) the geographical dispersion of the subordinates;
    (b) whether subordinates' work is all of a similar nature (wide span possible) or diversified;
    (c) the nature of problems that a supervisor might have to help subordinates with;
    (d) the degree of interaction between subordinates (with close interaction, a wider span of control should be possible);
    (e) the competence and abilities of both management and subordinates;
    (f) whether close group cohesion is desirable. Small groups will be more cohesive, with a better sense of team work. This would call for narrow spans of control;
    (g) the amount of help that supervisors receive from staff functions (such as the personnel department).

28. The is no universally 'correct' size for the span of management, and no current writer on organisations would suggest that a 'correct' span exists, without considering the particular circumstances of any particular individual organisation or department.

● **Line, staff and functional organisation**

29. There are two ways of looking at the distinction between line and staff management.

    (a) Line and staff can be used to denote functions in the organisation. Line management consists of those managers directly involved in achieving the objectives of an organisation (that is all production and sales managers in a manufacturing company). Every other manager is staff (for example accounting, marketing, research and development managers).

    > Rosemary Stewart wrote that 'Line functions are those which have direct responsibility for achieving the objectives of the company. Staff activities are those which primarily exist to provide advice and service.'

(b) As an alternative definition, line and staff can be used to denote relationships of authority. A line manager is one who has relatively unlimited authority over a subordinate to whom he gives orders. By this definition, any manager, no matter what department he works in (an operations department or an advisory department) will have line authority over his subordinates. Thus if the personnel department is a staff department, the manager in charge of recruitment and training will be subordinate in a line relationship to the personnel director. In other words, line authority can be a term used to describe the scalar chain of command in the management hierarchy.

30. Another popular distinction between line and staff is that:

- staff managers are thinkers and advisers; and
- line managers are doers.

31. Staff departments exist in many organisations where there is a need for specialisation of management. Accountants, personnel administrators, economists, data processing experts and statisticians are all experts in a specialised field of work. Where this expertise is 'syphoned off' into a separate department, the problem naturally arises as to whether:

(a) the experts exist to *advise* line managers, who may accept or reject the advice given; or

(b) the experts can step in to *direct* the line managers in what to do - to assume line authority themselves.

32. No organisation of substantial size can avoid operating problems unless there is a clear understanding as to the structure of the tasks and relationships of an organisation and as to where authority and responsibility rest. This means that managers must know whether they are 'line' or 'staff'.

33. Unfortunately, this is an aspect of organisation which causes enormous friction. Line managers are thought of as 'first class citizens' and staff are relegated in status to the second rank as expensive 'overheads', who are not contributing anything of worth to the organisation. Staff managers are therefore constantly trying to acquire line functions.

The classical approach: planning and structure

34. An organisation is divided into functions, such as production, finance and sales. The functions required by each business will depend on the individual situation of the business. For example, some businesses may need a research and development department, or an advertising department, and others will not need them. Other functions, such as market research and public relations, may be provided by external services. In small companies and other such organisations, most staff functions may be provided by external agencies: for example, a businessman might hire the services of a professional accountant for a few hours each week and the services of a solicitor when required; a computer bureau may take on many data processing applications, including the weekly and monthly payroll work. Typing and secretarial services may be 'farmed out' to an agency. Some small manufacturing organisations may sell all their products through an agent; for example, a printing company may obtain business through a sales 'broker' who takes a commission on all work he finds for the company.

35. Owing to specialisation of work, there must be both line and staff management within an organisation:

    (a) Line organisation establishes a direct relationship between the executive and his subordinates, and this order follows in the form of a *scalar chain* in a classical hierarchy.

    (b) Line and staff organisations are based on both direct and functional relationships. In this system the line organisation is supplemented by staff organisation. The staff officers have no direct authority over the line organisation, but they provide assistance and service to the line personnel in an advisory capacity.

36. The conflict between line management, who may resent specialist advice, and staff management, who may be frustrated when their advice is ignored, has no organisational solution. The problem can be lessened, however, if:

    (a) all vital activities of the business are line management functions; and
    (b) staff management are kept in close proximity (either physically or by communications links) to the line management they advise.

Functional organisation

37. A development in more recent years has been the recognition that some 'staff' management has become highly specialised in areas of work which form a fundamental part of the line management positions. Examples are usually found in the fields of industrial relations and capital expenditure. In these areas the line manager would allow the staff manager to assume some of his responsibilities while still retaining final authority and responsibility. A typical example would be where the personnel manager specifies the rules for disciplining and dismissal of employees. The line manager recognises that the staff manager has greater knowledge and expertise on this subject and acquiesces in the carrying out of the prescribed steps of the procedure.

38. This role is clearly different from that of the traditional staff manager (eg work study, organisation and methods, 'personal assistant to' positions etc). Urwick and Dale have defined the distinction as being 'functional staff' as opposed to 'general staff'. General staff positions are seen as purely advisory positions.

Example: line, staff and functional staff

39. On the next page is a typical organisation chart of an international company, far from complex if compared with hundreds of large organisations but complicated enough to illustrate the positions of authority and responsibility and the distinctions between line and staff.

> This organisation chart depicts a company with three businesses. It designs, makes and sells musical instruments, surgical instruments and sports equipment. It functions as a complete entity in three different countries to take account of the special needs of local markets.

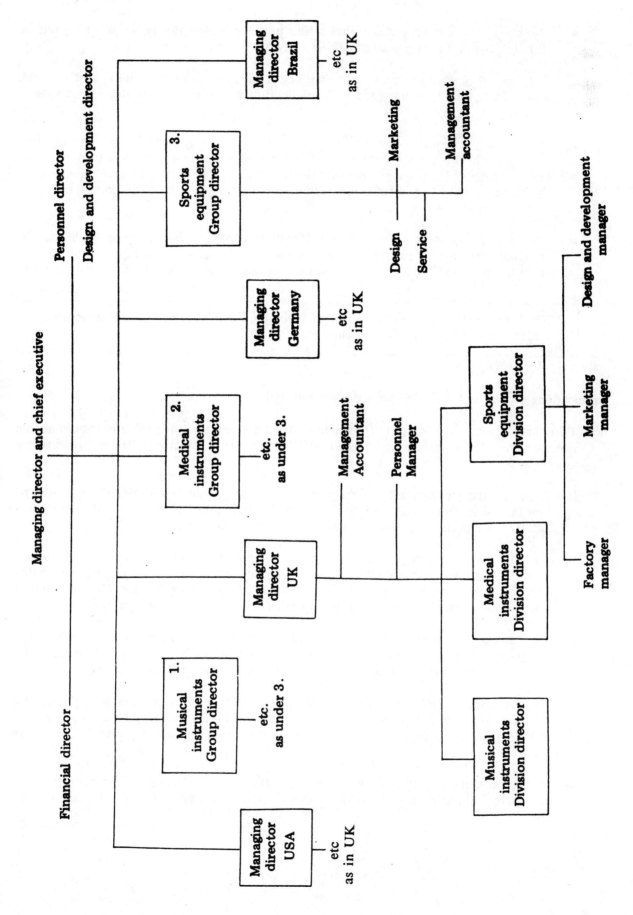

- The *chief executive* very clearly has a line job. His responsibility is for all aspects of all functions of the organisation. He is truly a chief executive.

- The regional *managing directors* take their places one down from the chief executive in the scalar chain; they have line jobs with responsibility for the organisational structures in each region.

- It is equally clear that the *financial director* and the *personnel director* are staff functions. They report to the managing director, they are there to provide information and to recommend policies and procedures related to their professional skills and knowledge of the business. They have a functional authority over the equivalent staff at various levels of the company, but not a line authority.

- The *three group* directors are more difficult to classify. They are responsible to the managing director for all aspects of their part of the business and yet they do not appear from the chart to have a line relationship with their opposite numbers at national level.

> This organisation structure may in fact be better classified as a 'matrix' structure, which is described later in this chapter.

Implications of line and staff for organisational design

40. There are drawbacks to using staff departments; a knowledge of the problems should enable management to deal with them, and thus use staff functions more effectively. These drawbacks are as follows.

(a) There is a danger that staff experts may, intentionally or not, undermine the authority of line managers. Subordinates might respect the 'expert power' of the staff man, and show a lesser willingness to accept the judgement of their line boss.

(b) Friction may also occur when staff managers report to a higher authority in the scalar chain of command. For example, a management accountant may submit reports about a line manager's performance to the production director or the managing director. The line manager might look on such reporting as 'telling tales' and resent the interference.

(c) Staff managers have no line authority and therefore no responsibility for what actually happens. If they give advice which is acted on, but fails to achieve desired results, staff men can blame the line managers for not acting on their advice properly.

(d) Because staff managers are 'thinkers' they may have their heads in the clouds. Their ideas may be unrealistic and impracticable; line managers, having received poor advice from one staff expert, might tar all staff managers with the same brush and resist all future expert help.

(e) Staff managers may attempt to usurp line authority. Any change in the boundaries of authority should be the result of conscious planning, and not surreptitious empire-building.

41. The solutions to these problems are easily stated, but not easy to implement in practice.

    (a) Authority must be clearly defined, and distinctions between line authority and staff advice clearly set out (eg in job descriptions).

    (b) Senior management must encourage line managers to make positive efforts to discuss work problems with staff advisers, and to be prepared to accept their advice. The use of experts should become an 'organisational way of life'.

    (c) Staff managers must be fully informed about the operational aspects of the business on which they are experts. By providing them with detailed information they should be less likely to offer impractical advice.

    (d) When staff advisers are used to plan and implement changes in the running of the business, they must be kept involved during the implementation, monitoring and review of the project. Staff managers must be prepared to accept responsibility for their failures and this is only really possible if they advise during the implementation and monitoring stages.

Finding a 'balance' of influence between line and staff management

42. There has to be a balance between operations managers (line) and managers of support functions (staff). The problem for organisation is seen, typically, as follows:

    (a) If operational managers had a superhuman ability to learn all the specialist skills necessary for management, there would be no need for support functions.

    (b) It is only because specialist support is essential (eg accountants, computer specialists) or advisable (eg personnel specialists) - because operational managers would on their own be unable to make well-informed decisions - that the problem arises of finding a balance of authority or influence between line and staff.

43. Undue authority to line managers might result in rapid short-term business development, and high short-term profits at high risk, with the danger that:
    (a) legal restrictions (eg the rules of the Companies Act) will be inadvertently broken;
    (b) personnel planning for the long term might be overlooked. Staff morale might be lowered;
    (c) up-to-date technology and management techniques might be overlooked;
    (d) important work not directly involved with day-to-day operations might be neglected.

    The cumulative long-term effect will be damaging to the organisation.

44. On the other hand, it is unwise to give *too much* authority or influence to staff management.

    (a) Staff management sometimes have divided loyalties between their organisation and their profession or speciality. Computer specialists might want to introduce up-to-date or 'perfect' computer systems when these might not be the most appropriate for the organisation. Accountants might show undue concern for the standards of their profession at the expense of the organisation's best interests.

(b) Many staff managers have skills which can be marketed to other organisations, so that their career is not necessarily tied to one company. Operational line managers, on the other hand, might be trained exclusively for service in one company, or one type of company or organisation (eg a bank or the Civil Service). When staff managers do not necessarily have a vested, long-term interest in their organisation, it might be argued that their authority should be kept under restraint.

(c) Staff managers tend to introduce rules and procedures - control systems, job evaluation and appraisal systems etc - and these tend to increase the bureaucratic nature of the formal organisation, with possible adverse repercussions on its efficiency due to excessive 'red tape'. This in turn might restrict an operational line manager's freedom of choice and flexibility. For example, a formal system of job descriptions might restrict the ability of management to make frequent reviews of their organisation's job structure.

(d) When an organisation has a multi-divisional structure, with international interests, each subsidiary or division (or sub-unit of a division) might have its own support functions. When there is staff management at group level, divisional level and below divisional level, a further organisational problem is created because of overlapping interests, boundaries of authority and influence, and conflicting advice and opinions between the different levels of functional staff.

(e) When staff departments build up an 'empire' of influence and authority, it may be difficult to measure the benefits to the organisation of various aspects of their work. Because the benefits of the work are 'indirect' they cannot always be measured in money terms. The only way to restrict the growth of costly, unjustifiable staff work might be to appoint outside consultants from time to time to carry out a cost-benefit analysis of a staff department on behalf of senior management.

45. In some cases, there might be a good argument for introducing elements of a matrix-management type of organisation (see later in this chapter) in which both operational (line) managers and support function (staff) managers have authority over the same managers below them in rank. For example:

(a) the group head of marketing and public relations might have some authority over operational managers throughout the group, who will have responsibility for marketing performance and accountability to the head of marketing in this respect. Operational managers would also have their lines of responsibility to their senior operational management;

(b) similarly, the group head of personnel might have some authority over operational managers, for example, with respect to job appraisal, manpower planning or recruiting and training.

46. The drawback to an excessive number of reporting lines (operational managers reporting to a number of different functional managers as well as their own operational superior) is that there will not be a clear source of authority in the organisation, and priorities might become uncertain and confused.

47. The argument of the classical school of management in favour of clear lines of authority is a valid one (although of course it is debatable whether a 'one boss for one subordinate' or 'unity of command' scalar chain of command is necessarily the only suitable way of establishing a clear authority structure).

48. Drucker argues that the traditional view of staff specialists as 'advisers with some authority' is a poor approach to organisation design. He suggested that 'as far as I have been able to grasp the concept, to be 'staff' means to have authority without having responsibility. And that is destructive'. It is much better that (staff) functional departments, which are necessary in any large organisation:

> (a)   should have their own clear objectives;
> (b)   should have clearly stated areas of authority; and
> (c)   should be responsible and accountable for their exercise of that authority.

Functional authority

49. *Functional authority* is a step further in the recognition that some 'staff' management has become highly specialised in areas of work which form a fundamental part of line management. This 'expert' power becomes formally recognised in the organisation/management structure, merging line and staff authority: the expert has formally delegated to him the authority to influence specific areas (those in which he is a specialist) of the work of other departments and their managers. Functional specialists in, for example, financial control, industrial relations or public relations have the power to direct line managers within the well-defined areas of their specialism.

50. This is a move towards dual authority, and carries elements of a matrix structure although the line manager retains ultimate authority for the functioning of his department. For this reason, and to avoid complex political problems, functional authority is usually exercised through the establishment of systems, procedures and standards, rather than by on-going direct intervention on the part of functional specialists.

Example: functional authority of the accounts department

51. Functional authority as described above is held by many different sorts of department but as an example let us examine how an understanding of functional authority underlies the organisation and management of an enterprise's accounting activity.

52. It is important for any function or department to understand the scope of its own authority, and to exercise that authority to an extent that is acceptable and effective in achieving organisational objectives.

53. If the accounts department of an organisation misunderstands the nature of functional authority, and assumes that it is in a 'staff' relationship with operational departments - or indeed if the accounts department *is* allocated a staff position in the organisation structure - the difficulties will be immense. If the department has no delegated authority to direct line managers in the areas of financial management and control, those activities will be at the mercy of line managers who may or may not choose to heed the advice which is all the accounts department can give.

54. The complexity of the commercial environment and the requirements of financial management make it impossible in any but the smallest organisations for line managers to fulfil their operational duties and handle financial control at the same time.

55. The application of functional authority, however, does have its problems, and an understanding of the nature of functional authority can again help in role definition and control with discretion: it is not 'staff' - but neither is it 'line' authority.

56. Functional accounts managers must understand the boundaries of their authority: the purpose is not to undermine or curtail the authority of line managers who, after all, still retain ultimate responsibility. Given that corporate financial control is necessary in most organisations, especially in large, decentralised ones (where departments or divisions have a degree of autonomy), the problem is to reconcile the functional authority of the accounting department with the line authority of other managers. An understanding of the scope and nature of the two types of authority will at least point out areas of difficulty: rationalisation and role definition can therefore be carried out. For example, the ambiguous position of finance and accounting staff working in line departments should not be allowed to become a source of stress, and will require sensitivity: dual reporting (to the department - line - manager and to the accounts manager) must be handled with discretion, if role conflict and divided loyalties are not to arise.

57. Organisations generally delegate the management and control of financial affairs to an accounting and finance function/department which is responsible for the establishment and control of policies and procedures to which line and staff managers must adhere. The organisational difficulties arising from this common situation are mainly caused by lack of role definition: the solution then is to redefine clearly the nature and boundaries of functional authority.

● **Departmentation**

58. As an organisation grows in size:

    (a) it is able to take advantage of economies of scale, which in turn may call for the establishment of departments of specialists or experts (eg research and development, management scientists etc);

    (b) the number of levels in the organisation hierarchy increases, so that problems of delegation of authority and control arise;

    (c) specialist support teams (eg service and maintenance, quality control, corporate planning, organisation and methods, data processing etc) are created to ease the burdens and complexities of line management. Such support teams need to be slotted into the hierarchical structure;

    (d) separate groups and departments continue to be formed as specialisation extends; new problems of communication and co-ordination (or integration) now arise.

59. When an organisation diversifies its activities into different products and markets, it is common for the structure to be 'divisionalised'. Large divisions of a company may in turn be sub-divided into smaller units.

Organisation by area, product, function, brand or customer

60. The creation of departments and divisions is known as departmentation. Different patterns of departmentation are possible, and the pattern selected will depend on the individual circumstances of the organisation. Various methods of departmentation are as follows.

   (a) By area: this method of organisation occurs when similar activities are carried out in widely different locations. The telecommunications service, for example, is divided into regions which in turn are sub-divided into Telephone Areas. Some authority is retained at Head Office (organised, perhaps, on a functional basis) but day-to-day service problems are handled on a territorial basis. Within many sales departments, the sales staff are organised territorially.

   The *advantage of territorial departmentation* is better local decision-making at the point of contact between the organisation (eg a salesman) and its customers. Localised knowledge is put to better use and in the right circumstances it may be less costly to establish area factories/offices than to control everything through Head Office (eg costs of transportation and travelling may be less).

   The *disadvantage of territorial departmentation* might be the duplication of management effort. For example, a national organisation divided into ten regions might have a customer liaison department in each regional office. If the organisation did all customer liaison work from head office it might need fewer managerial staff. In a similar way, there would be a tendency for regions to duplicate planning management, personnel and training management, accountancy management etc, thus increasing overhead costs and problems of co-ordination and integration.

   (b) By product: some organisations (such as ICI) group activities on the basis of products or product lines. Some functional departmentation remains (eg manufacturing, distribution, marketing and sales) but a divisional manager is given responsibility for the product or product line, with authority over personnel of different functions.

   The *advantages of product departmentation* are that:

   (i) individual managers can be held accountable for the *profitability* of individual products;

   (ii) specialisation can be developed. For example, some salesmen will be trained to sell a specific product in which they may develop technical expertise and thereby offer a better sales service to customers and for the company. Service engineers who specialise in a single product should also provide a better after-sales service;

   (iii) the different functional activities and efforts required to make and sell each product can be co-ordinated and integrated by the divisional/product manager.

   The *disadvantage of product departmentation* is that it increases the overhead costs and managerial complexity of the organisation.

(c) <u>By function</u>: this is a widely-used method of organisation. Primary functions in a manufacturing company might be production, sales, finance, and general administration. Sub-departments of the production function might be manufacturing (machining, finishing, assembly etc), production control, quality control, servicing and purchasing. Sub-departments of sales might be selling, marketing, distribution and warehousing. Departments of central Government include the Treasury, Home Office, Foreign Office, Department of Trade and Industry, Ministry of Defence, etc.

Functional organisation is logical and traditional and accommodates the division of work into specialist areas. Apart from the problems which may arise when 'line' management resents interference by 'staff' advisers in their functional area, the drawback to functional organisation is simply that more efficient structures might exist which would be more appropriate in a particular situation.

(d) <u>By brand</u> - business organisations are becoming increasingly marketing-led and as such they are aware of the value of their brands. A brand is the name or design which identifies the products or services of a manufacturer or provider and distinguishes them from those of competitors. Famous brand names include 'Kitkat', 'Persil' and 'Sugar Puffs'. Large organisations may produce a number of different brands of the same basic product, such as washing-powder or toothpaste. This is viable because branding brings the product to the attention of buyers and creates brand loyalty - often the customers do not realise that two 'rival' brands are in fact produced by the same manufacturer.

Because branding is linked with unique marketing positions it becomes necessary to have departmentation by brand. As with product departmentation, some functional departmentation remains (especially on the manufacturing side) but brand managers have responsibility for the brand's marketing and this can affect every function.

Brand departmentation has similar advantages and disadvantages to product departmentation. In particular, overhead costs and complexity of the management structure are increased, the relationships of a number of different brand departments with the one manufacturing department being particularly difficult.

(e) <u>By customer or market segment</u>: a manufacturing organisation may sell goods through wholesalers, export agents and by direct mail. It may therefore organise its sales, marketing and distribution functions on the basis of types of customer, or market segment. Departmentation by customer is commonly associated with sales departments and selling effort, but it might also be used by a jobbing or contracting firm where a team of managers may be given the responsibility of liaising with major customers (eg discussing specifications and completion dates, quality of work, progress-chasing etc).

(f) <u>By equipment specialisation</u>: the most obvious example of departmentation based on equipment specialisation is provided by the data processing departments of large organisations. Batch processing operations are conducted for other departments at a computer centre (where it is controlled by DP staff) because it would be uneconomical to provide each functional department with its own large mainframe computer.

(g) <u>By numbers</u>: when menial tasks are carried out by large numbers of workers, supervision can be divided by organising the people into gangs of equal size. Departmentation by numbers alone is rare; an example might be the organisation of a conscript army of infantrymen into divisions and battalions etc.

(h) <u>By shifts</u>: with shift-working employees organised on the basis of 'time of day'.

2: FORMAL ORGANISATION STRUCTURE

61. Simple typical examples of organisation charts are as follows:

(a) *Departmentation by area*

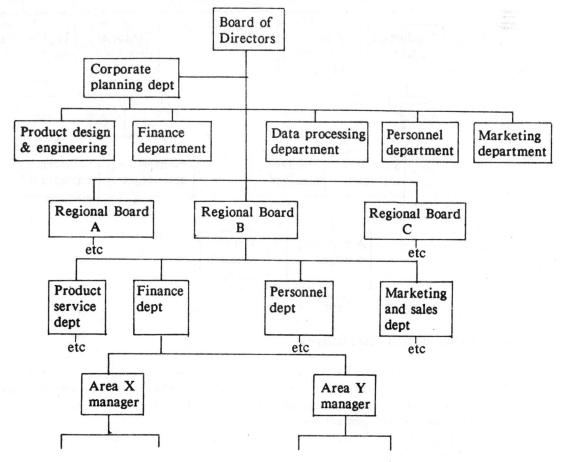

Functional divisions within areas

(b) *Departmentation by product or brand*

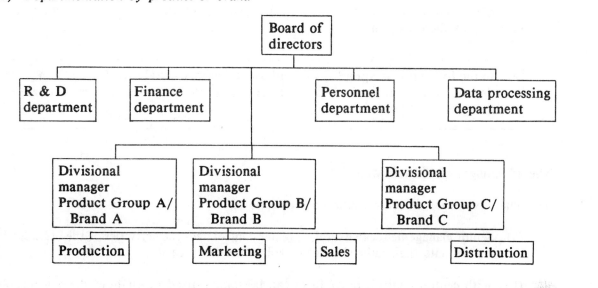

etcetera

(c) *Departmentation by function*

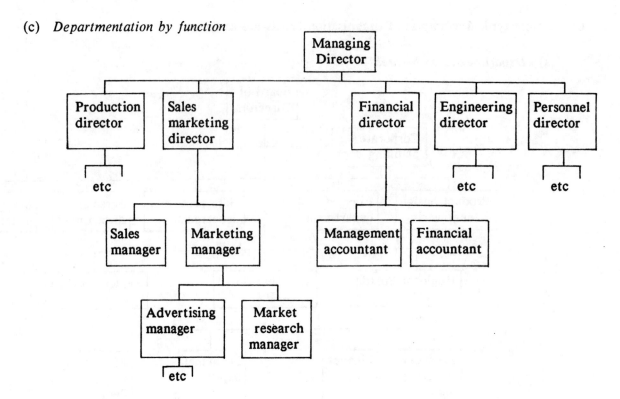

● **Centralisation and decentralisation**

62. *Centralisation* and *decentralisation* refer to the degree to which authority is delegated in an organisation. The terms are thereby used to describe the level at which decisions are taken in the management hierarchy.

63. Complete centralisation would mean that no authority at all was exercised by subordinates; complete decentralisation would mean that *all* authority was exercised by subordinates (there would be no co-ordination of subordinates). It is doubtful whether any organisation approaches to either of these extremes.

In the following paragraphs, we shall use the term 'centralisation' to mean a greater degree of central control, and 'decentralisation' to mean a greater degree of delegated authority.

The advantages of centralisation

64. The advantages of centralisation are as follows:

(a) Senior management can exercise greater control over the activities of the organisation and co-ordinate their subordinates or sub-units more easily.

(b) With central control, procedures can be standardised throughout the organisation.

(c) Senior managers can make decisions from the point of view of the organisation as a whole, whereas subordinates would tend to make decisions from the point of view of their own department or section. Sub-optimality occurs when one department makes a decision which appears to be a good one from the departmental point of view but which is actually damaging to the organisation as a whole. With centralisation, sub-optimality should not occur, but with decentralisation it would be a serious threat to the efficiency of the organisation.

(d) Centralised control enables an organisation to maintain a balance between different functions or departments. For example, if a company has only a limited amount of funds available to spend over the next few years, centralised management would be able to take a balanced view of how the funds should be shared out between production, marketing, research and development, motor vehicles, other fixed asset purchases in different departments etc.

(e) Senior managers ought to be more experienced and skilful in making decisions. In theory at least, centralised decisions by senior people should be better in 'quality' than decentralised decisions by less experienced subordinates. (Note: this raises the issues of trust and the capabilities of subordinates, which have already been discussed in this chapter.)

(f) Centralised management will often be cheaper in terms of managerial overheads. When authority is delegated, there is often a duplication of management effort (and a corresponding increase in staff numbers) at lower levels of hierarchy. To avoid such costs of duplication some specialised departments (eg data processing, the legal department) may remain centralised.

(g) In times of crisis, the organisation may need strong leadership by a central group of senior managers.

The advantages of delegation (decentralisation)

65. Some delegation is necessary in all organisations because of the limitations to the physical and mental capacity of senior managers. A greater degree of decentralisation - over and above the 'minimum' which is essential - has the following advantages:

(a) It reduces the stress and burdens of senior management.

(b) It provides subordinates with greater job satisfaction by giving them more say in decision-making which affects their work. Such participation in decisions, leading to job satisfaction, might motivate the subordinates to work harder and more efficiently and effectively to achieve the goals of the organisation.

(c) Subordinates may have a better knowledge of 'local' conditions affecting their area of work. With the benefits of such knowledge, they should be capable of more informed, well-judged management. Unfortunately, local managers often think in the short term, whereas senior managers think in the longer term. A subordinate might therefore make a well-informed decision to win a short-term advantage when a different decision would have been preferable in the longer-term view.

(d) Delegation should allow greater flexibility and a quicker response to changing conditions. If problems do not have to be referred up a scalar chain of command to senior managers for a decision, decision-making will be quicker. Since decisions are quicker, they are also more adaptable, and easier to change in the light of unforeseen circumstances which may arise.

(e) By allowing delegated authority to subordinates, management at middle and junior levels are 'groomed' for eventual senior management positions, because they are given the necessary experience of decision-making. Delegation is therefore important for management development.

(f) By establishing appropriate sub-units or profit centres to which authority is delegated, the system of control within the organisation might actually be improved. Targets for performance by each profit centre can be established, actual results monitored against targets and control action taken by appropriate subordinates with the necessary authority; the subordinates would then be held accountable and responsible for their results, and areas of efficiency or inefficiency within the organisation would be more easily identified and remedied.

SUMMARY

Arguments in favour of centralisation and decentralisation

Pro-centralisation

1. Decisions are made at one point, and so easier to co-ordinate.

2. Senior managers in an organisation can take a wider view of problems and consequences.

3. Senior management can keep a proper balance between different departments or functions - eg. by deciding on the resources to allocate to each.

4. Possibly cheaper, by reducing number of managers needed and so lower cost of overheads.

5. Crisis decisions are best taken at the centre.

Pro-decentralisation/delegation

1. Avoids overburdening top managers.

2. Improves motivation of more junior managers.

3. Greater awareness of local problems by decision makers. Geographically dispersed organisations should often be decentralised on a regional/area basis.

4. Greater speed of decision making, and response to changing events.

5. Helps junior managers to develop and helps the process of transition from functional to general management.

6. Separate spheres of responsibility can be identified, and control systems set up for junior management; controls, performance measurement and accountability are better.

---

66. Drucker argued in favour of more rather than less decentralisation, in order to provide a spur to management for better performance. An organisation should be structured so as to facilitate efficient and effective management. Drucker listed three major requirements for structuring:

(a) the organisation must be one which is directed towards *achieving business performance*. 'Organisation is the more efficient the more 'direct' and simple it is';

(b) the organisation should contain the *least possible number of management levels*, so that the chain of command is as short as possible. 'Every link in the chain sets up additional stresses, and creates one more source of inertia, friction and slack'. There is a tendency (identified by C Northcote Parkinson) for levels of management to increase in number, but this is both unnecessary and inefficient;

(c) the organisation structure should provide jobs in which *young managers can be properly trained and tested* for more senior management positions in the future. 'It must give people actual management responsibility in an autonomous position while they are still young enough to acquire new experience'.

● **Divisionalisation**

67.
The two structural principles which meet these requirements in classical theories of organisational structures are:

● *functional decentralisation*; and
● federal decentralisation, or *'divisionalisation'*.

These are alternative organisation structures to greater centralisation of authority but with some functionally-organised or divisional-based decentralisation.

Of these, Drucker considered federal decentralisation much better where it could be applied but it can only operate at fairly senior management level and cannot go below a certain level in the management hierarchy. At lower management levels, functional decentralisation should be applied.

Federal decentralisation

68. Federal decentralisation or divisionalisation is the division of a business into autonomous regions or product businesses, each with its own revenues, expenditures and capital asset purchase programmes, and therefore each with its own profit and loss responsibility. Each division of the organisation might be:
(a) subsidiary companies under the holding company; or
(b) profit centres or investment centres within a single company.

69. The rules for federal decentralisation should be as follows.

(a) It must have properly delegated authority, but strong 'control' should be retained at centre by head office. In other words, management of federal units are free to use their authority to do what they think is right for their part of the organisation, but they must be held properly accountable to head office (eg for profits earned).

(b) A decentralised unit must be large enough to support the quantity and quality of management it needs. It must not rely on head office for excessive management support.

(c) Each decentralised unit must have a potential for growth in its own area of operations.

(d) There should be scope and challenge in the job for the management of the decentralised unit.

(e) Federal units should exist side-by-side with each other. If they deal with each other, it should be as an 'arm's length' transaction. Where they touch, it should be in competition with each other. There should be no insistence on preferential treatment to be given to a 'fellow-unit' by another unit of the overall organisation'.

70. The *advantages* of federal decentralisation are that:

(a) it focuses the attention of management below 'top level' on business performance and results;

(b) it reduces the likelihood of unprofitable products and activities being continued;

(c) it therefore encourages a greater attention to efficiency, lower costs and higher profits;

(d) management by objectives can be applied more easily. 'The manager of the unit knows better than anyone else how he is doing, and needs no one to tell him';

(e) it gives more authority to junior managers, and therefore provides them with work which grooms them for more senior positions in the future;

(f) it tests junior managers in independent command early in their careers, and at a reasonably low level in the management hierarchy;

(g) it provides an organisation structure which reduces the number of levels of management. The top executives in each federal unit should be able to report direct to the chief executive of the holding company.

71. The *limitations* to federal decentralisation are that:

(a) in some businesses, it is impossible to identify completely independent products or markets. In the telecommunications system, for example:
   (i) federal decentralisation by region or area is not properly possible because customers in one region make inter-regional calls;
   (ii) federal decentralisation by service (eg telephones, data transmission, or local calls and trunk calls) is not properly feasible because different services use common equipment.

(b) federal decentralisation is only possible at a fairly senior management level, because there is a limit to how much independence in the division of work can be arranged. For example, every product needs a manufacturing function and a selling function. These functions cannot be separated into two federal units.

2: FORMAL ORGANISATION STRUCTURE

Functional decentralisation

72. Where federal decentralisation is not possible, Drucker argues in favour of functional decentralisation. This should operate throughout some businesses and at lower management levels in others. Functional decentralisation exists when an organisation is structured on the basis of functional departments, and authority is decentralised as far as possible within each department.

73. Functional decentralisation sets up integrated units with maximum responsibility and authority for a major and distinct phase of the business process (eg departments for Machining, Assembly, Personnel, Accounting and Marketing and Sales etc).

> 'Otherwise functional managers will not have objectives of performance and measurements of results that are really derived from business objectives and really focus on business results'.
>
> *Drucker*

● Matrix organisation

74. Matrix organisation is a structure which emerged in the USA during the 1950s and 1960s, and which is now widely practised in a variety of forms. Basically, a matrix organisation provides for the formalisation of management control between different functions, whilst at the same time maintaining functional departmentation.

75. A golden rule of classical management theory was unity of command - one man should have one boss. (Thus, staff management can only act in an advisory capacity, leaving authority in the province of line management alone.)

76. Matrix management may possibly be thought of as a reaction against the 'classical' form of bureaucracy by establishing a structure of dual command.

77. Matrix management first developed in the 1950s in the USA in the aerospace industry. Lockheed-California, the aircraft manufacturers, were organised in a functional hierarchy. Customers were unable to find a manager in Lockheed to whom they could take their problems and queries about their particular orders, and Lockheed found it necessary to employ 'project expediters' as customer liaison officials. From this developed 'project co-ordinators', responsible for co-ordinating line managers into solving a customer's problems. Up to this point, these new officials had no functional responsibilities.

78. Owing to increasingly heavy customer demands, Lockheed eventually created 'programme managers', with authority for project budgets and programme design and scheduling. These managers therefore had functional authority and responsibilities, thus a matrix management organisation was created. It may be shown diagrammatically as a management *grid*; for example:

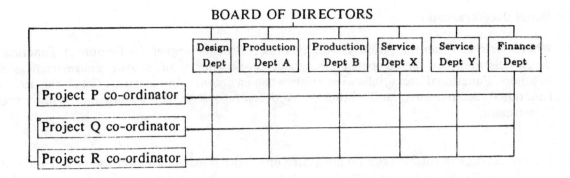

BOARD OF DIRECTORS

79. Authority would be shared between the project co-ordinators and the heads of the functional departments. Functional department heads are responsible for the organisation of the department, but project co-ordinators are responsible for all aspects of the project itself. An employee in a functional department might expect to receive directions/commands from a project co-ordinator as well as from the departmental head - so there may be dual command.

Product and brand management matrices

80. Departmentation by product and brand has already been described, but it is possible to have a product or brand management structure superimposed on top of a functional departmental structure in a matrix; product or brand managers may be responsible for the sales budget, production budget, pricing, marketing, distribution, quality and costs of their product or brand, but may have to co-ordinate with the R & D, production, finance and distribution departments in order to bring the product on to the market and achieve sales targets.

SENIOR MANAGEMENT

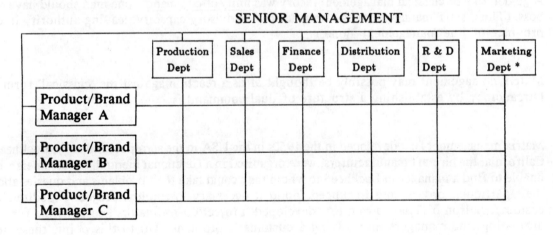

* The product or brand managers will each have their own marketing team; in which case the marketing department itself would be small or non-existent.

81. The authority of product and brand managers may vary from organisation to organisation. J K Galbraith drew up a range of alternative situations as shown on the next page:

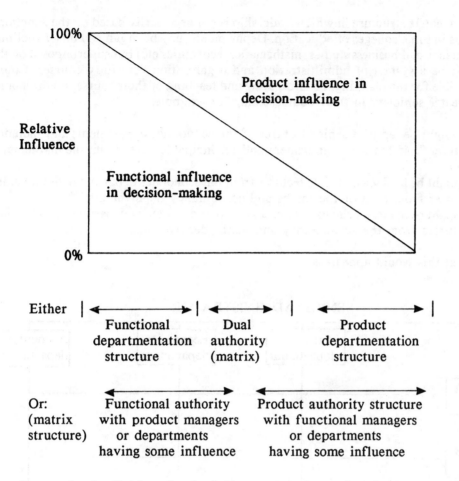

Once again, the division of authority between product or brand managers and functional managers must be carefully defined.

Project team matrices

82. Project teams are another example of a simple matrix structure. A project may be inter-disciplinary, and require the contributions of an engineer, a scientist, a statistician and a production expert, who would each be appointed to the team from their functional department, whilst still retaining membership and status within the department.

Level in departmental hierarchy	A	B	C	D	E
1	X	Ⓧ	X	X	Ⓧ
2	Ⓧ	X	X	X	X
3	X	X	Ⓧ	X	X
4	X	X	X	Ⓧ	X

Members of the project team (circled) would provide formal lateral lines of communication and authority, superimposed on the functional departmental structure. Leadership of the project team would probably go to one of the more senior members in the hierarchy, but this is not a requirement of the matrix structure.

83. An example of a matrix structure in which leadership is not necessarily based on the functional hierarchy occurs in some colleges of education. Departments may be organised on a functional basis (eg accountancy and business studies, mathematics, economics etc) but superimposed on this structure might be a system of administration and organisation for study courses. Course leaders, responsible for the planning, co-ordinating and teaching of their course, might include lecturers of greater seniority in their course team. For example:

(a) Course A might be led by a senior lecturer of the economics department, and include a junior lecturer from the same department and a principal lecturer from the mathematics department.

(b) Course B might be led by a principal lecturer from the economics department and include a senior lecturer from each of the maths and accountancy departments.

(c) Course C might be led by a principal lecturer from the accountancy department, and include junior lecturers from the accountancy and maths departments.

In a grid format this would appear as:

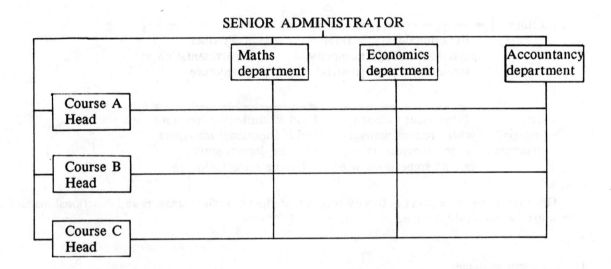

84. A more detailed organisation chart might be drawn as follows:

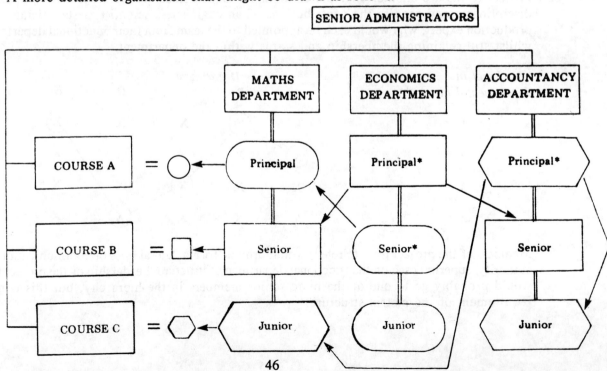

Key: *   Course leaders

_____   Lines of authority of course leaders

═════   Departmental lines of authority

85. Matrix management thus challenges classical ideas about organisation in two ways:

(a) it rejects the idea of one man, one boss (unity of command); and
(b) its subverts the bureaucratic ethic of authority based on status in the formal hierarchy.

Advantages of a matrix structure

86. The advantages of a matrix structure are said to be:

(a) greater flexibility:
    (i) of people. Employees adapt more quickly to a new challenge or new task, and develop an attitude which is geared to accepting change;
    (ii) of tasks and structure. The matrix structure may be short-term (as with project teams) or readily amended (eg a new product manager can be introduced by superimposing his tasks on those of the existing functional managers).
Flexibility should facilitate efficient operations in the face of change;

(b) dual authority gives the organisation multiple orientation. For example, a functional departmentation will often be production-oriented, whereas the superimposition of brand managers will provide the organisation with some market orientation;

(c) it provides a structure for allocating responsibility to managers for end-results. A product manager is responsible for product profitability, a project leader is responsible for ensuring that the task is completed, and a study course leader has direct responsibility for the provision of a complete, efficient and effective course to students;

(d) it provides for inter-disciplinary co-operation and a mixing of skills and expertise;

(e) arguably, it motivates employees to work harder and more efficiently by providing them with greater participation in planning and control decisions.

87. Argyris praised matrix organisations because they break down departmental monopolies and foster participative management styles based on teamwork, which he hoped would eliminate the traditional subordinate-superior relationships.

Disadvantages of matrix structure

88. The disadvantages of matrix organisation are said to be as follows.

(a) Dual authority threatens a conflict between functional managers and product/project managers. Where matrix structure exists it is important that the authority of superiors should not overlap and areas of authority must be clearly defined. A subordinate must know to which superior he is responsible for a particular aspect of his duties.

(b) One individual with two or more bosses is more likely to suffer stress at work.

(c) They are sometimes more costly - eg product managers are additional jobs which would not be required in a simple structure of functional departmentation.

(d) It may be difficult for the management of an organisation to accept a matrix structure. It is possible that a manager may feel threatened that another manager will usurp his authority. (Where authority is not clearly defined, this is likely to happen. The decision-making process would also be expected to slow down.)

89. Many companies have recently moved away from matrix management as being far too complex to handle. An article in the *Financial Times* in June 1989 pointed out the danger of reacting violently against what it describes as a management 'fad' such as matrices:

> "[moving away from matrix-management] helped push multinationals such as Philips towards over-simplistic structures, in which most national power (and much sense of motivation) was given up in favour of strong global product divisions. Philips and others are now having to backtrack towards a hybrid structure which is more acceptable to the many nationalities who work within it."

QUIZ

1. List the reasons in favour of and against 'tall' organisations.
   ● See paras 22-24

2. What factors influence the span of control appropriate to an organisation?
   ● See paras 25-28

3. What is functional authority as opposed to line/staff authority?
   ● See paras 37, 49-56

4. What are some of the problems associated with the existence of staff functions, and how can they be overcome?
   ● See paras 40-41

5. What effect does size have on organisation?
   ● See para 58

6. List the main ways in which work can be organised into departments - with some advantages and disadvantages of each.
   ● See para 60

7. List the advantages of (a) centralisation and (b) decentralisation.
   ● See paras 64-65

8. What is federal decentralisation? What are its advantages?
   ● See paras 68-70

9. What are the problems associated with matrix organisation?
   ● See paras 88,89

Chapter 3

SMALL BUSINESS MANAGEMENT

Topics covered in this chapter

- The problems of large organisations
- The management of small businesses
- The risks and problems of small businesses
- Financing the small business
  - o Problems and government measures to help
  - o Business expansion scheme
  - o Development agencies
  - o Enterprise agencies
  - o Checklist: information to be provided to potential lenders

---

Purpose of this chapter

To give you a broad awareness of the characteristics and common problems of the small business, and to indicate ways in which the small business can obtain resources for expansion.

● **The problems of large organisations**

1. A large organisation is one which has a large amount of resources at its disposal, and so, typically, employs a lot of people.

   The problems of large organisations stem mainly from the difficulties of getting a lot of people to work well together. How can large numbers of people share the work that has to be done, and how can their work be properly planned, co-ordinated and controlled?

PROBLEMS FACING A LARGE ORGANISATION

1. **Organisation structure**
1.1 Sharing out tasks and responsibilities. Who does what?
1.2 How much specialisation/functionalisation should there be?
1.3 What span of control is suitable? And so how tall/flat will the organisation be? There is a tendency for the management hierarchy to develop too many levels. The more management levels there are, the greater the problem of communication between top and bottom, and the greater the problems of control and direction by management at the top.
1.4 To what extent should authority be delegated? How much centralisation/decentralisation should there be? Can junior/middle managers be trusted to exercise discretion and make decisions? How should managers be trained and developed?

2. **Planning and control**
2.1 How should the organisation identify its objectives and set targets for achievement? In the case of large, diversified 'conglomerate' corporations, can the organisation have a major objective other than a financial one (profit maximisation)?
2.2 Developing formal management information systems to enable managers to plan and control properly. Communication problems.
2.3 The problem of making managers accountable, monitoring performance and setting up effective control systems.
2.4 The difficulties of co-ordinating the efforts of managers: problems of conflict (line versus staff; interdepartmental rivalries etc).
2.5 Difficulties of setting up an equitable system of rewards that is directly linked to performance appraisal and the achievement of objectives.

3. **Adapting to change**
3.1 Large organisations might be slow to adapt to change because of a bureaucratic system of operating and decision-making that stifles ideas for innovation.

4. **Motivation**
4.1 It is difficult for individuals to identify themselves with the objectives of a large organisation. The organisation's objectives and their personal objectives will differ.
4.2 Difficulties for individuals to see how their efforts contribute to achieving the organisation's objectives (due to narrow specialisation of jobs etc).
4.3 Possible problems in getting employees to enjoy working in a large organisation, where a bureaucratic 'role culture' predominates.
4.4 Decision-making might be slow, with managers not allowed the authority and discretion they would like.

---

2. An organisation might become so widely diversified in the range of products or services it offers that it becomes difficult, if not impossible, for management to integrate all of the organisation under a common objective and within a single 'management philosophy' and 'organisation spirit'. The different parts of the organisation will not complement each other, and might tend to pull the organisation in different directions. Drucker argued that 'this danger is particularly great in the business that originated in a common technology, such as chemistry or electrical engineering. As the technology unfolds, it creates more and more diversified products with different markets, different objectives for innovation and ultimately even with different technologies... The point may be reached where objectives and principles that fit one business (or group of businesses) endanger another'.

3.   The sheer size of an organisation provides both top management and more junior management with problems of co-ordination, planning, effective control and therefore the achievement of economies of scale and versatility in the range of products and services offered.

'Monster' organisations

For example, a junior manager might find the organisation so large that he has relatively little influence. Decisions which he regards as important must be continually referred up the line to his superiors, for inter-departmental consultations etc. At the same time, the top management might find the organisation so large and complex to understand, and changes in policy and procedures so difficult and time-consuming to implement, that they also feel unable to give direction to the organisation. The organisation is therefore a 'monster' which operates of its own accord, with neither senior nor junior managers able to manage it effectively.

---

4.   In a large organisation, many of the 'specialised' tasks for junior functional managers, and many day-to-day tasks of junior operational management are routine and boring. Even middle management might be frustrated by the restrictions on their authority, the impersonal nature of their organisation, the inability to earn a just reward for their special efforts (owing to the standardisation of pay and promotion procedures) and the lack of information about aspects of the organisation which should influence their work. These problems are likely to result in:

- poor motivation amongst managers;
- consequently, poor motivation amongst their junior staff; and
- a reluctance to accept responsibility.

Overcoming the problems of large size

5.   These difficulties of large organisations can, to some extent, be overcome by:

   (a)   decentralisation and delegation of authority, in particular in a policy of federal decentralisation plus functional decentralisation within federal units. This was described in Chapter 2. However, the aim of decentralisation should be to encourage decision-making at lower levels of management 'closer to the action'. Management motivation and management efficiency in target-setting, planning and control should improve;

   (b)   a pay policy, devised by the personnel department, which provides for just rewards (individual or team bonuses) for outstanding efforts and achievements;

   (c)   the introduction of comprehensive management and employee *information systems* which enable all managers and employees:

   - to understand their planned contribution towards achieving organisational objectives;
   - to compare their actual achievements against their targets;

   (d)   a task structure within the organisation which, through job enrichment, stimulates employee motivation towards better performance.

6. The large organisation does, however, have significant *advantages*.

   (a) A large-scale organisation should have access to sufficient resources to command a significant market share. This in turn will enable it to influence prices in the market so as to ensure continuing profitability.

   (b) A large organisation can provide for greater division of work and specialisation. Specialisation, and the development of a wide range of products or customer services, should enable the organisation to attract continuing customer support and market shares as well as diversifying risk. In contrast, a small or medium-sized business will require greater competence and versatility from its top management, because they will not have the benefits of support from functional specialists which are available to the top managers of large organisations.

   (c) A large organisation with a wide variety of products or customer services should be able to offer an attractive career to prospective employees, and it is therefore likely to receive job application requests from very talented people. This in turn should enable the large organisation to recruit and develop high-quality personnel for top management positions.

   (d) Specialisation brings with it the ability to provide expert services at a relatively low cost to the customer. A large organisation is also able to make use of the advantages of efficient 'large-scale' equipment (eg advanced computer systems or manufacturing equipment). For these (and other) reasons, large organisations are able to achieve *economies of scale* in the use of resources. Cheaper costs in turn mean either lower prices for customers or higher profits for the organisation.

   (e) A large organisation is more likely to provide continuity of goods or services, management philosophy, customer relations etc than a smaller organisation. A smaller organisation might be prone to sudden policy changes or changes of product when a new management team takes over.

● The management of small businesses

7. The management of small businesses contrasts directly, in many ways, with the problems of management of large organisations.

8. *Ownership and top management*
   The top manager of a small organisation is usually the founder and owner of the business. As such, he or she will often want to take a close and detailed interest in many management decisions that are taken, and the organisation will be characterised by centralised decision-making, and so be strongly influenced by the character and personality of the owner-leader.

9. The centralised control and decision-making by the owner-manager could act as a constraint on the growth of the organisation because eventually, as the organisation gets bigger, the burdens of authority will become too great for one individual, or just a handful of individuals.

10. Other features of the management of small businesses could be summarised as follows:

MANAGEMENT OF A SMALL BUSINESS

1. **Organisation structure, planning and control**
1.1 Less rigid definition of jobs than in large organisations, and less specialisation.
1.2 Authority often centralised, although the management hierarchy will be small and all managers should feel quite close to the decision-making process.
1.3 Planning, control and communication (management information systems) will be less formal than in larger organisations.
1.4 Fewer people than in large organisations, and so fewer problems of co-ordination. Greater sense of teamwork.
1.5 Not so much bound by formal rules and procedures as large organisations.
1.6 Decision-making procedures are relatively fast. Decisions can be taken quickly.
1.7 Individual managers have a better idea of the overall objectives of the business, and of how their sections and tasks relate to them.

2. **Adapting to change**
2.1 Small organisations are usually staffed by individuals who are more innovative in their ideas, and more responsive to change. Ideas for innovation and adapting to change are more accepted.

3. **Motivation**
3.1 Individuals have a wider range of duties, and are often able to contribute more to the achievements of the organisation, compared with the achievements of individuals in large organisations.
3.2 Individuals might develop a closer sense of identity with the organisation - say through personal association with the owner-managers.
3.3 Pay and reward systems are usually more personalised than in large organisations.
3.4 Management training and development are not encouraged as much as in large organisations. How many managers of small businesses are capable of stepping into a management job in a large organisation, and doing it well?
3.5 The 'culture' in small organisations is unlikely to be bureaucratic and will allow more scope for innovation and initiative.

● **The risks and problems of a small business**

11. Small businesses have limited resources, and this restriction imposes very serious constraints on what the organisation can do. A task of management is to achieve as much as possible within the limitations that a small size imposes.

12. *Finance:* Small businesses are considered risky investments, and lending organisations such as banks will be reluctant to lend much money without security. A small company's borrowing capability might therefore be limited to a small unsecured bank overdraft, plus a loan for which the assets of a company or the personal guarantees of its owners provide the security.

13. Small companies will also have difficulty in raising share capital. Many such companies are owner-managed, and the owners will only want to put in a certain amount of their own cash, and no more.

   (a) Retained profits can be a very important source of extra shareholder funds, but the company must be profitable in order to have access to extra funds from this source.

(b) If the existing shareholders are willing to allow other shareholders into the company, it might be possible to raise more finance by issuing new shares.

> In the UK, there is a tax incentive scheme called the Business Expansion Scheme (BES) which tries to encourage investors to buy new shares in unquoted companies. BES capital is a form of venture capital, and there are other organisations which specialise in providing venture capital for small companies either as a loan or in exchange for shares. The 3i group is the most well-known example in the UK. Another route to raising new finance from a share issue is a launch on to one of the stock markets for small companies, which in the UK are the Unlisted Securities Market (USM) and the Third Market.

14. Small companies will be restricted in what they can do because of their finance constraints, but the financial challenge for managers is to:

(a) create a profitable company;
(b) achieve a financially stable company (with good liquidity, and a good debt capital/share capital (gearing) ratio etc);
(c) develop attractive plans for the future which will encourage investors to want to put money into the company, or to be willing to lend to it.

Financing the small business is discussed in more detail later.

15. *Product/service development:* Small firms are often innovative and creative. Some are founded on the strength of their owner's original idea for a new product. A major problem for such small firms is the shortage of resources for new product development.

16. The small firm which succeeds in developing a new product with good commercial prospects will often need the support of a big company after a while. To develop a successful product, a high technology company will need:

(a) more capital than it can probably raise;
(b) cash for more R & D;
(c) more management skills to develop, produce, finance and market the new product;
(d) a marketing organisation through which to sell the product.

These are requirements which only a large company can usually satisfy.

17. A major challenge to management in small firms is therefore:

(a) to obtain the resources to maintain an effective product research and development unit, capable of producing a continual flow of new product ideas; and at the same time
(b) to avoid being taken over by a larger 'predator' company.

18. Further risk, especially in innovative (usually high-technology) product areas, is entailed by the comparative inability of small businesses to *diversify*. In theory, therefore, the small organisation may have 'all its eggs in one basket': loss or failure of one activity or product will not be 'covered' by the success of other areas – the company cannot spread the risk.

19. *Training and development:* All organisations need to recruit good, effective managers, and managers are likely to seek employment in organisations which offer:

   (a) career development; and
   (b) a satisfying job; as well as
   (c) good remuneration..

20. Training and management development are discussed fully in Chapter 21, but the problem for small companies is again one of limited resources.

   (a) Can they spare an individual's time to let him or her attend external training courses? (Small companies will usually be unable to provide in-house training of their own).

   (b) Do they have enough management tasks to provide a development programme for their managers? Or will all the key decisions be taken by one or two owner-managers, leaving little else for other managers?

   (c) Are there any trained 'understudies' to take over active management if someone leaves: are there the resources for a management succession plan?

21. In more general terms, according to Koontz, O'Donnell and Weihrich *(Management)*, 'a small corporation may not be able to afford specialised talent, managerial and technical, and yet its problems are the same, except in degree and scope, as those of a large corporation. The owner-manager of the typical small corporation frequently has severe limitations, both in education and experience.'

22. Koontz et al suggest that small business managers have particular problems of 'short-sightedness':

   (a) neglecting basic policy-making as they get bogged down in recurring operating problems;

   (b) failing to plan, particularly for sales and production fluctuations, unexpected expenses, drains on working capital etc. Small businesses are often tempted to accept orders without properly considering the capital required to meet them;

   (c) neglecting to review company objectives in the light of changes in technology, or the political, economic or legal environment.

Summary

Small businesses often encounter problems with:

- Raising finance
- Developing new products - without being taken over
- Inability to diversify and spread risks
- Management development and succession
- Management and staff expertise and experience
- Lack of economies of scale, marketing advantages etc arising from larger size and resources
- Strategic decisions neglected in favour of operational ones

- **Financing the small business**

23. The problems of small companies in raising funds for their investment programmes can be particularly severe. A small company, by definition, will not have much funds of its own for expansion, and it will need to find money from outside. However, the Stock Market is only prepared to list the securities of companies of at least a certain minimum size, and many small companies have no chance of going public.

24. The large institutional investors, such as pension funds and insurance companies, prefer to deal in large blocks of stocks and shares, through the Stock Market. Small companies are of little interest to them, because the amounts of money involved would be too small to justify the effort of managing investment in such organisations.

    Banks, which are an important source of funds (eg on overdraft), will probably place severe limits on the amounts they are prepared to lend a small company without adequate security, so as to limit the risk of default on repayments. Cash flow forecasts and other documentation to confirm the stability of small a company are not as readily believed and accepted as the forecasts of large companies. The risk element is therefore a serious drawback to investing in such companies.

25. Many venture capital funds will now not provide funds in amounts *less* than £250,000, indicating their reluctance to:

    (a) invest in high-risk small businesses; and
    (b) invest time and management resources in researching and monitoring a large number of small investments.

26.

> 'It is already becoming apparent that managers are having difficulty raising further funds because investors are not prepared to wait five years or more for their portfolio to start showing real returns.
>
> The venture capital industry has high hopes that the Third Market will provide for an additional 'exit route' for its investments, but it is still too early to tell if it will prove a success.' *(Financial Times, 29 April 1987)*

27. The Third Market was introduced by the Stock Exchange to challenge the position of the Over The Counter Market (OTC). There is no single OTC market in the UK. The OTC market is a collective term to describe a whole number of market makers in OTC shares, working in different locations and doing their business according to their own procedures and rules, not a single set of market rules.

In general terms, however, if a company wants to raise capital, but cannot get a full listing on the Stock Exchange or an Unlisted Securities Market (USM) quotation, it might approach an OTC market maker and ask him to sponsor the company on to the OTC.

> The main criticism of the OTC market has been the difficulty for shareholders wanting to sell to find buyers for their shares. 'OTC shareholders have often found it impossible to deal and have frequently been the last to discover their company was going bust.'
>
> *(Financial Times 23/1/88)*

28. A major problem of small businesses is therefore one of finding investors prepared to lend them money at a reasonable rate or to provide equity capital.

Government finance for the small business

29. Some financial institutions specialise in lending to small firms but the total amount of funds available is relatively low. The government has introduced a few schemes to encourage more lending to small firms and these include:

(a) the Business Expansion Scheme or BES. The BES is a tax incentive scheme to encourage investors to put up 'venture capital' for companies;

(b) its development agencies and other agencies or boards set up by either central or local government.

The Business Expansion Scheme

30. The Business Expansion Scheme (BES) was introduced in 1983 for an initial four-year period, and renewed for a further indefinite period in 1986.

It is a tax incentive to investors to purchase new shares in unquoted UK companies. Individuals are entitled to up to £40,000 per annum tax relief when they buy new shares in an unquoted company (shares in USM companies do not qualify under the scheme but Third Market companies' shares do).

31. There are two ways in which a company can obtain BES investment funds:

   (a) *They can approach a BES fund for equity funding.* BES funds are funds which have been set up especially to pool the BES investment capital of many individuals and to invest in a range of companies that qualify for BES funding. But an individual BES fund may not be willing to provide the full amount of money that a company wants.

   (b) *They can make an approach directly to private investors by means of issuing a prospectus.* Companies that choose this method of raising BES funds usually hire a 'sponsor' (eg Johnson Fry) to handle the administrative work etc. The costs of an issue can be quite high, however, and with sponsor's fees may amount to as much as 10% of the funds raised. The sponsor might also take options over a number of shares in the company, which it will eventually exercise if the company flourishes.

The attractions of the BES

32. The BES offers the following attractions to investors and small companies.

   (a) It gives individual investors the opportunity to shelter up to £40,000 of their income per annum against income tax, by investing in new equity shares of developing companies. If the shares were acquired after March 1986 and are held for more than 5 years, there is no capital gains tax payable on any gain.

   (b) It gives developing companies access to funds they might otherwise be unable to raise. The limit is £½m per year but this is to be raised to £750,000 per year, in the 1990 Finance Act, for shares issued after 1st May 1990. (Companies might raise sums through 'BES sponsorship' from investment brokers/ managers but smaller fund-raising schemes by companies would also give investors the income tax shelter they are looking for.)

This favourable tax treatment for BES investors explains the popularity of the scheme. Many companies, quite sensibly, have sought the opportunity to benefit from the scheme by offering new shares to BES investors. But the companies must be able to offer:

(a)   good 'asset backing' to attract investors; and
(b)   good prospects of making profits and prospects of expansion and growth.

BES funds

33. The obvious difficulty with the BES is matching investors and companies. If an individual wants to invest £20,000 in shares that will qualify for tax relief under the BES, how does he or she find a promising company that wants to issue new shares for £20,000?

34. This difficulty is overcome by Business Expansion Funds, or 'BES funds', which are a form of venture capital. These are funds set up by a number of financial institutions (investment managers, life assurance companies, investment brokers etc) which:

    (a) collect subscriptions from investors;

    (b) find companies which want to raise new capital and are prepared to issue new shares to obtain the finance. The companies must qualify under the BES; and

    (c) package together the subscriptions of individual investors into the fund, and buy the newly-issued shares of these companies.

    The fund charges a commission for its services.

Realising BES investments

35. Investors of BES funds will expect the company to have plans for how its shareholders who have invested under the BES scheme will be able to cash in their investment after 5 years, if that is what they want to do.

Planned 'exit routes' for shareholders might be:

(a) a launch of the company on to the USM after 5 years. The shares will then be more marketable than if they are traded on the Third Market;

(b) a management buy-back of the shares - the company's management arranging to purchase the shares of the BES investors from them;

(c) a takeover by a larger company.

Development agencies

36. The UK government has set up some development agencies (the Scottish and Welsh Development Agencies) which have been given the task of trying to encourage the development of trade and industry in their area.

37. The assistance that a development agency might give to a firm could include:

    (a) free factory accommodation, or factory accommodation at a low rent. Each development agency is given finance by the government to build factories, and the agency can build either:
    (i)   'bespoke' factories - tailored to the specific needs of a particular company; or
    (ii) 'advance' factories - factories built 'on spec' without any particular user in mind, which the agency will then hope to find someone to use;

    (b) financial assistance, in the form of:
    (i)   an interest relief grant for a bank loan - a company developing its business in an area might obtain a bank loan, and the development agency will agree to compensate the bank for providing the loan at a low rate of interest;
    (ii) direct financial assistance in the form of equity finance, preference share finance or loans.

38. There are several features of development agency assistance which are worth noting.

    (a) The assistance offered to a company comes in a package - eg the offer of free factory accommodation plus financial assistance. The package is co-ordinated by a project manager in the agency.

    (b) There is a 50% assistance limit - the company must put in at least as much finance into a development as the development agency.

    (c) A development agency will not give help to every company in its area. Obviously it must be satisfied that the business development will be successful and will provide jobs in the area. In addition, the agency's overriding concern is to assist depressed areas. Some parts of Wales or Scotland need help more than other parts, and so the particular area in which the development would take place is a matter of importance.

39.
> A development agency is therefore a potential source of *venture capital* for new or expanding companies.

40. There are no development agencies for any part of England, but firms wishing to develop business in England, particularly in depressed areas, can usually obtain similar government assistance, although from different and fragmented sources. Some of these are described below.

Enterprise boards

41. In England, three Enterprise Boards were set up by local authorities (Merseyside, West Yorkshire, West Midlands) to provide funds for local businesses, mainly by taking an equity stake in the businesses. The Enterprise Boards obtained their funding from the local authority or the pension funds of the local authority, but have also obtained some funds from various banks, in the form of guaranteed loans.

42. The Enterprise Boards have so far operated successfully and profitably.

    (a) The West Yorkshire EB was granted tax-avoiding enterprise agency status in 1986.
    (b) The West Midlands EB joined the British Venture Capital Association in 1987.

    These developments indicate the status that the Enterprise Boards have achieved as providers of venture capital for local firms.

Enterprise agencies

43. Enterprise agencies are centres where trained people are available to act as agents for small businesses, giving advice and consultancy, helping with problems and working as financial brokers etc for client firms. There are currently about 300 in Britain. The agencies receive most of their funds from successful big companies, and companies can set these contributions to enterprise agencies against their corporation tax liability. (An enterprise agency is defined by the government as an agency that qualifies for such tax relief.) The government itself also provides some funding.

44. Enterprise agencies do not provide funds themselves (with some exceptions, such as the West Yorkshire Enterprise Board) but their activities are intended to help small businesses to prosper by giving them suitable advice and assistance - eg about raising finance.

Enterprise initiatives

45. The much-vaunted Enterprise Initiative, developed by the Department of Trade and Industry, is a scheme whereby small and new businesses can obtain expert help in management consultancy, exporting, marketing etc. Part of the cost of this is met by the DTI.

Summary

46. The view of the government and many financial experts in the 1980s has been that the future of the UK economy depends on the growth and success of small firms.

47. The Stock Exchange, recognising the importance of smaller companies, set up the USM and then the Third Market as the OTC market developed. The Stock Exchange is still a major institution in the UK for channelling funds into companies. The institutional investors figure prominently in the workings of the stock market.

48. However, the Stock Exchange has not been a major source of funds for small or high risk companies, and the clearing banks on the whole have been reluctant to lend to high-risk ventures. As a result, the past few years have seen a growth in venture capital institutions to provide finance, normally in exchange for an equity stake in the company, to high risk (and often 'high-tech') areas of industry and commerce.

Checklist: presentation of information when seeking finance

Presentations to potential providers of finance should contain information about:

- *Business history*: main factors in development

- *Share capital and Articles* (limited companies); principal shareholders, restriction on borrowing etc in Articles

- *Management structure:* directors (if appropriate), managers and their experience, qualifications etc, management succession plan

- *Business activities*: turnover and profits from each product, details of markets, numbers of employees involved in each area

- *Trading results:* summarised financial information for current and previous years

- *Taxation aspects:* liabilities outstanding, matters in dispute with Inland Revenue etc

- *Reasons for additional finance:*
  - additional investment in fixed assets?
  - reduction in short-term borrowings?
  - enlargement of the business's trading base?
  - improvement of the balance sheet position?
  - meeting of seasonal trading peak?

- *Amount and period of loan required*

- *Existing liabilities*: current borrowings: lenders, amounts, repayment schedule, interest etc

- *Security:* assets offered to secure the loan, such as:
  - existing land and buildings, realistically valued
  - plant and machinery - age and value
  - personal guarantee (losing the protection of limited liability) or surrender value of insurance policies

- *Indication of repayment method and period*

- *Financial controls:* operation of systems to ensure effective application and management of funds

- *Future prospects*: cash flow forecast, projections for coming years - with statement of assumptions, sensitivity to factors outside firm's control etc.

QUIZ

1. What are the advantages of the large business?

   ● See para 6

2. What are the potential problems for the small business?

   ● See paras 9, 11–22

3. What are the possible consequences of the small business manager's immersion in operational decision-making?

   ● See para 22

4. What are the private sector sources of funds available to the small business?

   ● See paras 23–28

5. What are the government measures to help small businesses?

   ● See paras 29 et seq

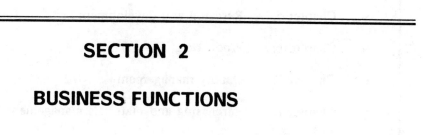

SECTION 2

BUSINESS FUNCTIONS

Topics covered in this section

- Chapter 4:   Marketing

- Chapter 5:   Research and development

- Chapter 6:   Production

- Chapter 7:   Quality management

- Chapter 8:   Purchasing and materials management

Objectives of this section

This section of the study text is designed to introduce the main-line functions of the organisation: marketing, production, research and development, purchasing and overall quality management. It covers the areas specified in the syllabus to give you a broad knowledge of the role of each.

Chapter 4

MARKETING

Topics covered in this chapter

- What is marketing?
- Marketing management
- Marketing philosophies: production, product and sales orientations
- The marketing concept
- Market orientation and organisational objectives
- Marketing organisation in a firm
- The marketing process
- Target marketing
- Marketing mix
- Marketing research
- Marketing financial services

Purpose of this chapter

To give you a broad awareness of the marketing concept and its implications for organisational strategy. To introduce the main decisions involved in distribution management.

● **What is marketing?**

1. Marketing is not simply the task of selling goods which are produced or services which are offered. <u>It is a means of trying to ensure beforehand that the goods produced or services offered conform to what potential customers want and will buy.</u>

2. A distinction should be made at the outset between the terms 'selling' and 'marketing'. Selling is only one aspect of the marketing process, whereas marketing itself is concerned with events before the act of selling (eg research and product development, product quality etc.) and after the act of selling (eg after-sales service).

4: MARKETING

3.

> (a) 'Marketing is the management process which identifies, anticipates and supplies customer requirements efficiently and profitably'.
>
> *(The Institute of Marketing)*
>
> (b) 'Marketing is not only much broader than selling, it is not a specialised activity at all. It encompasses the entire business. It is the whole business seen from the point of view of its final result, that is, from the customer's point of view. Concern and responsibility for marketing must therefore permeate all areas of the enterprise.'
>
> *(Peter F Drucker 1954)*
>
> (c) 'Marketing means working with markets, which in turn means attempting to actualise potential exchanges for the purpose of satisfying human needs and wants. Thus we return to our definition of marketing as human activity directed at satisfying needs and wants through exchange processes'.
>
> *(Philip Kotler 1980)*
>
> Marketing may therefore be considered as both a series of business activities (definitions (a) and (c) and also as a set of attitudes or a concept (definition (b)).

Marketing management defined

4. From the definition of marketing, it is possible to identify the role of management in the marketing process.

'Marketing management is the analysis, planning, implementation and control of programs designed to create, build, and maintain mutually beneficial exchanges and relationships with target markets for the purpose of achieving organisational objectives. It relies on a disciplined analysis of the needs, wants, perceptions and preferences of target and intermediary markets as the basis for effective product design, pricing, communication and distribution.'

(Kotler: *Marketing management, analysis, planning and control*)

5. Marketing management, if it is intended to create, build and maintain a market must inevitably try to *persuade* customers rather than allow the customer complete 'sovereignty' in the market. Kotler suggests that marketing management is *demand management*.

6. The immediate task of a marketing manager with respect to the products of his organisation may be to:

(a) create demand (where none exists);
(b) develop a latent demand;
(c) revitalise a sagging demand;
(d) attempt to smooth out (synchronise) uneven demand;
(e) sustain a buoyant demand (maintenance marketing); or even
(f) reduce overfull demand. Occasionally, a product will need to be 'killed off' (eg for safety or health reasons).

4: MARKETING

In many cases, the marketing manager will belong to an organisation which has direct control over the product; occasionally, however, an attempt may be made to influence customer demand for the products or services of another organisation (eg the UK government's attempts to discourage smoking (counter-marketing) and to develop the use of seat belts in cars).

The attitude of firms towards marketing

7. Since the process of marketing is controlled by the firms rather than the customers, the nature of marketing will inevitably be influenced by the attitudes of the firms. It has been suggested, for example, that the interest of a firm in its marketing effort is created by any of the following:
    (a) a decline in sales;
    (b) an unsatisfactory, slow rate of growth in sales or profits;
    (c) significant changes in the buying patterns of customers;
    (d) an increase in competition;
    (e) rising costs of marketing, sales and distribution expenditures.

    In other words, firms may only give serious consideration to their marketing effort when sales turnover or profits are threatened, or marketing costs increase so as to appear non-cost-effective. Such an attitude is short-sighted.

8. The attitude of firms towards marketing may also be considered in terms of their 'philosophy' towards production, their products and their customers.

Marketing philosophies: production, product and sales orientation

9. Some firms may be *production-oriented*, some *product-oriented* and others *sales-oriented*, although a firm should arguably be *marketing-oriented* to be successful in the longer term.

    (a) A *production-oriented firm* is one which believes that customers will favour products which are available and affordable. As a result, it believes that management time should be spent improving production and distribution efficiency.

    (b) A *product-oriented firm* is one which believes that if it can make a good quality product at a reasonable price, then customers will inevitably buy it with a minimum of marketing effort by the firm. The firm will probably concentrate on product developments and improvements. If there is a lack of competition in the market, or a shortage of goods to meet a basic demand, then product orientation should be successful. However, if there is competition and over-supply of a product, demand must be stimulated, and a product-oriented firm will resort to the 'hard sell' or 'product push' to 'convince' the customer of what he wants.

    (c) A *sales-oriented firm* is one which believes that in order to achieve cost efficiencies through large volumes of output, it must invest heavily in sales promotion. This attitude implies a belief that potential customers are by nature sales-resistant and have to be persuaded to buy (or buy more), so that the task of the firm is to develop a strong sales department, with well-trained salesmen. The popular image of a used car salesman or a door-to-door salesman would suggest that sales orientation is unlikely to achieve any long-term satisfaction of customer needs.

10. These three concepts have given way in many successful firms to the 'marketing concept' or *consumer sovereignty*. The earliest well-known example of the marketing approach is probably that of General Motors in the USA in the 1920s. In the early 1920s, the Ford Motor Company sold more than twice as many cars as General Motors. General Motors then analysed the needs of car buyers and users, and found that customers would pay more to drive *in comfort*. Technological developments in steel-making enabled the firm to produce a stamped-out car body shell which protected driver and passengers from the weather. The new product was developed and, with planned policies for sales promotion and car distribution, General Motors quickly took over the market leadership from Ford. The success of GM was in offering a 'total product proposition' which combined the main 'marketing mix' elements of <u>product, price, place and promotion</u> (discussed in more detail later).

● **The marketing concept**

11. The marketing concept may be defined as:

> 'a management orientation or outlook that accepts that the key task of the organisation is to determine the needs, wants and values of a target market and to adapt the organisation to delivering the desired satisfaction more effectively and efficiently than its competitors'.
>
> 'The organisation must learn to think of itself not as producing goods or services but as *buying customers*, as doing things that will make people *want* to do business with it. *(Levitt)*

12. In other words, customer needs are considered to be of paramount importance. Since technology, markets, the economy, social attitudes, fashions, the law, etc. are all constantly changing, customer needs are likely to change too. The marketing concept is that changing needs must be identified, and products or services adapted and developed to satisfy them. Only in this way can a supplier hope to operate successfully and profitably (if the supplier of the good or service is a profit-making organisation).

Some practical implications of the marketing concept

13. You might suppose, reading the definition of the marketing concept given above, that its practical implementation should present no great problems for management, and that the concept is a straightforward one. However, the needs of customers are not the same thing as what customers would like to have in an ideal world.

'A human *need* is defined as a state of felt deprivation of some basic satisfaction. Human *wants* are desires for specific satisfiers of these deeper needs' *(Kotler)*

Suppliers cannot satisfy all human needs with a single product, but they can try to identify what customers really want - what price they would be prepared to pay for goods that satisfied some of these needs. In a competitive environment, suppliers must be able to offer products that are either cheaper than rival products, or that satisfy certain customers' needs better, albeit at a higher price.

4: MARKETING

14. Car manufacturing is a good example of the application of the marketing concept of developing and selling products. The modern car is designed to provide the right balance between customer desires for high performance, fuel economy, comfort and style at a price the customer can afford, so that the car can compete successfully in the market place against the similar models of rival manufacturers.

15. Since the marketing concept is concerned with product design as well as cost and price, the application of the marketing concept to management decisions should begin at the strategic (long-term) planning stage, and continue through product development and testing to its eventual sale in the market.

● **Market orientation and organisational objectives**

16. You should not lose sight of the fact that the marketing concept should be applied by management only because it is the most practical philosophy for achieving the organisation's objective. A profit-making company's objective might be to achieve a growth in profits, earnings per share or return on shareholder funds. By applying the marketing concept to product design etc. the company might hope to make more attractive products, hence to achieve sustained sales growth and so make higher profits.

17. Another implication of the marketing concept is that an organisation's management should continually be asking 'What business are we in?'. This is a question which is fundamental to strategic planning too, and the importance of developing a market orientation to strategic planning is implicit in the marketing concept.

    (a) With the *product* concept and *selling* concept, an organisation produces goods or services, and then expects to sell them. The nature of the organisation's business is determined by what it has chosen to produce, and there will be a reluctance to change over to producing something different.

    (b) With the marketing concept, an organisation commits itself to supplying what customers need. As those needs change, so too must the goods or services which are produced.

18. You ought to be aware of examples of marketing management asking and answering the following question: 'What business are we in?' The question may be asked, but is not always answered successfully.

    > (a) Amstrad appears to be successful in its aim of developing electrical and electronic goods for certain target markets. The company's successes include CB radio (when many other CB radio manufacturers made heavy losses), microcomputers and word processors.
    >
    > (b) Atari, on the other hand, made heavy losses by identifying its business too narrowly (TV games) only to find itself being beaten in the market by home computer manufacturers and software producers.
    >
    > Try to take note of new developments in markets and products as they arise and see whether you can relate them to the marketing concept.

4: MARKETING

19. If the marketing concept is to be be applied successfully, it must be shared by all managers and supervisors in an organisation.

> 'Marketing is a force which should pervade the entire firm. It must enter into the thinking and behaviour of all decision-makers regardless of their level within the organisation and their functional area.' (*Boyd and Massy*).

'Marketing' in its broader sense covers not just selling, advertising, sales promotion and pricing, but also product design and quality, after-sales service, distribution, reliability of delivery dates and in many cases (eg the retailing industry) purchasing supplies. This is because customer needs relate to these items as well as more obvious 'marketing' factors such as sales price and how products are promoted.

Another way of expressing the important point made above is: 'most firms have a marketing or sales department, but the marketing concept should be shared by managers in every department.'

● **The marketing organisation in a firm**

20. There are various types of formal organisational structure for a marketing department. These are:

(a)

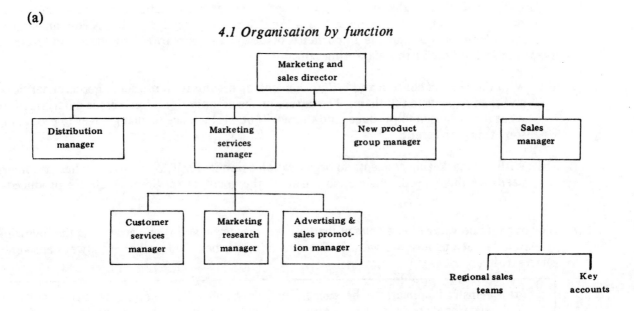

4.1 Organisation by function

The main advantage of functional organisation is its relative simplicity. However, in a large firm which offers a wide variety of products or brands to several markets, no manager is responsible for the success or failure of individual products. Control of product profitability might therefore be weak and inadequate. Equally, the profits from sales to particular market segments might be low and lack adequate control. Alternative forms of organisation which have developed as a means of controlling product or market profitability are product managers and market managers.

(b)

4.2 Product management organisation

```
                    ┌─────────────────┐
                    │  Marketing and  │
                    │  sales director │
                    └─────────────────┘
   ┌───────────┬──────────────┼──────────────────┐
┌──────────┐ ┌─────────┐ ┌──────────┐      ┌──────────┐
│Distribution│ │  Sales  │ │Marketing │      │ Products │
│  manager  │ │ manager │ │ services │      │ manager  │
└──────────┘ └─────────┘ │ manager  │      └──────────┘
                         └──────────┘            │
                    ┌─────────┴─────────┐   ┌──────────┐
              ┌──────────┐    ┌──────────┐  │ Product  │
              │Marketing │    │Advertising│  │  group   │
              │ research │    │& sales pro│  │ managers │
              └──────────┘    │  motion  │  └──────────┘
                              └──────────┘       │
                                            ┌──────────┐
                                            │  Brand   │
                                            │ managers │
                                            └──────────┘
```

(c)

4.3 Market management organisation

```
                    ┌─────────────────┐
                    │  Marketing &    │
                    │  sales director │
                    └─────────────────┘
   ┌───────────┬──────────────┼──────────────────┐
┌──────────┐ ┌─────────┐ ┌──────────┐      ┌──────────┐
│Distribution│ │  Sales  │ │Marketing │      │ Markets  │
│  manager  │ │ manager │ │ services │      │ manager  │
└──────────┘ └─────────┘ │ manager  │      └──────────┘
                         └──────────┘            │
              ┌──────────┬────┴─────┐       ┌──────────┐
        ┌──────────┐┌──────────┐┌──────────┐│ Markets  │
        │ Customer ││Marketing ││Advertising││ managers │
        │ services ││ research ││ & Sales  │└──────────┘
        └──────────┘└──────────┘│ promotion│
                                └──────────┘
```

● **The marketing process**

21. The whole activity of a business should be adjusted to the needs of the customer or potential customer (it should be consumer-oriented) and marketing should not be the sole concern of the sales and marketing departments.

   (a) There should be a complete integration of all departments in an organisation to achieve this end. (In practice, an organisation often suffers from internal squabbles between various departments, such as production, sales and finance, each having its own views on what is the best course of action for a company to take.)

(b) The benefits of customer-orientation are that the customer will want to buy the goods produced and companies will make a profit out of providing them with what they want. (In practice, this mutual satisfaction of companies and consumers is often not achieved because of deep mistrust of company self-interest by the general public). There has been a growth in recent years in efforts to protect the public by means of:

(i) government measures to protect the environment;
(ii) intense scrutiny of the potential danger to health of certain goods (eg cigarettes);
(iii) legislation, such as the Unsolicited Goods and Services Act, the Trade Descriptions Act, the Unfair Contract Terms Act, the Financial Services Act (discussed below) and the Consumer Protection Act.

22. The marketing process focuses on the vital requirement for *marketing planning*. The object of this is to come up with targets, budgets and action plans which will ensure that the organisation achieves its objectives. To do this the organisation must

- analyse market opportunities for new and existing products and markets; and
- select target markets in which the organisation is able to operate successfully.

23. Marketing planning is the blanket term then for many different sorts of analyses and plans:

(a) marketing research and target marketing (discussed below);
(b) product life-cycle analysis (discussed below);
(c) product development;
(d) the marketing mix (discussed below);
(e) sales planning and forecasting;
(f) media planning; and
(g) marketing and sales operations and control planning.

24. There must also be facilities to gain feedback information on how the plans are doing in practice.

25. In detail the marketing process can be concerned with very diverse elements. The following elements indicate how far a business ought to be marketing-oriented:

(a) research and development;
(b) product policy;
(c) production planning;
(d) quality control;
(e) stockholding policy;
(f) credit terms policy;
(g) price policy;
(h) after-sales service;
(i) sales organisation and manning the selling function;
(j) choice of distribution channels;
(k) dealer policies;
(l) advertising;
(m) branding;
(n) packaging;
(o) personal contact between employees and customers.

26.
> *Marketing* then is a comprehensive concept which includes within it the actual activity of selling. It is at the same time bigger and more important than *selling*, which only forms part of the whole.

● **Target marketing**

27. Target marketing by a company involves selecting its market and setting as an objective a target share of each market segment (or of the market as a whole).

28. If the company wants a leadership position, and cannot lead the entire market, it can attempt to gain the leadership position in a single market segment or in several segments. The market segments selected for a leadership position would ideally:
(a) have potential for future growth;
(b) be without a direct competitor;
(c) show a distinctive customer need for 'exploitation';
(d) be accessible and substantial.

29. It is not always possible to enter a market segment where there is direct competition, and a marketing problem for the firm will be the creation of some form of product differentiation (real or imagined) in the *marketing mix* of the product.

> 'Competitive positioning requires the firm to develop a general idea of what kind of offer to make to the target market in relation to competitors' offers.' (Kotler).

● **The marketing mix**

30. The marketing mix is defined by Kotler as 'the set of controllable variables and their levels that the firm uses to influence the target market'. It is of prime importance to marketing management because it represents the *controlled* use of a firm's resources allocated to the marketing budget.

31.
> The marketing mix may be simplified into the four Ps:
>
> (a) **Product** – factors concerning the product or service offered include quality, features, fashion, packaging and branding, after-sales service, guarantees, durability, etc.
>
> (b) **Price** – factors concerning price include not only the level of price, but also credit terms, bulk purchase discounts, discounts for early payment, trade-in allowances etc.
>
> (c) **Place** – factors here include the location of sales outlets and the number and type of sales outlets (shops, supermarkets, etc), the location of service departments, stock levels and transportation and delivery services.
>
> (d) **Promotion** – sales promotion includes the work of the sales team, advertising, merchandising and publicity.

32. Different marketing mixes will appeal to different market segments in any particular market. In addition to the items listed in (a) to (d) above, we could also add the need to obtain information about consumer preferences and to forecast the likely demand for a product. A further element in the marketing budget will therefore be expenditure on *market research* (discussed later).

33. It might be useful to consider some examples of how the marketing mix might be varied.

    (a) A manufacturer of chairs might wish to sell to both the consumer market and the commercial market for office furniture. The marketing mix selected for the consumer market might be low prices with attractive dealer discounts, sales largely through discount warehouses, modern design but fairly low quality and sales promotion relying on advertising by the retail outlets, together with personal selling by the manufacturing firm to the retailer.

    For the commercial market, the firm might develop a durable, robust product which sells at a higher price; selling may be by means of direct mail shots, backed by personal visits from salesmen.

    (b) An interesting comparison can be made between different firms in the same industry; for example, Avon and Yardley both sell cosmetics, but whereas Avon relies on personal selling in the consumer's own home, Yardley relies on an extensive dealer network and heavy advertising expenditure.

34. Other aspects of the marketing mix design which should be noted are:

    (a) a manufacturer of consumer goods will need a marketing mix for the end consumer, and an additional marketing mix for the retailers who act as middlemen in selling the product;

    (b) the optimum marketing mix will change over time as the marketing environment changes. The growth of discount stores and warehouses, for example, might persuade some manufacturers to switch to lower prices for selling through these outlets. The time of year might also be relevant to the mix; manufacturers of fires and central heating equipment might have to reduce prices in the summer months, increase advertising expenditure but reduce the product range on offer in order to achieve a reasonably profitable sales volume;

    (c) the marketing mix will also change over time as the product goes into different stages of its life cycle. When a product is in its 'growth' stages of life, the marketing mix might emphasise the development of sales outlets and advertising; in its 'mature' phase, there might need to be more concern for product quality; and to postpone the eventual decline, it may be necessary to reduce prices and spend more on advertising.

The product life cycle

35. The profitability and sale position (and the marketing mix) of a product can be expected to change over time. The 'product life cycle' is an attempt to recognise distinct stages in a product's sales history.

36. Marketing managers distinguish between:

    (a) *product class:* this is a broad category of product, such as cars, washing machines, newspapers;

(b) *product form:* within a product class there are different forms that the product can take, eg 5-door hatchback cars or 2-seater sports cars; twin-tub or front loading automatic washing machines; national daily newspapers or weekly local papers etc;

(c) *the particular brand or make* of the product form (eg Ford Escort, Vauxhall Astra; Hoover Electron, Zanussi 1100; *Financial Times, Daily Mail* etc).

37. The product life cycle has a differing degree of applicability in each of the three cases. A product-class may have a long maturity stage, and a particular make or brand might have an erratic life cycle. Product forms however tend to conform to the 'classic' life cycle pattern, commonly described by a curve as illustrated:

4.4 Product form life-cycle

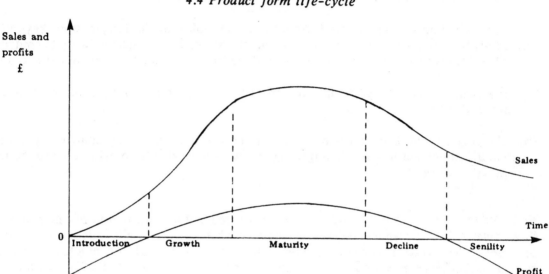

- *Introduction:* a new product takes time to find acceptance by would-be purchasers and there is a slow growth in sales. Only a few firms sell the product, unit costs are high because of low output, there may be early teething troubles with production technology and prices may be high to cover production costs and sales promotion expenditure as much as possible (eg pocket calculators, colour televisions and video cassette recorders were all very expensive when first launched). The product for the time being is a loss-maker.

- *Growth:* if the new product gains market acceptance, sales will eventually rise more sharply and the product will start to make profits. New customers buy the product and as production rises, unit costs fall. Since demand is strong, prices tend to remain fairly static for a time. However, the prospect of cheap mass-production and a strong market will attract competitors so that the number of producers is increasing. With the increase of competition, manufacturers must spend a lot of money on product improvement, sales promotion and distribution to obtain a dominant or strong position in the market.

- *Maturity:* the rate of sales growth slows down and the product reaches a period of maturity which is probably the longest period of a successful product's life. Most products on the market will be at the mature stage of their life. Eventually, sales will begin to decline as there is over-capacity of production in the industry. Severe competition occurs, profits fall and some producers leave the market. The remaining producers seek means of prolonging the product life by modifying it and searching for new market segments.

- *Decline:* most products reach a stage of decline which may be slow or fast. Many producers are reluctant to leave the market, although some inevitably do because of falling profits. If a product remains on the market too long, it will become unprofitable and the decline stage in its life cycle then gives way to a 'senility' stage.

38. Brands or individual makes can have a shorter life cycle than product forms, although the same 'pattern' applies to many of these too. For example, there are many different makes or brands of radial tyre. Some of these have a long life and others will have a much shorter life; however, all of them (or nearly all, at least) will have a shorter life cycle than the overall product form, 'radial tyres'.

The relevance of the product life cycle to planning and marketing

39. A company selling a range of products must try to look into the longer term, beyond the immediate budget period, and estimate how much each of its products is likely to contribute towards sales revenue and profitability. It is therefore necessary to make an assessment of:

    (a) the stage of its life cycle that any product class, product form, make or brand has reached; and

    (b) allowing for the price changes, other marketing strategies, cost control and product modifications, for how much longer the product will be able to contribute significantly to profits and sales.

40. In the 1970s and early 1980s, British Leyland was a well-publicised example of a company with 'life-cycle' difficulties which might be encountered when a company either does not or is unable to plan for the future of its ageing product range. In the 1970s, BL lost much of its share of the car market because its products were ageing and at a disadvantage to the new models being introduced by competitors. Because of the age of the models, the potential for generating profits was severely restricted.

    As a fairly short-term measure, BL gave urgent facelifts to its product range in order to lengthen its life, introduced the Ital and went into a joint venture with Honda to develop the Acclaim.

41. The marketing mix for a product at any time is likely to depend to a large extent on the stage it has reached in its life cycle. For example:

    (a) price competition is likely to be keener in a product's mature and declining phases than in its growth phase;

    (b) advertising and promotion might be crucial in the growth phase, to make customers aware of the product.

● Marketing research

42. Marketing decisions are inevitably made under conditions of uncertainty and risk. The use of marketing research cannot eliminate risk but can reduce it by indicating the likely outcome of a certain course of action.

> Markets are dynamic and competitive; success in business depends on greater investment and more frequent innovation so as not to lose ground to competitors. Important decisions have to be taken frequently, and in order to make decisions with confidence management needs relevant and comprehensive information. It is the task of marketing research to provide this information.

43. Marketing information needs can be classified into three broad categories:

   (a) information for *strategic decision-making* (eg product life cycle estimates, information to help with decisions about diversifying or to segment a market etc);

   (b) information for *tactical decisions* (eg planning sales territories, setting short-term marketing cost budgets etc);

   (c) information for a *marketing database* (eg for market share analysis, competitor analysis, substitute product analysis).

   The information system for marketing is referred to as *marketing research.*

44. > Marketing research can be defined as 'the objective gathering, recording and analysing of all facts about problems relating to the transfer and sales of goods and services from producer to consumer or user.'   *(British Institute of Marketing)*

The scope of marketing research

45. The scope of marketing research is to look at each element of the marketing mix, it may be listed as follows:

   - *Market research*, which includes:
     (i) analysis of the market potential for existing products;
     (ii) forecasting likely demand for new products;
     (iii) sales forecasting for all products;
     (iv) study of market trends;
     (v) study of the characteristics of the market;
     (vi) analysis of market shares.

   - *Product research*, which includes:
     (i) customer acceptance of proposed new products;
     (ii) comparative studies between competitive products;
     (iii) studies into packaging and design;
     (iv) forecasting new uses for existing products;
     (v) test marketing;
     (vi) research into the development of a product line (range).

   - *Price research*, which includes:
     (i) analysis of elasticities of demand;
     (ii) analysis of costs and contribution or profit margins;
     (iii) the effect of changes in credit policy on demand;
     (iv) customer perceptions of price (and quality).

- *Sales promotion research,* which includes:
  (i) motivation research for advertising and sales promotion effectiveness;
  (ii) analysing the effectiveness of advertising on sales demand;
  (iii) analysing the effectiveness of individual aspects of advertising (copy, use of media, etc);
  (iv) establishing sales territories;
  (v) analysing the effectiveness of salesmen;
  (vi) analysing the effectiveness of other sales promotion methods.

- *Distribution research,* which includes:
  (i) the location and design of distribution centres;
  (ii) the analysis of packaging for transportation and shelving;
  (iii) dealer supply requirements;
  (iv) dealer advertising requirements;
  (v) the cost of different methods of transportation and warehousing.

46. Marketing research also extends into other areas, such as:

    (a) the study of corporate responsibility (eg towards the environment);
    (b) economic forecasting;
    (c) international and export studies; and
    (d) long-term business forecasting.

47. Marketing research has been a growing source of organisation expenditure in recent years. The reasons for this development are probably as follows.

    (a) As organisations become larger, and concentrate production to achieve economies of scale, the communications gap between the customer and the supplier increases. The supplier is no longer close to his markets and does not have any deep personal knowledge of them. Since the supplier is remote from the customer, information about the customer must be provided.

    (b) As organisations expand into larger markets, perhaps international and export markets, the business risk of collapse and failure grows. A larger amount of money is invested and unless a firm is well-diversified, a change in the size or nature of demand in some of the market could mean that this investment may be lost. Marketing research is a method of reducing the business risk by providing better information for decision-making.

    (c) Organisations have become aware that customers can be persuaded to buy, not just on the basis of price, but also on other grounds. This has led to *non-price competition -* competing with other firms' products with 'inducements' other than lower prices (eg location of sales outlets, advertising, sales promotion, etc) - and marketing research information has been found useful as a means of analysing the effectiveness of various marketing tools.

    (d) If organisations adopt the marketing concept, and become customer-oriented, the need to find out more about consumer needs will arise. (Indeed, it can be argued that in an economic recession, when market sizes are too small for production capacities, market-oriented firms will survive whilst product-oriented firms will lose their markets.)

48. Two important types of forecast are derived from market research.

    (a) *Market forecast*

    This is a forecast for the market as a whole. It is mainly involved in the assessment of environmental factors, outside the organisation's control, which will affect the demand for its products/services. Often it consists of three components:

    (i) the economic review (national economy, government policy, covering forecasts on investment, population, gross national product, etc);

    (ii) specific market research (to obtain data about specific markets and forecasts concerning total market demand);

    (iii) evaluation of total market demand for the firm's and similar products - eg profitability, market potential etc.

    (b) *Sales forecasts*

    These are estimates of sales of a product in a future period:

    (i) at a given price;
    (ii) using a stated method(s) of sales promotion which will cost a given amount of money.

    Unlike the market forecast, a sales forecast concerns the firm's activity directly. it takes into account such aspects as sales to certain categories of customer, sales promotion activities, the extent of competition, product life cycle, performance of major products.

    Sales forecasts are expressed in volume, value and profit, and in the case of national and international organisations regional forecasts are usual, by product.

49. Market research is an important element in setting objectives. Decisions must be made about:

    (a) whether the organisation wants to be the market leader or not;
    (b) whether the product range needs to be expanded;
    (c) whether the organisation relies too heavily on one product or market and should diversify;
    (d) whether the organisation should aim to shift position in the market (eg from producing low-cost standard items for the main market to higher-cost and higher-priced specialist products for individual segments of the market);
    (e) how much of each product to make - the production mix according to sales potential.

QUIZ

1. What is marketing management?

   ● See para 4

2. What is the marketing concept?

   ● See paras 11-12

3. What business activities concern the marketing function?

   ● See para 25

4. What comprises the marketing mix?

   ● See paras 30, 31

5. What are the stages in a product form life-cycle?

   ● See para 37

6. What is the scope of marketing research?

   ● See para 45

Chapter 5

RESEARCH AND DEVELOPMENT

Topics covered in this chapter

- Research or development
- R&D in practice
- The R&D department
- Financing research and development
- Problems of R & D management

Purpose of this chapter

This brief chapter is intended to introduce you to the role played by the research and development function in a modern organisation.

- **Research or development?**

1. It is useful when discussing research and development (R&D) to have clear definitions of what these terms actually mean. SSAP 13, *Accounting for Research and Development*, splits R&D expenditure into the following categories:

   - *Pure research* is original research to obtain new scientific or technical knowledge or understanding. There is no clear commercial end in view and such research work does not have a practical application. Companies and other business entities might carry out this type of research in the hope that it will provide new knowledge which can subsequently be exploited.

   - *Applied research* is original research work which also seeks to obtain new scientific or technical knowledge, but which has a specific practical aim or application (eg research on improvements in the effectiveness of toothpastes or medicines etc). Applied research may develop from 'pioneering' pure research, but many companies have full-time research teams working on applied research projects.

   - *Development* is the use of existing scientific and technical knowledge to produce new (or substantially improved) products or systems, prior to starting commercial production operations.

2. The dividing line between each of these categories will often be indistinct in practice, and some expenditure might be classified both as research and development. It may be even more difficult to distinguish development costs from production costs. For example, if a prototype model of a new product is developed and then sold to a customer, the costs of the prototype will include both development and production expenditure.

3. Pure research and much applied research is carried out by government departments or agencies (eg medical research in hospitals and research into improved agricultural products by the Ministry of Agriculture etc). Profit-making organisations use an R & D department principally for development work, although some large organisations also fund some research work (usually applied research).

4. Within a profit-making organisation, the role of R & D could be stated more specifically as contributing towards the discovery and development of new and improved products or processes whereby the organisation can continue to compete commercially in its markets and to attract customers. New product design and development is essential to the survival of many companies, and they must therefore use some of their resources to fund R & D work. The faster the pace of change in the industry, the greater is the need for R & D effort.

5. Some organisations lead their industry in R & D, and the role of their R & D department will be innovative, aimed at developing new products and processes before any of their competitors. Other organisations adopt a more defensive and 'follow-my-leader' approach to development work, imitating the new products of a rival company as quickly as possible after the rival has initially developed them.

6. The functions of R & D may therefore be summarised as follows:

    (a) Providing the organisation with knowledge of current opportunities and threats presented by developments in the technological environment.

    (b) Contributing to corporate planning by identifying threats and opportunities in the current and potential product bases and processes of the organisation. Influencing marketing strategies ie whether they are rooted in active innovation, defensive 'following' etc.

    (c) Developing new products, or prolonging the lifespan of old products, in response to market changes, competition, changing cost structures and the stage of the product life cycle reached by existing products.

    (d) Developing new production processes, in response to the need for increased productivity or cost reduction, or to the availability of new technologies.

    (e) Creating and supporting the organisation culture of adaptability and innovation.

7. Examples given by SSAP 13 (revised) of activities that would normally be included as R&D expenditure are:

    • experimental, theoretical or other work aimed at the discovery of new knowledge or the advancement of existing knowledge;

    • searching for applications of that knowledge;

    • formulation and design of possible applications for such work;

    • testing in search for, or evaluation of, product, service or process alternatives;

    • design, construction and testing of pre-production prototypes and models and development batches;

- design of products, services, processes or systems involving new technology or substantially improving those already produced or installed;

- construction and operation of pilot plants.

• R&D in practice

8. *Research* then is generally carried out in order:

   (a) to acquire and understand new knowledge;
   (b) to seek and examine opportunities for technical improvements in products and services;
   (c) to seek and examine ways to improve the methods and costs of production of goods and services; or
   (d) to seek and examine ways to enhance the quality of provision.

9. Industrial research, to the extent that it goes on at all, is applied research – it is conducted with the intention of identifying areas in which new findings can be commercially exploited, eg a more effective toothpaste or a better means of cleaning teeth.

10. *Development* is the function of translating useful research results into production. The development of a product might follow the stages set out below:

    (a) preparing a 'duty' specification for the new products;
    (b) preparing a 'model shop' sample;
    (c) preparing drawings of components;
    (d) preparing methods of assembly and assembly procedures;
    (e) supervising first product runs;
    (f) a field test;
    (g) releasing the product for full production and selling to the market.

11. Clearly, development stages will differ, and the timescale of development will differ, according to the nature of the product. Developing a new model of aeroplane will be more complex and lengthy than developing a better way of packaging toothpaste, for example.

• The research and development department

12. The director or manager of research and development is a senior executive often reporting directly to the chief executive officer or managing director. He has a line responsibility for his own staff and staff relationship with other first line executives. An organisation chart for the R & D department is shown over the page.

5: RESEARCH AND DEVELOPMENT

5.1 R & D department organisation chart

13. The *objectives* of a R&D department are amongst the most difficult to define. They may include:

    (a)   producing new product plans by an agreed date and at a predetermined cost;

    (b)   making possible production of new products in line with phasing out old ones;

    (c)   providing meaningful estimates of costs of manufacture of new products, including both capital and production costs;

    (d)   getting ahead of or catching up with competitive technology;

    (e)   achieving a predetermined percentage of 'new products' in the company's line of saleable products; or

    (f)   running the department at a pre-planned cost.

> It is the task of R&D management to plan and control R&D work (timescales, product development programmes, costs etc) and to ensure that innovation and the exercise of creative imagination are encouraged amongst employees. This clearly is tied in with the marketing orientation of a firm and with its commitment to quality.

14. *Product management* is the task of planning new products, updating existing products, examining competitive products, and making prototypes to duty specifications required by the marketing organisation. We saw in Chapter 4 that firms with a marketing orientation are likely to have a product management structure.

The R&D department's design and development engineers provide the link between the marketing operations and the factories. They are concerned not only with ensuring that planned costs of manufacture bear a satisfactory relationship to market selling prices, but also with ensuring that the goods produced are what customers want to buy.

15. *Quality control* is essential in this process because it is well recognised in industry that satisfactory quality stems from good design. Designing good quality products and ensuring that systems are developed to monitor quality are also part of the R & D department's role, in liaison with the quality control section.

> We shall look at quality control in more detail in Chapter 7.

16. *The research and development laboratory.* Many organisations (eg drugs companies) need a laboratory for research work, which might be concerned with study of materials, power, electrical characteristics, 'finishing' (ie plating techniques), painting, foods, drugs etc.

17. The laboratory, product management and quality control might need a 'mini production unit' to test their products and the products of competitors, and to make prototypes for proposed future products. This will be purpose of a *model shop*.

● **Financing research and development**

18. Deciding how much should be spent on research and development is a difficult management decision. Comparisons with competitor companies' expenditure may help. Comparisons with previous years, bearing in mind the success or failure of these years, may be useful. The remaining life of existing products will also be an important consideration because replacement products or improved versions of existing products must be scheduled if an organisation is to keep its customers. If the end of a product's life can be reasonably estimated then this may help to decide when new products must reach the market place and the cost of meeting this need.

19. Many large manufacturers, particularly of highly technical machine tools and pharmaceuticals, now pay universities and other professional research bodies to carry out both pure and applied research in their sphere of interest. Increasingly it is *development* only which is carried out in the firm itself.

20. Funds spent on developing new or existing products can, in some cases, be capitalised and carried forward to future years. They are then written off against income generated by the successful new product. SSAP13 allows this policy to be followed when:

(a) there is a clearly defined development project for which the related expenditure is separately identifable;

(b) the outcomes of the project have been assessed, and it is reasonably certain that the outcomes are technically feasible and commercially viable;

    (c)   the eventual profits from the developed products are reasonably expected to cover the costs of past and future development; and

    (d)   the company has adequate resources to complete the development project.

● **Problems of R & D management**

21.   *Organisational problems.* Problems of authority relationships arise with the management of Research and Development. The function will have to liaise closely with marketing, and with production, as well as with senior management responsible for corporate planning: its role is both strategic and technical. Aspects of the R and D role are relevant to product/market/price decisions and to product planning and control. To whom does the R and D manager report? What is the 'crossover' point at which the relationship between R and D, marketing and production is the responsibility of one person? Should R and D have functional or staff authority over process development or product specification activities carried out by other departments? Should R and D be left altogether to outside agencies, rather than in-house specialists?

22.   *Financial control problems.* Evaluation is by nature not easily planned in advance, and financial performance targets are not easily set. Budgeting for long-term, complex development projects with uncertain returns can be a nightmare of management accounting.

23.   *Evaluation and control problems.* Evaluation could be based on successful application of new ideas, ie patents obtained, commercial viability etc. Investment appraisal methods, or analysis of probable risk and payoff might be used, subject to each enterprise's risk aversion, current financial situation and market position etc.

24.   *Staff problems.* Research staff are usually highly qualified and profession-oriented, with consequences for the style of supervision and level of remuneration offered to them. Staff will have more career mobility in some fields than others, but the fact remains that the organisation will need to make concessions if it wants to stimulate innovation.

25.   *Cultural problems.* Encouraging innovation means trial and error, flexibility, tolerance of mistakes in the interests of experimentation, high incentives etc. If this is merely a subculture in an essentially bureaucratic organisation, it will not only be difficult to sustain, but a source of immense 'political' conflict and potential organisational identity crisis.

QUIZ

1. Define pure and applied research. In what ways is development different from research?

   ● See paras 1 and 2.

2. What is the object of research?

   ● See para 5.

3. What are the functions of the R & D department?

   ● See para 6

4. List seven examples of development activity.

   ● See para 10.

5. How does the R&D department link in with an organisation's marketing and production departments?

   ● See para 14, 15.

6. In what circumstances may development expenditure be carried forward to future years?

   ● See paras 19 and 20.

7. What are the problems associated with R & D management?

   ● See paras 21 - 25.

Chapter 6

PRODUCTION

Topics covered in this chapter

- Production and operations management
- Types of production
- Just In Time techniques
- Capital-intensive and labour-intensive organisation
- Control in production
- Plant management
- Production planning
- Production control
- Progress control

Purpose of this chapter

To give you a broad knowledge of production and operations management, and of just-in-time production techniques.

● **Production and operations management**

1. The function of the organisation and management of production is to plan, organise, direct and control the necessary activities to provide products and services.

    (a) The first concern of the production manager is to provide *inputs* to the production 'system', such as plant facilities, materials, labour etc - to acquire machinery and equipment, raw materials and production workers.

    (b) Once the inputs have been assembled, the *creation of value* can take place. This is the stage which occupies most of the production manager's attention, in some of the following ways:
        (i)   scheduling jobs on machines;
        (ii)   assigning labour to jobs;
        (iii) controlling the quality of production;
        (iv)   improving methods of work;
        (v)   handling materials efficiently - so as to avoid costly waste.

    (c) The final stage of production is the completion of *'outputs'*, ie finished products and services.

2.   The objective of the production manager is to maximise the value created.

Production manager

Inputs ———→ Creation of value ———→ Outputs (which have *added value* over the value of inputs)

A production system is a framework within which the creation of value can take place.

3.   An example of inputs, operations and outputs might provide a helpful illustration. Take a furniture manufacturer.

(a)   Inputs   – timber, screws, nails, adhesives, varnish, stain, templates, cutting tools, carpenters;
(b)   Operations   – sawing, sanding, assembly, finishing;
(c)   Outputs   – tables, chairs, cabinets, etc;
(d)   Intermediate
        activities   – progressing, inspection, storage.

4.   A simplified production system can be illustrated as follows. Notice that the link between production management and the physical production work is usually *information* - reports and records.

Activity	*Reports/records*	*Responsibility*
Inputs of raw materials	Goods inward notes and inventory records	
Inspection and storage	Work schedules Route sheets for progressing work	Production manager
Operations	Production reports Time and cost records	
Final inspection		
Finished goods Storage	Inspection and stock reports	
Despatch	Despatch notes	

5.   There are three main stages in any production system:

●   the logistical and validation work required before manufacture, or operation of the service, can begin;
●   the manufacture or performance of the service itself;
●   the testing, inspection and measuring of overall performance.

6: PRODUCTION

6.   These can be summed up as:
   ● prepare;
   ● do;
   ● monitor, control and adapt.

---

7.   Production organisation and management is essentially about producing on time the required quantity of products or services of the correct quality or standard, by the most efficient and economical means compatible with cost parameters.

---

8.   Production management is concerned with two main groups of decisions:

   (a)   the longer term decisions related to setting up the organisation, such as:
      (i)   design of the product;
      (ii)   selection of equipment and processes;
      (iii) job design and methods;
      (iv)   factory location and layout;

   (b)   the short-term decisions concerned with the running and control of the organisation, for example:
      (i)   production and stock control;
      (ii)   inspection and quality control;
      (iii) maintenance;
      (iv)   labour control and supervision.

● Types of production

9.   There are several ways of classifying systems for manufacturing or service industries. Different forms of production are often classified in terms of their economic character. The three best known are:
   (a) job production;
   (b) batch production;
   (c) flow production.

10.   The kind of industry that a company is in will naturally affect the character, type and size of operations, and therefore determine the method of production. In turn, the methods of production will influence the company's organisation, plant, tooling and labour. For example, the use of robots for production work because of their expense will be largely confined to mass production or large volume flow production, or to jobbing work where the value of individual jobs is very high and jobs are fairly standard.

The main factors determining the most appropriate form of production in a particular situation are:
   ●   the type of product and its characteristics;
   ●   the demand for the product - is it big or small, regular or occasional?
   ●   the process involved, including such things as the degree of standardisation possible and the qualities of material and workmanship required.

Job production

11. Jobbing work is the production of units in separate identifiable jobs. This is normally used when a product is being made to a customer's special order - often a 'one-off' product which is unlikely to be repeated, such as in shipbuilding, bridgebuilding, or where special machines are being made. It is also common in printing, repair shops, and jobbing foundries.

   The main features of job production are as follows.

   (a) Most of the work is done specially for each order.
   (b) Work does not normally start until an order has been received.
   (c) Most of the parts and materials cannot be stocked in advance.
   (d) The company may need a wide range of general purpose tools, plant and equipment.
   (e) The workforce is usually versatile and highly skilled, to deal with the special problems of production.
   (f) There is no regular rhythm to production; each job needs individual planning and production.
   (g) The supply of materials can only be maintained with plenty of early warning because it is usually difficult to balance capacity and requirements.

Batch production

12. This is the production 'in one go' of a quantity of the same product, where the items produced are not intended for sale to a specific single customer. Batch production is used when the product is being made at regular intervals in specific quantities, often at a specific price. Therefore the quantities involved must be large enough to justify dividing up the work into a number of separate operations. Each operation is completed before the batch is passed on to the next stage.

   The main features of batch production are as follows.

   (a) Each batch of work passes from one machine or process to the next stage as work is completed.

   (b) Groups of general purpose machines are needed to cope with the variety of work.

   (c) Comparatively expensive tooling arrangements are needed to cater for this variety of products (and the larger the batch, or the more often a batch is repeated, the more special tooling is justified).

   (d) The greater division of labour in batch production compared with job production means that less skill is needed by the individual operator; but more skill is needed by the machine setter and the production engineer.

   (e) Efficient planning and control of production is necessary to cope with routing, changes of programme and the variety of jobs and operations.

   (f) Good facilities must be provided for transferring work from operation to operation.

   (g) There is a greater need for forward planning of materials as the volume and the variety of output increases.

6: PRODUCTION

Flow production

13. Where a product is made on a continuous basis, with an unbroken flow of production passing from one operation to the next, this is called flow production. There are two main types of flow production:

    (a) where a single product, such as oil or paper, is treated through a fixed sequence of processes in a continuous flow. (This is often called '*process production*');

    (b) where individual products such as cars , domestic appliances etc are made in a series of repetitive operations in a fixed sequence, sometimes on an assembly line. (This is often referred to as '*mass production*').

14. The main features of flow production are:

    (a) a rigid specification based on development work for the production processes or operations;

    (b) highly specialised tools and equipment or plant laid out to facilitate continuous flow. Flow production lends itself readily to the use of robotics;

    (c) a high degree of standardisation of methods, tools, equipment and materials;

    (d) a carefully balanced work load at each station in the production process;

    (e) sufficient continuous demand to justify the expenditure involved;

    (f) continuous maintenance to prevent breakdown in the flow line;

    (g) a carefully scheduled supply of materials to avoid costly stoppages in production.

15. Note that many factories have more than one of the types of production described above. For example in a factory making cars, the final assembly of the car may be carried out in flow production while some parts, like the chassis and certain components, may be made in batch production, and the special jigs and tools needed, as well as the maintenance and repair work, may be carried out under job production.

● **Just In Time production techniques**

16. Just In Time (JIT) is a system of production which aims to eliminate waste. Waste can be described as the use of resources that fail to add value to the product. There are two main aspects of it:

    (a) *JIT purchasing* - this seeks to match as closely as possible the usage of raw materials in production with the delivery of materials from suppliers. Stock is therefore kept at the near-zero level.

    (b) *JIT production* - production only takes place when there is actual customer demand for the output. This means that work in progress and finished goods stock levels are at a minimum.

17. A JIT manufacturing strategy has other important implications.

   (a) A manufacturer who uses JIT will want its *suppliers* to deliver materials and components 'just in time' and in small quantities rather than in large deliveries. This calls for a close relationship with suppliers, and so the manufacturer is likely to have just one or two suppliers for each component or material item.

   (b) Keeping stocks of components to a minimum also means that their quality standard must be high, because there is no safety margin if some of them turn out to be defective.

   (c) Low levels of work in progress and finished goods mean that:

      (i) production quality must be high, because many rejects will halt the production line, and there will be insufficient safety stock of finished goods to meet customer demand;
      (ii) the production process may need to be shortened and simplified. Flexible manufacturing systems (FMS) are an example of this. Changing the shopfloor layout to reduce the movement of materials is another;
      (iii) the manufacture of components and sub-assemblies needs to be synchronised, so that they are available when they are needed, and neither too soon (causing excess stocks) nor too late (causing delay in production).

   (d) Quality may need to be controlled and improved through measures such as:

      (i) statistical checks on output quality;
      (ii) training workers. 'Training workers fits in well with another tenet of the JIT philosophy: "total employee involvement". Workers need to have diverse skills so they can move from one task to another keeping production flowing smoothly.' (Diane Coyle, *Investors Chronicle*, 5 May 1989).

   (e) 'Production systems must have flexibility, and the workforce contributes to this. "Kanban" is a system of markers for passing components around the factory - but only when they are needed. One worker cannot produce his next item until the next worker along the line has taken the last one; instead he does something else useful - like sweeping the floor.'
   (Diane Coyle)

18. The characteristics of JIT were summarised by consultant Martin Cocker *(Management Accounting*, March 1989) as follows.

   'A Just In Time environment is composed of the following:

   - the elimination of waste
   - a move towards zero inventory
   - an emphasis on perfect quality
   - stable production rates
   - increased people responsibility
   - short set-ups
   - moving towards a batch size of one
   - preventive maintenance
   - balanced capacity.'

   To this, we should add the demand-pull emphasis on the physical flow of goods through the factory.

Numerical control machines

19. NC machines are programmable manufacturing machines, controlled by either a 'local' or a central computer, which carry out tasks under programmed instructions within predetermined performance criteria. The implications of NC machine technology include:

    (a) reduced set-up times;
    (b) better quality of output;
    (c) fewer reworked items and less scrap;
    (d) less reliance on direct labour.

20. A feature of the modern manufacturing environment is the *work cell*, which is a grouping of NC machines and a small direct labour team, for performing a manufacturing task.

Flexible manufacturing systems (FMS)

21. A flexible manufacturing system (FMS) is a highly-automated manufacturing system, which is computer-controlled and capable of producing a broad 'family' of parts in a flexible manner. It is characterised by small batch production, the ability to change quickly from one job to another and very fast response times, so that output can be produced quickly in response to specific orders that come in.

22. The sophistication of an FMS can vary from one system to another, but features can include:

    (a) a JIT system;
    (b) full computer-integrated manufacturing (CIM), or perhaps just islands of automation (IAs);
    (c) a computerised materials handling system (MHS); or
    (d) an automated storage and retrieval system (ASRs) for raw materials and parts.

23. The possibilities of FMS have been excellently described by Anna Kochan in the *Financial Times* (31 May 1989) as follows.

    "Small batch production helps to provide the flexibility needed for *just-in-time manufacturing*, which involves producing only to customer order and eliminating stock.

    The problem with small batches is the set-up time. Even with the most modern of machine tools, it can take several hours, or several days, to prepare a machine before production can start.

    The target of an FMS is to avoid this delay by separating the set-up operation from the machining process. While an operator at one station is preparing a pallet, its fixtures and the component for machining, machine tools at other stations are cutting the prepared components.

    To keep production going continuously, an FMS has to incorporate tool stores, pallet stores and an automated cart that transfers the pallets between the different stations and stores. The whole operation is computer controlled.

    With the automated equipment and the organising software, FMS is a big investment for a company. So although its flexibility makes it the obvious technology for small subcontractors few have adopted it."

6: PRODUCTION

- **Capital-intensive and labour-intensive organisations**

24. One method of classifying production organisations or business units is by the capital and labour employed within them, usually under two headings:
    (a) capital-intensive organisations; and
    (b) labour-intensive organisations.

25. A <u>capital-intensive organisation</u> is one in which there are exceptionally large investments of capital in machinery, plant, buildings and equipment in relation to the workforce. Usually these are large-scale business organisations using flow production methods in industries that are technologically based.

> An example is the motor car industry, where vast sums are spent on specialised machinery (such as transfer line machines to produce an engine block completely machined), and on special tooling (such as car body dies to produce the body pressings).

26. Capital-intensive industry also makes use of automated production, particularly in the continuous flow process types of industry such as oil refining and chemicals and steel manufacture.

27. The objective of capital-intensive industry is to produce at the lowest unit cost, by using specialised plant and relying on mechanisation and automation rather than labour.

    This type of industry needs continuous outlets for its products, a continuous supply of raw materials and bought-out items, and continuously running plant to achieve the maximum return on the huge capital investments involved.

28. Capital-intensive industry also requires a different mix in the labour force. Although the labour content in relation to output is much smaller than in other industries, and the direct production labour may only be semi-skilled, it is highly dependent on a comparatively small number of highly skilled and qualified technicians and specialists to service and control the plant. These are people like systems engineers and analysts, computer programmers and production engineers capable of planning for automated processes, as well as professional engineers and technicians to carry out the maintenance function.

29. A <u>labour-intensive organisation</u> uses a larger proportion of labour relative to its capital investment. In manufacturing these tend to be firms producing in one-off or batch quantity items requiring craft skills, or assembling large quantities of output which cannot be mechanised.

> It is the service type industries which are normally the most labour-intensive, for example local and central government services such as refuse collection, postal and hospital services.
>
> In the private sector the retail and distributive trades are also labour-intensive, although supermarkets represent an attempt to reduce labour input in retailing.

6: PRODUCTION

30. Labour-intensive operations need good personnel policies, supervision and attention to industrial relations.

31. Recent years in the UK have seen high labour costs in both labour-intensive and capital-intensive industries. These have prompted senior management to reduce employment levels and become more efficient (eg in service industries and government departments) or more capital-intensive (eg newspaper printing).

● **Plant management**

32.
> Hicks and Gullet (*'Management'* 1981) see the task of plant management as embracing:
>
> ● product design (although this task might be subordinated to the *research and development* department);
>
> ● methods of production;
>
> ● production control; and
>
> ● materials handling (although this task may be subordinated to a *purchasing/ buying* department, which might not report to the production director).
>
> To this list could be added:
>
> ● production administration (eg production planning, the collection and reporting of production statistics, plant location and layout, capital expenditure decisions); and
>
> ● process engineering.

33. *Process engineering* is a technical planning operation, which:

(a) decides how much work is to be done and measures work (work study, methods study);

(b) investigates processes and operations in order to establish the correct or the most efficient procedures - eg to eliminate unnecessary working or reduce fatigue or stress in work operations;

(c) arranges the preparation of or provision of drawings, jigs, tools and inspection equipment;

(d) maintains an up-to-date awareness of current manufacturing trends and methods;

(e) ensures that personnel policy with regard to training (training on-the-job etc) is implemented; and

(f) obtains cost reports and investigates excessive production costs.

Production planning

34. The task of production planning is to:

    (a) decide what production work ought to be done in the planning period, say in the next week; and

    (b) inform the manufacturing manager and supervisory staff about the work that has been scheduled and is required to be done.

35. Detailed planning arrangements will vary from workplace to workplace, but essentially, production planning involves:

    (a) establishing the production demand - the jobs that have been ordered, the batches that have to be made, or the quantities of output required in flow production;

    (b) establishing what resources are available to do the work. In the case of jobbing work or batch production, this involves deciding how many resources will be required to do each job or complete each batch:

    (i) raw material requirements must be established;
    (ii) labour time requirements, for each skill and in each production section, must be estimated;
    (iii) machine time requirements on each type of machine must also be estimated;

    (c) when there are different jobs or batches on the order book, a priority schedule must be established to decide which jobs or batches should be attended to first;

    (d) making suitable provision for maintenance time, repair time and any other down-time;

    (e) scheduling the work to be done in the planning period, and informing the manufacturing department about the schedule and about individual jobs/batches within the schedule.

36. Scheduling production in a jobbing or batch process industry calls for the preparation of job 'cards' (job 'sheets' or route cards) or batch cards.

    (a) With job cards, details of the job number, drawings or jigs etc required, estimated production times, machines required, and materials required will be sent to the supervisor of each section. For example, if a job must go through production sections A and C, and assembly section G, three job cards might be prepared, one each for the supervisors of sections A, C and G, with each card specifying the work to be done in the particular section.

    (b) With route cards, a single job card is prepared for the entire job, and the card accompanies the job on its progress through the factory.

37. When the manufacturing manager receives the production schedules, he or his subordinates can arrange for:

    (a) the requisition of the necessary materials and components from store; and
    (b) any overtime working likely to be needed in the period.

6: PRODUCTION

• Production control

38. Production control is the task of monitoring actual production, comparing actual production with planned or standard production levels and, where there is a significant difference between actual and standard, investigating the reasons for the difference. Where appropriate, control action should be taken, either to 'mend the damage' (eg re-make a faulty batch, or catch up lost production time with overtime) or to make sure that similar faults do not occur again in the future.

39. Controls should be applied to:

   (a) total output volumes;
   (b) progress - for example, are jobs completed on time? What number or percentage of jobs were late?
   (c) quality of output or service;
   (d) efficiency of working. Was the use of materials, labour and machines and equipment as efficient as it should have been, or were resources wasted?
   (e) costs. Were actual costs not more than they should have been? As accountancy students, you will be familiar with the concept of budgetary control.

40.
> In summary, production control is concerned with the overall effectiveness and efficiency of the production function - is the factory achieving its production targets on time and efficiently, at suitable costs and to a suitable standard of quality? If not, control action should be taken at factory foreman level, at production director level, or at a suitable level in the production management hierarchy in between.

41. Control measures might involve:

   (a) moving to a better factory location;
   (b) improving factory layout;
   (c) improving work methods;
   (d) tightening up supervisory controls, perhaps to reduce the wastage of materials or to improve the diligence of operatives;
   (e) buying new machinery or improving maintenance work to reduce the incidence of breakdowns.

42. Measuring actual results and comparing them with planned production varies from organisation to organisation.

   (a) In mass production or process production (and possibly in batch production) where standard products are made in large quantities, standard times and costs can be established. Actual costs and times for total output are then compared with the standard costs and times that should have been expected, and variances calculated.

   (b) In jobbing work (and possibly in batch production) each job will have an estimated completion time and cost. Actual times and costs can be recorded on each job card or route card, compared with the estimate for that job, and variances calculated.

(c) Machine performance can be measured by machine records - keeping a record for each machine or group of machines of actual running times and comparing this with budgeted running times. A utilisation percentage can be measured - eg a machine might be used 70% of the time available, with say 5% of the time spent on routine maintenance, 15% say on breakdown time and 10% of the time idle waiting for work.

(d) Labour performance can be measured in a similar way, with employee time records (eg records of arrival time at work and leaving time, records of time spent by each individual on various jobs, and idle time records).

(e) Materials usage can be recorded on individual job cards, but there will also be materials requisition notes (recording the delivery from stores of specified quantities of materials for a particular work section, job number or batch number) and materials returns notes (recording the return of unused materials to store). Material usage costs can be established from these records.

---

43. | The very important area of quality control in production is covered in Chapter 7.

● **Progress control**

44. The control aspects of production planning and control, as mentioned above, include progress control. This is the task of ensuring that work is completed as scheduled, and that production flows smoothly. Late work is 'chased' to find out why there is a hold-up and to urge the manufacturing department concerned to speed up the work. Progress control personnel cannot usually give orders about what to do to manufacturing staff, and so reports on late production or production bottlenecks have to be sent up to more senior management in the production department for their attention.

45. Variations in production timetabling from the planned schedule might be caused by:

(a) hold-ups arising from a stock-out of raw materials, a lack of work because of hold-ups in other departments responsible for earlier stages of processing, a shortage of labour, a strike or a shortage of machine time, perhaps because of breakdowns;

(b) changes to specifications by customers, which might involve a delay in doing the work because time is needed to redesign or re-plan the work;

(c) the need to introduce a 'crash programme' to expedite an urgent order, which will involve a rescheduling of all other work in hand.

46. Progress control is particularly important when the order book is full because if work is processed quickly, the business can take on more work and still provide a good service to customers. In addition, customers will want to know when a job can be finished for them, and progress control will be responsible for:

(a) giving a promised completion date in the quotation to the customer;

(b) informing production management about these promised dates, because having made such a promise, it will be necessary to ensure that the resources are available to complete the work on time, in the event that the customer accepts the quotation and places the order.

47. Effective progress control depends on accuracy and having up-to-date knowledge of what the manufacturing departments are doing and what spare capacity they have. It can be very helpful to use a range of visual aid or charting techniques to help keep track of progress of jobs, and machine loadings etc, and techniques such as network analysis, Gantt charts and bar charts are all particularly useful for progress control. For example, a network analysis diagram can be used to:

(a) check whether activities on the critical path are being completed on time;

(b) check whether non-critical activities are being delayed for too long, so that they are threatening to become time-critical themselves;

(c) record actual finishing times and start times on the network chart by the side of the planned times.

48. Some organisations employ *progress chasers* to maintain up-to-the-minute information about the current progress of particular jobs, and to remind managers responsible for production about the completion times they must meet. Progress chasing is particularly useful in situations where failing to complete on time would have serious consequences for a customer but several different people must each complete a part of a job, and if one person is late, the entire job will be late. For example, an advertising agency might be required to provide an advertisement for a journal by a particular deadline, and a progress chaser would be responsible for checking that photographs, artwork and copy are all available by the required times so that their client's advertisement appears in the journal as planned.

49. As the name implies, progress *control* is intended to initiate control action when jobs are late or when urgent jobs have to be crashed, by reporting regularly to the management responsible. It is a never-ending job, because there must be a continual chasing-up of activities to ensure that lost time is made up, or at least that delays do not get any worse (eg that an overfull order book is not made more full by promising customers completion dates that cannot be met).

QUIZ

1. Describe the three main types of production.

   ● See para 9-15

2. What is just-in-time production?

   ● See paras 16-23

3. Distinguish between capital- and labour-intensive organisations

   ● See paras 25-29

4. What is production planning?

   ● See paras 34-35

5. What are the nature and importance of progress control?

   ● See paras 44-49

Chapter 7

QUALITY MANAGEMENT

Topics covered in this chapter

- What is quality management?
- Quality control and inspection
- Quality measures
- Total quality management (TQM)
- Quality assurance
- Quality circles

Purpose of this chapter

To give a broad coverage of the techniques for control and management of quality.

● **What is quality management?**

1. In ordinary language, quality implies some degree of excellence or superiority. In an industrial context, it is defined in a much more functional way. Here, quality is more concerned with 'fitness for purpose', and quality management (or control) is about ensuring that products or services meet their planned level of quality, and conform to specifications.

2.

Quality management may be defined as the process of:

- establishing standards of quality for a product or service;
- establishing procedures or production methods which ought to ensure that these required standards of quality are met in a suitably high proportion of cases;
- monitoring actual quality; and
- taking control action when actual quality falls below standard.

---

3. As an example, the postal service might establish a standard that 90% of first class letters will be delivered on the day after they are posted, and 99% will be delivered within two days of posting. Procedures would have to be established for ensuring that these standards could be met (eg. frequency of collections, automated letter sorting, frequency of deliveries and number of staff employed etc). Actual performance could be monitored, perhaps by taking samples from time to time of letters that are posted and delivered. If the quality standard is not being achieved,

the management of the postal service could take control action (eg. employ more postmen or advertise again the use of postcodes) or reduce the standard of quality of the service being provided.

● Quality control and inspection

4. The position of the quality control and inspection department within an organisation may vary. In manufacturing industries, quality control is often seen as a manufacturing responsibility based on the inspection of output by 'quality control' staff. The quality control manager might have a semi-independent position in the organisation, reporting details of rejected or defective items to the manufacturing manager, but not taking orders from him. Instead, the quality control manager might be accountable to the production director - to management at a senior level.

5. Inspection is only one aspect of quality control, however, and a distinction has to be made between *quality control* in its wider sense and *inspection*.

   (a) *Quality control* is concerned with trying to make sure that a product is manufactured, or a service is provided, so as to meet certain design specifications. This involves setting controls for the process of manufacture or provision of a service. It is a 'technique' aimed at *preventing* the manufacture of defective items (or the provision of defective services).

   (b) *Inspection* is concerned with looking at products that have been made, supplies which have been delivered and services that have been provided, to establish whether they have been up to specification. It is a technique of *identifying* when defective items are being manufactured at an excessive and unacceptable level.

   Inspection is normally carried out at three main points:

   (i)   receiving inspection - for raw materials and bought out components;
   (ii) floor or process inspection; and
   (iii) final inspection or testing.

6. Quality control therefore represents process planning and process control, whereas inspection deals with the identification of faulty output. There is a connection between them, and quality control staff ought to tell inspection staff:

   (a) what needs inspecting;
   (b) when it ought to be inspected; and
   (c) how many items ought to be inspected.

7. Inspection management would decide *how* products or services ought to be inspected.

● Where and when are quality control measures taken?

8. Quality control happens at various stages in the process of designing and providing a product or service.

(a) *Product design stage*

At the product design stage, quality control means trying to design a product or service so that its specifications provide a suitable balance between price and quality (of sales and delivery, as well as manufacture) which will make the product or service competitive. Quality is a characteristic which distinguishes the goods or services of one business from those of its competitors. However, higher quality will cost more and so a suitable balance has to be struck between quality and price. One technique for exercising quality control at the product design stage is *value analysis*. This is based on the idea that goods should be produced in the most economic way harmonious with value to the customer.

(b) *Production engineering stage*

Production engineering is the process of designing the methods for making a product (or service) to the design specification. It sets out to make production methods as efficient as possible, and to avoid the making of sub-standard items.

One aspect of quality control in production engineering is manufacturing tolerances. Production engineers must decide how much variation or 'tolerance' can be allowed in the manufacture of an item, before the item fails to meet its design specification. If tolerances are too lax, too many sub-standard products will be made. If tolerances are unnecessarily tight - an accuracy of plus or minus 0.005 cm when plus or minus 0.03 cm would be perfectly adequate - production costs will be higher than they need be. Surface finish is another area where production engineering might incur unnecessary costs by arranging for products to be 'over-finished'.

(c) *Quality assurance of goods inwards*

The quality of output depends on the quality of input materials, and so quality control should include procedures for acceptance inspection of goods inwards. Inspection methods, like inspection of finished goods within the organisation, will normally be based on statistical sampling techniques and the concept of an *acceptance quality level* (AQL). Another approach that can be used is to give each supplier a 'rating' for the quality of the goods they tend to supply, and give preference with purchase orders to well-rated suppliers. (This method is referred to as 'vendor rating').

(d) *Inspection of output*, perhaps at various stages in the production process. Inspection, based on sampling and other statistical techniques, will provide a continual check that the production process is under control. (This is sometimes called quality assurance.) The aim of inspection is not really to sort out the bad products from the good ones after the work has been done. The aim is to satisfy management that quality control in production is being maintained. More will be said about inspection methods later.

(e) *Monitoring customer complaints* with a view to deciding whether changes are needed in product design, product engineering or inspection methods.

Some sub-standard items will inevitably be produced. Inspection will identify some bad output, but other items will reach the customer. Customer quality complaints have to be dealt with, as part of the organisation's service. As far as quality control is concerned, complaints ought to be monitored, with a view to identifying quality weaknesses in product design, production engineering, production standards or the quality of raw materials in use.

How is quality performance measured?

9. If no defective items are allowed, and all output must be perfect, there would have to be 100% inspection. However, it is usual to accept that some defective output will be made and it is not the end of the world if they get through to the customer.

   When some defectives are allowed to get through, the measurement of quality can be based on the inspection of *samples* of output (or goods inwards). This is known as *acceptance sampling*.

10. The inspection of samples rather than 100% testing of all items will keep inspection costs down, and smaller samples will be less costly to inspect than larger samples. The greater the confidence in the reliability of production methods and process control, the smaller the samples will be. For example, if a production process has a fairly high proportion of defectives, 10% of all output might be inspected; whereas if the process rarely goes out of control, the sample sizes for inspection might be 1% or less of output.

11. The acceptance quality level (AQL) is the maximum percentage of defectives that will be tolerated, on economic grounds, in the samples that are tested. If the AQL is 2%, say, this would mean that the organisation is taking the view that a maximum of 2% of output can be allowed to be defective, because the costs of reducing the proportion of defectives further would not be worth the costs of improved quality control. When defectives exceed the AQL, the quality-related costs will be too high, and improvements in quality would be called for.

Statistical quality control charts

12. Statistical quality control charts might be used to record and monitor the accuracy of the physical dimensions of products. The theory recognises that the exact dimensions may vary in a random manner due to the effects of chance. A typical control chart is shown below. The horizontal axis on the graph is time, the vertical axis is the physical dimension of the product in appropriate units. Above and below the level of the expected dimension of the product are the control limits. The graph shows inner warning limits and outer action limits although in many cases only one limit is used. The limits are set such a distance from the expected dimension that a value outside the limits is very unlikely to have occurred by chance and consequently the size of the deviation from the expected dimension indicates that something may have gone wrong with the manufacturing process. Normally, the values plotted on the chart would be the mean of a small sample taken at regular points in time.

7.1 Quality control chart

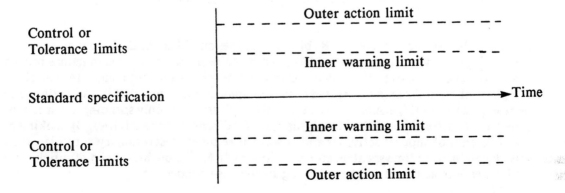

13. Samples of an output manufacturing process may be taken daily or even every hour, and faults in the manufacturing process which are revealed may be fairly simple to correct by adjusting the appropriate machinery. If output exceeds the control limits consistently, more urgent management action would be called for, because this would indicate:

    (a) inefficiency in production, by labour or the machines;
    (b) inadequacy in production methods;
    (c) inadequate quality of raw materials and components; or
    (d) excessively tight tolerances in the first place.

● **Total quality management (TQM)**

14. Total quality management (TQM) is a management technique, derived from Japanese companies, which focuses on the belief that 'total quality is essential to survival in a global market'.

15. The basic principle of TQM is that the cost of preventing mistakes is less than the cost of correcting them once they occur. The aim should therefore be to get things right first time consistently.

> "Every mistake, every delay and misunderstanding, directly costs a company money through wasted time and effort, including time taken in pacifying customers. Whilst this cost is important, the impact of poor customer service in terms of lost potential for future sales has also to be taken into account."
> (Robin Bellis-Jones and Max Hard of Develin and Partners,
> in an article on TQM in *Management Accounting* May 1989)

16. There are several different TQM programmes, all aimed at identifying and then reducing/ eliminating causes of wasted time and effort. One such programme is called Qualified Total Quality (QTQ). In QTQ, a work group is asked to analyse its activities and classify these into three groups:

    (a) *core activities,* which are the reason for the existence of the work group and which add value to the business;

    (b) *support activities* which support core activities but do not themselves add value; and

    (c) *discretionary activities* such as checking, progress chasing, dealing with complaints etc, which are all symptoms of failure within the organisation.

17. In the article referred to earlier by Robin Bellis-Jones and Max Hard, there is an example of an engineering company, with a group of 400 product engineers, which needed to reduce product lead times from about 4 years to 18 months to compete more efficiently with major foreign rivals. The company introduced computer assisted design equipment, but found that it was having to employ more engineers. A QTQ exercise revealed that the engineers were only spending about 12% of their time on core activities and the rest on support and discretionary activities. By looking hard at the efficiency of support activities and at ways of reducing discretionary activities, the group was able to increase time spent on core activities to 41%. The business need of quicker product lead times was achieved, without having to increase headcount.

18. Two approaches to controlling quality and quality costs are:

    (a) *Approach 1:* minimise total quality costs by budgeting for a level of quality which minimises prevention costs plus inspection costs on the one hand and internal and external failure costs on the other.

    (b) *Approach 2:* aim for zero rejects and 100% quality. The desired standard of production is contained within the product specification and every unit produced ought to achieve this standard; in other words, there ought to be no defects. Zero-defect targets are one aspect of Japanese management philosophy. However, the actual level of defects must be recorded and reported, even if the quality costs are not measured.

19. Both approaches show a concern for quality and quality standard control. They both accept the need to incur quality costs: with a zero defect target, there must be costs incurred in preventing defects and testing output. However, there is a fundamental difference of view in the sense that approach 1 accepts some level of defects and approach 2 takes the view that *all* defects are undesirable.

    > Eventually, as modern manufacturing systems are introduced and Just In Time systems are employed, approach 1 is likely to result in the conclusion that the costs of failure are so high (because they hold up production) that the only acceptable quality standard is a zero defect limit (approach 2).

● **Quality assurance**

20. The essentials of quality assurance are that the supplier guarantees the quality of his goods and allows the customers' inspectors access while the items are being manufactured. Usually agreed inspection procedures and quality control standards are worked out by customer and supplier between them, and checks are made to ensure that they are being adhered to.

    (a) The main advantage to the customer is that he can almost eliminate goods inwards inspection and items can be directed straight to production. This can give large savings in cost and time in flow production assembly plant, and can facilitate JIT production.

    (b) The advantage to the supplier is that he produces to the customers' requirement, therefore reducing rejects. Also the cost of returning reject material from the customer is saved.

21. Suppliers' quality assurance schemes are being used increasingly, particularly where extensive sub-contracting work is carried out, eg the motor industries.

● **Quality circles**

22. Quality circles emerged first in the United States, but it was in Japan that they were adopted most enthusiastically. The modern success story of Japanese industry has prompted Western countries to imitate many of the Japanese working methods, with the result that quality circles are re-appearing in American and West European companies.

A quality circle consists of a group of employees, perhaps about eight in number, which meets regularly to discuss problems of quality and quality control in their area of work, and perhaps to suggest ways of improving quality. The quality circle has a leader or supervisor who directs discussions and possibly also helps to train other members of the circle. It is also a way to encourage innovation.

23. Some training in methods of quality control (eg quality testing methods) will be necessary for each member of the circle. Equally, it is important to ensure that good communications exist within the circle, perhaps by formal training in techniques of communication.

24. A problem with quality circles in many Western companies arises from the separation of the functions of:

   (a) product design/quality design/work methods; and
   (b) operations.

25. Design is often the function of the production engineering department whilst operations is the function of the production department.

   (a) If a quality circle consists of production workers, their role may be restricted to controlling quality within pre-designed specifications.

   (b) If the quality circle consists of design staff, quality decisions might be taken without any consultation with production staff.

   (c) A quality circle that consists of both engineering and production staff might need a supervisor whose level of seniority is quite high.

26. If the problem of seniority and areas of discretion can be resolved, quality circles can provide motivation for employees to become more involved in quality matters, and thereby help to improve the quality of output.

27. Quality circles are not random groups of employees. To make the system work a number of factors must be considered when the circle is being formed.

   (a) A quality circle is a *voluntary* grouping. There is no point in coercing employees to join because the whole point is to develop a spontaneous concern for quality amongst workers.

   (b) Quality circles do not function automatically. Training may be needed in methods of quality control, problem-solving techniques and methods of communication.

   (c) The right leader must be chosen. The person required is one who is capable of directing discussions and drawing out contributions from each member of the circle.

28. Ideally, quality circles should be given more responsibility than merely suggesting improvements. Shop-floor commitment may be increased if the members of quality circles also have responsibility for implementing their recommendations.

29.
> Benefits claimed to arise from the use of quality circles include:
> - greater motivation of employees;
> - improved productivity;
> - improved quality of output;
> - greater awareness of problems by shop-floor staff.

QUIZ

1. Define quality management.

   - See para 2

2. At what stages of design and production are quality control measures taken?

   - See para 8

3. How is a statistical quality control chart used?

   - See paras 12-13

4. What is Total Quality Management and why is it followed?

   - See para 15

5. What are the advantages of quality assurance agreements?

   - See para 20

6. What problems are associated with quality circles?

   - See para 25.

Chapter 8

PURCHASING AND MATERIALS MANAGEMENT

Topics covered in this chapter

- The purchasing function
- Objectives of the purchasing officer
- Structure of the purchasing department
- The purchasing mix
- Just In Time procurement
- Supply strategy
- Materials requirement planning (MRP)
- Manufacturing resource planning (MRPII)
- World Class Manufacturing (WCM)

Purpose of this chapter

To give you a broad knowledge of the techniques and importance of purchasing and materials management.

- **The purchasing function**

1. The purchasing officer or buyer is probably the most under-estimated executive in manufacturing industries. He is usually responsible for a major part of the company's expenditure and rarely gets subjected to the planning and control constraints that are experienced by other executives with less responsibility.

2. This comment is not true of other branches of industry and commerce such as high street stores, where 'buying' is recognised as one of the most important functions of the business.

3. Peter Drucker in *Managing for results* says:

   'This is what people have in mind when they speak of 'materials management' instead of 'purchasing'. There are a good many techniques for the job available now; for instance, value engineering, which looks at each part of a product and asks of it: What is the simplest and least expensive way to do this particular job?

   Some of the large buyers - for instance, in the automobile companies - have become highly sophisticated materials managers and fully integrate design and purchasing. But most manufacturers still have to learn what some of the large retailers grasped thirty or forty years ago; buying is as important as selling, and the best selling cannot make up for a mediocre buying specification.'

4. The purchasing officer's position in the hierarchy of business organisation varies. In some cases he is a first line executive reporting to the managing director, and in others he reports to the production director or manager. In any case he will have to exercise his responsibilities in close co-operation with colleagues in Finance, Production and Marketing.

The purchasing officer's objectives

5. To implement the firm's buying policies, he must provide much of the information which will enable the firm to establish its policies. His responsibilities include:

    (a) the economic acquisition of raw materials, components, sub-assemblies, consumable stores and capital equipment;

    (b) purchasing supplies and capital equipment for offices (eg microcomputers, motor cars, telephone systems, office furniture , paper and other stationery items etc);

    (c) liaising with the design and development department to find suppliers for materials which are to the specifications required by the designers.

    He will discuss prices, discounts, delivery lead times, specifications with suppliers, chase late deliveries, and sanction payments for deliveries.

6.
    > The purchasing department may be responsible for:
    >
    > - Locating and selecting suppliers
    > - Provision of up-to-date information on availability, quality, prices, distribution and suppliers for the evaluation of purchasing alternatives
    > - The purchase of goods and services at prices which (in the long term) represent best value
    > - Maintenance of stock levels (chasing deliveries etc)
    > - Establishing and maintaining necessary relationships with internal departments (Production, Finance, Marketing, R & D) and suppliers.

Structure of the purchasing department

7. Purchasing is a function which in medium and large organisations lends itself to co-ordinated decentralisation. This is de-centralisation of authority to make purchases, whilst still retaining some guidance and control from a central authority. In other words, to carry out the work in the most efficient way requires the facility of providing local management with control over purchasing, but without losing the advantages of large scale negotiations from a central source.

8. In a large organisation the executive responsible for purchasing will have a central staff providing corporate purchasing policies, practices and procedures, possibly retaining line authority for purchases beyond agreed amounts. He will monitor quality, seek out competitive sources and maximise quantity discount opportunities where several sources are buying from the same supplier.

9. The purchasing staff will assist design departments to locate sources of new materials. It is then the task of local managers, given authority to purchase orders up to a ceiling value and within a purchasing budget, to take the buying decisions and place the orders directly themselves.

10. The administrative tasks of purchasing departments involve a tremendous amount of data processing. Most manufacturing organisations spend more than 60% of costs in purchasing. The importance of efficient administrative handling is vital to the success of the company.

11. The tasks include:

    ● receipt of requisitions for goods
    ● invitations to tender or quote; examination of tenders
    ● planning and placing purchase orders
    ● matching purchase orders with goods inwards documentation
    ● progressing orders to ensure good delivery
    ● checking suppliers' invoices and quotations
    ● controlling returned goods and obtaining credit notes
    ● maintaining records of orders made, fulfilled, delivery dates, invoices, defects etc
    ● arranging for the requisitioning department to receive goods etc direct from supplier or via stores.

12. In view of the heavy routine administrative burdens, it has become common to computerise many purchasing functions, but responsibility for ensuring that the work is done efficiently must remain with the purchasing department's management and staff.

● **The purchasing mix**

13. The 'purchasing mix' includes consideration of the following factors:

    (a) *Quantity.* The size and timing of orders will be dictated by the balance between:

        (i) delays in production caused by insufficient stock; and
        (ii) the costs of stock-holding - tied up capital, storage space, deterioration, insurance, risk of pilferage.

    A system of stock control should be devised, whereby *optimum re-order levels*) (the stock level at which supplies must be replenished so as to arrive in time to meet demand) can be set, and *Economic Order Quantities* (EOQ) obtained for individual stock items. Environmental considerations (eg seasonal peaks, political pressures) will also influence the decisions about future supply.

8.1: Stock control system

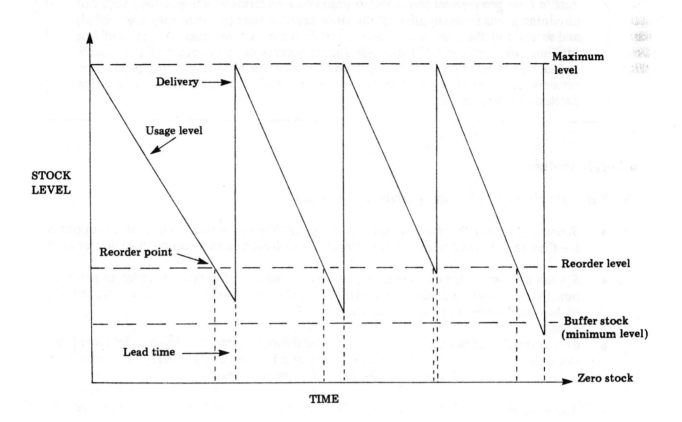

(b) *Quality*. The production department will need to be consulted about the quality of goods required for the manufacturing process, and the marketing department about the quantity of goods acceptable to customers.

(c) *Price*. Favourable short-term trends in prices may influence the buying decision, but purchasing should have an eye to the best value over a period of time - considering quality, delivery, urgency of order, stock-holding requirements etc.

(d) *Delivery*. As you will note from the stock control diagram above, the lead time between placing and delivery of an order can be crucial to efficient stock control and production planning. The reliability of suppliers' delivery arrangements must also be assessed.

● **Just In Time procurement**

14. In recent years, there have been developments in the inventory policy of some manufacturing companies, which have sought to reduce their inventories of raw materials and components to as low a level as possible.

> *Just In Time procurement* and *stockless production* are terms which describe a policy of obtaining goods from suppliers at the latest possible time (ie when they are needed) and so avoiding the need to carry any materials or components stock. A system of Just In Time procurement (JIT) depends for its success on a smooth and predictable production flow, and so a JIT policy must also be aimed at improving production systems, eliminating waste (rejects and re-worked items), avoiding production bottlenecks, and so on.

• Supply strategy

15. There are six aspects to supply strategy. These are:

- *Sources of supply.* What are the sources available? Where are they? What sort of suppliers are they and are they reliable? Are they likely to treat you as a valued customer or not?

- *Spread of supply.* Should there be just a single source of supply in order to get bulk purchase discounts and minimise costs, or should there be dual sourcing to avoid the risk of lost production and supplier complacency?

- *Cost of supplies.* How quickly can cost discounts through volume purchases be achieved? Can the supplier be convinced that if he supplies at a low price to encourage low-cost high volume sales, he will soon reap the benefit of large orders?

- The *make or buy* decision. Is it more efficient to make the goods in house or buy them in?

- *The suitability of the existing supplier.* Can existing suppliers produce goods to the required standard? If new standards of quality are required, can existing suppliers match them or not?

- *The image or reputation of the supplier.* This could be a selling point for the buyer's own customers - eg major car rental firms are pleased to admit that they rent Ford, GM or other makes of car.

• Materials requirement planning (MRP)

16. One aspect of materials management is materials requirement planning, and this aspect of strategic planning deserves some further attention.

17.
> Wild defines MRP as a 'technique by which known customer demand requirements are exploded to produce gross parts, components or activity requirements. These gross requirements are compared with available inventories to produce net requirements which are then scheduled within available capacity limitations. MRP is thus used for scheduling, inventory management and capacity management'.

18. Wild identifies four uses of MRP.

    (a) *The bill of requirements*. This identifies the total materials needed for the final product, and how they are to come together. It will identify in the short term what is readily available, and in the long term what is needed to be developed or bought in (and perhaps what is at risk from unstable or unreliable suppliers). The analysis will embrace not only the bought-in raw materials and components, but also the manufactured major sub-assemblies.

    (b) *The master production schedule*. If the product is scheduled for a long production run, the planning period for inventory levels and plant capacity will clearly be longer than for a short run. In general, however, Wild suggests that the planning period should be such that all the required materials can be acquired and all components prepared with parts and sub-assemblies ready for the assembly of the final product. There may be a learning curve effect: clearly with a new product, with perhaps new designs and methods, early assembly may be both slow and wasteful of material, requiring more material to be made available.

    (c) *The opening inventory*. This is very much a short-term planning problem. When any new project starts, especially if it is based on standard components, consideration must be given to the available levels of uncommitted inventory, ie stock not already allocated to existing orders, so that the level of purchases and lead times can be accurately computed.

    (d) *Opening production capacity*. Capacity planning decisions are likely to be a long-term consideration: the planned production capacity and the planned materials requirements will obviously be inter-related matters.

19. From this, Wild identifies five outputs from MRP:

    (a) short-term and long-term purchase requirements;
    (b) short-term and long-term activity schedules expressed in terms of manufacturing demands, quantities and deadlines;
    (c) the probabilities of expected shortages;
    (d) 'free' inventory; and
    (e) the possible available surplus capacity.

20. Two other short-term factors that can be considered are:

    (a) the batch sizes or production runs, bearing in mind the level of both short-term sales and levels of finished goods inventory required; and

    (b) the level of safety stock that is needed in case the sales forecasts prove to be conservative and demand starts to outstrip production.

● **Manufacturing resource planning (MRP II)**

21. Manufacturing resource planning (MRP II) developed out of material requirements planning (MRP).

    (a) MRP was devised in the late 1960s as a system for calculating the total quantities of materials required to manufacture finished products. The aim was stock control - ie to make sure that the materials would be available in sufficient quantities to meet production demand, but that excessive quantities of unwanted items would not be held.

(b) MRPII emerged in the 1970s, and involves the building of a computer model of the manufacturing environment, which provides:

- material requirements planning
- capacity planning and production scheduling
- shopfloor control
- a reporting system for actual progress
- control through a comparison of actual achievements and costs against the plan.

22. MRPII is used by many companies for manufacturing planning, but with the advent of Just in Time manufacturing (JIT) it has been criticised as a planning system.

> "The primary criticism of the MRPII approach is that by modelling the reality of manufacturing plant, it builds in all the bad habits. It takes account of long leadtimes, shopfloor queues, large batch sizes, scrap and quality problems. Instead of accommodating these things, it should be driving towards their elimination. Poor productivity is built into MRPII and planned into the production process."
>
> (Brian Maskell, *Management Accounting*, January 1989)

23. Even so, MRPII has advantages as a system for planning and controlling manufacturing systems, especially when JIT methods are unsuitable.

• World Class Manufacturing (WCM)

24. World Class Manufacturing (WCM) is a term used by Professor Schonberger in 1986 to describe the fundamental changes taking place in manufacturing companies. WCM is a very broad terms, but it can be taken to have four key elements.

(a) *A new approach to product quality*. Instead of a policy of trying to detect defects or poor quality in production as and when they occur, WCM sets out to identify the root causes of poor quality, eliminate them, and achieve zero defects - ie 100% quality. Eliminating waste is likely to involve building better quality into the product.

(b) *Just in Time manufacturing (JIT)*. This is the system of manufacturing that aims to eliminate waste. Wasteful activities include:

- inspection of goods
- shopfloor queues
- re-working of defective items
- excessive storage
- unnecessary movement of materials.

(c) *Managing people*. The aim of WCM is to utilise the skills and abilities of the work force to the full. Employees are given training in a variety of skills, so that they can switch from one task to another. They are also given more responsibility for production scheduling and quality. A *team approach* is encouraged, with strong trust between management and workers.

(d) *Flexible approach to customer requirements*. The WCM policy is to develop close relationships with customers:

(i)   to know what their requirements are;
(ii) to supply customers on time, with short delivery lead times; and
(iii) to change the product mix quickly and develop new products or modify existing products as customer needs change.

QUIZ

1.   What is meant by the phrase "materials management"?

  ● See para 3

2.   For what is the purchasing department responsible and what are its tasks?

  ● See paras 6 and 11

3.   What is the 'purchasing mix'?

  ● See para 13

4.   What is Just In Time procurement?

  ● See para 14

5.   Identify the uses of materials requirement planning.

  ● See para 18

6.   How does MRPII differ from MRP?

  ● See para 21

7.   What are the key elements of World Class Manufacturing?

  ● See para 24

SECTION 3

PRINCIPLES OF MANAGEMENT

Topics covered in this section

- Chapter 9:   Introduction to management principles

- Chapter 10:   Motivation

- Chapter 11:   Delegation, authority and responsibility

- Chapter 12:   The communication process

- Chapter 13:   Monitoring and controlling performance

- Chapter 14:   Boundary management

Objectives of this section

In this section we look at the important principles which underlie the practice of effective management. Particular attention is paid to motivation, delegation, communication and control. We also look at how effective management must take into account the external and internal environment in which it operates.

Chapter 9

INTRODUCTION TO MANAGEMENT PRINCIPLES

Topics covered in this chapter

- Theories of management
- Classical school
- Scientific management
- Human relations school
- Systems approach to management
- Contingency approach
- The Japanese experience

Purpose of this chapter

To introduce you to the major 'schools of thought' in the theory of management as a background to this section on management principles. Some of the ideas inform the concepts in the following chapters on motivation and control.

● **Theories of management**

1.

> Writers on management hold the view that if certain principles of management or organisation are put into practice, the management will be more successful in ensuring that the objectives of the organisation are achieved in an efficient manner. Their aim is to encourage effectiveness and efficiency in the use of resources to achieve organisational goals.

2. The idea of 'principles' of management might suggest to you that there are some 'correct' ways of being a good manager or supervisor. Early 'schools' of thinking about this were:

    (a) the classical and scientific management schools; and
    (b) the human relations or behavioural school.

● Classical school of management

3. The Classical school of management thought popularised the concept of 'universality of management principles', which nevertheless could be applied flexibly.

4. Henri Fayol, the leading Classical theorist, argued that as managers rise up the 'scalar chain', or organisation hierarchy, they need to show an increasing amount of managerial ability. For top executives, managerial ability is of paramount importance; however, when he wrote, there were no accepted theories or principles of management and there was no concept of training to be a manager. This was a gap which Fayol set out to close.

5. He said that applying the classical principles of management is a 'difficult art requiring intelligence, experience, decision and proportion'. Among them he listed the following.

   (a) *Division of work* or *specialisation*. The object of specialisation is to produce more and to obtain better results.

   (b) *Authority and responsibility*: Fayol distinguished between a manager's official authority (deriving from his office) and personal authority (deriving from his experience, moral worth, intelligence etc). The principles associated with these terms are discussed in detail in Chapter 11.

   (c) *Discipline*: A fair disciplinary system, with penalties judiciously applied by worthy superiors, can be a chief strength in an organisation.

   (d) *Unity of command*: for any action, a subordinate should receive orders from one boss only. Fayol saw dual command as a disease, whether it is caused by imperfect demarcation between departments, or by a superior giving orders to an employee, without going via the intermediate superior.

   (This 'principle' immediately gives rise to problems concerning the role of 'staff' as opposed to 'line' management as we saw in Chapter 2).

   (e) *Unity of direction*: there should be one head and one plan for each activity. Unity of direction relates to the organisation itself, whereas unity of command relates to the personnel in the organisation.

   (f) The interest of one employee or group of employees should not prevail over that of the general interest of the organisation.

   (g) *Remuneration* of personnel should be fair, satisfying both employer and employee alike.

   (h) *Scalar chain*: as described earlier in Chapter 2.

   (i) *Stability of tenure of personnel*: 'It has often been recorded that a mediocre manager who stays is infinitely preferable to outstanding managers who merely come and go'.

   (j) *Esprit de corps*: personnel must not be split up. 'In union, there is strength.' Verbal communication is preferable to written communication which is frequently abused, causing friction between departments.

   (k) *Initiative*: 'it is essential to encourage and develop this capacity to the full'.

(1) *Centralisation*: although he did not use the term 'centralisation' of authority, Fayol argued that circumstances would dictate whether overall efficiency would be optimised by concentrating or by dispersing authority.

6. Fayol himself would probably not have accepted the view, held by many other people who have adopted his principles, that there is such a thing as a universal manager who can manage any type of organisation with equal success. While he said that the need for technical knowledge decreases with a rise in the management hierarchy, he felt that even top managers could not depend on administrative skills alone.

> In fact, in discussing the qualities needed by top management, he gave administrative ability a weight of only 50% in the case of a manager of a very large firm, and only 25% in the case of a small firm top executive.

● Scientific management

7. Frederick W Taylor was a Classicist who was the 'father' of the 'scientific management' movement.

> He argued that management should be based on 'well-recognised, clearly defined and fixed principles, instead of depending on more or less hazy ideas'.
>
> His purpose was to maximise efficiency and he suggested that by offering workers more money for being efficient, both the workers and the employers would benefit.

8. Productivity would not be improved by the offer of more money alone, and Taylor argued that a radical change of attitudes, on the part of both management and workers, was essential if his system were to be successful.

9. His famous four principles of scientific management were as follows.

(a) *Development of a true science of work:* all knowledge which has hitherto been kept in the heads of workmen should be gathered and recorded by management. 'Every single subject, large and small, becomes the question for scientific investigation, for reduction to law'. Very simply, he argued that management should apply techniques to the solution of problems and should not rely on experience and 'seat-of-the-pants' judgements.

(b) *Scientific selection and progressive development of workmen:* workmen should be carefully trained, and given jobs to which they are best suited. Although 'training' is an important element in his principles of management, 'nurturing' might be a more apt description of his ideas of worker development.

(c) *Bringing together of the science and the scientifically selected and trained people:* the application of the techniques to decide what should be done, using workmen who are both properly trained and willing to maximise output, should result in maximum productivity.

(d) *Constant and intimate co-operation between management and workers:* 'the relations between employers and men form without question the most important part of this art' (Taylor, *'Shop Management'* 1903)

10. The four principles should be applied together; unfortunately, it is possible to apply 'scientific management' techniques in order to improve productivity, without training the workforce or paying them for the improvement in output. This resulted in great hostility from trade union leaders, who condemned scientific management as a means of overworking the labour force and reducing the number of jobs. Taylor was eventually obliged to defend his ideas before a committee of the House of Representatives (US Congress) in 1912.

A criticism of scientific management

11. Hicks wrote 'by the end of the scientific management period, the worker had been reduced to the role of an impersonal cog in the machine of production. His work became more and more narrowly specialised until he had little appreciation for his contribution to the total product ... Although very significant technological advances were made ... the serious weakness of the scientific approach to management was that it de-humanised the organisational member, who became a person without emotion and capable of being scientifically manipulated, just like machines'.

Conclusion: Scientific management

12.
> The scientific management approach may be summarised as follows:
> * an organisation should be an alliance of management and workers, to increase efficiency and productivity, so as to improve profitability;
> * management should contribute towards this greater efficiency by the application of scientific techniques, and certain principles of management;
> * the attitude of workers should not be ignored, and attention must be given to industrial psychology. Human attitudes began to attract increasing attention from management theorists so that a sociological approach to management and the 'behavioural' school of thought began to emerge as an alternative to scientific management.

● **The human relations school**

13. From about 1930 a school of management thought developed which emphasised the importance of human relationships in organisations. In many ways, it was a reaction against the de-humanising aspects of the scientific management school of thought. (Note: 'de-humanising' refers not so much to the thinking of Taylor himself, but to the tendency of (scientific) management techniques to be introduced without the co-operation and approval of the workforce).

14. Elton Mayo was perhaps the most important contributor to this school of thought, as a result of his experiments at the Hawthorne plant of the Western Electric Company (known as the 'Hawthorne experiments').

15. Like Taylor and most of the other members of the scientific management movement, Mayo was primarily interested in management as it affected those at the rank and file level. But his viewpoint was entirely different.

- He not only agreed with the critics of the movement who felt that it paid insufficient attention to the human factor in productivity; but

- he also believed that the economic motive, on which Taylor laid such stress, was unimportant compared to emotional and non-logical attitudes and sentiments in improving the efficiency and productivity of the employees at work.

16. Following the Hawthorne experiments (which found that a feeling of group solidarity and importance had a more productive effect than improved working conditions) a hypothesis was developed that motivation to work, productivity and the quality of output were all related to:

   (a) the 'psychology of the work group' - social relations among the workers; and
   (b) the relationship between the workers and their supervisor/boss.

17. Further experiments by Roethlisberger and Dickson appeared to confirm that human attitudes (both of individuals and work groups) and the relationship between management and work groups or individual subordinates were of key importance in establishing motivation to work and production efficiency.

   Motivation will be discussed separately and in detail in Chapter 10.

● The systems approach to management

18. The early 'systems approach' took the view that an organisation is a social system, consisting of individuals who co-operate together within a formal framework, taking inputs from and sending outputs to the surrounding environment.

19. The earliest leading theorist of this approach was Chester Barnard. His views, briefly summarised, are as follows.

   - Human beings are physically incapable of doing everything they need for themselves, therefore they must co-operate with each other. Once co-operation begins out of physical needs, the concept of a co-operative is reinforced by psychological and social attitudes.

   - Co-operation inevitably leads to the establishment of *co-operative systems* - being organisations.

   - Organisations can be 'formal' (consciously co-ordinated systems of human interactions, with a common purpose) or 'informal' (social interactions without a conspicuous structure or common purpose).

   - Formal organisation depends on:

      (i)   the ability of individuals in the system to communicate with each other;
      (ii) a willingness to contribute towards group action;
      (iii) having a known 'conscious' common purpose.

   - Formal organisations must have:

      (i)   a system of dividing work into functional groupings, so that members can specialise;

(ii)   a system of incentives which will make group members contribute towards the common purpose;

(iii)   a system of authority (or power) so that group members accept the decisions of supervision management; and

(iv)   a system of logical decision-making.

A diagram of the organisation as an open system with sub-systems might appear as follows.

PROCESS

Organisation structure and methods of operation
Technology
Social structure and individual psychologies
Management and control system
Organisation's goals

Inputs
from the
environment

Outputs
to the
environment

9.1
Open system

20.   General systems theory makes a distinction between open and closed systems.

(a)   A *closed system* is a system which is isolated from its environment and independent of it, so that no environmental influences affect the behaviour of the system - the way it operates - nor does the system exert any influence on its environment. Such a system is likely to suffer entropy - it will deteriorate or wear out.

(b)   An *open system* is a system connected to and interacting with its environment. It takes in influences (or 'energy') from its environment, that is inputs and outputs from other systems and, through a series of activities, converts these inputs into outputs (or inputs into other systems). In other words it influences its environment by its behaviour. An open system is a stable system which is nevertheless continually changing or evolving. All social systems are open systems.

Inputs to the organisation include labour, finance, raw materials, components, equipment and information. Outputs include information, services provided, goods produced etc.

21.   The 'open system' organisation must remain sensitive to its external environment, with which it is in constant interaction: it must respond to threats and opportunities, restrictions and challenges posed by markets, consumer trends, competitors, the government etc. Changes in input will influence output. This phenomenon is known as equifinality - because there is no single best way of achieving objectives, an open system allows the organisation to vary its input, processes and methods. Managers have more discretion and decision-making freedom.

22.   An organisation is not simply a structure: an organisation chart reflects only one sub-system of the overall organisation. Trist and his associates at the Tavistock Institute have suggested that an organisation is a 'structured sociotechnical system' - consisting of at least 3 sub-systems:

(a)   a structure;

(b) a technological system (concerning the work to be done, and the machines, tools and other facilities available to do it); and

(c) a social system (concerning the people within the organisation, the ways they think and the ways they interact with each other).

> The systems model therefore emphasises the interdependence of the component parts comprising the system: one facet can rarely be changed without impacting on another.

The contribution of the systems approach

23. General systems theory can contribute to the principles and practice of management in several ways, not least by enabling managers to learn from the experience of experts and researchers in other disciplines. But like any other approach, managers should take what they find useful in practice in the systems view, without making a 'religion' of it.

(a) It draws attention to the *dynamic* aspects of organisation, and the factors influencing the growth and development of all its sub-systems.

(b) It creates an awareness of sub-systems, each with potentially conflicting goals which must be integrated. *Sub-optimisation* (where sub-systems pursue their own goals to the detriment of the system as a whole) is a feature of organisational behaviour.

(c) It focuses attention on interrelationships between aspects of the organisation, and between it and its environment, that is the needs of the system as a whole: management should not get so bogged down in detail and small political arenas that they lose sight of the overall objectives and processes. Organisations should be looked at from a holistic viewpoint - because the whole is greater than the sum of its parts.

(d) It teaches managers to reject the deterministic idea that A will always cause B to happen. 'Linear causality' may occur, but only rarely, because of the unpredictability and uncontrollability of many inputs.

(e) The importance of the *environment* on a system is acknowledged. One product of this may be customer orientation, which Peters and Waterman note is an important cultural element of successful, adaptive companies.

24. The systems school has developed and extended the views of the behaviouralists, and suggests that:

(a) the efficiency or inefficiency of an organisation depends on the structure of the system or organisation, rather than on the characters of individual people who work in the system;

(b) an organisation should be viewed as a complex whole of inter-acting parts, and as isolated units or groups wherein human attitudes prevail.

The socio-technical systems approach

25. Trist, who is associated with the socio-technical systems approach to management, put forward the view that the behaviour of groups or individuals within an organisation is significantly affected by the technology employed within the organisation (the equipment used, and the methods

of working which follow on from the use of this equipment). The technology of the organisation interacts with the social system and human behaviour within the organisation. (In systems theory, both the technology and also the social inter-relationships between employees, employees and management etc are sub-systems of the overall system - the organisation. Their inter-relationships should therefore be studied and co-ordinated in a way which ensures the most efficient and effective use of the organisation's resources).

Technology, people and environment as variables in the 'organisation mix' become important areas of study as part of a development of the systems approach: the *contingency* approach.

● The contingency approach

26. Contingency theory, which is now the generally-held view, is that there isn't a universally-best organisation structure, but that there could well be a best structure for each individual organisation, which will depend on 'contingent factors'.

27. Essentially, it takes the view of 'different horses for different courses' - what a manager should do in practice will depend on the particular circumstances or situations he is in; similarly, the optimal organisational structure will depend on the individual circumstances or situation of the organisation. This approach is an important one because it rejects the belief, which is inherent in scientific management especially, that there is a universally correct answer to a given problem in every case whenever and wherever it crops up.

28. Conclusions may be drawn from a study of general principles about what type of organisation or style of management appears to be best for different situations, but specific conclusions should be reached with care and caution. For instance, size is not the only factor which will affect the optimal structure of the organisation. Charles Handy identified:

   ● history and ownership;
   ● technology;
   ● goals and objectives;
   ● the environment; and
   ● the people involved

as other contributory factors.

29.
> The contingency approach states that there is a structure which would improve the efficiency of an organisation, but that this ideal structure will vary in type according to the situation or circumstances of each particular individual organisation.

30. The structure which is actually selected is likely to be a 'compromise' between pressures which pull in opposite directions.

   (a) There are pressures for *uniformity*:
      (i)   standardisation of methods, rules and procedures might result in economies of scale;
      (ii) where uniform procedures exist, it is easier to impose centralised control;

      (iii)   the interchangeability of personnel from one part of an organisation to another is made easier;

      (iv)   specialised skills can be developed and applied throughout the organisation.

  (b) There are also strong pressures for *diversity*. Differences in regional characteristics, markets, customers or products, differences in the technology used in various aspects of the organisation's work, the greater readiness of individuals to identify with smaller work groups than with an entire organisation, and the desire of subordinates to have more authority ('decentralisation') are all factors which shape diversity in different parts of an organisation.

31. The contingency approach suggests that the factors which help to determine the optimal structure in any particular situation are:

  (a) *environment*. The organisational structure most conducive to high performance depends on whether the environment is stable and simple, or changing and complex. In a stable environment, the pressures for uniformity are strong; any unforeseen events will be rare and can be dealt with by top management.

Lawrence and Lorsch compared the structural characteristics of a 'high-performing' container firm, which existed in a relatively stable environment, and a 'high-performing' plastics firm which existed in a rapidly changing environment. They concluded that:

      (i)   in a stable environment (the container firm) the most efficient structure was one in which the influence and authority of senior managers were relatively high and that of middle managers low;

      (ii)   in a dynamic environment (the plastics firm) the most efficient structure was one in which the influence and authority of senior managers were somewhat less, and of middle managers correspondingly greater;

  (b) *diversity*. Lawrence and Lorsch referred to 'differentiated' organisations, which are organisations in which work practices, goods and planning time horizons varied widely between different parts of the organisation.

Successful firms will employ an organisation structure which reduces uncertainty:

      (i)   'staff' experts will be employed to act as an interface between the organisation and its environment, and to gather information from the environment;

      (ii)   there may be pressure to delegate decisions to the line manager 'on the spot';

      (iii)   there will be less formalisation and a greater emphasis on discussions, participation in decision-making, co-ordination and dissemination of information.

For example in an environment of rapid change, some managers (eg in research and corporate planning) concentrate on longer-term goals and time horizons; development engineers and sales staff might be more conscious of changes in the short term, and production management might be steeped in problems of day-to-day manufacture. Lawrence and Lorsch argued that the more widely differentiated an organisation becomes, the greater will be the pressures for a diversified organisation structure. A more obvious example might be 'conglomerate' companies, which are commonly organised on a decentralised, divisionalised basis;

   (c)   *size*. It has already been suggested that as an organisation grows larger, its systems tend to formalise into a bureaucracy. Contingency theory suggests that although an informal structure is more efficient for smaller firms, in large organisations formalisation and bureaucracy is often the most efficient type of structure available;

   (d)   *type of personnel*. Some employees like to be told what to do and prefer a standardised, uniform structure of organisation with authoritarian leadership; other employees (often those with a broader and greater education) prefer to be given responsibilities and to work in teams, and to make decisions in their own ways;

   (e)   the '*culture*' of the organisation, or the shared values and beliefs that make up 'the way things are done around here';

   (f)   *technology* of the organisation.

32.
> Contingency theory does have its critics, such as John Child: 'One major limitation of the contemporary contingency approach lies in the lack of conclusive evidence to demonstrate that matching organisational designs to prevailing contingencies contributes *importantly* to performance.'

Socio-technical systems

33. Joan Woodward developed the so-called 'socio-technical systems' view that the structure of organisations and nature of management depended on the nature of the technology used within the organisation. In other words, organisations varied widely in character, and a major factor contributing to the variations was technology, as a contingent variable.

34. Woodward categorised the levels of technology into:
   (a)   unit production, or small batch production;
   (b)   mass production, or large batch production;
   (c)   process production, or continuous flow production.

This categorisation also describes a rising scale of technical complexity - process production is more complex than mass production, which is more complex than unit production.

By 'technical complexity' she meant the extent to which the production process is controllable and its results predictable.

35. Joan Woodward described the findings of a survey of firms in Essex.

> "When the firms were grouped according to similarity of objectives and techniques of production, and classified in order of technical complexity of their production systems, each production system was found to be associated with a characteristic pattern of organisation. It appeared that technical methods were the most important factor in determining organisational structure and of setting the tone of human relationships inside the firms."

36. Elaborating further on the survey, she said that:

    (a) different objectives of different firms controlled and limited the techniques of production they could use (eg a firm developing prototypes of electronic equipment cannot go in for mass production);

    (b) analysing the firms into a continuum of ten levels of technical complexity (sub-divisions, slightly overlapping, of the three main levels described earlier) ranging from basically simple technology up to the complex, she found that firms using similar technical methods also had similar organisational structures. 'It appeared that different technologies imposed different kinds of demands on individuals and organisations and that these demands had to be met through an appropriate form of organisation.'

37. Specific findings were that:

    (a) the number of levels in the management hierarchy increased with technical complexity, so that complex technologies lead to 'tall' organisation structures and simpler technologies can operate with a 'flat' structure;

    (b) the span of control of first line supervisors was at its highest in mass production, and then decreased in process production;

9.2 Span of control related to technological complexity

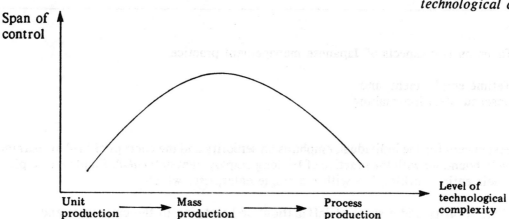

    (c) labour costs decreased as technology advanced;

    (d) the ratio of indirect labour to direct labour increased with the level of technical advance;

    (e) the span of control of the chief executive widened with technical advance;

    (f) the proportion of graduates in supervisory positions increased with technical advance;

    (g) the organisation was more flexible at both ends of the scale (simple unit production for customer orders at one end; continuous process production at the other) so that duties and responsibilities were less clearly defined. In mass production, duties and responsibilities are clearly set out, largely due to the nature of the technology, and this favours a formal, authoritarian structure;

    (h) the amount of written, as opposed to verbal, communication, peaked with mass assembly line production; written communication is a feature of bureaucracy and formal structures;

(i) specialisation between the functions of management was most frequent in large batch and mass production companies; the clear cut demarcation (and resultant conflicts) between 'line' and 'staff' management was also most frequent here;

(j) the planning of production (the 'brainwork') and the actual supervision of production work are the most widely separated in large-batch and mass production companies;

(k) industrial and human relations were better at both extremes of the scale than in large-batch and mass production companies, possibly due to heavier pressure on all individuals in this type of organisation;

(l) the size of the firm was not related to its technical complexity, so it is not possible to attribute the 'faults' of mass production to the size of the firm rather than to the nature of its technology.

● **The Japanese experience**

38. Koontz, O'Donnell and Weihrich note (*Management*) that

> "Japan, one of the leading industrial nations in the world, has adopted managerial practices that are quite different from those of other economically advanced countries in the Western world".

39. They focus on two aspects of Japanese management practice:

● lifetime employment; and
● consensus decision-making.

40. Japanese concern for the individual, emphasis on seniority and the concept of '*wa*' or 'harmony' are closely bound up with the practice of lifelong employment or '*nenko*'. Employees typically spend their entire working life within a single enterprise, which:

(a) offers security and a sense of 'affiliation' or belonging to the employee; and
(b) fosters employee loyalty and commitment to the organisation; but also
(c) adds to payroll costs even when there is insufficient work; and
(d) 'carries' weak employees and may discourage ambitious ones.

41. This practice, used only by large firms (and now decreasingly, even there - an estimated one-third of the population - and excluding women) creates a population of older employees who have spent a lifetime with the enterprise. The seniority system has traditionally provided privileges for these individuals. However there are signs that younger people are now being given greater opportunities for advancement.

> "The managerial practice of decision-making is also considerably different from that in the United States. It is built on the concept that change and new ideas should come primarily from below."
>
> *Koontz et al*

42. Ideas are submitted for questioning, suggestions, discussion etc to the next level up the hierarchy until they reach the senior manager: this is decision-making by consensus. The initiator of a proposal is then encouraged to implement it: the method of reaching a decision may be time-consuming, but it is then ripe for implementation without further persuasion or acceptance. Moreover, Japanese methods of decision-making are aimed at relevance and effectiveness: time is spent discussing and defining the *problem* (and finding out whether there *is* a problem) before any attempt is made to find the *solution*.

43. In an article in the *Student's Newsletter* in February 1988, L R Gray put forward two illustrations of the *'wa'* and *'nenko'* concepts:

    (a) Quality Circles (QC - discussed in Chapter 7); and
    (b) industrial relations.

44. | "QCs are the result of the development of an organisational climate which emphasises both high productivity and high quality.... The QCs are based on *'wa'* and on the sound idea that the person most knowledgeable of the production process is the operative on the shop floor. Similarly, the participative nature of decision-making ensures that decisions *are* taken at shop-floor level which relate to shop-floor matters. The Japanese are well aware that the profits are made on the shop-floor, not in the boardroom." *Gray*

45. Japanese workforces and unions identify with the company and adopt a 'unitary' perspective on industrial relations: employer and employee can agree common goals and pursue them together.

46. As we have noted, however, the practice of *'nenko'* is declining, and has its detractors. There are suggestions that factors other than the 'cultural' framework might be instrumental in Japanese success, such as:

    (a) limited interference by central government;
    (b) investment in industry, via banks, by small investors (*Nakagawa and Ota*);
    (c) ability to identify overseas markets and consumer needs (*Kenichi*);
    (d) diverse product lines, large scale joint ventures (eg General Motors and Toyota) etc (*Kast and Rosenweig*).

QUIZ

1. What are the classical principles of management as listed by Fayol?

   ● See para 5

2. Criticise the idea of scientific management.

   ● See para 11

3. What is the contribution of the systems view of organisation to the practice of management?

   ● See paras 18-24

4. How do the findings of Joan Woodward support a contingency approach to delegation?

   ● See paras 33,36

5. What are the two key elements of the 'Japanese experience of management' and how do they affect quality and industrial relations?

   ● See paras 38-46

Chapter 10

MOTIVATION

Topics covered in this chapter

- Motivation
- Motivation theories
    - o   Hierarchy of needs
    - o   Job satisfaction
    - o   The job as motivator
- Systems and contingency approach to motivation
- Motivation in practice
    - o   Job design
    - o   Pay
    - o   Participation
- Management style
- Theories about the worker - theories X, Y and Z

Purpose of this chapter

To consider what motivation is, why it matters and how it occurs, or can be created in practice. This involves the introduction of topics covered in other areas of the syllabus, particularly the management function of work organisation.

● Motivation

1.   An organisation has goals which can only be achieved by the efforts of the people who work in the organisation. Individual people also have their own 'goals' in life, and these are likely to be different from those of the organisation. A major consideration for supervisors and management is the problem of getting the employees to work in such a way that the organisation achieves its goals; in other words, employees must be *motivated*.

Why is motivation important?

2.   You may be wondering why motivation is important. It could be argued that if a person is employed to do a job, he will do that job and no question of motivation arises. If the person doesn't want to do the work, he can resign.

3.   The point at issue, however, is the *efficiency* with which the job is done. It is suggested that if individuals can be motivated, by one means or another, they will work more efficiently (productivity will rise) or they will produce a better quality of work. There is some debate as to what the actual effects of improved motivation are, efficiency or quality, but it has become widely accepted that motivation is beneficial to the organisation.

> "If we could understand, and could then predict , the ways in which individuals were motivated we could influence them by changing the components of that motivation process. Is that manipulation - or management?"
>
> *Charles Handy - Understanding Organisations*

Motivators and motivation

4.   In the most basic terms, an individual has needs which he wishes to satisfy. The means of satisfying his needs are 'wants'. For example, an individual might feel the need for power, and to fulfil this need, he might want money and a position of authority. Depending on the strength of his needs and wants, he may take action to achieve them. If he is successful in achieving them, he will be satisfied. This can be shown in a simple diagram.

10.1 From needs to satisfaction ...

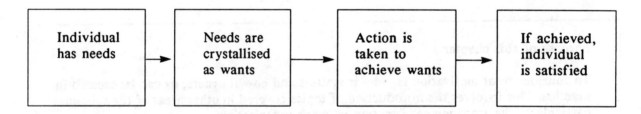

'Motivation' then is the urge or drive to take action to satisfy wants. Motivation to work is often part of a trade-off with a person's motivation to do something else. For example, an individual might want to be promoted, but he might not be sufficiently motivated to work harder or more efficiently in order to win the promotion: he might also want leisure, or he may not believe that the company really will promote him if he does work harder. Management has the problem of creating or 'manipulating' motivators which will actually motivate employees to perform in a desired way.

● Motivation theories

5.   The kind of theory that we subscribe to, about what motivation is and what can be 'done' with it, will influence all our attitudes to our management style and to individuals in organisations. There are various ways of looking at motivation. Early motivation theories can be grouped under three headings:

- *satisfaction theories*. These theories are based on the assumption that a 'satisfied' worker will work harder, although there is little evidence to support the assumption. Satisfaction may reduce labour turnover and absenteeism, but will not necessarily increase individual productivity. Some theories hold that people work best within a compatible work group, or under a well-liked leader;

- *incentive theories*. These theories are based on the assumption that individuals will work harder in order to obtain a desired reward - this is positive reinforcement, although most studies are concentrated on money as a motivator. Incentive theories *can* work, if:

  (i)   the individual perceives the increased reward to be worth the extra effort;
  (ii)   the performance can be measured and clearly attributed to that individual;
  (iii)   the individual wants that particular kind of reward; and
  (iv)   the increased performance will not become the new minimum standard;

- *intrinsic theories*. These theories are based on the belief that higher-order needs are more prevalent in modern man than we give him credit for. People will work hard in response to factors in the work itself - participation, responsibility etc: effective performance is its own reward.

Hierarchy of needs

6.   The American psychologist Abraham Maslow argued that man has seven innate needs.

- physiological needs	- the need for food, shelter etc.
- safety needs	- freedom from threat, but also security, order and predictability
- love needs	- for relationships, affection, sense of belonging
- esteem needs	- for competence, achievement, independence, confidence and their reflection in the perception of others, that is recognition, appreciation, status, respect
- self-actualisation needs	- for the fulfilment of personal potential: 'the desire to become more and more what one is, to become everything that one is capable of becoming'
- freedom of inquiry and expression needs	- for social conditions permitting free speech and encouraging justice, fairness and honesty
- knowledge and understanding needs	- to gain and order knowledge of the environment, to explore, learn, experiment etc.

According to Maslow, the last two needs are the channels through which we find ways of satisfying all the other needs - they are the basis of satisfaction. The first two needs are essential to human survival. Satisfaction of the next two is essential for a sense of adequacy and psychological health. Maslow regarded self-actualisation as the ultimate human goal, although few people ever reach it.

7. Roethlisberger and Dickson add on to physiological and safety needs:

- Friendship and belonging needs
- Needs for justice and fair treatment
- Dependence-independence
- Needs for achievement

8. In his motivation theory, Maslow put forward certain propositions about the motivating power of these needs and how they actually dictate the process by which they are fulfilled.

(a) Man's needs can be arranged in a 'hierarchy of needs'.

(b) Each 'level' of need is dominant until satisfied; only then does the next level of need become a motivating factor.

(c) A need which has been satisfied no longer motivates an individual's behaviour. The need for self-actualisation can never be satisfied.

10.2 Maslow's hierarchy of needs

9. There is a certain intuitive appeal to Maslow's theory. After all, you are unlikely to be concerned with status or recognition while you are hungry or thirsty - primary survival needs will take precedence. Likewise, once your hunger is assuaged, the need for food is unlikely to be a motivating factor.

10. Maslow's theories may be of general interest, but they have no clear practical application. It has not been proved that stimulating an individual's needs (providing motivators) will in its turn spark off a desired behavioural reaction.

- The same need may cause different behaviour in different individuals. One person might seek to satisfy his need for esteem by winning promotion whereas another individual might seek esteem by leading a challenge against authority.

- It is occasionally difficult to reconcile the willingness of individuals to forego the immediate satisfaction of needs and to accept current 'suffering' to fulfil a long-term goal (eg the long studentship of the medical or accounting professions), in view of the supposed 'hierarchy'.

Job satisfaction

11. Frederick Herzberg in his book *'Work and the Nature of Man'* (1966) identified the elements which cause job dissatisfaction (hygiene factors), and those which can cause job satisfaction (motivator factors).

    Factors which cause dissatisfaction at work are:
    (a) company policy and administration;
    (b) salary;
    (c) the quality of supervision;
    (d) interpersonal relations;
    (e) working conditions;
    (f) job security.

    > 'When people are dissatisfied with their work it is usually because of discontent with the environmental factors' (Herzberg).

    He calls such factors *'hygiene'* or *'maintenance'* factors; hygiene because they are essentially preventative. They prevent or minimise dissatisfaction but do not give satisfaction, in the same way that sanitation minimises threats to health, but does not give 'good' health. They also have to be continually reviewed. Satisfaction with environmental factors is not lasting. In time dissatisfactions will occur.

12. The important point is that motivation through the above-mentioned factors is a necessary but thankless task. It is never-ending. Even if effective it will still not motivate the employee to work well (at a higher than usual level of performance) except for a short period of time.

    On the other hand, if the environment is deficient in some way then the subordinates are likely to become annoyed and show their displeasure by industrial conflict, decreased productivity, grumbling etc. Yet if the deficiency is corrected the best that can be expected is that output/effort will return to 'normal'.

13. *Motivator factors* actively create job satisfaction and *are* effective in motivating an individual to superior performance and effort. These factors consist of:

    (a) status (although this may be a hygiene factor as well as a motivator factor);
    (b) advancement;
    (c) gaining recognition;
    (d) being given responsibility;
    (e) challenging work;
    (f) achievement;
    (g) growth in the job.

14. Herzberg saw two separate 'need systems' of individuals:

    (a) there is a need to avoid unpleasantness. This need is satisfied at work by hygiene factors. Hygiene satisfactions are short-lived; individuals come back for more, in the nature of drug addicts;

    (b) there is a need for personal growth, which is satisfied by motivator factors, and not by hygiene factors.

    A lack of motivators at work will encourage employees to concentrate on bad hygiene (real or imagined) such as to demand more pay. Some individuals are not mature enough to want personal growth; these are 'hygiene seekers' because they can only ever be satisfied by hygiene factors.

The job as motivator

15. The job itself can be interesting and 'exciting'. It can satisfy the desire for a feeling of 'accomplishing something', for responsibility, for professional recognition, for advancement and so on, and the need for self-esteem.

16. 'Dissatisfaction arises from environment factors - satisfaction can only arise from the job.' (Herzberg).

    If there is sufficient challenge, scope and interest in the job, there will be a lasting increase in satisfaction and the employee will work well; productivity will be above 'normal' levels.

    The extent to which a job must be challenging or creative to a motivator seeker will, in relation to each individual, depend on
    (a) his ability; and
    (b) his tolerance for delayed success.

17. Herzberg suggested means by which motivator satisfactions could be supplied. Stemming from his fundamental division of motivator and hygiene factors, he encourages managers to study the job itself (the type of work done, the nature of tasks, levels of responsibility) rather than conditions of work. Only this way will motivation improve. (Concentrating on environmental factors will merely stave off job dissatisfaction.)

    He specified three typical means whereby work can be revised to improve motivation. These are:

    (a) *job enrichment:* this is the main method of improving job satisfaction and can be defined as 'the planned process of up-grading the responsibility, challenge and content of the work'. Typically, this would involve increasing delegation to provide more interesting work and problem-solving at lower levels within an organisation;

    (b) *job enlargement:* although often linked with job enrichment, it is a separate technique and is rather limited in its ability to improve staff motivation. Job enlargement is the process of increasing the number of operations in which a worker is engaged and so moving away from narrow specialisation of work. Herzberg tells us that this is more limited in value, since a man who is required to complete several tedious tasks is unlikely to be much more highly motivated than a man performing one continuous tedious task;

(c) *job rotation:* this is the planned operation of a system whereby staff members exchange positions with the intention of breaking monotony in the work and providing fresh job challenge.

Job enrichment, job enlargement and job rotation are described in more detail later on.

Expectancy theory

18. Expectancy theory states that the strength of an individual's motivation to do something will depend on the extent to which he *expects* the results of his efforts to contribute towards his personal needs or goals, to reward him or to punish him.

19. Put another way, expectancy theory states that people will decide how much they are going to put into their work, according:

   ● to what they perceive they are going to get out of it (expectancy)
   ● to the value that they place on this outcome (whether the positive value of a reward, or the negative value of a punishment) which Vroom called 'Valence', and
   ● to the strength of their expectation that behaving in a certain way will in fact bring out the desired outcome (force of motivation).

Expectancy x **V**alence = **F**orce of motivation.

The motivation calculus

20. Charles Handy (*Understanding Organisations*) puts forward an 'admittedly theoretical' form of expectancy model.

21. Handy suggests that for any individual decision, there is a conscious or unconscious 'motivation calculus' which is an assessment of three factors:

   (a) the individual's own set of needs;

   (b) the desired results - what the individual is expected to do in his job;

   (c) 'E' factors. Handy suggests that motivational theories have been too preoccupied with 'effort'. He notes that there seems to be a set of words, coincidentally beginning with 'e', that might be more helpful. As well as effort, there is energy, excitement in achieving desired results, enthusiasm, emotion, and expenditure (of time, money etc).

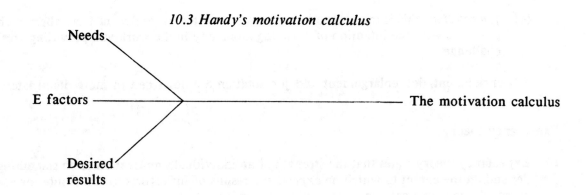

10.3 Handy's motivation calculus

22. The 'motivation decision' - how strong the motivation to achieve the desired results will be - will depend on the individual person's judgement about:

    (a) the strength of his needs;
    (b) the *expectancy* that expending 'E' will lead to a desired result; and
    (c) how far the result will be 'instrumental' in satisfying his needs.

> A man may have a high need for power. To the degree that he believes that a particular result, such as a completed task, will gain him promotion (expectancy) *and* that promotion will in fact satisfy his need for power ('instrumentality') he will expend 'E' on the task.

23. In terms of organisation practice, Handy suggests that several factors are necessary for the individual to complete the calculus, and to be motivated.

    (a) *Intended results* should be made clear, so that the individual can complete his 'calculation', and know what is expected of him, what will be rewarded and how much 'E' it will take.

    (b) Without knowledge of *actual results*, there is no check that the 'E' expenditure was justified (and will be justified in future). *Feedback* on performance - good or bad - is essential, not only for performance but for confidence, prevention of hostility etc.

24. Handy's calculus helps to explain various phenomena of individual behaviour at work.

    (a) Individuals are more committed to specific goals - particularly those which they have helped to set themselves.

    (b) If an individual is *rewarded* according to performance tied to standards ('management by objectives'), however, he may well set *lower* standards: the 'instrumentality' part of the calculus (likelihood of success and reward) is greater if the standard is lower, so less expense of 'E' is indicated.

Systems and contingency approaches to motivation

25. Stemming from the early research work of Elton Mayo, a systems and contingency approach to motivation has been developed by a number of writers, notably Kurt Lewin. A systems and contingency approach means that:

    (a) the motivation of an individual cannot be seen in isolation. It depends on the system within which he operates, his work group and his environment;

    (b) the motivation of the individual will also depend on circumstances. Different people react to the same environment in different ways, and a person's motivation is likely to vary from day to day, according to his mood, events at work and his fatigue as well as 'hygiene' and 'motivator' factors in his work.

26. Writing in 1938, Lewin developed his 'field theory' in which he compared an individual's environment to a magnetic field, with various forces in that field pulling him in different directions and affecting his attitudes from day to day. His formula for human behaviour was:

    $B = (P,E)$ where

    B is a person's behaviour, which depends on
    P (the person himself/herself) and
    E (his or her environment).

27. This means that an individual's motivation, varying over time, could be illustrated on a graph as follows:

Amount or
degree of
motivation
of individual

10.4 Individual's motivation graph

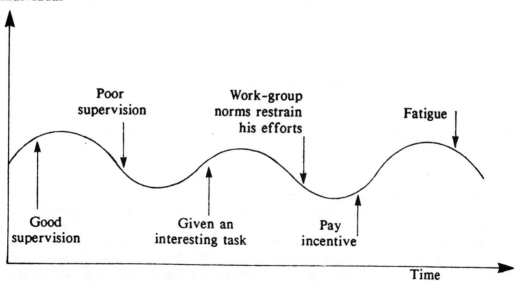

28. The systems and contingency school of thought is that if a manager wishes to improve the motivation of subordinates, he must take all the circumstances of the particular situation into account, being differences between individuals, the external environment, individuals' expectations, work groups, variations in circumstances from day to day or month to month etc.

29.

> One conclusion from this approach might be that motivation depends on so many interrelated factors that a manager wishing to improve motivation is faced with a complex problem for which there may be no obvious ready-made solution.

Carrot or stick?

30. You might have noted that 'motivation' can be a negative process (appealing to an individual's need to *avoid* unpleasantness, pain, fear etc.) as well as a positive one (appealing to the individual's need to attain certain goals).

    (a) Negative motivation is 'wielding the big stick: threatening dismissal or demotion, reprimand etc - it is negative reinforcement.

    (b) Positive motivation is 'dangling the carrot', and may be achieved by:

        (i)   the offer of 'extrinsic' rewards, such as pay incentives, promotion, better working conditions etc;
        (ii) 'internal' or psychological satisfaction for the individual - 'virtue is its own reward', a sense of achievement, a sense of responsibility and value etc.

> "Have managers outsmarted motivational theory, and become cynical about carrots, world-weary about sticks?" (Ray Proctor: *Finance for the perplexed executive*)

● Motivation in practice

31. Drucker (writing before Herzberg) suggested that motivation through 'employee satisfaction' is not a useful concept because employee satisfaction is such a wishy-washy idea. It doesn't mean anything in particular, and if it is to have some meaning, it must be defined more constructively. His suggestion was that employee satisfaction comes about through encouraging - if need be, by 'pushing' - employees to accept *responsibility*. There are four ingredients to this.

    (a) *Careful placement of people in jobs*. The selection or recruitment process is an important one, because the person selected should see the job as one which provides a challenge to his abilities. There will be no motivation for a university graduate in the job of shop assistant, whereas the same job can provide a worthwhile challenge to someone of lesser academic training and intelligence.

    (b) *High standards of performance in the job*. Targets for achievement should be challenging. However, they should not be imposed in an authoritarian way by the employee's bosses. The employee should be encouraged to expect high standards of performance from himself.

    (c) *Providing the worker with the information he needs to control his own performance*. The employee should receive routine information about how well or badly he is doing without having to be told by his boss. (The design of a reporting system is important in this respect.) Being told by a boss comes as a praise or reprimand, and the fear of reprimand will inhibit performance. Access to information as a routine matter overcomes this problem of inhibition.

(d) *Opportunities for participation in decisions that will give the employee managerial vision.* Participation means having some say and influence in the way the employee's work is organised and the targets for his work are set. Participation does not mean that his boss relinquishes the job of managing the business! However, bosses should manage people to make them efficient; and managing people to manage themselves is a potentially valuable way of achieving such efficiency.

Methods of improving motivation

32. There are various ways in which management can attempt to increase the motivation of their subordinates:

(a) Herzberg and others recommended better job design - job enrichment, job enlargement and job rotation;

(b) pay and incentive schemes are frequently regarded as powerful motivators;

(c) various writers have suggested that participation by subordinates in decision-making will improve motivation through self- realisation.

> We shall discuss each of these ways in turn.

● Job design

33. Job design is the process of deciding:

- on the content of a job in terms of its duties and responsibilities;

- on the methods to be used in carrying out the job, in terms of techniques, system and procedures; and

- on the relationship that should exist between the job holder and his/her superiors, colleagues and subordinates.

34. As its objectives, the job design process seeks to improve productivity, efficiency and quality and to satisfy the individual's needs for interest, challenge and accomplishment.

35. The process has two main steps:

(a) job analysis - analysing and establishing what work has to be done; and
(b) job enrichment - allowing the individual greater opportunity for personal achievement.

> In this chapter we shall concentrate on job enrichment, the size of the job and job rotation. Job analysis is covered in Chapters 21-23.

Job enrichment

36. Job enrichment is planned, deliberate action to build greater responsibility, breadth and challenge of work into a job. A job may be enriched by:

    (a) giving it greater variety (although this could perhaps also be described as job enlargement);

    (b) allowing the employee in the job greater freedom to decide for himself how the job should be done;

    (c) encouraging employees to participate in the planning decisions of their superiors;

    (d) ensuring that the employee receives regular feedback on his performance, comparing his actual results against his targets.

37. Job enrichment attempts to add further responsibilities to a job by giving the job holder decision-making capabilities of a 'higher' order.

38. For instance, an administrator's responsibilities for producing quarterly management reports ended at the stage of producing the figures. These duties were then extended so that he prepared the actual reports and submitted them, under his own name, to the senior management. This alteration in responsibilities not only enriched his job but also increased his work-load. This in turn led him to delegate certain responsibilities to clerks within the department. These duties were in themselves job enrichment to the clerks and so a cascading effect was obtained.

> This highlights one of the basic elements of job enrichment - that what is tedious, mundane detail at a high level can represent significant job interest and challenge at a lower level in the organisation where a person's experience and scope is much less.

39. Some experiments have been made whereby *work-groups* were given collective job enrichment. Child (in *'Organisation: A Guide to Problems and Practice'*) cited the example in the UK of Phillips. A work group responsible for manufacturing black and white television sets carried out the entire assembly operation and also had authority to deal directly with purchasing, stores and quality control, without a supervisor acting as intermediary. The change in work organisation meant, however, that the company had to incur additional costs in re-equipment and training.

40. Perhaps a more well-known example is the case of Volvo in Sweden, where a new factory was built so as to facilitate greater flexibility for work groups, with considerable responsibilities for major stages of manufacture, to organise their jobs as they considered best. Once again, job enrichment necessitated large capital expenditure.

41. Job enrichment has not been widely developed, and only a few reported cases exist in both the USA and Europe, although there may be other schemes 'masquerading' as job enrichments which are not thorough-going applications of the principle. The reasons for its slow progress may be:

    (a) the technology of working conditions. It would be difficult to introduce a scheme of job enrichment into mass production and assembly line working without spending considerable amounts of money on re-organisation of working conditions and equipment. Child suggested that 'in some cases, the conditions for job enrichment via autonomous group working involve capital investment which is more expensive than in traditional technologies; examples are Volvo's Kalmar automobile plant and Renault's Le Mans axle factory';

(b) jobs with a low level of skill may be difficult to enrich (but it should be easier to enrich jobs of subordinate managers);

(c) job enrichment should be wanted by subordinates. An attempt by senior managers to impose job enrichment schemes according to their own particular views as to what job enrichment actually means is unlikely to be long-lasting or productive.

42. It would be wrong, however, to suppose that job enrichment alone will automatically make employees more productive.

> 'Even those who want their jobs enriched will expect to be rewarded with more than job satisfaction. Job enrichment is not a cheaper way to greater productivity. Its pay-off will come in the less visible costs of morale, climate and working relationships'. (Handy).

43. If jobs are enriched, employees will expect to be paid fairly for what they are doing. It might be more correct therefore to say that job enrichment might improve productivity through greater motivation, but only if it is rewarded fairly.

Job enlargement versus micro-division of labour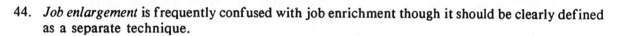

44. *Job enlargement* is frequently confused with job enrichment though it should be clearly defined as a separate technique.

> Job enlargement, as the name suggests, is the attempt to widen jobs by increasing the number of operations in which a job holder is involved.
>
> This has the effect of lengthening the 'time cycle' of repeated operations; by reducing the number of repetitions of the same work, the dullness of the job should also be reduced. Job enlargement is therefore a 'horizontal' extension of an individual's work, whereas job enrichment is a 'vertical' extension.

45. Job enlargement has often been described as an approach to a job design which is at the opposite end of a spectrum to the *'micro-division'* of labour. The micro-division of labour is based on a production line approach to the organisation of work:

(a) a job is divided up into the smallest number of sequential tasks possible. Each task is so simple and straightforward that it can be learned with very little training;

(b) if labour turnover is high, this does not matter because unskilled replacements can be found and trained to do the work in a very short time;

(c) since the skill required is low, workers can be shifted from one task to another very easily. The production flow will therefore be unaffected by absenteeism;

(d) if tasks are closely defined and standard times set for their completion, production is easier to predict and control;

(e) standardisation of work into simple tasks means that quality is easier to predict. There is less scope for doing a task badly.

46. The arguments against the micro-division of labour are:

(a) the work is monotonous and makes employees tired, bored and dissatisfied. The consequences will be high labour turnover, absenteeism and spoilage;

(b) the boredom of employees in their work will provide a breeding ground for industrial unrest and strikes;

(c) people, unlike machines, work more efficiently when their work is variable;

(d) an individual doing a simple task feels like a small cog in a large machine. This prevents him from having any sense of his contribution to the organisation's end product;

(e) excessive specialisation isolates the individual in his work and inhibits social contacts with 'work-mates'.

47. A well-designed job should therefore:

(a) give the individual scope for setting his own work standards and targets;
(b) give the individual control over the pace and methods of working;
(c) provide variety by allowing for inter-locking tasks to be done by the same person;
(d) give the individual a chance to add his comments about the design of the product, or his job;
(e) provide feedback of information to the individual about his performance.

48. Arguably, job enlargement is limited in its ability to improve motivation since, as Herzberg points out, to ask a worker to complete three separate tedious, unchallenging tasks is unlikely to motivate him more than asking him to fulfil one singe tedious, unchallenging task.

> 'To paraphrase Herzberg, adding one Mickey Mouse job to another does not make any more than two Mickey Mouse jobs' (Child).

(The same criticism would be applied to job rotation, which has a similar purpose to job enlargement - giving subordinates more varied work to do, but of a similar nature or degree of difficulty.)

Job enrichment and job enlargement combined

49. Job enlargement might succeed in providing job enrichment as well, provided that the nature of the extra tasks to be done in the bigger job are possible and give the employee a greater challenge and incentive.

(a) When work is organised as a production line, with each employee responsible for just a small part of the total work, the dullness and monotony of the employee's work will be exceptionally high. Just by giving an employee a task which spans a larger part of the total production work - by enlarging the job - the dullness and monotony are likely to be reduced.

(b) Enlarged jobs can provide a challenge and incentive. For example, a trusted employee might be given added responsibilities for:

   (i) checking the quality of output. (There is a view that concern for quality of manufactured goods is a major reason for the success of Japanese industry. An employee who is allowed to monitor his own work quality, as well as the work of others, might easily see a challenging responsibility in such a job);

   (ii) training new recruits.

50. Enlarged jobs might also be regarded as 'status' jobs within the department, and as stepping stones towards promotion.

51. *Participation* in decision-making by employees (which will be discussed more fully later) is a form of both job enlargement and job enrichment. Drucker (in *'The Practice of Management'* (1955)) quoted the example of IBM where the final details of the design of the first electronic computers by the company were worked out on the factory floor in consultation with the workforce. Workers were able to offer suggestions based on their experience and practical know-how for the improvement of the computer design. The effects of this innovation in job design were found by IBM management to be:

(a) better product design;
(b) lower production costs;
(c) greater speed of production;
(d) greater worker satisfaction.

Job enrichment and enlargement and delegation of authority

52. *Delegation* is another factor in the design of jobs. Job enlargement and enrichment cannot be taken too far unless more authority is delegated to subordinates. Handy suggests that although delegation is one of those 'good' words which managers pay lip service to, they are often reluctant to delegate in practice. This is because by delegating, a manager loses to his subordinates control over decisions, and he does not necessarily trust his subordinates to do the job as well as he could himself.

53. This is what Handy calls a *'trust control' dilemma:* the manager wants to have control over decisions, but would like to delegate and so show his trust in the subordinates' abilities. He cannot show more trust (delegate) without losing more control.

'Trust...is cheap. Trust leaves the superior free to do other things; trust, if given and accepted, breeds responsibility and obviates the need for controls, as the controls become, in a sense, self-administered (the secretary refers the letters she is worried about to her boss, the salesman consults his manager in doubtful cases). But trust is risky, for the superior is held accountable for things that others did, even if they did them in ways he would not himself have chosen.

Trust can be misplaced, trust can be abused. And since trust means the absence of superior-administered controls, trust can leave the superior feeling naked and a little lonely (what are they all up to, I wonder?), like an anxious mother when the children are mysteriously quiet.'
Handy

Job rotation

54. Job rotation may take two forms:

    (a) an employee might be transferred to another job after a period of, say, 2-4 years in an existing job in order to give him or her a new interest and challenge, and to bring a fresh person to the job being vacated;

    (b) job rotation might be regarded as a form of training. Trainees might be expected to learn a bit about a number of different jobs, by spending six months or one year in each job before being moved on. The employee is regarded as a 'trainee' rather than as an experienced person holding down a demanding job.

55. No doubt you will have your own views about the value of job rotation as a method of training or career development. It is interesting to note Drucker's view: 'The whole idea of training jobs is contrary to all rules and experience. A man should never be given a job that is not a real job, that does not require performance from him'.

It is generally accepted that the value of job rotation as a motivator is limited.

Pay as a motivator

56. We must remember that an employee needs income to live. The size of his income will affect his standard of living, and although he would obviously like to earn more, he is probably more concerned:

    (a) that he should earn *enough* pay; and

    (b) that his pay should be fair in comparison with the pay of others both inside and outside the organisation.

57. It should be apparent that pay as a motivator is commonly associated with payment by results, whereby a worker's pay is directly dependent upon his output.

All such schemes are based on the principle that people are willing to work harder to obtain more money. But there are several constraints which can nullify this basic principle. For example:

(a) the average worker is generally capable of influencing the timings and control systems used by management, and so can 'fiddle the figures';

(b) workers remain suspicious that if they achieved high levels of output and earnings then management would alter the basis of the incentive rates to reduce future earnings;

(c) generally, workers conform to a group output norm and the need to have the approval of their fellow workers by conforming to that norm is more important than the money urge.

58. Further drawbacks to the use of money as a form of motivation are:

(a) rates of pay are perhaps more useful as a means of keeping an organisation adequately staffed by competent, qualified people rather than as a means of getting them to work harder;

(b) in most large companies, salary levels and pay levels are usually structured carefully so as to be 'equitable' or fair. Managers and workers will *compare* the pay of each other, or with people working in other organisations in the same area, and will be dissatisfied if the comparison is unfavourable (Drucker calls this phenomenon 'the toxic side-effect of the carrot'). Pay is therefore more likely to be a 'hygiene' factor at work than a motivator;

(c) when employees expect a regular annual review of salary, increases in pay will not motivate them to work harder. Indeed, if the increase is not high enough, it may be a source of dissatisfaction.

59. A major problem with using pay systems as forms of motivator for employees is that management want to achieve other objectives with the pay structure they set up than simply motivation; it isn't the only factor to consider when we think about pay. How much pay costs the organisation and eats into its profits are also very important considerations.

60. Child has suggested that there are six management criteria for a reward system.

(a) It should encourage people to fill job vacancies and to stay in their job (ie. not leave).

(b) It should increase the predictability of employees' behaviour, so that employees can be depended on to carry out their duties consistently and to a reasonable standard.

(c) It should motivate (increase commitment and effort).

(d) It should increase willingness to accept change and flexibility. (Changes in work practices are often 'bought' from trade unions with higher pay.)

(e) It should foster and encourage *innovative behaviour*.

(f) Pay differentials should reflect the nature of jobs in the organisation and the skills or experience required. The reward system should therefore be consistent with seniority of position in the organisation structure, and should be thought *fair* by all employees.

---

61. On the other hand, money *can* be a motivator, depending on the individual's need for money. Thus a young married man with a family to support may want money very badly, so that he can afford enough to achieve a desired standard of living. Money is not usually an end in itself, but it provides the means of buying the things an individual wants in order to satisfy his physiological, safety, social, esteem and self-actualisation needs.

> It is generally agreed that if there is a clear, short-term and direct link between extra effort, results and higher pay, then an individual can be considerably motivated by money. Salesmen paid on a commission basis could be a clear example of this principle in practice.

62. Drucker suggested that pay is an incentive to produce better output only where a willingness to perform better already exists.

63. Some companies have moved from individual to group incentive schemes. Where this has been linked to a job enrichment programme, effective working groups with healthy rivalry can be formed, thus gaining some advantages from both worlds. On the other hand, an individual will not work harder unless the group as a whole raises its norms, and there will be some resentment against group members who are seen to be 'shirking'.

64. It has become clear from the experiences of many companies that profit-sharing schemes, incentive schemes (productivity bonuses) and joint consultation machinery do not in themselves improve productivity or ease the way for work to get done. Company-wide profit sharing schemes cannot be related directly to extra effort by individuals and are probably a 'hygiene' factor rather than a motivator.

Better organisation, better technology and motivation of employees are also needed to improve productivity; a major problem is to put all these into practice together.

● Participation as a means of motivation

65. There is a theory that if a superior invites his subordinates to participate in planning decisions which affect their work, if the subordinates voluntarily accept the invitation, and if results about actual performance are fed back regularly to the subordinates so that they can make their own control decisions, then the subordinate will be motivated:

  (a) to be more efficient;
  (b) to be more conscious of the organisation's goals;
  (c) to raise his planning targets to reasonably challenging levels; and
  (d) to be ready to take appropriate control actions when necessary.

66. It is obvious that participation will only be feasible if the superior is willing to apply it.

What does participation mean and why is it desirable?

67. Handy commented that: 'Participation is sometimes regarded as a form of job enlargement. At other times it is a way of gaining commitment by workers to some proposal on the grounds that if you have been involved in discussing it, you will be more interested in its success. In part, it is the outcome of almost cultural belief in the norms of democratic leadership. It is one of those 'good' words with which it is hard to disagree'.

68. The advantages of participation should perhaps be considered from the opposite end - what would be the disadvantages of not having participation? The answer to this is that employees would be told what to do, and would presumably comply with orders. However, their compliance would not be enthusiastic, and they would not be psychologically committed to their work.

69. Participation can involve employees and make them committed to their task, but only if:

    (a) participation is *genuine*. It is very easy for a boss to pretend to invite participation from his subordinates but end up issuing orders. If subordinates feel the decision has already been taken, they might resent the falsehood of management efforts to discuss the decision with them. A good example would be the offer by management to discuss redundancies with its employees when employees believe that the decisions about redundancies have already been taken, and management's offer of discussions is false;

    (b) the efforts to establish participation by employees are *continual* and pushed over a long period of time and with a lot of energy. However, 'if the issue or the task is trivial...and everyone realises it, participitative methods will boomerang. Issues that do not affect the individuals concerned will not, on the whole, engage their interest'. (Handy);

    (c) the *purpose* of the participation of employees in a decision is made quite clear from the outset. 'If employees are consulted to make a decision, their views should carry the decision. If, however, they are consulted for advice, their views need not necessarily be accepted';

    (d) the individuals really have the *abilities* and the *information* to join in decision-making effectively;

    (e) the supervisor or manager *wishes* for participation from his subordinates, and does not suggest it merely because he thinks it is the 'done thing'.

Motivation through participation in practice

70. Present social and educational trends show that people's expectations have risen above the basic requirement for money. The current demand is for more interesting work and to have a say in decision-making. These expectations are a basic part of the movement towards greater participation at work. Participation should involve the work group.

> This movement towards greater participation is not limited to the UK. In most industrially developed countries (USA, West Germany, Sweden, Australia, France) there is the desire for increased involvement in decisions on the part of those people who will be affected by them.

71. The methods of achieving increased involvement have largely crystallised into two main streams. These can be described as:

    (a) industrial action towards greater day-to-day involvement and participation in the process of management; and

    (b) political action towards industrial democracy.

72. These two streams have been described as *immediate* and *distant* participation.

    (a) *Immediate participation* is used to refer to the involvement of employees in the day-to-day decisions of their work group. Typical examples of this type of participation in the past have come from Scandinavia, eg Volvo, Saab, etc.

    (b) *Distant participation* refers to the process of including company employees at the top levels of the organisation which deal with long-term policy issues (eg investment, employment *et al*). Typical examples of this type of participation would be found in any major West German company with the two tier board structure. (In 1951, a German law was passed which required labour representatives on the supervisory board and executive committee of certain large companies. The executive committee should include one labour representative as a director. The UK is still some way off from having such 'worker-directors'.)

73. Because the word 'participation' is so emotive, it has tended to become a catch phrase, being used by individuals in different contexts without definition, thereby causing much misunderstanding. In business, participation can cover a range of views, depending on the point of view from which one looks.

Conclusions on motivation of individuals

74. The following conclusions might be drawn about motivation of individuals.

    (a) Individuals vary in the kind of needs they have and the satisfactions they want. Supervisors and managers should study these needs and try to satisfy the needs of their employees by providing satisfaction in their work.

    (b) When employees are recruited, the capacity of an individual to be motivated might be just as important as the individual's basic abilities and paper qualifications.

    (c) Supervisors and managers should continually seek ways of trying to generate motivation through job design: the job should:
        (i) have a clear meaning and purpose in relation to the objectives of the organisation;
        (ii) be as self-contained as possible, so that the employee will be doing a 'complete' job;
        (iii) provide opportunities for making decisions or participating in decisions which affect his work and targets (eg in deciding the methods for doing work). In this respect, a decentralisation of authority throughout the organisation is likely to encourage employee motivation;
        (iv) provide a regular feedback of information to the employee about his performance;
        (v) avoid monotony and repetitiveness.

(d) There are numerous problems in using pay incentives and salary schemes as a means of motivation, due to the complex ways in which people respond to matters affecting the pay of themselves and others. However, pay remains a potential motivator, in spite of Herzberg's doubts on this subject.

● **Management style and assumptions about the worker**

75. In Chapter 18 on leadership we shall examine in detail various theories and techniques of leadership. At this stage, however, it is worth pointing out that the ways in which a manager chooses to motivate his or her staff have a great effect on the style he or she adopts as a manager generally. In turn, many theorists argue, his or her style and choice of motivation technique depend (to some extent) on the assumptions he or she makes about workers.

76. Douglas McGregor in his book *The Human Side of Enterprise* claims that a manager's choice of leadership style will stem from the theories he has about how his subordinates behave.

He offers two theories, which he calls Theory X and Theory Y. Note that these are not supposed to be descriptions of how people *are* but of how managers *see them to be*.

Theory X

77. This is the theory that <u>the average human being has an inherent dislike of work and will avoid it if he can</u>. Because of this human characteristic of dislike of work, most people must be coerced, controlled, directed and/or threatened with punishment to get them to put forth adequate effort towards the achievement of organisation objectives. The human being prefers to be directed, wishing to avoid responsibility. He has relatively little ambition and wants security above all.

Theory Y

78. <u>The expenditure of physical and mental effort in work is as natural as play or rest</u>. The ordinary person does not inherently dislike work: according to the conditions it may be a source of satisfaction or punishment. Extensive control is not the only means of obtaining effort. Man will exercise self-direction and self-control in the service of objectives to which he is committed.

The most significant reward that can be offered in order to obtain commitment is the satisfaction of the individual's self-actualising needs. The average human being learns, under proper conditions, not only to accept but to seek responsibility. Many more people are able to contribute creatively to the solution of organisational problems than do so. At present the potentialities of the average person are not being fully used.

> Inevitably a manager's choice of leadership strategy will arise from his theories on the causes of behaviour of his subordinates.

79. McGregor supported the ideas of Maslow about man's hierarchy of needs, and suggested that a manager with a Theory X approach will be successful where workers are concerned with physiological and safety needs. 'But the "carrot and stick" theory does not work at all once workers have reached an adequate subsistence level and are motivated by higher needs....'. Theory Y assumptions would be more useful at such a point.

80. Theory X stresses domination and dependence in work relationships; Theory Y emphasises independence. But the seeming 'either/or' conflict suggested by these opposing views does not exist; leadership styles can vary in degrees, ranging from extreme Theory X to extreme Theory Y. McGregor was unable to prove that one extreme was objectively better than another (ie more productive) nor could he disprove that a middle of the road leadership style might not be better.

    (a) Theory X supervision, when the 'rules' are properly applied, should be successful in achieving stated objectives. It is unlikely, however, that the stated objectives will be surpassed, so the minimum objectives become the maximum objectives as well. Much potential might be unrealised.

    (b) Theory Y supervision has been implemented on occasions. For example, the Lincoln Electric Company in the USA made each employee responsible for his own supplies (both purchasing and control) and for setting the quality and quantity of his own output. Theory Y, however, depends on mature individuals; maturity, given the influence of group psychology etc, does not exist sufficiently on the shop floor to be practicable in its extreme form. *Progress along the road to Theory Y is all that is realistically possible.*

> McGregor concluded that 'Theory Y is an invitation to innovation'. In general, however, lip service is often paid to Theory Y while practice is based on Theory X.

81. A manager who has Theory X assumptions will closely direct and control workers and will operate through specific instructions and detailed control. On the other hand, the Theory Y based manager will naturally delegate and develop his staff and encourage them to take greater responsibility and tackle more challenging work.

Theory Z - the importance of cultural values

82. Theory Z attempts to draw on the successful management techniques of large Japanese companies, and suggests how the key elements of successful Japanese management methods can be applied to Western management and organisation.

> It probably has more application to organisation design than to management style or motivation, but it is linked to Theories X and Y in that it assumes that the beliefs held by managers about their workers affect the ways in which managers habitually act.

83. William Ouchi researched the reason for Japanese big business success by comparing American and Japanese cultural values, and formulated an ideal cultural system called Theory Z, based on the Japanese concepts of 'wa' and paternalism, but incorporating the best elements of Western practice.

Ouchi concluded that the American big business should re-create their companies to incorporate the 'family-like' qualities of the Japanese culture, as some already have to a certain extent – such as IBM and Hewlett Packard.

84. Theory Z is based on the belief that it is the spirit of co-operation, and the consensus approach to decision-making, that gives Japanese firms the advantages of higher employee motivation, better productivity and higher output quality. Theory Z argues that:

(a) although individual managers might have to accept responsibility for decisions, there should be a *consensus in decision-making*, reached by agreement with the manager's subordinates and colleagues. In Japan, the concept of collective responsibility is sometimes used;

(b) although there is a formal organisation and management hierarchy, *decisions are nevertheless democratic and based on trust* between managers and subordinates;

(c) this participative approach to decision-making encourages the free flow of information between departments as well as between managers and subordinates;

(d) work activities should be 'humanised'. Individual employees should not simply be regarded as functional cogs in the wheel.

	Theory J (Japanese)	Theory A (American)	Theory Z (Ideal)
Degree of corporate concern with employee	entire, all aspects of life, including housing, family, and schooling	focused on performance only	whole person and all aspects of life
Personnel appraisal	appraisal based on loyalty to firm	appraisal based on performance	primarily loyalty
Length of employment	lifetime	varies, but mainly short	long
Career path	progression and exposure in many areas	specialised in chosen area	less specialised than Theory A
Promotion	slow	rapid	slow
Responsibility	collective (as a result of decision making)	individual (as a result of decision making)	individual
Decision making	consensus by many, communication upward, as well as downward	individual by managers	consensus by many

10.5 *William Ouchi's outline of Theories J, A and Z*

85. For consensus decision-making to work and so that an atmosphere of trust develops between managers and subordinates, there must be an erosion of status-consciousness. Separate canteens for managers and workers cannot be permitted and managers should really dress in the same way as workers, in standard-type overalls. Employees must also be rewarded for their commitment to the firm, but not in such a way that the desire for rewards affects what they think and do - eg secure lifetime employment is a more effective reward than early promotion.

QUIZ

1. Illustrate Maslow's hierarchy of needs theory in a simple diagram.

   ● See para 8

2. What are the practical implications of Herzberg's two-factor theory?

   ● See paras 12, 16, 17

3. Outline expectancy theory and its practical implications.

   ● See paras 18-22, 23-24

4. What are the four elements Herzberg defined as being part of a policy to get employees to accept responsibility?

   ● See para 31

5. Distinguish between job design, enrichment, enlargement and rotation.

   ● See paras 33-35, 36, 44, 54

6. What is wrong with money as a motivator, and particularly payment by results, in practice?

   ● See para 57-58

7. Under what conditions might participation increase employee commitment?

   ● See para 69

8. What do Theories X and Y describe?

   ● See paras 77-78

9. Describe the components of the 'ideal' Theory Z.

   ● See paras 83-85.

Chapter 11

DELEGATION, AUTHORITY
AND RESPONSIBILITY

Topics covered in this chapter

- Authority, responsibility and delegation
- Delegation of authority
  - ○ Principles
  - ○ Problems
  - ○ When to delegate
- Systems of appeal and pooled authority

Purpose of this chapter

To explain the nature of authority and responsibility, and to explore delegation as it occurs (or fails to occur) in management practice. (The *extent* to which authority is delegated in the organisation as a whole has already been discussed in relation to centralisation and decentralisation in Chapter 2.)

● Authority, responsibility and delegation

1.   It is easy to confuse these three concepts since they are all to do with the allocation of power within an organisation. We shall begin therefore by defining and discussing each of them in turn.

Authority

2.   *Organisational authority* refers to the scope and amount of discretion given to a person to make decisions, by virtue of the position he or she holds in the organisation.

The authority and power structure of an organisation defines:

(a)   the part which each member of the organisation is expected to perform; and
(b)   the relationship between the members

so that their concerted efforts should be effective in achieving the purpose of the organisation.

---

3.   A person's (or office's) *authority* can come from a variety of sources, including from above (supervisors) or below (subordinates).

(a) Top-down authority is associated with formal organisations and is *organisational authority* or *position power*.

(b) Bottom-up authority comes from subordinates, and may be related to an individual's personal qualities or social rank. It is not generally associated with formal organisations although it can be argued that it exists in a democratic trade union.

Responsibility

4.   *Responsibility* refers to the liability of a person to be called to account for his/her actions and results. A subordinate may have a responsibility for which he will be called to account by his superior; a board of directors may have a responsibility to its shareholders; and a government in a democracy has a responsibility to the electorate.

> Responsibility is therefore the obligation to do something; in an organisation, it is the duty of an official to carry out his assigned tasks.

5.   Unlike authority, responsibility cannot be delegated. Where a supervisor delegates authority to his subordinate, he remains responsible for ensuring that the work gets done, albeit by the subordinate rather than by himself personally. The superior will exact responsibility from the subordinate for the authority delegated but he will remain responsible himself too.

6.   With responsibility, we must associate *accountability*. A manager is accountable to his superiors in the organisation for his actions and he is obliged to report to his superior how well he has exercised his responsibility and the use of the authority delegated to him.

Delegation

7.   *Delegation of authority* occurs in an organisation where a superior gives to a subordinate the discretion to make decisions within a certain sphere of influence. This can only occur if the superior initially possesses the authority to delegate; a subordinate cannot be given organisational authority to make decisions unless it would otherwise be the superior's right to make those decisions himself.

> Delegation of authority thus refers to the process by which a superior gives a subordinate the authority to carry out an aspect of the superior's job. Without delegation, a formal organisation could not exist.

8.   In a formal organisation, the source of all authority (eg shareholders) delegates authority to a subordinate or representative (eg the board of directors) but retains some of the authority itself (eg shareholders retain certain authority, as established by company law and the Articles of Association of the company).

The subordinate in turn delegates some authority to its own subordinates (eg individual executive directors) whilst retaining some exclusively for its own discretion. The process of delegation is repeated, stage by stage (or scale by scale) down a chain of command to the lowest level of subordinates given delegated authority.

9. The command structure of authority may be shown by an *organisation chart* (which we saw in Chapter 2), or it may be documented in schedules or manuals. It may be easily appreciated that authority, responsibility and delegation are critical aspects of an organisation structure, and are significant factors in determining the efficiency with which an organisation operates.

Authority and power

10. If an organisation is to function as a co-operative system of individuals, some people must have authority or power over others. Authority and power flow *downwards* through the formal organisation.

    (a) Authority is the right to do something; in an organisation it is the right of a manager to require a subordinate to do something in order to achieve the goals of the organisation. Managerial authority thus consists of:
        (i)   making decisions within the scope of one's own managerial authority;
        (ii) assigning tasks to subordinates;
        (iii) expecting and requiring satisfactory performance of these tasks by subordinates.

    (b) Power is distinct from authority, but is often associated with it. Whereas authority is the *right* to do something, power is the *ability* to do it.

11. Three aspects of authority developed by Hicks and Gullet *('Management')* are as follows.

    (a) *Responsibility and accountability* are coupled with managerial authority. When a manager is given the *authority* to do something, it is automatically presupposed that he has the ability to do it and the facilities that he needs, and that the desired results will be achieved.

        The manager is *responsible* for the actual results achieved, and he is held *accountable* because information about his achievements will be fed back to his superiors, and they can then call him to account to explain his performance.

    (b) *Authority is subjective.* Amitai Etzioni made a study of authority and motivation in differing environments. He found that the way in which authority and power are exercised will differ according to the environment, relationships and type of subordinates. Thus the way a prison warder, or even a shopfloor supervisor, exercises authority to get subordinates to do what he wants will be different from the way in which the director of a public company or the managing partner of an audit firm will exercise theirs. It will differ again in the case of the captain of the rugby team, or a parish priest. In general, at the bottom end of the management hierarchy, authority must be exercised with more coercion whilst at the top end of the hierarchy authority is more discreet and immediate subordinates more self-motivated.

(c) *Sources of authority*. The authority of a manager might come from one or more sources.

    (i) *Top-down authority* refers to the authority conferred on a *manager* because of the position he holds in the organisation's hierarchy and the extent to which authority has been delegated. It is the official authority 'traditionally' associated with management, which goes down the scalar chain. In most organisations, top-down authority goes hand-in-hand with departmentalisation and the division of work, so that a senior manager in department A cannot tell a junior manager in department B what to do, because his authority does not cross department or sectional boundaries.

    (ii) *Bottom-up authority* refers to the authority conferred on a *leader* from the people at lower levels in the organisation. Elected leaders, such as politicians and many trade union officials, have such authority, which they will be expected to exercise in the interests of the electors/union members.

    (iii) *Rank*. In some organisations, such as the armed forces, rank is a clear expression of authority and orders gain credibility because they come from someone of higher rank.

    (iv) *Personal authority or charisma*. Some managers acquire authority through their personal charisma, and as a consequence are capable of influencing the behaviour of others.

    (v) *Tradition*. Some individuals acquire authority by tradition. In old established family firms, the elder members of the family might continue to be obeyed and held in respect, even after they have officially retired.

● **Delegation of authority**

12. It is generally recognised that in any large complex organisation, management must delegate some authority because:

(a) there are physical and mental limitations to the possible workload of any individual or group in authority;

(b) routine or less important decisions are passed 'down the line' to subordinates, and the superior is free to concentrate on the more important aspects of the work (eg planning), which only he is competent (and paid) to do;

(c) the increasing size and complexity of organisations calls for specialisation, both managerial and technical. This is the principle of division of work.

> However, by delegating authority to subordinates, the superior takes on the extra tasks of calling the subordinates to account for their decisions and performance, and also of co-ordinating the efforts of different subordinates.

13. To be truly effective, the process of delegation should consist of four stages.

(1) The expected *performance levels* (the expected results) of the subordinate should be clearly specified (to determine the required results). These should be fully understood and accepted by the subordinate.

(2) Tasks should be *assigned* to the subordinate who should agree to do them.

3. *Resources* should be allocated to the subordinate to enable him to carry out his tasks at the expected level of performance, and *authority* should be delegated to enable the subordinate to do this job.

4. *Responsibility* should be exacted from the subordinate by the superior for results obtained (because ultimate responsibility remains with the superior).

14. The subordinate's ability and experience must be borne in mind when allocating tasks and responsibilities, since it is highly damaging to allocate tasks beyond a subordinate's capabilities both for the organisation and for the employee, who may suffer severe 'role overload' or stress. In addition frequent contact must be maintained between the boss and subordinate to review the progress made and to discuss constructive criticism. *Feedback* is essential for control, and also as part of the learning process.

15. A subordinate may have written or unwritten authority to do his job. Written authority is preferable because it removes room for doubt and argument. Authority may also be general or specific:

   (a) it is general if the subordinate is given authority to make any decisions with regard to a certain (specified) area of the operations - he is put in charge;

   (b) it is specific if the subordinate has authority to make certain limited and identified decisions within that area of operations. General authority gives the subordinate greater discretion and flexibility.

Principles of delegation

16. There are certain principles of delegation, recommended by classical theorists, and many of them are still relevant in the context of formal organisation structure. These are as follows.

   (a) Authority (and power) and responsibility (and accountability) must be properly balanced within an organisation; there must be parity between authority and responsibility:

   (i) a manager who is not held accountable for any of his authority or power may well exercise his authority in a capricious way. It is a common human trait to wish to maximise power and minimise accountability;

   (ii) a manager who is held accountable for aspects of performance which he has no power or authority to control is in an impossible position.

   (b) Responsibility cannot be delegated. A subordinate should be responsible to his superior for achievements within delegated authority, but the superior in his turn remains responsible to his own boss for the achievements of his subordinates.

   (c) There should be delegation of authority according to the results required; a subordinate must be given sufficient authority to do all that is expected of him.

   (d) Once authority has been delegated, a superior should not expect his subordinate to refer decisions back up the chain of command to him for confirmation (or ratification) provided that the decision is within the subordinate's scope of delegated authority.

(e) There must be no doubts about the boundaries of authority because where doubts exist, decision-making will be weak, confused and possibly contradictory (if boundaries of authority overlap). Classical theorists such as Fayol therefore argued that the chain of command must be clearly specified in terms of who holds what authority and who is accountable to whom and for what. Information flow does not have to be restricted to passing up and down the chain, but authority should.

(f) The greater the clarity of:

(i)   the functions given to each department;
(ii)   the activities and authority of each department;
(iii) the ways in which departments are meant to inter-act and co-operate

the greater will be the ability of individuals with authority in each department to contribute towards the achievement of the organisation's goals.

(g) Classical theorists such as Fayol argued in favour of the principle of *unity of command*. Each individual should report to only one superior so as to avoid conflicts created by dual command. A subordinate who reports to a single boss will accept responsibility more readily, because there will be no stress or confusion created by having two bosses with conflicting demands. The principle of unity of command is not accepted by supporters of organisation structures which include matrix management or inter-disciplinary project teams, however.

17. When authority is delegated, the relationship between subordinate and superior is critically important. Drucker has argued that although authority is passed down to subordinates, the relationship between subordinates and superiors, and their responsibilities, have three dimensions.

(a) Every manager has the task of contributing towards what his superior's section must do to achieve its objectives.

(b) Every manager has a responsibility towards the organisation as a whole, and must define the activities of his own unit so as to contribute towards achieving the organisation's objectives.

(c) Every manager has a responsibility towards his subordinates (to make sure they know what is expected of them, to help them set their own objectives, to help them attain their objectives, to offer counsel and advice etc).

> 'The vision of a manager should always be upward - towards the enterprise as a whole. But his responsibility runs downwards as well to the managers on his team'. (Drucker)

18. It is interesting to ask why, in a formal organisation built up in the 'classical' hierarchical manner, there should be so many levels of management. After all, the purpose of management is to see that the work of the organisation gets done, and the only managers who supervise 'actual work' directly are the 'front-line' or 'first line' supervisors.

19. If a first line supervisor has a superior, the work of the superior must derive from the supervisor. Drucker noted that 'the managers on the firing line have the basic management jobs - the ones on whose performance everything else ultimately rests. Seen this way, the jobs of higher management are derivative and, in the last analysis, are aimed at helping the firing line manager do his job. Viewed structurally and organically, it is the firing line manager in whom all authority and responsibility centre; only what he cannot do himself passes up to higher management'.

20. Yet authority is passed down or delegated through the formal organisation; it is not passed up from supervisors to senior managers. Although the front-line supervisor manages the 'real' work, the authority to do so comes from higher up.

    (a) A front-line supervisor only has authority over his part of the work of the organisation and cannot issue instructions to another part. For example, the manager of the Oldham branch of a clearing bank cannot issue instructions to employees in the Huddersfield branch. Senior managers are required to co-ordinate the work of subordinates by having authority over a wider area of work, right up to the chief executive and board of directors.

    (b) Front line supervisors make short-term day-to-day decisions and have no time for longer-term plans and decisions. Longer-term decisions are kept within the authority of more senior managers.

Problems of delegation

21. In practice many managers are reluctant to delegate and attempt to do many routine matters themselves in addition to their more important duties. Amongst the reasons for this reluctance one can commonly identify:

    (a) low confidence and trust in the abilities of the subordinates - the suspicion that 'if you want it done well, you have to do it yourself';

    (b) the burden of responsibility and accountability for the mistakes of subordinates, aggravated by (a) above;

    (c) a desire to 'stay in touch' with the department or team - both in terms of workload and staff - particularly if the manager does not feel 'at home' in a management role, and/or misses aspects of the subordinate job, camaraderie etc;

    (d) an unwillingness to admit that subordinates have developed to the extent that they could perform some of the manager's duties. The manager may feel threatened by this sense of 'redundancy';

    (e) poor control and communication systems in the organisation, so that the manager feels he has to do everything himself if he is to retain real control and responsibility for a task, and if he wants to know what is going on;

    (f) an organisational culture that has failed to reward or recognise effective delegation by superiors, so that the manager may not realise that delegation is positively regarded (rather than seen as a 'shirking' of responsibility);

    (g) lack of understanding of what delegation involves - *not* giving subordinates total control, making the manager himself redundant etc.

22. Handy *('Understanding Organisations')* writes of a 'trust dilemma' in a superior-subordinate relationship, in which the sum of trust + control is a constant amount:

> $T + C = Y$
>
> where T = the trust the superior has in the subordinate, and the trust which the subordinate feels the superior has in him;
> C = the degree of control exercised by the superior over the subordinate;
> Y = a constant, unchanging value.

Any increase in C, that is the superior retains more 'control' or authority, will mean that the subordinate will immediately recognise that he is being trusted less. If the superior wishes to show more trust in the subordinate, he can only do so by reducing control (C), that is by delegating more authority.

23. To overcome the reluctance of managers to delegate, it is necessary to:

    (a) provide a system of selecting subordinates who will be capable of handling delegated authority in a responsible way. If subordinates are of the right 'quality', superiors will be prepared to trust them more;

    (b) have a system of open communications, in which the superior and subordinates freely interchange ideas and information. If the subordinate is given all the information he needs to do his job, and if the superior is aware of what the subordinate is doing:
        (i)   the subordinate will make better-informed decisions;
        (ii)   the superior will not 'panic' because he does not know what is going on.

        Although open lines of communication are important, they should not be used by the superior to command the subordinate in a matter where authority has been delegated to the subordinate; communication links must not be used by superiors as a means of reclaiming authority;

    (c) ensure that a system of control is established. Superiors are reluctant to delegate authority because they retain absolute responsibility for the performance of their subordinates. If an efficient control system is in operation, responsibility and accountability will be monitored at all levels of the management hierarchy, and the 'dangers' of relinquishing authority and control to subordinates are significantly lessened;

    (d) reward effective delegation by superiors and the efficient assumption of authority by subordinates. Rewards may be given in terms of pay, promotion, status, 'official' approval etc.

When to delegate

24. A manager should be coached, if necessary, about the particular instances in which he should or should not delegate. He will have to consider:

    (a) whether he requires the *acceptance* of subordinates - for morale, relationships, ease of implementation of the decision etc. If so, he would be advised at least to consult his subordinates; if acceptance is the primary need and the decision itself is largely routine, such as in the case of canteen arrangements, office decor etc, then he should delegate;

(b) whether the '*quality*' of the decision is most important, and acceptance less so. Many financial decisions may be of this type, and authority should be retained by the superior, who alone may be capable of making them. If acceptance and quality are equally important, eg for changes in work methods or the introduction of new technology, consultation is advisable;

(c) whether the *expertise or experience* of subordinates is relevant or necessary to the task, or will enhance the quality of the decision. If a manager is required to perform a task which is not within his own specialised knowledge, he should delegate to the appropriate person: the office manager may delegate repair and maintenance of machinery to an operations supervisor, perhaps;

(d) whether, being as objective as possible, he feels he can trust in the competence and reliability of his subordinates. As Handy notes, there is bound to be a dilemma here, but the manager is accountable for his own area of authority, and should not delegate if he *genuinely* lacks confidence in his team (in which case, he has other problems to solve);

(e) whether the task of decision-making requires tact and confidentiality or, on the other hand, maximum exposure and assimilation by employees. Disciplinary action, for example, should not be delegated (say, to a peer of the individual concerned), whereas tasks involving new procedures to which employees will have to get accustomed should be delegated as soon as possible.

25. In instances where *reference upwards* in the scalar chain to the manager's own superior may be necessary, the manager should consider:

(a) whether the decision is *relevant* to the superior: will it have any impact on his area of responsibility, such as strategy, staffing, or the departmental budget?;

(b) whether the superior has *authority* or *information* relevant to the decision that the manager does not possess: eg. authority over issues which affect other departments or interdepartmental relations, or information only available at senior levels;

(c) the *political climate* of the organisation: will the superior expect to be consulted, and resent any attempt to make the decision without his authority? Are there, on the other hand, useful 'points' to be scored for showing initiative and independence (especially if the decision is a success)?

26. The general structure and accepted practices of the organisation will partly decide the extent to which a manager will delegate decisions to subordinates, or refer them to his superior: eg. if the corporate culture favours participation, group decision-making, a consultative style of management etc.

● Systems of appeal and pooled authority

27. Further problems with delegation occur when:

(a) subordinates who must co-ordinate their activities cannot agree about how things should be done; or

(b) the collective authority of subordinates may be required to make a decision.

28. Disagreements will inevitably occur within any formal organisation. The general rule is that problems which cannot be solved at lower levels are referred upward through the organisation structure until the problem reaches an official with enough authority and power to solve the problem. The channel for appeals would be described by an organisation chart:

11.1 Organisation chart

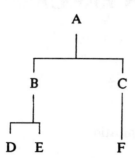

A disagreement between D and E could be settled by B, whereas a disagreement between D and F would need to be settled either by B and C together (using their pooled authority) or by appealing up the scalar chain to A.

29. Some organisations may have a special *appeals* procedure, with problems or grievances referred to an independent arbitrator. Pooled authority (or 'splintered' authority) refers to a situation in which two subordinates join together and use their collective authority to make a decision, instead of referring the matter up the chain of command to a superior. In the preceding 'organisation chain' B and C might pool their authority to make a decision affecting their common area of work, or affecting subordinates D, E and F, instead of referring their problem to A. Management conferences are an example of attempts to exchange ideas and reach collective decisions on the basis of pooled authority.

QUIZ

1. Define authority, responsibility and accountability.

   ● See paras 2, 4, 6

2. What steps should a manager take when delegating – and what will he have to bear in mind as he does so?

   ● See paras 13, 14, 16

3. In what ways might communication and 'clarity' be important in ensuring effective delegation?

   ● See paras 13, 16(e) and (f), 17(c), 23(b)

2. If an organisation has problems with its managers being reluctant to delegate, what areas should it consider?

   ● See para 23

Chapter 12

THE COMMUNICATION PROCESS

Topics covered in this chapter

- The need for communication
- The management problem of communication
  - Barriers to communication
  - Communication between superiors and subordinates
- Informal channels
  - The grapevine
- Communication methods
- Communication networks
- Face-to-face communication
  - Meetings
  - Interviews
  - Committees
  - Brainstorming
  - Chairing and minuting
  - Conferences
- Communication in practice

Purpose of this chapter

To consider the need for communication by and for management, to examine the communication process, and to suggest how communication can be established or improved in practice.

- **The need for communication**

1. In any organisation, the communication of information is necessary:

   (a) for management, to make the necessary decisions for *planning, co-ordination* and *control;* managers should be aware of what their departments are achieving, what they are not achieving and what they *should* be achieving;

   (b) between departments, so that all the interdependent systems for purchasing, production, marketing and administration can be synchronised to perform the right actions at the right times to *co-operate* in accomplishing the organisation's aims;

(c) by individuals. Each employee should know what is expected from him. Otherwise he may be off-target, working without understanding, interest or motivation, and without any sense of belonging and contributing to the organisation. Effective communication gives an employee's job meaning, makes personal development possible, and acts as a motivator, as well as oiling the wheels of labour relations.

2. Communication in the organisation may take the form of:
   (a) giving instructions;
   (b) giving or receiving information;
   (c) exchanging ideas;
   (d) announcing plans or strategies;
   (e) comparing actual results against a plan;
   (f) laying down rules or procedures;
   (g) job descriptions, organisation charts or manuals (communication about the structure of the organisation and individual roles).

Direction of communication

3. Communication within the formal organisation structure may be:

   (a) *vertical:*
      (i) downwards (from superior to subordinate);
      (ii) upwards (from subordinate to superior); or

   (b) *horizontal or lateral* (between people of the same rank, in the same section or department, or in different sections or departments).

4. Communication is perhaps most routine between people at the same or similar level in the organisation, that is horizontal communication. It is necessary for two reasons:

   (a) *formally:* to co-ordinate the work of several people, and perhaps departments, who have to co-operate to carry out a certain operation;

   (b) *informally:* to furnish emotional and social support to an individual.

   > Horizontal communication between 'peer groups' is usually easier and more direct then vertical communication, being less inhibited by considerations of rank. It has to be tactfully handled, however, to avoid situations where one manager accuses another of putting his nose into affairs which shouldn't concern him.

5. Communication may be said to be 'diagonal' when it involves interdepartmental communication by people of different ranks. Specialist departments which serve the organisation in general, such as Personnel, Filing or Data Processing, have no clear line of authority linking them to managers in other departments who need their involvement. A Sales supervisor, for example, may find himself 'requiring' the services of the Personnel Manager in a disciplinary procedure: who reports to whom? Particular effort, goodwill and tact will be required in such situations.

● **The management problem of communication**

6.
> Rosemary Stewart reported a survey of 160 managers in British companies (1967) in which it was found that 78% of their time was spent communicating (talking took up 50% and reading and writing 28% of their time).

7. Good communication is essential to getting any job done: co-operation is impossible without it. Difficulties occur because of general faults in the communication process:

   (a) distortion or omission of information by the sender;
   (b) misunderstanding due to lack of clarity or technical jargon;
   (c) non-verbal signs (gesture, posture, facial expression) contradicting the verbal message, so that its meaning is in doubt;
   (d) 'overload' - a person being given too much information to digest in the time available;
   (e) differences in social, racial or educational background, compounded by age and personality differences, creating barriers to understanding and co-operation;
   (f) people hearing only what they want to hear in a message.

8. There may also be particular difficulties in a work situation:

   (a) a general tendency to distrust a message in its re-telling from one person to another;
   (b) a subordinate mistrusting his superior and looking for 'hidden meanings' in a message;
   (c) the relative status in the hierarchy of the sender and receiver of information. A senior manager's words are listened to more closely and a colleague's perhaps discounted;
   (d) people from different job or specialist backgrounds (eg. accountants, personnel managers, DP experts) having difficulty in talking on a non-specialist's wavelength;
   (e) people or departments having different priorities or perspectives so that one person places more or less emphasis on a situation than another;
   (f) subordinates giving superiors incorrect or incomplete information (eg. to protect a colleague, to avoid 'bothering' the superior); also a senior manager may only be able to handle edited information because he does not have time to sift through details;
   (g) managers who are prepared to make decisions on a 'hunch' without proper regard to the communications they may or may not have received;
   (h) information which has no immediate use tending to be forgotten;
   (i) lack of opportunity, formal or informal, for a subordinate to say what he thinks or feels;
   (j) conflict in the organisation. Where there is conflict between individuals or departments, communications will be withdrawn and information withheld.

Barriers to communication

9. The barriers to good communication arising from differences in social, racial or educational backgrounds, compounded by age differences and personality differences, can be particularly severe.

   (a) A working class person with a comprehensive school background might feel resentful towards a fellow employee with an upper class background and public school education. The ex-public school employee might consider himself superior to the other. The different backgrounds and inferior/superior attitudes will make communication difficult.

(b) A young person might be resented by an older person of the same grade or status in the organisation. The young person might look down on the older one as someone who has failed to advance his career, and is therefore second-rate. Difficulties in seeing each other's point of view might be compounded by different methods of expression (slang words and phrases etc).

(c) Personality differences might occur where one person appears fairly happy-go-lucky, and another is more serious in his application to work and his outlook on life. Frustration may occur in communication between the two because their different values give them conflicting views about what is important and what is less so.

10. Differences in background might result in:

(a) failure to understand the other's point of view and sense of values and priorities;

(b) failure to listen to the information the other person is giving. The information is judged according to the person who gives it;

(c) a tendency to give the other person ready-formulated opinions (which the other does not accept) instead of factual information which will enable the other person to formulate his own opinions;

(d) lack of shared 'vocabulary' - whether linguistic or symbolic - which might lead to lack of understanding of the message.

11. Personal conflict or antagonisms will cause further communication problems.

(a) Emotions (anger, fear, frustration) will creep into communications and further hinder the transmission of clear information.

(b) The recipient of information will tend to:
(i) hear what he wants to hear in any message;
(ii) ignore anything he does not want to accept in a message;
- and blame it on the other person if problems arise later on.

Communication between superiors and subordinates

12. In a well known 'real-world' study into three companies in the USA (1962) W Read showed how the mobility aspirations of subordinates in a large organisation strongly affect the amount of communication that takes place.

> The more a subordinate wanted promotion, the less likely he would be to transmit 'negative' aspects of his work performance. This relationship was conditioned or modified by the degree of inter-personal trust that existed between the superior and the subordinate.

13. O'Reilly and Roberts (1974) developed this argument in a laboratory study from which they concluded about the upward flow of communication that: 'If the information is important but unfavourable to the sender it is likely to be blocked. This has implications for top-level decision-making and policy formulation because it may mean that organisational resources are often committed in a vacuum of relevant (particularly non-favourable) information'.

● **Informal communication channels**

14. The formal pattern of communication in an organisation is *always* supplemented by an informal one, which is sometimes referred to as the 'grapevine' or 'bush telegraph'. People like to gossip, and talk about rumours and events, on the telephone, over a cup of tea in the office, on the way home from work, in the corridor, at lunch, and so on.

15. The danger with informal communication is that it might be malicious, contain inaccurate rumour or half-truths, or simply be wild speculation. This type of gossip can be unsettling to people in an organisation, and make colleagues mistrust one another or act cautiously.

16. For example, suppose that you work for a company in London, and your friend from another department telephones to say that he has heard from someone who knows someone else in the personnel department that your office is going to be moved to Cardiff, and anyone refusing to go will be given the sack. This sort of news would be certain to upset you for a while, even if it turns out eventually to be wrong.

17. Formal communication systems need the support of a good – and accurate – informal system, and some ideas have been put forward about how this might be done.

> ● One idea is to set up 'official' corporate communications that will feed information into the informal system. House journals or briefings groups can be used to provide accurate bits of information, which individuals can pick up and gossip about.
>
> ● Another idea, put forward by Nancy Foy (1985), is that an organisation should encourage 'networking'. *Networking* describes 'a collection of people, usually with a shared interest, who tend to keep in touch to exchange informal information'.

The grapevine

18. The grapevine is one aspect of informal communication. A well-known study into how the grapevine works was carried out by K Davis (1953) using his 'echo-analysis' technique: the recipient of some information, A, was asked to name the source of his information, B. B was then asked to name his source, C etc until the information was traced back to its originator. His research findings were that:

(a) the grapevine acts fast;

(b) the working of the grapevine is selective: information is not divulged randomly;

(c) the grapevine usually operates at the place of work and not outside it;

    (d) perhaps surprisingly, the grapevine is only active when the formal communication network is active: the grapevine does not fill a gap created by an ineffective formal communication system;

    (e) it was also surprising to discover that higher level executives were better communicators and better informed than their subordinates. 'If a foreman at the sixth level had an accident, a larger proportion of executives at the third level knew of it than at the fourth level, or even at the sixth level where the accident happened';

    (f) more staff executives were in the know about events than line managers (because the staff executives are more mobile and get involved with more different functions in their work).

19. Davis concluded that since the grapevine exists, and cannot be got rid of, management should learn both to accept it and to use it, by harnessing it towards achieving the objectives of the organisation.

● Communication methods

20. Various media and channels of communication are available to the organisation:

    (a) face-to-face communication:
        (i)   formal meetings;
        (ii)   interviews;
        (iii) informal contact;
        (iv) the grapevine;

    (b) oral communication:
        (i)   the telephone;
        (ii)   public address systems;

    (c) written communication:
        (i)   letters: external mail system;
        (ii)   memoranda; internal mail system;
        (iii) reports;
        (iv) forms;
        (v)   notice boards;
        (vi) house journals, bulletins, newsletters;
        (vii) organisation manual;

    (d) visual communication:
        (i)   charts;
        (ii)   films and slides.

Oral and written communication are discussed below. Meetings, interviews and committees are discussed later in this chapter.

Oral communication

21. *The telephone* is of course the most common method of oral communication between individuals in remote locations, or even within an organisation's premises. It provides all the interactive and feedback advantages of face to face communication, while saving the travel time. It is, however,

more 'distant' and impersonal than an interview for the discussion of sensitive personal matters, and it does not *by itself* provide the concreteness of written media. The latter disadvantage can be remedied by written confirmation of a telephone call.

British Telecom offer a range of facilities to telephone users, for external communication (direct dialling is now possible to most countries in the world) and internal (ranging from simple extensions, to sophisticated computerised message-managing switchboards).

22. *Public address systems.* A simple public address system might operate through loudspeakers placed at strategic points eg. in workshops or yards, where staff cannot be located or reached by telephone and the noise would not be too disturbing. The more recent, electronic method of paging individuals who move around and cannot be located is the 'bleeper' (eg. British Telecom's Radiopaging service), which alerts the user to a message waiting for him at a pre-arranged telephone number.

Written communication

23. *The letter* is flexible in a wide variety of situations, and useful in providing a written record and confirmation of the matters discussed. It is widely used for external communication, via the *external mailing system*. Various facilities are provided by the Post Office for the delivery of letters, with special arrangements for guaranteed, insured or urgent deliveries in the UK or internationally. An external messenger, taxi, or courier may also be used for urgent or important letters and documents.

> A direct letter may be used internally in certain situations where a confidential written record is necessary or personal handling required: to confirm an oral briefing; to announce redundancy, or urge employees against strike action, resignation etc.

24. *The memorandum.* This is the equivalent of the letter in internal communication: versatile and concrete. It is sent via the *internal mail system* of an organisation: taken by hand to recipients within the organisation or to offices for collection (eg. from departmental or individual pigeon holes) or forwarding. If parts of an organisation are in separate locations, provision may be made for internal messengers to collect and distribute mail by van or motorcycle. 'Internal mail envelopes', re-usable envelopes on which each successive recipient's name is simply crossed off and the next added, are a useful and cost-effective way of keeping internal mail safe and confidential.

> Memoranda are useful for exchanging many sorts of message and particularly for confirming telephone conversations: sometimes, however, they are used *instead* of telephone conversations, where the call would have been quicker, cheaper and just as effective. Many memoranda are unnecessarily typed where a short handwritten note would be adequate.

25. *Reports.* The function of a formal report is to allow a number of people to review the complex facts and arguments relating to an issue on which they have to base a plan or make a decision. This is primarily an internal medium used by management, but can be used externally for the

information of shareholders, the general public, government agencies etc. (eg. the company's Annual Report, which the organisation is required by law to issue to shareholders, but is often available to employees and the general public on request).

> The written report does not allow for effective discussion or immediate feedback, as does a meeting, and can be a time-consuming and expensive document to produce. However, as a medium for putting across a body of ideas to a group of people, it has the advantages that:
>
> (a) people can study the material in their own time, rather than arranging to be present at one place and time;
> (b) no time need be wasted on irrelevancies and the formulation of arguments, such as may occur in meetings;
> (c) the report should be presented objectively and impartially, in a formal and impersonal style: emotional reactions or conflicts will be avoided.

26. Annual reports are now issued by some organisations for their employees, similar to the shareholder's report but simplified and adapted to the information needs of employees, including a review of, for example, manpower and attendance records, industrial relations, health and safety, and costs of maintaining wages, welfare, facilities etc.

27. Progress and completion reports may also be commissioned to review the progress and eventual effectiveness of long-term operations such as the conversion of files, restructuring of a department or move of office accommodation.

> How to communicate effectively via letters, reports and memoranda is covered fully in Chapter 24.

28. *Forms*. Routine information flow is largely achieved through the use of forms. A well-designed form can be filled quickly and easily with brief, relevant and specifically identified details of a request or instruction. They are simple to file, and information is quickly retrieved and confirmed. Examples include: expense forms, timesheets, insurance forms, stock request forms etc. Staff do not usually have to exercise discretion in the selection and use of this medium: a form either is, or is not, available to meet a particular need.

29. *Notice board*. This is a channel through which various written media can be cheaply transmitted to a large number of people. It allows the organisation to present a variety of information to any or all employees: items may have a limited time span of relevance but will at least be available for verification and recollection for a while. The drawbacks to notice boards are that:

(a) they can easily fall into neglect, and become untidy or irrelevant (or be sabotaged by graffitti); and
(b) they are wholly dependent on the intended recipient's curiosity or desire to receive information.

30. *House journal*. Larger companies frequently run an internal magazine or newspaper to inform employees about:

   - staff appointments and retirements
   - meetings, sports and social events
   - results and successes; customer feedback
   - new products or machinery
   - motivating competitions eg. for suggestions, office maintenance, safety.

31. The journal usually avoids being controversial: it may not deal with sensitive issues such as industrial relations or pollution of the environment, and may stop short of criticising policy, management, products etc: it is, after all, designed to improve rather than threaten communication and morale, and it may be seen by outsiders (especially customers) who might get an unfavourable impression of the organisation. Journals are sometimes regarded by the workforce as predictable, uninteresting and not to be taken seriously: on the other hand, they can provide a legitimate means of expression and a sense of corporate identity.

32. *Organisation manual or handbook*. An organisation (or office) manual is useful for drawing together and keeping up to date all relevant information for the guidance of individuals and groups as to:

   (a) the structure of the organisation (perhaps an organisation chart);
   (b) background: the organisation's history, geography, 'who's who' of senior executives;
   (c) the organisation's products, services and customers;
   (d) rules and regulations;
   (e) conditions of employment: pay structure, hours, holidays, notice etc;
   (f) standards and procedures for health and safety;
   (g) procedures for grievance, discipline, salary review etc.;
   (h) policy on trade union membership;
   (i) facilities for employees.

33. The manual is thus not only a useful survival kit for new members of the organisation, but a work of reference and a symbol of corporate identity. Manuals and handbooks will have to be regularly updated and reissued, which can be expensive and time-consuming: a looseleaf format permitting additions and amendments is a common solution (though in practice the circulation of loose amendment sheets - which may or may not get inserted - may not prove efficient).

● **Communication networks**

34. Every individual cannot communicate, either formally or informally, with every other individual in his organisation (except in very small organisations). The way in which information is channelled between individuals forms a communication pattern or network and some research has been conducted into whether one type of network pattern is more effective than another.

35. In a well-known 'laboratory' test (1951) H J Leavitt examined the effectiveness of four communication networks for *written* communication between members of a small group. The four network patterns were:

(a)   the circle:

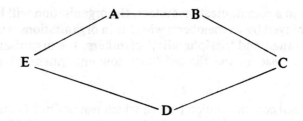

in which each member of the group could communicate with only two others in the group, as shown:

(b)   the chain: A - B - C - D - E

Similar to the circle, except that A and E cannot communicate with each other and are therefore at both ends of a communication chain;

(c)   the 'Y':

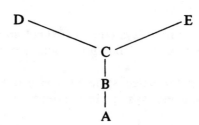

(d)   the wheel:

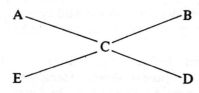

In both the 'Y' and the 'wheel' patterns, C occupies a more central position in the network. In Leavitt's experiment, each member of a group of five people has to solve a problem and each has an essential piece of information. Only written communication, channelled according to one of the four patterns described above, was allowed.

36. The findings of the experiment were as follows:

(a) *speed of problem-solving*: the wheel was fastest, followed by the Y, the chain and finally the circle;

(b) *leadership*: in the circle, no member was seen as the leader, but in the other three types of groups, C was regarded as a leader (more so in the wheel and the Y);

(c) *job satisfaction*: the enjoyment of the job was greatest among members of a circle, followed by the chain, the Y and lastly the wheel (but see paragraph 39(c) below).

37. The progression (one way or the other) of Circle-Chain-Y-Wheel emerged in all these findings. Leavitt wrote 'the Circle, one extreme, is active, leaderless, unorganised, erratic and yet is enjoyed by its members. The Wheel at the other extreme is less active, has a distinct leader, is well and stably organised, is less erratic and yet is unsatisfying to most of its members'. He concluded that in organisations where there is minimal 'centrality' and 'peripherality' of

individuals in a communication system, the organisation will be active, error-prone, leaderless, slow and enjoyed by its members; whereas in organisations where there is greater 'centrality' of some individuals and 'peripherality' of others, the organisation will be stable and efficient, consisting of leaders and the led (with low enjoyment among the members).

38. One significant communication pattern which was omitted from Leavitt's experiment was the 'all-channel' communication system which might be practically employed in group working:

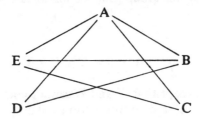

39. In a comparison of the all-channel system, the Wheel and the Circle as methods of group communication and operations, the following results emerged:

   (a) *Simple problem-solving*: the Wheel system solves problems quickest, and the Circle is the slowest, with the all-channel system in between.

   (b) *Complex problem-solving*: the all-channel system, with its participatory style, and more open communication system, generally provides the best solutions to complex problems. The efficiency of the Wheel depends on the ability of the leader, or central figure. In the Circle, there is a lack of co-ordination and solutions to problems are poor.

   (c) *Job satisfaction*: contrary to Leavitt's findings, it is now argued that job satisfaction in the Circle is low because of poor or slow performance in decision-making and a lack of co-ordination; although job satisfaction in the Wheel system is low for individuals away from the centre, the person at the centre has high satisfaction. The all-channel system provides fairly high job satisfaction to all group members (although the size of the group must not be so large that some individuals feel excluded from participation).

40. It must not be supposed that an all-channel system is best under all circumstances. It solves complex problems well, but slowly, and it tends to disintegrate under pressure (eg time pressure to get results) into a wheel system.

● **Face-to-face communication**

41. Face-to-face communcation (meetings etc) plays an important part in the life of any organisation, whether it is required by government legislation or the Articles of a company, or is held informally for information exchange, problem-solving and decision-making.

42.

> Face to face communication in general and group discussion (meetings) in particular offer several advantages for:
>
> (a) generating new ideas;
> (b) 'on the spot' feedback, constructive criticism and exchange of views;
> (c) encouraging co-operation and sensitivity to personal factors;
> (d) spreading information quickly through a group of people.
>
> However, meetings can be non- or counter-productive if:
>
> (a) the terms of reference (defining the purpose and power of the meeting) are not clear;
> (b) the people attending are unskilled or unwilling communicators;
> (c) there is insufficient guidance or leadership to control proceedings.

Meetings

43. Formal meetings, such as the Board meeting of a company, the Annual General Meeting (AGM) of a society, or a Local Council meeting, are governed by strict rules and conventions. These may establish procedure on such matters as:

   (a) attendance rights (for members of the public, shareholders etc.);
   (b) adequate notice of forthcoming meetings;
   (c) the minimum number of members required to hold the meeting (the 'quorum') and other details;
   (d) the timing of meetings;
   (e) the type of business to be discussed; and
   (f) the binding power of decisions made upon the participants.

> Many people regard such rules and conventions as a hindrance to free and effective communication, with elaborate courtesies, 'politics' and voting procedures.

44. But a well-organised, well-aimed and well-led meeting can be extremely effective in many different contexts, such as:

   (a) executive decision-making eg. by a group of directors, managers, government officials;
   (b) the relaying of decisions and instructions eg. briefings;
   (c) the provision of advice and information for management planning and decision-making;
   (d) participative problem solving, by consultation with people in different departments or fields, eg. a task force or working party;
   (e) brainstorming: free exchanges with a view to generating new approaches and ideas.

45. We shall see later in this chapter how a meeting can be well-organised and well-led when we look at chairing and minuting of meetings.

Interviews

46. The interview is an excellent internal system for handling the problems or queries of individuals, allowing confidentiality and flexible response to personal factors where necessary. Interviews are, however, costly in terms of managerial time: few interviews are built into the formal communication system (although a one-to-one meeting may be requested at need).

47. Grievance and disciplinary interviews are important in maintaining morale and performance: the employee's complaints or dissatisfactions (about his job, conditions of work, mistreatment etc) can be aired in private; the organisation's displeasure with an employee (for disobedience or unacceptable behaviour, persistent lateness, dangerous recklessness etc) can be expressed without humiliating the individual in front of his peers.

48. Appraisal interviews are used to discuss the employee's performance, progress and possible need for improvement (and will therefore need to be carefully handled in an open and friendly manner if they are not to be regarded with fear and resentment.) A similar type of interview is used as part of the staff selection process: see the job interview which is discussed in Chapter 20 on Personnel Management: Manpower Resourcing.

Committees

49. Committees are frequently used within an organisation as a means of delegating authority. The disadvantages and advantages of committees extend beyond considerations of authority and responsibility and they are described here in full.

50. Within an organisation, committees can consist entirely of executives (eg board meetings, budget approvals, project teams, feasibility studies). Alternatively, committees can be an instrument for joint consultation between employers and employees (eg works councils, joint productivity groups, staff advisory councils).

Classification of committees

51. Committees may be classified according to the power they exercise, distinguishing between those having the power to bind the parent body and those without such power.

52. It is also important to consider the function and duration of committees so that the following categories may be defined:

    (a) *executive committees* which have the power to govern or administer. It can be argued that the board of directors of a limited company is itself a 'committee' appointed by the shareholders, to the extent that it governs or administers;

    (b) *standing committees* which are formed for a particular purpose on a permanent basis. Their role is to deal with routine business delegated to them at weekly or monthly meetings;

    (c) *ad hoc committees* are formed to complete a particular task. An ad hoc committee can be described as a fact-finding or special committee which is short lived and, having achieved its purpose, reports back to the parent body and then ceases to exist;

(d) *sub-committees* may be appointed by committees to relieve the parent committee of some of its routine work;

(e) *joint committees* may be formed to co-ordinate the activities of two or more committees, eg representatives from employers and employees may meet in a Joint Consultative Committee. This kind of committee can either be permanent or appointed for a special purpose.

Advantages of committees

53. Committees may give rise to significant advantages.

(a) Consolidation of power and authority: whereas an individual may not have sufficient authority to make a decision himself, the pooled authority of a committee may be sufficient to enable the decision to be made. A committee may be referred to in this type of instance as a plural executive. Examples of a plural executive include a board of directors or the Cabinet of the government, which are policy-making and policy-executing committees.

(b) Blurring responsibility: when a committee makes a decision, no individual will be held responsible for the consequences of the decision. This is both an advantage and a disadvantage of committee decisions.

(c) Creating new ideas: group creativity may be achieved by a 'brainstorming committee' or 'think tank' (see below).

(d) They are an excellent means of communication. For example:
   (i)   to exchange ideas on a wide number of interests before a decision affecting the organisation is taken;
   (ii) to inform managers about policies, plans, actual results etc.

(e) They are democratic, because they allow for greater participation in the decision-making process.

(f) Combining abilities: committees enable the differing skills of its various members to be brought together to deal with a problem. In theory, the quality of committee decisions should be of a high standard.

(g) Co-ordination: they should enable the maximum co-ordination of all parties involved in a decision to be achieved, for example:
   (i)   in appraising performance throughout the organisation and modifying policy as necessary;
   (ii) in developing and improving operational procedures;
   (iii) in establishing and co-ordinating time relationships between the activities of each department, in order to achieve the optimum production cycle;
   (iv) in ensuring full co-operation between each department and special efforts, where necessary, to obviate bottlenecks arising in the flow of production;
   (v)   in co-ordinating the budgets of each department and compiling a master budget.

(h) They can exercise purely executive functions, such as the management of funds of a staff superannuation scheme, as opposed to those of an advisory character which require ratification by the board of directors.

(i) Advisory capacity: a committee is frequently used to offer advice to a decision-maker.

(j) Representative: they enable all relevant interests to be involved in the decision-making process and they bring together the specialised knowledge of working people into a working combination.

(k) Through participation, they may improve the motivation of committee members (and even of their subordinates).

(l) Delay: a committee is used to gain time, eg a manager may set up a committee to investigate a problem when he wants to delay his decision, or a company may refer a labour relations problem to a committee to defer a crisis with a trade union.

(m) A committee may be set up by a board of directors to do 'spade work' and avoid detailed discussions at board meetings.

Disadvantages of committees

54. The disadvantages of committees may be summarised as follows:

(a) They are apt to be too large for constructive action, since the time taken by a committee to resolve a problem tends to be in direct proportion to its size. The optimum number of members will, of course, vary according to the committee's functions, so that it is difficult to dogmatise; however, in an industrial organisation, the complement should be rather lower than that found in local and public authorities, where the profit motive is absent. The ideal number may perhaps range from three to six or seven persons.

(b) Committees are time-consuming and expensive. In addition to the cost of highly paid executives' time, secretarial costs will be incurred in the preparation of agendas, recording of proceedings and the production and distribution of minutes.

(c) Delays may occur in the production cycle if matters of a routine nature are entrusted to committees; committees must not be given responsibilities which they would carry out inefficiently.

(d) Operations of the enterprise may be jeopardised by the frequent attendance of executives at meetings, and by distracting them from their real duties.

(e) Incorrect or ineffective decisions may be made, owing to the fact that members of a committee are unfamiliar with the deeper aspects of issues under discussion, which may only be fully appreciated by the directorate, or by those employees actually carrying out the work in question. Occasionally, there may be a total failure to reach any decision at all.

(f) Certain members may be apathetic, owing to pressure of work or lack of interest, resulting in superficial action.

(g) The fact that there is no individual responsibility for decisions might invite compromise instead of clear-cut decisions, besides weakening individual responsibility throughout the organisation. Moreover, members may thereby be enabled to avoid direct responsibility for poor results arising from decisions taken in committee. Weak management can hide behind committee decisions.

(h) Committees lack conscience.

(i) Proceedings may be dominated by outspoken or aggressive members, thus unduly influencing decisions and subsequent action, perhaps adversely; there may be 'tyranny' by a minority.

55. The writer E C Lindeman strongly disapproved of the committee function and he felt that the best kind of committee was the 'committee of one'. He felt that their function was discontinuous, contained irrelevant discussion, members tried to impress superiors, and chairmen to prohibit opinions; there is a tendency to jump to conclusions, committees are soulless, expensive and encourage irresponsibility. He also felt that committees were introduced to cover up the fact that those responsible had not decided what to do, that they enable individuals to escape responsibility and that they are consistent with the fear of assigning executive responsibility to individuals.

56. A committee may be mis-used for a number of 'wrong' purposes, such as:

   (a) to replace managers. A committee cannot do all the tasks of management (eg leadership) and therefore cannot replace managers entirely;

   (b) to carry out research work. A committee may be used to create new ideas, but work on those ideas cannot be done effectively by a committee itself;

   (c) to make unimportant decisions. This would be expensive and time-consuming;

   (d) to discuss decisions beyond the authority of its participants. This might occur, for example, when an international committee of government ministers is created, but ministers send deputies in their place to meetings, without giving the deputy sufficient authority to enable the committee to make important decisions.

Using committees successfully

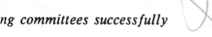

57. It is difficult to create a truly efficient committee, but the following factors will help to foster efficiency:

   ● Well-defined areas of authority, time-scales of operations and purpose must be specified in writing.

   ● The chairman must have the qualities of leadership to co-ordinate and motivate the other committee members (see below).

   ● The committee should not be so large as to be unmanageable.

   ● The members of the committee must have the necessary skills and experience to do the committee's work; where the committee is expected to liaise with functional departments, the members must also have sufficient status and influence with those departments.

   ● Minutes of the meetings should be taken and circulated, with any action points arising out of the meetings notified to the members responsible for doing the work (see below).

   ● Above all, an efficient committee must provide benefits which justify its cost.

   ● Finally, if at all possible, the committee should be allowed plenty of time to reach decisions, enabling members to form sub-groups.

Brainstorming

58. Brainstorming sessions are problem-solving conferences of 6-12 people who produce spontaneous 'free-wheeling' ideas to solve a particular problem. Ideas are produced but not evaluated at these meetings, so that originality is not stifled in fear of criticism. Brainstorming sessions rely on the ability of conference members to feed off each other's ideas. They have been used in many organisations and might typically occur, for example, in advertising agencies to produce ideas for a forthcoming campaign.

59. In the 1950s W J Gordon of the Arthur D Little company, a consulting firm in Massachussets, developed the *Gordon technique*. The company offered, among its other business lines, the services of an invention design group which could invent a product to order. The Gordon technique relies on brainstorming sessions with the unique difference that only the conference leader knows the nature of the problem and it is his task to steer the ideas of the group towards a solution 'in the dark.' This prevents any member from getting addicted to a single idea, which is an inherent danger in a normal brainstorming session.

Chairing a meeting

60. An open public meeting would usually be presided over by a chairman appointed for the occasion by the promoter or organiser of the meeting. In the case of the more restricted and regular meetings of an established body, it is possible - and desirable - to aim for greater suitability, consistency and continuity in the chairmanship. This can best be achieved if the body chooses one individual, for his experience and personal qualities, to hold office as chairman for a certain period, and to take the chair at *all* meetings held within his period of office.

61. The chairman may be appointed for a *fixed term*, eg. one year, or he may be appointed to hold office *indefinitely*, until he vacates office or is removed.

62. If the regulations *do not* provide for the appointment of a chairman, a meeting has an inherent right to appoint a person present to be chairman of that meeting. If the regulations *do* provide for the appointment of a chairman but

     (a) he is not present, at a meeting properly convened; or
     (b) he withdraws before the meeting has completed its business or adjourned,

     the meeting may replace him with a chairman of its own choice.

63. If the chairman has been *appointed* under the regulations, which is the normal case, he can only be *removed* under the regulations: the meeting cannot usually vote him out of the chair. But a meeting which has properly chosen its own chairman may similarly remove him, by carrying a vote of no confidence and electing another chairman.

64. Appointing an individual as chairman for a period enables the members (or the managing committee) to select someone who is likely to have and/or develop the required personal qualities for a position which can be rather demanding. In particular, the chairman will often have obtained experience as deputy to the previous chairman, or as a long-serving member of the managing committee, so that he is well acquainted with its affairs and procedure.

65. There are a number of recognised qualities of a good chairman (though common sense may dictate many others, varying with the circumstances of the meeting).

   (a) He will have to give immediate rulings on points of dispute or doubt, so he should have:

      (i)   a sound knowledge of the relevant regulations;
      (ii) an ability to make up his mind without dithering; and
      (iii) skill in communicating his rulings clearly, but tactfully and in a courteous manner.

   (b) He should be, and be seen to be, impartial. There will be times when criticism is expressed which he personally may find unfair, or there is a strong clash of opinion between other members present. In either situation, whatever his personal views, the chairman should treat opponents with equal fairness - and his *own* opponents with as much consideration as his supporters. In particular, he should give them a reasonable opportunity to express their views, along with any minority interests at the meeting.

   (c) He should have the discretion to know when to insist on strict observance of correct procedure, and when a certain amount of relaxation will ease the tension. (If in doubt, proper adherence to procedure may on the whole be safer.)

   (d) He should be punctual and regular in his attendance at meetings. If he cannot give his duties the appropriate amount of time and attention, he should consider resigning.

What does the chairman do?

66. The main tasks of a meeting's chairman are:

   (a) to preserve order;
   (b) to make sure that correct procedure is observed; and
   (c) to ascertain the 'sense' of the meeting on relevant issues.

67. However, the Chairman (or 'Chair') also has a very important personal contribution to make.

   (a) Before starting the meeting the chairman should be satisfied that it has been properly convened by notice and is properly constituted by the attendance of a quorum. He should be watchful to ensure that a quorum is maintained throughout the meeting, of persons entitled to vote on each item of business under discussion.

   (b) He should do his best to maintain order and harmony (or at least courtesy) and should take appropriate action in face of disorder.

   (c) He should guide the meeting through its business:

      (i)   making sure that each motion and amendment is valid and within the bounds of the notice convening the meeting (if appropriate);

      (ii) taking one subject at a time, in the order set out in the agenda (or any modification of it which may be agreed by the meeting);

      (iii) making sure that those who are eligible to speak are invited to do so, and that nobody dominates the meeting so that other people cannot put their views.

(d) He should <u>permit an adequate amount of discussion</u> on each point, giving sufficient (but not excessive) opportunity for the expression of different points of view. He should deal firmly with irrelevance, long-windedness, interruption and signs of temper.

(e) If '<u>points of order</u>' are raised, that is complaints or queries regarding procedure, he should give immediate rulings on them.

(f) At the end of a debate he must <u>ascertain 'the sense of the meeting'</u> in an appropriate way.

    (i) At a small and informal meeting it may suffice for him to *sum up* the general agreement of the members on a particular conclusion.

    (ii) In case of disagreement, however, and at any larger or more formal meeting, he should put the issue to the *vote*. If amendments to the motion have been proposed, they should be put to the vote in the appropriate order, before the original or substantive motion finally comes to the vote.

    (iii) It is the chairman's duty to *count* the votes (though this may be delegated to scrutineers in a vote on a poll at a company meeting) and to *declare the result*. Unless his declaration is challenged at the time, it cannot usually be disputed later (unless the declaration itself is glaringly wrong - eg. '4 in favour, 5 against, I declare the motion carried').

(g) When the minutes of the meeting have been prepared, the chairman should satisfy himself that they are an accurate and complete record. If he is satisfied, he should <u>sign the minutes</u>. There may be procedures for consulting other members of a small board or committee before the minutes are signed.

(h) In addition to his formal and public duties at the meeting itself, the chairman may have a part to play in the preparations for it. The secretary may seek his views in preparing an agenda, or may work with him on a statement which the chairman may be required to make at a general meeting of a public company or other large body.

68. Although there are no formal restrictions on the use of a casting vote, the general view is that the chairman, whatever his views on the motion, should endeavour to be impartial.

Minuting a meeting

69. Companies and local authorities are required by law to keep minutes of their meetings, being a written record of the business done at meetings. Other bodies may have regulations which impose a similar requirement. It is certainly the general practice of all established bodies to keep minutes, in case there is a later dispute as to exactly what was decided, or there is need to refer back to the business of a previous meeting.

70. Minutes are likely to be of value to a body which holds meetings, as:

(a) a record of events for reference at a later date, or by members who missed the meeting. This will also be a useful control for the implementation of policy decisions taken at the meeting;

(b) evidence of exactly what was decided, in case of later uncertainty or dispute. The minutes will be authenticated by signature as a true record of proceedings;

(c) a precedent and authority for future proposals;

(d) an aid to compiling the next agenda - picking up unfinished business, considering 'matters arising' etc.;

(e) a check on ill-considered action at meetings. Participants are more accountable for views and decisions which are put into the minutes. They may also request to 'go on record' with views they hold particularly strongly, or wish to be recalled later (to prove the soundness of their judgement, after the event etc).

71. *Minutes* of a meeting should be distinguished from a *report* of a meeting.

- If press representatives are present at a meeting, reports may appear in the newspapers, written by the reporters. These are often selective and incomplete (if not wildly inaccurate); they tend to give more space to an account of the debate, and the personalities involved, than to the decision reached.

- By contrast minutes are a formal and complete record, in concise form, of decisions taken and other things done, but not usually of the course of debate.

72. The minutes of each meeting should be headed to show:

(a) what the meeting was, such as the annual general meeting of a specified body;

(b) the date of the meeting and the place where it was held;

(c) the names of the persons 'present', if this is practicable. In the case of a large meeting it may be better to invite those who attend to sign an attendance book or attendance sheets (with different sheets for eg. shareholders and other persons such as the press). The minutes then simply refer to the attendance record, which should be preserved;

(d) the names of those 'in attendance': technically, the word 'present' in this context should be reserved for persons who have a right to be there. Thus in the minutes of a board meeting, only the directors are 'present'; the secretary, if he is not also a director, is 'in attendance'.

Note: If any person is present for only part of a meeting, eg. because he arrives late or leaves early, the minutes should, if possible, record the period when he was there. For example, 'Mr Smith during items 205 to 215'.

73. At the foot of the last (or only) page of the minutes of the meeting there is a space for the chairman's signature. This is sometimes marked for convenience by:

....
Chairman

74. The body of the minutes should follow the order of business set out in the agenda, and should be:
    (a) divided into paragraphs; and
    (b) numbered for reference.

75. Minutes may be set out as 'action minutes', with a slightly different format. A marginal column is provided, in which a note is made against any action to be taken, arising from an item of business, with the name of the person (if any) who is to be responsible.

76. Minutes should always be concise, but sufficiently detailed to avoid ambiguity. It is not correct to include in a minute any account of the discussion leading up to a decision. The reasons or arguments advanced by one speaker may not, after all, be the factors which led others to vote in the same way. The decision is a collective act; each speaker speaks only for himself. The decision itself, however, should be given in full.

77. It is always necessary to include in the minutes sufficient detail to enable a reader to understand the decision. If anything unusual has arisen, it is better that it should be mentioned.

78. If some person votes against a motion, or abstains from voting, and expressly requests that this be minuted, it is usual and courteous to comply with his request. This point is most likely to come up at a meeting of a board of directors, when an individual strongly disagrees with the decision of the majority, or wishes to have it recorded that he abstained from voting on a matter in which he had a personal interest.

79. In order for the minutes to fulfil their purpose, they should be:

    (a) concise, but sufficiently detailed to make the sense of the meeting clear;
    (b) precise and unambiguous; factually accurate and fair in implication;
    (c) impersonal, impartial and uniform in style - not 'coloured' by the 'author';
    (d) written in the past tense (with reported speech as appropriate ie: 'X requested that his abstention be minuted', rather than 'X said: "I wish my abstention to be minuted"');
    (e) clearly laid out, paragraphed and cross-referenced.

Conferences

80. A body which has a large membership spread over a wide area, such as a professional body or a trade union, may find *conferences* a useful means of improving contact between the organisation and the body of the membership. The central administration may appear too remote, and representative committees, though useful, do not always reflect the views of the general membership.

> A well-organised annual conference is a means of bringing together a much larger number of members to discuss matters of current interest or concern. It can 'bridge the gap', and give members:
> (a) a better understanding of what their organisation is trying to do for them; and
> (b) a greater commitment to it.

81. In a typical case, a conference lasts several days, sometimes spread over the long weekend of a public holiday: Easter is a favourite time for conferences. As the conference will entail hotel accommodation, it is often held at a seaside resort or inland spa which will have the facilities, and may provide them more cheaply 'out of season'.

82. There will be *social events* for the entertainment of members (and their spouses). The town chosen for the conference will usually encourage the organisation to come again by offering a civic reception or visits to places of interest. There may be a dinner for the conference delegates on one evening of the period. The social aspect of conferences is an important element.

● **Communication in practice**

83. In 1986 a survey was carried out by Vista Communications, an employee consultancy company. 222 large UK companies were asked to complete questionnaires on their methods of internal communication.

84. The most popular methods of communication proved to be internal memos, circulars and notice boards (used by 92% of companies who completed the questionnaire), followed by team or line briefings (86%) and the company newspaper (81%). Lower down the list came management conferences (65%), employee reports (63%) and communication via trade union representatives (62%).

85. The most discouraging finding of the survey was that few companies made any systematic efforts to find out the views of their own workers on the quality of communications within the firm (although most respondents claimed that communications in their firm were good or very good). Asked how they checked the effectiveness of their communications with employees, most said by feedback through line management. (A smaller proportion mentioned the state of their industrial relations as a good indicator.)

86. Commenting on this, the managing director of Vista Communications said: 'That is like asking the salesman what he thinks of the product he is selling, rather than asking the consumer'.

QUIZ

1. What are some of the problems and barriers to communication?

    - See paras 7-11

2. What is informal communication, and how can the organisation utilise it?

    - See paras 14-19

3. List four methods of face-to-face communication and seven methods of written communication.

    - See para 20

4. Why is an internal written report a useful method of communication?

    - See para 25

5. What are the advantages and disadvantages of the various communication networks or patterns?

    - See paras 36-40

6. In what ways may meetings be useful?

    - See para 44

7. What are the advantages and disadvantages of the use of committees?

    - See paras 53-54

8. What are recognised as being the qualities of a good chairman?

    - See para 65

9. What does a meeting's chairman do?

    - See para 67

10. How should minutes be written?

    - See para 79

Chapter 13

MONITORING AND CONTROLLING PERFORMANCE

Topics covered in this chapter

- Planning and control: an introduction
- Planning
  - Barriers to good planning
  - Aspects of planning
  - Types of plan
  - Steps in planning
  - Planning horizons
- Performance standards and measurement criteria
- Control
  - The manager as controller
  - The control cycle
  - Feedback, double loop feedback and feedforward control
- Design choices for a management control system

Purpose of this chapter

To look at the principles behind and practice of the management functions of planning and control, and how they are interrelated parts of a management control system.

● Planning and control: an introduction

1. Managers should be held accountable for what they do with their authority and the resources at their disposal. Making managers accountable is achieved through the processes of planning and control.

(a) Planning is the process of deciding what should be done.
(b) Control is the process of checking whether planned targets are being achieved, and if not, doing something about it.

The combined processes of planning and control are known as a *control system.*

---

2. Accountability is a process whereby a manager's actual results and achievements are reviewed by his superiors. In other words, the consequences of a manager's planning and control decisions, and the manager's achievements with the resources at his disposal, are held up for inspection by his boss or bosses.

● **Planning**

3.   If individuals and groups within an organisation are to be effective in working for the achievement of the organisation's objectives, they need to know what it is that they are expected to do. This is the purpose of planning:

(a)   to decide objectives for the organisation;

(b)   to identify alternative ways of achieving the objectives; and

(c)   to select from amongst these alternatives for the organisation as a whole, and for individual departments, sections and groups within it.

4.   Planning involves decisions by management about:
(a)   what to do in the future;
(b)   how to do it;
(c)   when to do it; and
(d)   who is to do it.

The future cannot be foreseen with certainty, and even the best-laid plans will go wrong to a greater or lesser degree; nevertheless, plans give direction to an organisation. Without plans, events will be left to chance.

Barriers to good planning

5.   There are many managers in practice who are reluctant to make formal plans, and prefer to operate without them, dealing with problems only when and if they arise. The reason for their reluctance to plan might be one or more of the following.

(a)   *A lack of knowledge (or interest) about the purpose and goals of the organisation.* Unless a manager knows what the organisation's goals are, and how other departments and sections are trying to work towards those goals, his own efforts might well either:
(i)   duplicate the efforts of someone else, thereby causing a waste of time and resources; or
(ii)   conflict with the efforts of someone else.
Good planning encourages the co-ordination of efforts within an organisation.

(b)   *A reluctance to be committed to one set of targets.* Planning involves making a choice about what to do from amongst many different alternative courses of action. A manager might want to keep his options open, which means that he will not want to have specific goals. Whereas this might be feasible in a very small organisation, it is unsatisfactory in any organisation where managers must co-ordinate their efforts and work together for the achievement of organisational goals. Freedom of choice could well be a recipe for lack of preparation for environmental changes, and a lack of co-ordinated response to economic, technological, social and political developments etc with which the organisation will be faced.

(c)   *A fear of blame or criticism for failing to achieve planned targets.* It is possible to identify success or failure by setting targets, plans and standards to be met, as well as performance criteria to measure success, and later comparing actual performance against plans. When failure is 'punished' in any way (eg in the form or lower salaries or bonuses, or thwarted promotion prospects and career ambitions, or even the displeasure of superior managers) managers might resent planning, because planning is the start of a process by which they might later be labelled as failures.

(d) *A manager's lack of confidence* in himself to perform his job efficiently and effectively, or a lack of confidence in the organisation's senior management to provide him with the resources he needs to achieve his planned targets.

For example, suppose that the manager of a retail store is asked to plan the target volume of turnover and profits for the store in the next two or three years. The manager might lack confidence in the company's senior management to provide him with enough resources (staff, equipment, product ranges, money for sales promotion etc) to achieve a reasonable targeted performance; or if he did have sufficient resources, he might doubt his own ability to ensure that the targets are achieved. The manager would then prefer instead not to have any plans or targets at all.

(e) *A manager's lack of information about what is going on in the 'environment'.* Managers need to know about the needs of customers, the nature of their markets and their competition, the strength of public opinion or government pressures, the state of the economy etc. Without such information, they will be unable to make plans for the future which are achievable in view of environmental conditions. For example, when a government announces its intention to introduce legislation to ban lead in petrol, car manufacturers and oil companies must know about the timing and nature of such legislation before they can plan properly for its consequences.

6. A further problem in planning is that some managers have plans *imposed* upon them without any prior consultation at all. If a manager is *told* what he must do and what his targets are, he is likely to resist the plan, and find reasons why it is unachievable.

7. The barriers to good planning must be overcome.

(a) All levels of staff should be involved (to a greater or lesser degree) in the planning process. Plans should not be imposed on staff without their participation, or without their opinions being sought.

(b) Planners must be provided with the *information* they need (and access to sources of future information, when it arises) to plan properly. The source of information might be:

(i) from outside the organisation concerning environmental factors;
(ii) from inside the organisation concerning facts about the organisation itself. This information is called '*feedback*'.

(c) A system of rewards for successful achievement of plans might be beneficial. However, a system of rewards is also a system of punishment for those managers who fail to earn rewards. The motivational problems of rewards and punishments are not easily overcome, and are likely to be a continual barrier to good planning.

(d) Managers should be taught the virtues of planning, and the techniques of good planning. For example, managers should learn the value of co-ordinating the efforts of all staff in the organisation for the achievement of common goals; and the managers should also learn that a subordinate can only be expected to achieve certain targets if he is given sufficient resources to do his job properly.

Aspects of planning

8. There are four major aspects to planning.

   (a) The purpose of every plan (and of every subsidiary plan within the framework of an overall plan) is *to make it easier for management to achieve a goal or objective*. Planning allows managers to identify:

      (i) what actions will serve towards achieving a stated objective;
      (ii) what actions will be counter-productive and serve to obstruct the achievements of an objective; and
      (iii) what actions will be irrelevant to the achievement of an objective.

   (b) *Planning precedes all other management functions*. An organisation must have an idea of its objectives and of what actions must be performed to achieve them before management can:

      (i) provide a formal organisation structure to carry out the activities;
      (ii) identify the style and qualities of leadership necessary to get the best out of the staff; and
      (iii) set standards and targets of performance for groups and individuals, by which control can be exercised.

      Planning therefore precedes organisation, staffing, commanding, leading and control as management functions, and planning is also an essential feature of co-ordination.

   (c) *Planning is a function of all managers*. Some managers do more planning than others, but all managers, even first-line supervisors and foremen, do some planning.

   (d) Plans enable managers *to decide whether the achievement of certain targets is worth the cost of putting the plan into operation*. An efficient plan is one whose costs of implementation are less than the benefits obtained from its contribution to the organisation's goals and objectives. The planning process enables managers to evaluate the efficiency (or cost effectiveness) of their proposed actions and intended targets.

Types of plan

9. There are a number of different types of plan, which may be classified as follows:

   (a) *Objectives for the organisation as a whole*. This might be to earn a profit, or provide a certain service. It might also be possible to distinguish between a *mission* for the organisation (eg to provide a certain type of product in order to satisfy a certain type of customer need or need of society) and an objective (eg to make a profit whilst accomplishing the organisation's mission). The company's mission is often the answer to the question "What business are we in?"

An objective is an end goal towards which all activities should be aimed.

   (b) *Objectives for individual departments or divisions* within the objectives for the organisation as a whole. For example, within an international company separate objectives might be identified for the domestic division and the international division.

(c) *Strategies* follow on from the determination of long-term goals and objectives.

> *Strategies* are plans of activity (mainly long-term) and plans for the allocation of resources which will achieve the organisation's objectives.

There are different types of strategy. For example:

(i)   a product/market strategy is a plan about the types of product or service an organisation should provide (in order to obtain a sufficient volume of customer demand) and about the types of market in which it should be trying to sell those products or services. A product/market strategy is also a plan for competition against other producers of the same products in the same markets;

(ii) a manpower strategy is a plan about the number and types of staff which will be required in the long term to achieve the organisation's goals.

(d) *Policies* are general statements or 'understandings' which provide guidelines for management decision-making. Company policies might be, for example:

(i)   to offer 5 year guarantees on all products sold and to give money back to customers with valid complaints;

(ii) to promote managers from within the organisation, wherever possible, instead of recruiting managers to senior positions from 'outside';

(iii) to encourage all recruits to certain jobs within the organisation to work towards obtaining an appropriate professional qualification;

(iv) to be price-competitive in the market;

(v)   that employees in the purchasing department should decline gifts from suppliers (subject, perhaps, to certain exceptions or purchase limits).

> *Policy* guidelines should allow managers to exercise their own discretion and freedom of choice, within certain acceptable limits.

(e) *Procedures* exist at all levels of management (eg even a board of directors will have procedures for the conduct of board meetings) but procedures become more numerous, onerous and extensive lower down in an organisation's hierarchy.

> *Procedures* are a chronological sequence of required actions for performing a certain task.

The advantages of procedures for routine work are:

(i)   efficiency. Procedures should prescribe the most efficient way of getting a job done;

(ii) the absence of any need for the exercise of discretion in routine tasks;

(iii) familiarity. Staff will find jobs easier to do when they are familiar with established procedures;

(iv) standardisation of work. Prescribed procedures ensure that a task of a certain type will be done in the same way throughout the organisation;

(v)   continuity. The work will be done the same way even when a different person starts in a job or takes over from the previous holder;

(vi) a written record of required procedures can be kept in a procedures manual. People unfamiliar with how a job should be done can learn quickly and easily by referring to the manual;

(vii) they reduce the likelihood of inter-departmental friction. For example, work done by the warehousing department of a factory will affect the work of the sales force, delivery and distribution department and production department. The warehousing department will require documentation from production giving details of goods put into store, and documentation about sales orders from the sales force. It will issue delivery instructions to the delivery crews. By having established procedures, disputes between departments about who should do what, and when, and how, should be avoided.

(f)

> A *rule* is a specific, definite course of action that must be taken in a given situation.

Unlike a procedure, it does not set out the sequence or chronology of events (but a procedure is a chronological sequence of rules). For example, the following are rules but not procedures:

(i) employees in department X are allowed 10 minutes exactly at the end of their shift for clearing up and cleaning their work-bench;

(ii) employees with access to a telephone must not use the telephone for personal calls.

Rules allow no deviations or exceptions, unlike policies which are general guidelines allowing the exercise of some management discretion.

(g) *Programmes* are co-ordinated groups of plans (goals, policies, procedures, rules) for the achievement of a particular objective. A company might undertake an expansion or rationalisation programme; in the USA, the government's space agency has a number of programmes, such as the Strategic Defence Initiative ('Star Wars') programme.

> A *programme* of any importance is usually a complex of plans which stands by itself and has a clear, separate identity within the organisation and its planning structure.

(h)

> A *budget* is a formal statement of expected results set out in numerical terms, and summarised in money values.

It is a plan for carrying out certain activities within a given period of time, in order to achieve certain targets. The budget indicates how many resources will be allocated to each department or activity in order to carry out the planned activities.

The budget is usually prepared on a company-wide or organisation-wide basis, so that all the activities of the organisation are co-ordinated within a single plan. In order to compare the plans and targets of each department, section, group and individual manager, budgets are expressed in money terms as well as in terms of physical quantities.

Budgets are numerical statements and, as such, tend to ignore *'qualitative'* aspects of planning and achievement.

Steps in planning

10. The steps in a planning decision are as follows.

- recognise an opportunity to be exploited or a problem to be dealt with;

- establish goals or objectives as the end result of exploiting the opportunity or solving the problem;

- forecast relevant information (eg about products, markets, competition, prices, wage rates, technology etc). Some planning premises should be established which are agreed and used by managers throughout the organisation. An accepted set of premises about the environment in which the organisation will operate, and the resources it will have at its disposal, will provide guidelines for planning decisions.

> For example, suppose that a forecast is made that the market for product Z has reached saturation, and prices are likely to fall in the future because of over-supply. Costs are expected to rise, and the profitability of the product will go into decline for reasons outside management control. Given these planning premises, management's plans for dealing with the problem of product profitability, or any opportunities provided by spare production capacity, would not be to spend on advertising to sell more of the product, or to use the spare capacity to make more of the product and introduce more price competition into the market! Planning decisions would be channelled towards different solutions for the company's problems;

- consider alternative 'realistic' courses of action for the achievement of the objectives;

- compare the alternative courses of action and select the best course;

- formulate detailed plans for carrying out the chosen course of action. These plans consist of:
  - (a) supporting plans for the provision of the required resources (materials, equipment, trained labour, finance etc);
  - (b) standards of performance required (quality, time-scale etc) and measurement criteria; and
  - (c) numerical plans or budgets indicating targets for achievement, sales prices, budgeted sales and production quantities, expenditure budgets etc.

11. These steps in planning apply to:
    (a) 'one-off' as well as routine plans or projects; and
    (b) planning at senior management, middle management and junior management levels.

Planning horizons

12. Planning should cover the long term as well as the short term.

   (a) There is a planning period or 'time horizon' which is the length of time between making a planning decision and the implementation of the decision. For example, a decision to relocate to new premises might have a time horizon of many years, a decision to develop and launch a new product might take several years, a normal capital budget might span a five year period, an operating budget will span a one-year period, and a production schedule might be produced weekly.

Plans of varied duration will be made within an organisation, although the longer the planning horizon, the more senior the management planner is likely to be.

(b) Long-term planning indicates a commitment by an organisation to a certain course of action. In other words, plans are tangible evidence of a commitment to decisions already taken. The length of a planning period should be long enough for the commitment to these past decisions to be reflected in the determination of objectives, strategies and resource allocations.

(c) Long-term objectives might conflict with short-term plans, and a feature of planning should be to reconcile the needs of the long and short terms. For example, if a company has a short term problem of resource availability, and has only limited funds for expenditure, it might be tempting to devote all the resources to maintaining current profitability. However, if longer term spending on capital investment or research and development are ignored, the company's profitability in the long-term might be sacrificed.

(d) In the short-term, a company might consider profitability as the major objective. In the longer term, profitability will also be important; however other qualitative considerations such as social responsibility, employee welfare, corporate image, standards of service and reputation etc might take on added importance. If long-term planning recognises non-profit goals, there will be a greater likelihood of short-term planning also making some concessions to these goals.

(e) Plans, once formulated, should not be rigid because the future is uncertain and plans should be changed whenever necessary to meet unforeseen circumstances which arise. The need for flexibility in planning is an argument in favour of having shorter planning periods, and so avoiding wasted time on long-term plans which will inevitably change.

A compromise should be found between the need for flexibility (keep plans short-term) and the need for commitment to decisions already made (make plans as long-term as the planning horizon requires). The best compromise is perhaps that plans should be reviewed regularly, and redrawn if necessary. Short-term plans will be more detailed than long-term ones, so the latter are more flexible.

● **Performance standards and measurement criteria**

13. Identifying and establishing *performance standards* is an important feature of management control (and also of operational control). Performance standards may be:

(a) *quantitative:* eg volume of output or sales, market shares, levels of scrap and inventory, cost levels, timescales etc. Performance can be measured on criteria of desired versus actual costs and profits; or

(b) *qualitative:* eg attitudes of employees and customers.

14. At middle management level, any quantitative performance standards will be largely expressed in terms of money (costs, revenues, profits). Hence budgets and forecasts are usually expressed in monetary terms, although they may derive from information on the number of units produced, hours worked etc.

15. Performance standards provide a means of both planning and control. Where they are quantitative, control will be initiated by the preparation of a report or control document (eg production cost report, selling cost report, distribution cost report, monthly operating statement, profit and loss account etc).

16. The criteria used to measure how successfully performance standards have been met depend on how the standards are expressed *and* on the overall objectives of the organisation:

    ● an organisation which expects 20% return on capital employed will measure performance in terms of the extent to which this target has been met;

    ● an organisation with a mission to provide the customer with the products he wants at the time and price he wants them may use the number of complaints received or refunds made. If these exceed a certain level (say, 5% of all sales) then it could be said that performance has failed to measure up to the standard.

● Control

17. We have seen that planning and the setting of targets and standards are part of the management control system. In this chapter, we are concerned mainly with *formalised* systems of control, although the principles also apply to more informal and 'one-off' control measures - for example, a supervisor telling off a subordinate who is not performing as he should (eg taking too much time off at lunchtime, or working too slowly etc).

The manager as controller

18. The objective of the management function of control is the measurement and correction of the activities of subordinates in order to make sure that the goals of the organisation, or planning targets, are achieved.

> 'In an undertaking, control consists in verifying whether everything occurs in conformity with the plan adopted, the instructions issued and the principles established.
>
> [Its object is] to point out weaknesses and errors in order to rectify them and prevent recurrence. It operates on everything; things, people, actions'. (Henri Fayol)

Control is a necessary management function at all levels in the management hierarchy.

19. In order to carry out their control functions, managers must have:

    (a) plans, which indicate not only the targets and goals which the efforts of themselves and their subordinates should be directed towards achieving but also the rules and procedures for achieving them;

    (b) an organisation structure; in particular a clear indication of the managers responsible for the actual results achieved and deviations from plan (and the managers who should therefore have the authority to instigate corrective action).

The control cycle

20. The basic control process or control cycle in management has six stages:

    (a) making a plan: deciding what to do and identifying the desired results. Without plans there can be no control;

    (b) recording the plan formally or informally, in writing or by other means, statistically or descriptively. The plan should incorporate standards of efficiency, targets of performance and measurement criteria;

    (c) carrying out the plan, or having it carried out by subordinates, and measuring actual results achieved;

    (d) comparing actual results against the plans. This is sometimes referred to as the provision of 'feedback';

    (e) evaluating the comparison, and deciding whether further action is necessary to ensure the plan is achieved; and

    (f) implementing corrective action as necessary.

21. Control is dependent upon the receipt and processing of *information*. Within organisations, information may be received from:
    (a) formal sources within the organisation;
    (b) informally from sources within the organisation;
    (c) formal sources outside the organisation, from the environment;
    (d) informally from environmental sources.

22. Examples of information requirements are as follows:

Activity in control cycle	Information required
Make plan	Resources available, value to the company if the plan is successfully carried out, comparison with alternative plans which could be carried out.
Record the plan	The way in which the plan will fit into the company's operations as a whole, so that other people/departments affected by the plan can be informed.
Carry out the plan	Details of the quantity and quality of resources for the job: specifying time and place.
Comparison of actual against plan	What happened?
Evaluation and control action	Changes which have taken place since the original plan, outside the framework of the plan itself; the goal of the original plan may need to be amended and control action should be adjusted accordingly.

23. A business must be controlled to keep it steady or enable it to change safely, so each business must have its control system. Control is required because unpredictable events occur so that actual results deviate from the expected results or goals. Examples of unplanned and unforeseen events would range, in a business, from the entry of a powerful new competitor into the market, an unexpected rise in labour costs, or the failure of a supplier to deliver promised raw materials, to the tendency of employees to stop working in order to chatter or gossip. A control system must ensure that the business is capable of surviving these 'disturbances' by dealing with them in an appropriate manner.

Feedback and the control loop

24. *Feedback* for management control is information which is measured from business operations and reported as control information to the managers responsible for those operations so that corrective action may be taken. Measuring results, comparing results against plans and taking control action is known as the *control loop*.

25. A business organisation uses feedback for control; however, external influences are not ignored. A management information system must be designed to provide both proper feedback and also sufficient environmental information to optimise the control system.

26. *Negative feedback* is information which indicates that results are deviating from their planned or prescribed course, and that some re-adjustment is necessary to bring the plan back on to course. This feedback is called 'negative' because control action would seek to reverse the direction or movement of the system back towards it planned course.

13.1 Negative feedback

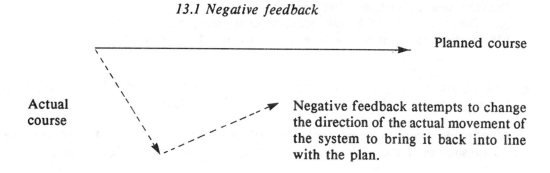

Planned course

Actual
course

Negative feedback attempts to change
the direction of the actual movement of
the system to bring it back into line
with the plan.

Thus if the budgeted sales for June and July were £100,000 in each month, whereas the report of actual sales in June showed that only £90,000 had been reached, this negative feedback would indicate that control action was necessary to raise sales in July to £110,000 in order to get back on the planned course. Negative feedback in this case would necessitate July sales exceeding the budget by £10,000 because June sales fell short of budget.

27. A control system might be drawn as a 'black box' diagram, in which the system being controlled is shown simply as a box, and the inputs, outputs, feedback and control actions are shown relating to that box.

13.2 Control system

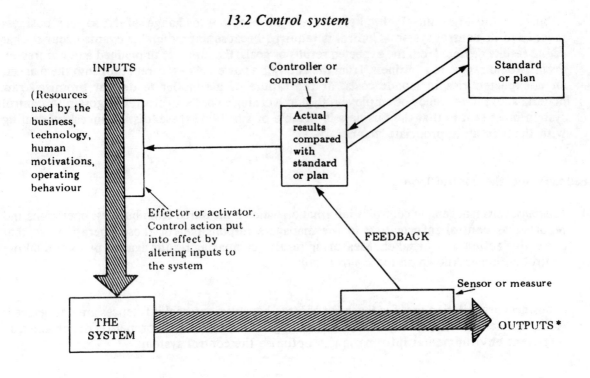

28. This control system can be said to consist of four key elements:

    (a)   the plan for the system - the 'condition to be controlled';
    (b)   the measure or 'sensor' of results;
    (c)   the comparison of actual results against plan ('the comparator');
    (d)   putting any control action into effect (the 'effector' or 'activator').

29. This diagram is as yet incomplete, but it may be helpful at this stage to relate the control system to a practical example, such as monthly budgetary control variance reports.

    (a)   Standard costs and a master budget are prepared for the year. Management organises the resources of the business (inputs) so as to achieve the budget targets.

    (b)   At the end of each month, actual results (output, sales, costs, revenues etc) are reported back to management. The reports are the measured output of the control system, and the process of sending them to the managers responsible provides the feedback loop.

    (c)   Managers compare actual results against the plan and where necessary, take corrective action to adjust the workings of the system, probably by amending the inputs to the system. Where appropriate the standard may have to be revised.

30. In this example, however, we have not allowed for several factors:

    (a)   the influence of the environment on both plans and system inputs;

    (b)   whether control action is possible. For example, a manager might not be able to do anything about the effect of inflation on the costs of his department;

(c) how much information should be measured and fed back to the managers responsible for the activities. Not all output is measured, either because it would not have any useful value as information, or because the system does not provide for its measurement.

31. It is also important to bear in mind that the standard or plan might need to be changed and a comparison of actual results against the existing plan might be invalid. Environmental influences could be responsible for the need to change the standard.

32. For example, in variance reporting for a budgetary control system:

(a) unmeasured output might include the morale and motivation of staff, the number of labour hours wasted as idle time or the volume of complaints received about a particular product or service;

(b) as a consequence of reported variances, it may be decided that the standard costs should be revised because, for some reason, they are not valid. Similarly, the master budget might be changed if it is realised that actual sales volumes will be radically different from those budgeted;

(c) there will be environmental influences (such as government legislation about safety standards, changing consumer demand, an unexpected rise in raw material prices, or a long strike in a supplier industry) affecting both inputs to the system and also how the budget is established or amended;

(d) not all inputs to the system are controllable; a rise in raw material prices, or a change in weather conditions which affects production (eg in the building industry) or sales (eg ice creams, soft drinks) are outside the scope of management control. Other inputs might be controllable, but are not controlled due to lax or inattentive management (eg poor labour morale and a high labour turnover, or difficulties in recruiting staff which might be controllable by improving the quality of job content, training or pay).

33. An important feature of any control system is the *timeliness* of control information. In a formal management reporting system, for example, there ought to be established feedback periods, which are "the frequency of transmitting feedback information to the control function, which will be determined by such factors as the likelihood of the process going out of control, availability of information and cost of collection." (CIMA Official Terminology).

Double loop feedback

34. Higher level feedback or *double loop feedback* is control information transmitted to a higher level in the system. In a business system, higher level feedback is reported to a more senior level of management. Whereas single loop feedback is concerned with 'task control' (the control loop), higher level feedback is concerned with 'multiple (overall) task control'. The term 'double loop' feedback indicates that the information is reported to indicate both divergencies between the observed and expected results where control action might be required, and also the need for adjustments to the plan itself, perhaps in response to changing environmental conditions. The scale of control action at a higher level will be wider than at the level of single loop feedback - there will be larger variances requiring control measures. Higher level feedback consists not only of information gathered from measuring outputs of the system itself, but also of *environmental information*.

Feedforward control

35. With feedback control, *historical* actual results are measured and reported, so that control action can be taken where necessary. As we have seen, there can be a *control delay,* and the time lag in reporting or taking action could damage the effectiveness of the control system.

> Where some control delay is inevitable with feedback reporting, management might be able to use *feedforward control* instead.

36. Feedforward control is based on *trying to anticipate what will happen in the future,* unless something is done to correct or change matters now, and *comparing this anticipated outcome with the planned outcome.*

    If the anticipated outcome does not match up adequately to the plan, control action can be taken now, before it is too late to do anything effective to put matters right. By providing control information sooner (before an event happens rather than after it has happened), a feedforward control system can prevent control delay which might be harmful and unavoidable in some circumstances.

37. To maintain an effective feedforward control system, management must:

    (a) identify all the critical activities or events;
    (b) develop an overall plan, including targets for these critical activities or events;
    (c) keep the model updated, as events or circumstances change;
    (d) report deviations in anticipated results from the planned (model) results as soon as they become apparent.

38. Child has developed the control cycle to suggest how the process of *management* control operates.

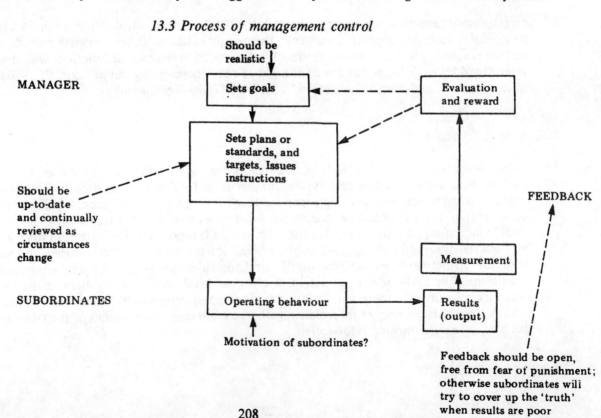

13.3 Process of management control

● **Design choices for a management control system**

39. Child has suggested that there are three main design choices in the structure of a control system:

    (a) the degree of centralisation or decentralisation of decision-making;

    (b) the degree of formality or informality in control. Organisation growth sets up pressures for decentralisation but also for greater formality in control. The disadvantage of decentralisation and formality in control systems is that rules, procedures and bureaucracy can take over;

    (c) the degree of personal supervision that managers exercise over subordinates. This is the issue of *span of control*.

40. Child goes on to suggest that there are four alternative strategies for control in an organisation.

1. *Personal centralised control*
    Centralised decision making.
    Personal leadership; direct supervision.
 	
    Often a feature of small owner-managed companies.

2. *Bureaucratic control*
    Based on rules and procedures, budgets and budgetary control.
    As much programmed decision-taking as possible.
 	
    Control is based on the principles of scientific management - specialisation of work, simplification of work methods, and standardisation of procedures.

3. *Output control*   The organisation of work is structured so as to identify groups that can be made responsible for a particular output. Systems of *'responsibility accounting'* are operated. Authority for operational matters regarding the output is delegated to the operational managers. Divisional organisation structures fall into this category.

4. *Cultural control*
    Cultural control is achieved where all employees develop a strong personal identification with the goals of the organisation. There is often semi-autonomous working, with few formal controls. Employees are motivated by prospects of career progression; selection, training and development of staff are important features of management policy.
 	
    Examples of organisations where cultural control exists are firms of chartered accountants and companies such as Japanese corporations, in which a strong composite identity is built up, and which Ouchi and Price (1978) have called the 'industrial clan' mentality.

41. The most appropriate control strategy, Child argues, will depend on contingent factors, such as

		Control strategy likely to be suitable
Market demand for the organisation's output bureaucratic	Strong Weak	Output and/or cultural Centralised and/or
Employee skills and education bureaucratic	High Low	Output and/or cultural Centralised and/or
Change bureaucratic	Rapid Slow	Output and/or cultural Centralised and/or
Size of organisation	Small Not small	Centralised Any other

Control measurement: standards

42. It is worth stressing the point that control measurements can relate to qualitative factors as well as to quantifiable factors. However, there should be *targets* for qualitative performance (eg ethical standards of behaviour) because unless there is a standard or target, it will be impossible to establish whether or not actual achievements have been satisfactory.

43. Management's attention should be directed at critical control points - points about performance that require special attention because they are judged critical to the success of operations. The points selected for control should be critical in the sense that they indicate better than other factors whether actual results are working out according to plan.

44. Critical control points will vary between different organisations and different departments within the same organisation. The types of critical control point and the standards of performance which might be used are:

   (a) physical standards (eg units of raw material per unit produced, labour hours per unit produced, labour hours per working week etc);

   (b) cost standards. These convert physical standards into a money measurement by the application of standard prices. For example, the standard labour cost of making product X might be 4 hours at £5 per hour = £20;

   (c) capital standards. These establish some form of standard for capital invested (eg the ratio of current assets to current liabilities, or gearing (the ratio of fixed interest capital to equity capital)).

   (d) revenue standards. These measure expected performance in terms of revenue earned, such as turnover per square metre of shelf space (in a supermarket) or value of sales orders per salesman, or revenue per passenger-mile (for transport services) etc;

(f)   the achievement of stated goals;

(g)   intangible standards. These may be difficult to measure objectively, but they should only be used if objectivity can be achieved. Intangible standards might relate to employee motivation, quality of service, customer goodwill, corporate image, product image etc.

Cost-effectiveness of control

45.   Controls should be economical and worth their cost in terms of the benefits obtained. Large organisations can probably afford a larger control system because its potential benefits or savings are higher. Control will probably be economical if it is tailored to:

(a)   the critical control points of the organisation's work; and
(b)   the size of the organisation.

46.   It could be argued, however, that although large scale organisations can afford more complex control systems, the organisations themselves are so large and complex that they have:

(a)   more control problems, of a greater magnitude than small organisations;
(b)   more problems of efficient communication;
(c)   a wider area of planning; and therefore
(d)   greater problems of communication.

Hence a large organisation needs a more complex control system to avoid its 'in-built' organisational inefficiencies, so that an argument can be put forward that smaller organisations are easier to control, even with a less complex control system.

47.
> A guiding principle of control economy is that controls are efficient when they identify and explain the causes of important differences between actual performance and planned results with the minimum of costs.

Control flexibility

48.   Controls should continue to be workable even when events show that original plans are un-achievable (and should therefore be changed) perhaps due to unforeseen circumstances which arise. In other words, controls must be flexible and adaptable to new circumstances.

49.   Perhaps the most clear example of the need for flexibility is the budget. Suppose that a company has an annual marketing costs budget of £500,000 and a distribution costs budget of £300,000. These budgets were based on expected sales demand of £6,000,000 per annum, or £500,000 per month. Now if actual sales turn out to be much higher than expected, and start running at, say, £750,000 per month, it would be reasonable to expect marketing and distribution costs to exceed the original budget. This means that a monthly or weekly comparison of actual costs against budgeted costs, as the year progresses, will be pointless, because the control information will merely indicate overspending which might reasonably be expected.

To overcome this problem, it is possible to prepare a flexible budget, which adjusts planned spending to a level which ought to be expected in view of the increase in sales. Actual spending is then compared against expected spending in the flexible budget, and any deviations and variances would then provide more meaningful control information about over-or underspending.

Other features of a good control system

50. Other features of a good control system include the following.

(a) The control system should be acceptable to the organisation's members.

   (i) Employees who are used to a rigid, disciplinarian management will perhaps accept strict measures of control and procedures or rules for investigating exceptional variations between actual results and plans.

   (ii) Employees who are accustomed to participating in planning decisions, and are encouraged to use their initiative, will react unfavourably to rigid controls 'imposed' on them by senior management.

   The purpose of a control system is to stimulate control action, and it must therefore be tailored to the 'culture' of the organisation or the department within the organisation.

(b) Controls should be tailored to the capabilities and personalities of individual managers. If a manager cannot or will not understand control information given to him, he will not trust it, and if he does not trust it, he will not use it. Some managers (eg accountants, statisticians) might prefer numerical reports of some complexity, whereas other managers might prefer simpler reports (perhaps with charts or diagrams). The providers of information might compile long reports in a computer printout, which managers will not use because of their length and complexity.

(c) Controls should not be too sophisticated, using techniques of measurement and analysis which only a statistical or accounting 'expert' might understand. Non-technical managers are easily put off by technical reports, and would react more favourably to a control system which is more crude, but nevertheless more comprehensible.

(d) A control system will serve no useful function at all unless it leads management into taking corrective action.

QUIZ

1. List the possible barriers which prevent or discourage managers from making plans. How might these barriers be overcome?

   - See paras 5, 6, 7

2. What types of plans are there?

   - See para 9

3. What types of performance standard are there?

   - See para 13

4. What are the stages in the control cycle?

   - See para 20

5. What is feedback?

   - See 24-26

6. Sketch a control system.

   - See paras 27 or 38

7. Child identifies four strategies for control. What are they? Suggest what types of organisation for which each of these strategies might be appropriate.

   - See paras 40, 41

8. What are critical control points?

   - See paras 43-44

Chapter 14

BOUNDARY MANAGEMENT

Topics covered in this chapter

- Political and legal constraints on organisations
- The social and ethical environment
- The social responsibility of managers
- Management as a profession
  - o Professional code of conduct
  - o Codes of conduct issued by organisations themselves
- Stakeholder analysis
  - o Influence of stakeholders
- Management responsibilities
  - o Employees (including recruitment, retirement, redundancies)
  - o Customers
  - o Suppliers
  - o Competitors
  - o The community
- PR and corporate image
- Accountability of management

Purpose of this chapter

To consider the environmental, legal and other contraints on the exercise of managerial responsibility. We also look at the responsibilities of management to consumers, suppliers, employees, the environment and the general public, and at the way in which the organisation is perceived by the public.

- **Boundary management**

1. A business supplies goods and services to customers, and employs people; it is therefore an integral part of society and is subject to the pressures of that society. Most companies:

   (a) seek a good public image;

   (b) are increasingly conscious of the need to conserve energy, and to protect the environment from the pollution of industrial wastage and spillages;

   (c) attempt to be good employers;

(d) attempt to provide facilities or welfare to the local community or the country as a whole (eg. the sponsorship of sports, which is not always associated with a blaze of advertising and publicity, donations to charity etc.).

2. There are differing views about the extent to which external environmental constraints modify business objectives and form *boundaries* to the exercise of management discretion.

(a) The *stakeholder view* of company objectives is that many groups of people have a stake in what the company does. Shareholders own the business, but there are also suppliers, managers, workers and customers. Each of these groups has its own objectives, so that a compromise or balance is required. Management must balance the profit objective with the pressures from the non-shareholder groups in deciding the strategic targets of the business.

(b) The *consensus theory* of company objectives was developed by Cyert and March. They argued that managers run a business but do not own it and that 'organisations do not have objectives, only people have objectives'. Managers do not necessarily set objectives for the company, but they rather look for objectives which suit their own inclinations. However, objectives emerge as a consensus of the differing views of shareholders, managers, employees, suppliers, customers and society at large, but (in contrast to the stakeholder view) they are not all selected or controlled by management.

3. Ansoff suggested that a company has:

(a) a primary objective, which is financial or economic, aimed at optimising the efficiency and effectiveness of the firm's 'total resource-conversion process';

(b) social or non-economic objectives, which are secondary and modify management behaviour. These social objectives are the result of inter-action among the individual objectives of the differing groups of 'stakeholders';

(c) in addition to economic and non-economic objectives, there are two other factors exerting influence on management behaviour:

(i) *responsibilities*: these are obligations which a company undertakes, but which do not form a part of its 'internal guidance or control mechanism'. Responsibilities would include charitable donations, contributions to the life of local communities etc;

(ii) *boundaries*: these are rules which restrict management's freedom of action, and include government legislation (on pollution levels, health and safety at work, employment protection, redundancy, monopolies, illegal business practices etc) and agreements with trade unions.

● **Political and legal restraints on management**

4. The government acts as a restraining influence on managers of other organisations, in both the public and private sectors.

(a)   In the public sector, senior management is accountable to a government department, and decisions taken by the management might be dictated by government policy.

(b)   For both the public and private sectors, the government enacts and enforces the law. Managers are sometimes compelled to take certain actions, because of the law. Examples are company law (filing of accounts etc), consumer law (pollution controls, dangerous goods legislation), employment law (minimum wage, health and safety) and contract law (limitations on exclusion of liability).

(c)   The government is also able to exert considerable influence on organisations without the need for legal backing.

    (i)   Fiscal policy and economic policy have implications for corporate taxes, interest rates, foreign exchange rates, inflation, and so on, which influence the corporate planning decisions by organisations.

    (ii)   The government might provide financial incentives (eg grants) to encourage organisations to make certain investments, employ more people, or provide more training.

---

5. There is a two-way relationship between government and management, and management can influence the policy decisions of a government, perhaps by means of organised lobbying - eg lobbying by the book trade in the mid 1980s to persuade the government not to impose VAT on newspapers and books.

6. The legal constraints or controls affecting the management of an organisation come from the Companies Act and a wide range of legislation and case law. The controls can be categorised under six broad headings:

(a)   *personnel*: employment law might extend to minimum wages, sex and racial discrimination, dismissal, hours of work, redundancy payments, formal worker participation in Board decisions;

(b)   *operations*: laws might place restrictions on the operations of the organisation; for example, health and safety at work and product safety standards, the banning of dangerous materials or substances in products. In the case of the transport of goods, legislation might extend to permitted routes for lorries or maximum hours/distances per driver per day;

(c)   *marketing*: the selling of goods might be restricted by laws on the description of goods, sending unsolicited goods to customers, dangerous packaging, misleading advertising, weights and measures;

(d) *environmental*: certain products or production operations might be banned because they are damaging to mind and health, or pollute the environment. Major construction works (eg new power plants and oil pipelines) might be required to cater for protection of the environment. Organisations might be forbidden to pollute rivers, the air or land with dangerous effluent materials. There are likely to be continuing pressures from environmental and scientific groups for further legislation to protect the environment (eg to take steps to prevent acid rain or nuclear radiation and to restrict damage to the ozone layer);

(e) *finance*: legislation on financial matters involves, for instance, consumer credit. Taxation affects organisations in two ways:
   (i)   they act as tax collectors for the government (PAYE income tax, VAT);
   (ii) they pay tax to the government (corporation tax).
   There are also legal requirements to produce financial information (eg annual returns, annual report and accounts);

(f) *organisation*: legislation might affect the organisation structure of an organisation, eg by establishing the duties of directors of a company.

7.   An organisation may also act to prevent changes in the law from taking place. A well-publicised example is the success of the firearms manufacturers in the USA in preventing anti-gun legislation from being enacted. Other organisations have attempted to delay legislation which would affect their operations (eg cigarette manufacturers have successfully postponed anti-smoking legislation in the UK).

On a larger scale, national governments may be frustrated in their attempts to regulate the activities of multi-national companies by the fact that companies can switch their activities to other countries where similar legislation and controls do not exist.

• The social and ethical environment

8.   Whereas the political environment in which an organisation operates consists of laws, regulations and government agencies

> • the social environment consists of the customs, attitudes, beliefs and education of society as a whole, or of different groups in society; and
>
> • the ethical environment consists of a set (or sets) of well-established rules of personal and organisational behaviour.

9.   Social attitudes, such as a belief in the merits of education, progress through science and technology, and fair competition, are significant for the management of a business organisation. Other beliefs which have either gained strength or been eroded in recent years include the following.

(a) There is a growing belief in preserving and improving the quality of life by reducing working hours, reversing the spread of pollution, developing leisure activities etc. Pressures on organisations to consider the environment are particularly strong because most environmental damage is irreversible and some is fatal to humans and wildlife.

(b) Many pressure groups have been organised in recent years to protect social minorities and under-privileged groups. Legislation has been passed in an attempt to prevent racial discrimination and discrimination against women and disabled people.

(c) The conflict between 'them and us' - management and workers - has bedevilled British industry for many years and shows signs of abating only in restricted areas. To some extent, this view is the product of social attitudes which exist outside a particular work situation.

(d) There has possibly been some erosion in respect for authority.

(e) A growth in materialism and consumerism has meant that money is once again a very strong motivator.

10. The ethical environment refers to justice, respect for the law and a moral code. The conduct of an organisation, its management and employees will be measured against ethical standards by the customers, suppliers and other members of the public with whom they deal.

Ethical problems facing managers

11. Managers have a duty (in most enterprises) to aim for profit. At the same time, modern ethical standards impose a duty to guard, preserve and enhance the value of the enterprise for the good of all touched by it, including the general public. Large organisations tend to be more often held to account over this than small ones.

12. The types of ethical problem a manager may meet with in practice are very numerous. A few of them are suggested in the following paragraphs.

13. In the area of products and production, managers have responsibility to ensure that the public and their own employees are protected from danger. Attempts to increase profitability by cutting costs may lead to dangerous working conditions or to inadequate safety standards in products. In the United States, product liability litigation is so common that this legal threat may be a more effective deterrent than general ethical standards. The Consumer Protection Act 1987 is beginning to ensure that ethical standards are similarly 'enforced' in the UK.

14. The pharmaceutical industry is one where this problem is particularly acute. On the one hand managers may be influenced by a genuine desire to benefit the community by developing new drugs which at the same time will lead to profits; on the other hand, they must not skimp their research on possible side-effects in rushing to launch the new product. In the UK, the Consumer Protection Act 1987 attempts to recognise this dilemma. Drugs companies are not held liable for side-effects which could not have been foreseen by scientific knowledge as it existed at the time the drug was developed - the 'development risk' defence.

15. Another ethical problem concerns payments by companies to officials (particularly officials in foreign countries) who have power to help or hinder the payers' operations. In *The ethics of corporate conduct* Clarence Walton refers to the fine distinctions which exist in this area:

(a) *Extortion.* Foreign officials have been known to threaten companies with the complete closure of their local operations unless suitable payments are made.

(b) *Bribery.* This refers to payments for services to which a company is not legally entitled. There are some fine distinctions to be drawn; for example, some managers regard political contributions as bribery.

(c) *Grease money.* Multinational companies are sometimes unable to obtain services to which they are legally entitled because of deliberate stalling by local officials. Cash payments to the right people may then be enough to oil the machinery of bureaucracy.

(d) *Gifts.* In some cultures (such as Japan) gifts are regarded as an essential part of civilised negotiation, even in circumstances where to Western eyes they might appear ethically dubious. Managers operating in such a culture may feel at liberty to adopt the local customs.

16. Another difficult area for managers concerns the extent to which an organisation's activities may appear to give support to undesirable political policies. In modern times, the conspicuous example of this has been the apparent support given to apartheid by companies with South African trading links. Supermarkets find themselves under pressure not to stock South African fruit, and increasingly companies are quietly withdrawing from their South African links.

Examples of social and ethical objectives

17. However, companies are not passive in the social and ethical environment. Many organisations pursue a variety of social and ethical objectives. The following list is not comprehensive.

(a) For employees:
   (i) a minimum wage, perhaps with adequate differentials for skilled labour;
   (ii) job security (over and above the protection afforded to employees by government legislation);
   (iii) good conditions of work (above the legal minima);
   (iv) job satisfaction.

(b) For customers:
   (i) to provide a product of a certain quality at a reasonable price;
   (ii) to make products that should last a certain number of years (eg. for consumer durable goods).

(c) For suppliers, to offer regular orders in return for reliable delivery and good service.

(d) For shareholders, to remain independent and resist takeover offers.

(e) For society as a whole:
   (i) to control pollution, noise and smell;
   (ii) to provide financial assistance to charities, sports and community activities;
   (iii) to co-operate with government authorities in identifying and preventing health hazards in the products sold.

18. As far as it is possible, social and ethical objectives should be expressed quantitatively, so that actual results can be monitored to ensure that the targets are achieved. This is often easier said than done - more often, they are expressed in the organisation's mission statement which is rarely a quanitfied amount.

● **The social responsibility of organisations and managers**

19. It willbbe apparent from the preceding paragraphs that not only does the environment have a significant influence on the structure and behaviour of organisations, but also the organisation will have some influence on its environment.

20. Since organisations have an effect on their environment, it is arguable that they should act in a way which shows social awareness and responsibility.

> 'A society, awakened and vocal with respect to the urgency of social problems, is asking the managers of all kinds of organisations, particularly those at the top, what they are doing to discharge their social responsibilities and why they are not doing more.' (Koontz, O'Donnell and Weihrich)

21. Social responsibility is expected from all types of organisation, be they businesses, governments, universities and colleges, the church, charities etc.

   (a) Local government is expected to provide services to the local community, and to preserve or improve the character of that community, but at an acceptable cost to the ratepayers.

   (b) Businesses are expected to provide goods and services, which reflect the needs of users and society as a whole. These needs may not be in harmony - arguably, the development of the Concorde aeroplane and supersonic passenger travel did not contribute to the public interest, and caused considerable inconvenience to residents near airports who suffer from excessive aircraft noise. A business should also be expected to anticipate the future needs of society; an example of socially useful products might be energy-saving devices and alternative sources of power.

   Pollution control is a particularly important example of social responsibility by industrial organisations, and some progress has been made in the development of commercial processes for re-cycling waste material. British Coal attempts to restore the environment by planting on old slag heaps.

   (c) Universities and schools are expected to produce students whose abilities and qualifications will prove beneficial to society. One view of education, by no means universally shared, is that greater emphasis should be placed on vocational training for students.

   (d) In some cases, legislation may be required to enforce social need, for example to regulate the materials used to make crash helmets for motor cyclists, or to regulate safety standards in motor cars and furniture. Ideally, however, organisations should avoid the need for legislation by taking earlier self-regulating action.

● **Management as a profession**

22. If it is accepted that the managers of organisations should have certain social and ethical responsibilities, the next question is 'should there by a formal code of behaviour for managers, and if so, who should issue such a code?'

23. A code of social and ethical behaviour might be issued:
    (a) by a professional or management institution; or
    (b) by an organisation, as a guide for its own managers and employees.

24. Professional bodies such as those for accountants, lawyers and doctors issue and enforce a code of ethical conduct for their members. Breaches of the code are punishable, *in extremis*, by expulsion from the profession.

25. There is a view that, in a broader sense, management is a profession too, and managers of all organisations ought to share a common code of professional ethics. One such code in the UK has been issued by the British Institute of Management (BIM).

The BIM's Code of Conduct

26. A *Code of conduct* (and supporting *Guides to good management practice*) is published by the British Institute of Management and gives guidance on the ethical and professional standards required of BIM members.

27. According to the *Code* managers should:
    (a) comply with the law;
    (b) respect the customs and practices of any country in which they work as managers;
    (c) not misuse their authority or office for personal or other gains.

28. The supporting *Guides* lay down a number of professional ethics.

(a) In pursuing their personal ambitions, managers shall take account of the interests of others.

(b) Managers should never maliciously injure the professional reputation or career prospects of others, nor the business of others.

(c) Managers should make immediate and full declaration of any personal interests which may conflict with the interests of the organisation.

(d) Managers should be concerned in the working environment for the health, safety and well-being of all, especially those for whom they are responsible.

(e) Managers should respect the confidentiality of any information if so requested by customers and suppliers.

(f) Managers should neither offer nor accept any gift, favour or hospitality intended as, or having the effect of, bribery and corruption.

(g) Managers should ensure that all public communications are true and not misleading.

---

29. The need for this kind of ethical guidance may not be immediately obvious. You might think that adequate legislation exists to prevent any abuse of their position by managers. But professional standards go beyond compliance with the law to ensure that not even an appearance of unethical conduct is given. 'The law is a floor. Ethical business conduct should normally exist at a level well above the minimum required by law.'

30. It is not clear to what extent moral ethics will determine the decisions of management. An international survey reported in 1983 found that even with a published code of ethics, the business executive is still more likely to make the expedient rather than the moral decision. The problem, it appears, is 'group think' - a result of companies, especially multi-nationals, creating their own morality. A group of managers, especially when working closely together on an important project, tends to come to a consensus view of the world which may not always be the same as the views held by outsiders or be in accordance with society's normal codes of morality.

Codes of conduct issued by organisations themselves

31. If this is so, it would seem to follow that the imposition of social and ethical responsibilities on its management should come from within the organisation itself, and the organisation should issue its own code of conduct for its employees.

32. One such set of guidelines has been issued by United Biscuits plc as follows.

> "These 'guiding principles', taken in conjunction with our budget and strategic objectives, are important as a description of the way in which we operate.
>
> United Biscuits' business ethics are not negotiable - a well-founded reputation for scrupulous dealing is itself a priceless company asset and the most important single factor in our success is faithful adherence to our beliefs. While our tactical plans and many other elements constantly change, our basic philosophy does not. To meet the challenges of a changing world, we are prepared to change everything about ourselves except our values.
>
> Some employees might have the mistaken idea that we do not care how results are obtained, as long as we get results. This would be wrong: we do care how we get results. We expect compliance with our standard of integrity throughout the company, and we will support an employee who passes up an opportunity or advantage that can only be secured at the sacrifice of a principle.
>
> While it is the responsibility of top management to keep a company honest and honourable, perpetuating ethical values is not a function only of the chief executive or a handful of senior managers. Every employee is expected to take on the responsibility of always behaving ethically whatever the circumstances. Beliefs and values must always come before policies, practices and goals; the latter must be altered if they violate fundamental beliefs."

33. It is easier for a single 'family' organisation than it is for a large organisation to hold firmly to ethical beliefs, because there are fewer employees to give direction to. A published code of conduct, which has the backing of top management, is arguably needed for large organisations, in order to foster a proper sense of ethical and social behaviour.

● Stakeholder analysis

34. The 'stakeholder view' is a way of looking at an organisation's social responsibility which states that many different groups of people have a 'stake' in what the organisation does. From their various perspectives they have different objectives which they would like to see the organisation fulfil.

35. There are three broad types of stakeholder in an organisation, such as a company, as follows:

    (1) internal stakeholders - employees, management
    (2) connected stakeholders - shareholders, customers, suppliers, financiers
    (3) external stakeholders - the community, government, pressure groups.

    These types are indicated in the diagram below.

14.1 Stakeholders in a company

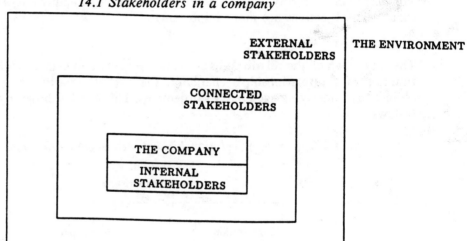

We shall consider each of them in turn.

36. *Internal stakeholders*
    Because employees and management (which includes the Chairman and the Board of Directors) are so intimately connected with the company, their objectives are likely to have a strong and immediate influence on how it is run.

37. *Connected stakeholders*
    The objective of shareholders - which is generally that of making a profit - is often taken as the prime objective which the company's management seeks to fulfil. But clearly financiers such as banks have similar objectives which must be met (usually the payment of loan interest is a contractual obligation whilst the payment of dividends is not), whilst the customer's objectives, in a market-led company, must also be fulfilled if the company is to be successful. Other stakeholders directly 'connected' with the company are suppliers, trade unions and distributors.

38. *External stakeholders*
    These groups - the government, local authorities, pressure groups, the community at large, professional bodies - are likely to have quite diverse objectives and have a varying ability to ensure that the company meets them.

39. How stakeholders relate to the management of the company depends very much on what type of stakeholder they are - internal, connected or external - and on the level in the management hierarchy at which they are able to apply pressure. Clearly a company's management will respond differently to the demands of, say, its shareholders and the community at large. This is because both the character of the relationship and the means by which the relationship is conducted depend on the relative bargaining power and philosophy of the stakeholder on the one hand and the company on the other.

40. The relationship may be characterised by a number of stances. Each party (stakeholder and company) may actively seek dominance or they may each adopt defensive roles. Ideally they should seek a balance of objectives but in turn this can mean that they may actively seek agreement or may merely react to circumstances as they arise. Hence the company and its employees/trade unions may have a relationship characterised by each party seeking dominance over the other, whilst with its customers the company may find itself reacting to the demands made of it by them. This shows that the ability to influence management does not necessarily arise from mere closeness to the company (employees are internal to the company but often the shareholders' and customers' objectives are more important).

41. The way in which the relationship between company and stakeholders is conducted again is a function of the relationship's character, the parties' relative bargaining strength and the philosophy underlying each party's objectives. This can be shown by means of a spectrum as follows.

14.2 Spectrum of relationship between organisation and stakeholders

			Stakeholders' bargaining strength			
Weak						Strong

| Company's
conduct
of
relation-
ship | Command/
dictat by
company | Consultation
and
consideration
of
stakeholders'
views | Negotiation | Participation
and
acceptance
of
stakeholders'
views | Democratic
voting by
stakeholders | Command/
dictat by
stakeholders |

Influence of stakeholders

42. Stakeholders can influence and constrain the management of the company at a number of different levels, which can be defined at the *strategic level* (the main mission and objectives of the company), the *planning level* (how those objectives are going to be met) and the *operations level* (how plans are put in practice day-to-day). But in addition management is constrained at every level by the legal environment in which it exists and the regulations with which it must comply. These can be said to arise from the objectives of the community at large and of the government, and can affect things such as employment rights, financial control and reporting, safety and environmental protection and the way in which competition is handled.

Strategic level

43. When deciding on the company's mission and objectives, and the strategies to be adopted in meeting them, the company's board will almost certainly be constrained primarily by the interests of the shareholders (profit) but also by those of the customers (price, variety,

reliability) and of other financiers (interest and capital repayments, value of security, value of shares). But the extent to which management has discretion to make profits for shareholders is itself constrained by the demands of customers for value and of financiers for reducing risk to their investment. A balance must clearly be reached.

44. The company must comply with identifiable constraints such as its statutory duty to exercise 'stewardship' over its shareholders' assets, its contractual duty to pay interest on loans and its legal duties regarding employment and environment protection. These may come into conflict with other stakeholders' interests and even with the company's preferred strategy such as to be 'market-led'.

45. Finally the company's strategy may be influenced by intangible constraints from the external stakeholders and the environment as a whole such as 'green' culture and concern for Third World development and good employment practices.

Planning level

46. In order to achieve objectives and ultimately fulfil the company's mission, the management must make tactical plans. These will be influenced to a greater or lesser extent by stakeholders.

   (a) *Customers'* demands will dictate decisions for investment in new products, development of existing ones and setting-up of new outlets. They will also affect the standards adopted for quality control, and the extent to which they can be enticed away by competitors' products will affect the planned advertising spend.

   (b) *Suppliers'* and *distributors'* demands will affect the timing and amount of production, the amount of raw material and finished goods stock held and hence the financial planning which allows production to take place.

   (c) *Employees'* attitudes and objectives will greatly affect the organisation and co-ordination required to put production plans into effect. Construction of departments and work groups, job design, workflow and the amount of training undertaken will all be matters in which management will have to take the employees' stake into account.

   (d) *Specialised or professional employees* have two sets of priorities - their jobs, and the requirements of their professional bodies. The management must be careful not to bring these two into conflict, say by asking a qualified construction engineer to operate with untrained staff.

   (e) *Trade unions* represent employees *en masse* and seek to ensure that pay, terms and conditions of employment, disciplinary and grievance procedures and employment protection policies are formulated with the employees in mind. Management will have to consider these and will have to involve unions in the planning process in order to preserve good industrial relations.

   (f) *Legislation, regulations and the community at large.* At the planning level management discretion can be contrained by a great number of restrictions which are put in place to protect the community as a whole. Examples are planning restrictions on a construction company, pollution controls on a chemical works and disclosure requirements for a financial services group.

Operations level

47. Clearly many of the constraints affecting management at the strategic and planning levels will also filter down to the running of day-to-day operations. Certainly consumers will affect production aims (size, quality, colour) and procedures (planning, stockholding, computerisation etc) when demand is variable (as in the fashion and high-tech industries). Health and safety legislation for employees and consumer protection legislation also mean that day-to-day operations must be constantly reviewed for compliance.

• Management responsibilities

48. Management is be responsible not only to the organisation's owners (shareholders) but also to:

   (a)   employees;
   (b)   customers;
   (c)   suppliers;
   (d)   competitors;
   (e)   the local community; and
   (f)   the general public (and government).

Responsibilities to employees

49. An organisation's broad responsibilities to its employees are well set out by United Biscuits plc as follows:

> To achieve the dynamic morale and team spirit based on mutual confidence without which a business cannot be successful, people have to be cared for during their working lives and in retirement. In return we expect from all our staff loyalty and commitment to the company. We respect the rights and innate worth of the individual. In addition to being financially rewarding, working life should provide as much job satisfaction as possible. The company encourages all employees to be trained and developed to achieve their full potential.
>
> United Biscuits takes a responsible attitude towards employment legislation requirements and codes of practice, union activities and communications with staff.
>
> We place the highest priority on promoting and preserving the health and safety of employees. Employees, for their part, have a clear duty to take every reasonable precaution to avoid injury to themselves, their colleagues and members of the public.

50. General principles have to be converted into practice, and should take the form of good pay and working conditions, and good training and development schemes. They should also extend into:

   (a)   recruitment policy;
   (b)   redundancy and retirement policies.

51. *Recruitment* of new staff should be done as carefully as possible, because if an organisation recruits an individual who turns out to be bad at his job the company has to sack him. Dismissals will be inevitable in any large organisation, but careful recruitment methods should manage to keep such demoralising incidents down to a small number.

52. Staff who are about to retire, after years of service with the organisation, should be provided for in their *retirement*.

    (a) The organisation might have a good pension scheme.

    (b) One of the problems for retired people is learning what to do with their leisure time. Some organisations provide training courses and discussion groups for employees who are coming up for retirement, to help them to plan their future time constructively.

53. Dealing with *redundancies* is a more difficult problem. Even for organisations which show an ethical sense of responsibility towards their employees, there may be occasions when parts of the business have to be closed down, and jobs lost. In such a situation, the organisation:

    (a) should try to redeploy as many staff as possible, without making them redundant; and
    (b) where necessary, should provide retraining to give staff the skills to do their new job.

54. For those staff who *are* made redundant, the organisation should take steps to help them to get a job elsewhere. Measures could include:

    (a) counselling individuals to give them suggestions about what they might try to do;

    (b) providing retraining, or funds for training, in other skills which the employees could use in other organisations and industries;

    (c) arranging 'job fairs', by inviting other employers to come and display the jobs that they have on offer, and to discuss job opportunities with redundant employees;

    (d) providing good redundancy payments, which employees might be able to use to set up in business themselves or which at least should tide them over until they find employment again.

Responsibilities to customers

55. Ethical responsibilities towards customers are mainly those of providing a product or service of a quality that customers expect, and to deal honestly and fairly with customers.

56. The guidelines of United Biscuits plc again provide a good example of how these responsibilities might be expressed.

UB's reputation for integrity is the foundation on which the mutual trust between the company and its customers is based. That relationship is the key to our trading success.

Both employees and customers need to know that products sold by any of our operating companies will always meet their highest expectations. The integrity of our products is sacrosanct and implicit in the commitment is an absolute and uncompromising dedication to quality. We will never compromise on recipes or specification of products in order to save costs. Quality improvement must always be our goal.

No employee may give money or any gift of significant value to a customer if it could reasonably be viewed as being done to gain a business advantage. Winning an order by violating this policy or by providing free or extra services, or unauthorised contract terms, is contrary to our trading policy.

Responsibilities to suppliers

57. The responsibilities of an organisation towards its suppliers are expressed mainly in terms of trading relationships.

    (a) The organisation's size could give it considerable power as a buyer. One ethical guideline might be that the organisation shouldn't use its power unscrupulously (say to force the supplier to lower his prices under threat of withdrawing business).

    (b) Suppliers might rely on getting prompt payment in accordance with the terms of trade negotiated with its customers. Another ethical guideline is that an organisation should not delay payments to suppliers beyond the agreed credit period.

    (c) All information obtained from suppliers and potential suppliers should be kept confidential.

    (d) All suppliers should be treated fairly, and this means:

        (i) giving potential new suppliers a chance to win some business; and also

        (ii) maintaining long-standing relationships that have been built up over the years with some suppliers. Long-established suppliers should not be replaced unless there is a significant commercial advantage for the organisation from such a move.

Responsibilities to competitors

58. Some ethical responsibilities should exist towards competitors.

> "We compete vigorously, energetically, untiringly but we also compete ethically and honestly. Our competitive success is founded on excellence - of product and service. We have no need to disparage our competitors either directly or by implication or innuendo....
>
> No-one may attempt improperly to acquire a competitor's trade secrets or other proprietary or confidential information. 'Improper' means are activities such as industrial espionage, hiring competitors' employees to get confidential information, urging competitive personnel or customers to disclose confidential information, or any other approach which is not completely open and above board."
>
> (United Biscuits plc)

Responsibilities towards the community

59. An organisation is a part of the community that it serves, and it should be responsible for:

    (a) upholding the social and ethical values of the community;

    (b) contributing towards the well-being of the community, eg by sponsoring local events and charities, or providing facilities for the community to use (eg sports fields);

    (c) responding constructively to complaints from local residents or politicians (eg about problems for local traffic caused by the organisation's delivery vehicles).

• Public relations and corporate image

60. The Institute of Public Relations defines the role of public relations (PR) as 'a planned and sustained effort to establish and maintain mutual understanding between an organisation and its public.'

    A large organisation is likely to have a PR department, and smaller companies might hire the services of a PR agency to perform the same function for them. PR is a form of boundary within which management must act because it is always better to have good relations with the public than bad. This can involve doing something which is good for PR and/or not doing something which is bad.

61. An important element of public relations is publicity. Publicity can be a useful selling aid, depending on:

    (a) the newsworthiness of any item;
    (b) relations between the public relations department and the news media; and
    (c) the item's credibility.

62. Publicity is often relatively inexpensive in comparison with the cost of advertising. The need for publicity probably varies significantly from industry to industry. The tourist trade, for example, relies heavily on publicity to attract customers, whereas a small industrial firm might restrict its interest in PR and publicity to the locality of its factories and offices (as a local employer, a firm ought to be conscious of its relationship with the local community).

63. The role and purpose of a PR department are:

(a) to obtain favourable publicity for the organisation, usually through the national and local press or television, and to prevent adverse publicity. The publicity sought is through an 'independent' channel, and is not paid for – advertising and sales promotions are paid for by an organisation, and would not normally be handled by PR staff;

(b) in some cases, to obtain a high profile for the organisation in the public mind;

(c) to arrange for the announcement of events to the news media. For example, if one company decided to take over another company, its PR department would call a press conference to announce the event, and hope to obtain widespread coverage;

(d) to provide information about new products – eg by inviting the press to a 'product launch';

(e) to establish a good working relationship with journalists and other news reporters, so that 'official leaks' to the press can be made through favoured contacts;

(f) to deal with all other relations with the press (except for advertising matters) – eg most public companies will arrange to pay for the inclusion of their shares in the price lists in the *Financial Times*;

(g) to liaise with the customer relations department about the response of customers to the organisation's products and services;

(h) to produce the in-house journal and be responsible for all internal communications of this type – eg distributing to employees statements made by the MD or chairman;

(i) if appropriate, to organise exhibitions and visits by the general public to the organisation's premises;

(j) to be involved, perhaps, in sponsored events paid for by the company (eg sports events, many of which are now sponsored);

(k) to lobby the government and other authorities for decisions which would be of benefit to the organisation; and

(l) to identify and perhaps to establish a relationship with stakeholder groups (eg environmental groups, local interest groups etc) with a view to establishing a communications link for liaising with them.

Corporate image

64. Corporate image describes the public attitude towards a company, or the image of the company in the mind of the general public, and perhaps more specifically in the minds of potential customers. It is possible to promote a desired corporate image through a combination of PR,

advertising and the experience and attitudes built up by customers over the years (for example, the favourable corporate image of Marks and Spencer grew up over the years, without the need for excessive PR or advertising).

65. There are various reasons why an organisation might attempt to build up a corporate image.

   (a) The organisation may want to strengthen customer loyalty, and so a corporate image of good quality products and services, and concern for the customer's interests, could be fostered. British Home Stores, for instance, have successfully built up such an image in recent years, partly through advertising.

   (b) Rather than strengthen customer loyalty, a corporate image might be developed to create customer awareness. Some companies have faced the problem that customers do not know what they are, and have never heard of them. A corporate image is then needed to give the company a public identity (eg fairly recently, Racal plc spent large sums advertising itself as one of the largest companies no one had ever heard of).

   (c) Corporate image can strengthen an employee's attachment to the company he or she works for, because of corporate identity. People may want to work for a company because of its image in the mind of the public ('prestige' jobs) or because the company has a 'get-ahead' image.

   (d) Some companies may wish to develop a corporate image of social responsibility, in order to avoid unfavourable legislation, to prevent adverse publicity or to prevent pressure from stakeholder groups. Examples of this motive are:

   (i)   the attempt by oil companies to establish an image of care for the environment and for the future needs of society;
   (ii) the attempt by British Nuclear Fuels to promote an image of deepest concern for the safety of nuclear waste;
   (iii) the attempt by fur traders to counter the adverse publicity built up against them by the efforts of animal rights activists; and
   (iv) the efforts of independent TV companies to promote an image of 'quality' programme-makers, to strengthen their chances of winning a bid for franchises.

   (e) Some companies may wish to have a favourable corporate image which they can subsequently use to win public and political support. For example, the corporate image of Land Rover as a successful and very British manufacturer of a quality product was used in 1986 to stir up public and political support against a takeover by the US company General Motors.

   (f) A good corporate image has a variety of benefits for management, in addition to strengthening customer loyalty. An image of a sound, well-established company might encourage investors to put more money into the business, and suppliers to grant longer credit.

66. As mentioned above, the most commonly used methods of communicating information about a company and company image are:

   (a) public relations (PR); and
   (b) advertising, especially TV advertising, although this is expensive.

231

Market research by MORI has shown that:

(a) two out of every three people in the UK believe that a company which has a good reputation would not sell poor quality products (this suggests that customers would be more willing to try a new product if it is promoted by a well-known corporate name than if it is made by an unknown company); and

(b) nine times out of ten, the better known a company is, the more highly it is regarded.

67. In an article on the subject, the *Financial Times* made the following interesting comments about corporate advertising:

> 'Anyone who doubts the efficacy of corporate messages might consider the famous McGraw-Hill advertisement which features a daunting company executive who asks: "I don't know who you are. I don't know your company. I don't know your company's product. I don't know what your company stands for. I don't know your company's customers. I don't know your company's reputation. Now - what was it you wanted to sell me?"
>
> Some industries have learnt the corporate lesson. Banks and building societies have shown consistent commitment to pushing the corporate 'brand' ... remember 'the listening bank', 'the action bank' and 'a thoroughbred among banks'?
>
> Before them, the oil companies knew well the dividends reaped by keeping the public informed. They handled a messy product which carried a pollution risk, involved an unsightly production process and had a premium price tag (as customers saw it). Which is why Shell, BP, Esso, Mobil and the rest have kept up a constant public information programme.'

68. A popular way for UK companies to project a corporate image is to identify itself with an animal - on the basis that British people love animals more than anything else. Hence we have the Esso tiger, the Peugeot lion and the black horse of Lloyds Bank. In 1989, Woolworth plc adopted the name 'Kingfisher', the qualities of this bird being deemed appropriate in some way to represent the organisation's corporate objectives. Moreover, it was felt necessary to get away from the much-loved but essentially downmarket image associated with the threepenny store's name.

● **Accountability of management**

69. Social responsibility, which is desirable in theory, is not easily achieved in practice, because managers are commonly judged by a different set of results - profits, sales growth, market share, earnings per share etc - and not in terms of achievements for society. After all, why should company A incur high costs on improving the safety standards of its product when a competitor, company B, does not spend any money on such improvements, and would therefore be able to undercut company A's prices on the market?

70. Managers are unlikely to act with proper responsibility unless they are made accountable for what they do. Social and ethical responsibilities are unlikely to be anything more than fine words and phrases unless managers are judged according to their achievements.

71. If an organisation sets its own social and ethical guidelines, managers should be given objectives to achieve, and actual performance should be measured against those objectives in a formal system of control reporting. For example, any manager found guilty of a breach of the code of conduct should be reprimanded, or other disciplinary measures should be taken against him.

72. Social responsibility is to some extent forced on managers by the wishes of consumers.

> *Consumerism* has been defined (by Mann and Thornton) as a 'social movement seeking to augment the rights and powers of buyers in relation to sellers up to the point where the consumer is able to defend his interests'.

73. Aspects of business activity on which consumer organisations have focused include:

- dangerous products (such as cigarettes and the content of car exhaust emissions);
- dishonest marketing or promotion. In the UK there is legislation designed to deal with this kind of abuse;
- the abuse of power by organisations which are large enough to disregard external constraints and even government pressure;
- the availability of information. Consumers are anxious, for example, to be informed of any artificial additives in foodstuffs.

The accountability of managers in the public sector

74. Social responsibility ought to be particularly important for the management of public sector organisations, such as local authorities, and it could be argued that management in central or local government ought to be accountable, not just to their political 'bosses' but also to the general public.

75. However, the concept of checks and balances in the British Constitution results in a system of government in which no single department or agency is entirely responsible for anything. Several different departments will always be involved, none of them entirely responsible for the tasks in hand and so none of them fully accountable. It is all too easy to 'pass the buck' and blame another department when members of the general public complain.

76. Some examples of shared responsibilities, and so the lack of management accountability to the public, were described in an article by Richard C Carr in the *Administrator* (January 1988).

    (a) *Education.* Local authorities build schools and employ teachers. Central government sets rules about how education should be provided and even what should be taught. Because central government provides much of the finance for schools, it can also put indirect pressure (the threat of refusing to give payments of grants) on local authorities. And what 'powers' do school governors have to direct the running of their school?

    (b) *Police.* Similarly, the police are employed by local authorities to enforce laws made mainly by central government. Police activity is constrained by decisions of the courts and the local chief constable of police is also answerable to a police authority.

(c) *Gypsy encampments*. The article described a problem in Cambridgeshire with unauthorised gypsy encampments, and public complaints about them. County councils have a duty to provide official encampments, but local residents near such proposed sites complain. The costs of developing official sites are paid for by central government. District councils have to manage the sites, and are also involved as planning authorities. The police, county highway authority and district council environment health officers and planning officers are all involved in dealing with or acting against unauthorised encampments. Central government might issue instructions that dwellers on unauthorised encampments should not be harrassed. So who should members of the general public complain to, with a demand for action?

77. The points being made here are that:

(a) management might only feel socially responsible, in the long run, if they are held accountable;

(b) how can managers be made accountable to the public? For private companies, we have seen that accountability can be achieved through the exercise of law, or adverse public reaction and the threat of lost customer demand. For public sector organisations, however, where social responsibility *ought* to be strong, management might choose to escape their responsibility by passing the blame on to someone else. Responsibility does not lie with just one department, nor even just one organisation.

QUIZ

1. List some of the social and ethical objectives that an organisation might pursue.

    ● See para 3

2. What are the legal constraints affecting management?

    ● See paras 6-7

3. What ethical problems face management?

    ● See paras 11-16

4. To whom does management arguably have responsibilities, and what are some of those responsibilities?

    ● See paras 19-21

5. What are the professional ethics of the British Institute of Management?

    ● See para 28

6. What is stakeholder analysis?

    ● See paras 34-38

7. At what levels do stakeholders influence an organisation?

    ● See paras 42-47

8. What responsibilities have managers to persons other than their organisation?

    ● See paras 48-59

9. What is the role of the PR department?

    ● See para 63

SECTION 4

MANAGEMENT SKILLS AND FUNCTIONS

Topics covered in this section

- Chapter 15:   Functions of management
- Chapter 16:   Organising
- Chapter 17:   Co-ordination
- Chapter 18:   Leadership
- Chapter 19:   Organisational culture
- Chapter 20:   Business development
- Chapter 21:   Personnel management: manpower resourcing
- Chapter 22:   Personnel management: training, appraisal and termination
- Chapter 23:   Personnel management: developing teamwork
- Chapter 24:   Management communication skills
- Chapter 25:   Management of professionally qualified staff
- Chapter 26:   Business planning: objectives
- Chapter 27:   Business planning: strategic management
- Chapter 28:   The international perspective

Objectives of this section

This section builds on the material covered in Section 3 (Principles of Management) to discuss the functions of management and how they can be carried out in business organisations.

Chapter 15

FUNCTIONS OF MANAGEMENT

Topics covered in this chapter

- The role of managers
- The functions of management: Fayol
- The management process: Drucker
- Being a manager: Handy
- Managerial roles: Mintzburg

Purpose of this chapter

To introduce some views of the functions of management and the manager's role, as a foreword to this section of the text.

• The role of managers

1. In broad terms, the collective role of managers in an organisation is:

    (a) to act on behalf of the owners of the organisation. In a company, these are the shareholders, to whom the senior management should ultimately be accountable;

    (b) to set objectives for the organisation;

    (c) to achieve those objectives through the process of managing; and

    (d) to sustain corporate values in their dealings with other organisations, customers, employees and the general public.

2. In a public sector organisation, management acts on behalf of the government and its 'political masters'. Politicians in a democracy are in turn accountable to the general public. A possible difference of some importance between public and private sector organisations is that some of the objectives of a public sector organisation might be set by the 'owners' - the government - rather than by the management. The government might also tell senior management to carry out certain policies or plans, thereby restricting management's discretion.

3. As just one example, when the UK government in 1988 announced its plans to privatise the electricity industry:

    (a) not all managers in the industry agreed with the government's objective/policy of denationalising the industry; and

    (b) the chief executive of the industry was reported to disagree strongly with major points of detail in the plan for privatisation, which the government was imposing on the industry's senior management.

4. Given some such differences, though, the role and functions of management in both the private and public sectors are similar.

5. It is worth emphasising one of the roles of managers - and all employees - *is to sustain corporate values*. This is an aspect of management which can easily be overlooked. In United Biscuits plc's handbook for its staff on the company's ethics and operating principles it is stated that:

    > 'A company is more than a legal entity engaged in the production and sale of goods and services for profit. It is also the embodiment of the principles and beliefs of the men and women who give it substance; it is characterised by guiding principles which define its view of itself and describe the values it embraces. Such values have, for our company, existed implicitly for very many years - United Biscuits is what it is and as good as it is because a great many individuals over a long period of time have contributed their own best efforts to preserving and enhancing the values that cause it to endure'.

    We shall look at managerial roles in more detail later in this chapter.

● **The functions of management**

6. The process of management and the functions of management have been analysed many times in various ways by different writers, who have taken the view that:

    (a) management is an operational process, which can be understood by a close study of management functions;

    (b) the study of management should then lead to the development of certain principles of good management, which will be of value when put into practice.

7. Henri Fayol, the French management theorist working in the early decades of this century, listed the functions of management as follows:

    (a) <u>Planning</u>. This involves selecting objectives and the strategies, policies, programmes and procedures for achieving the objectives either for the organisation as a whole or for a part of it. Planning might be done exclusively by line managers who will later be responsible for performance: however, *advice* on planning decisions might also be provided by 'staff management' who do not have 'line' authority for putting the plans into practice. Expert advice is nevertheless a part of the management planning function.

(b) Organising. This involves the establishment of a structure of tasks which need to be performed to achieve the goals of the organisation, grouping these tasks into jobs for an individual, creating groups of jobs within sections and departments, delegating authority to carry out the jobs, providing systems of information and communication and co-ordinating activities within the organisation.

(c) Commanding. This involves giving instructions to subordinates to carry out tasks over which the manager has authority for decisions and responsibility for performance.

(d) Co-ordinating. This is the task of harmonising the activities of individuals and groups within the organisation, which will inevitably have different ideas about what their own goals should be. Management must reconcile differences in approach, effort, interest and timing of these separate individuals and groups. This is best achieved by making the individuals and groups aware of how their work is contributing to the goals of the overall organisation.

(e) Controlling. This is the task of measuring and correcting the activities of individuals and groups, to ensure that their performance is in accordance with plans. Plans must be made, but they will not be achieved unless activities are monitored, and deviations from plan identified and corrected as soon as they become apparent.

8. Fayol's analysis of management functions is only one of several similar types of analysis. Other functions which might be identified, for example, are *staffing* (filling positions in the organisation with people), *leading* (unlike commanding, 'leading' is concerned with the impersonal nature of management) and *acting as the organisation's representative* in dealing with other organisations (an ambassadorial or public relations role).

> Some theorists reject Fayol's argument that managers are commanders, and argue instead that they are persuaders and motivators.

● Drucker on the management process

9. Peter Drucker worked in the 1940s and 1950s as a business adviser to a number of US corporations. He was also a prolific writer on management. Drucker grouped the operations of management into five categories:

(a) *Setting objectives for the organisation.* Managers decide what the objectives of the organisation should be and quantify the targets of achievement for each objective. They must then communicate these targets to other people in the organisation.

(b) *Organising the work.* The work to be done in the organisation must be divided into manageable activities and manageable jobs. The jobs must be integrated into a formal organisation structure, and people must be selected to do the jobs.

(c) *Motivating* employees and communicating information to them to enable them to do their work.

(d) *The job of measurement.* Management must:
   (i)   establish objectives or yardsticks of performance for every person in the organisation;
   (ii) analyse actual performance, appraise it against the objectives or yardsticks which have been set, and analyse the comparison;
   (iii) communicate the findings and explain their significance both to subordinate employees and to superiors.

(e) *Developing people.* The manager 'brings out what is in them or he stifles them. He strengthens their integrity or he corrupts them'.

---

10. Every manager performs all five functions listed above, no matter how good or bad a manager he is. A bad manager performs these functions badly, whereas a good manager performs them well. Drucker emphasised the importance of *communication* in the functions of management, which should be evident in items (a), (c) and (d) above.

11. Drucker has also argued that the manager of a business has a basic function of management - economic performance. In this respect, the business manager is different from the manager of any other type of organisation. Management of a business can only justify its existence and its authority by the economic results it produces, even though as a consequence of their actions, significant non-economic results occur as well.

12. He then described the jobs of management within this basic function of economic performance as follows. (It is worth noting in particular the inclusion of *innovation* in this list. Innovation will be discussed in Chapter 20.)

   (a) *Managing a business.* The purposes of the business are:
      (i)   to create a customer; and
      (ii) innovation;

   (b) *Managing managers.* The requirements here are:
      (i)   management by objectives;
      (ii)   proper structure of managers' jobs;
      (iii) creating the right spirit in the organisation;
      (iv)   making a provision for the managers of tomorrow;
      (v)   arriving at sound principles of organisation structure;

   (c) *Managing worker and work.*

13. A manager can improve his performance in all areas of management, including management of the business, by a study of the principles of management, the acquisition of 'organised knowledge' (eg management techniques) and the systematic appraisal of his own performance in all aspects of his work, at whatever level of management this happens to be.

14. The three jobs in paragraph 12 are carried out within a time dimension.

   (a) Management must always consider both the short-term and longer-term consequences of their actions. A business must be kept profitable into the long-term future, but at the same time short-term profitability must be maintained to avoid the danger that the long term will never be reached, and the business liquidated or taken over.

   (b) Decisions taken by management are for the future, and some have a very long 'planning horizon' - the time between making the decision and seeing the consequences of that decision can be very long. For example, if a decision is made to build a factory, it might be years before the building is erected, equipped and in operation, and years more before it earns sufficient profits to pay back the investment.

● **Being a manager: the views of Handy**

15. Charles Handy suggested that a definition of a manager or a manager's role is likely to be so broad as to be fairly meaningless. His own analysis of being a manager was divided into three aspects:

   ● the manager as a general practitioner;
   ● managerial dilemmas; and
   ● the manager as a person.

16. <u>The manager as a general practitioner</u>. A manager is the first recipient of an organisation's health problem and he must:

   (a) identify the symptoms in the situation (eg low productivity, high labour turnover, severe industrial relations problems etc);
   (b) diagnose the disease or cause of the trouble;
   (c) decide how it might be dealt with by developing a strategy for better health; and
   (d) start the treatment.

17. Typical strategies for health were listed as:

   (a) *People:* changing people, either literally or figuratively, by:
      (i) hiring and firing;
      (ii) re-assignment;
      (iii) training and education;
      (iv) selective pay increases;
      (v) counselling or admonition;

   (b) *The work and the structure:*
      (i) re-organisation of reporting relationships;
      (ii re-definition of the work task;
      (iii) job enrichment;
      (iv) re-definition of roles;

(c) *The systems and procedures:* to amend or introduce:
  (i) communication systems;
  (ii) rewards systems (payment methods, salary guides);
  (iii) information and reporting systems;
  (iv) budgets or other decision-making systems (eg stock control, debtor control).

18. <u>The managerial dilemmas</u>. Managers are paid more than workers because they must face some constant dilemmas which have to be resolved, and it is management's job to resolve them. These dilemmas are:

(a) the dilemma of the cultures. It is management's task to decide which culture of organisation and management is required for his particular task. As a manager rises in seniority, he will find it necessary to behave in a culturally diverse manner to satisfy the requirements of his job and the expectations of his employees. In other words, managers must be prepared to show flexibility and good judgement in their choice of organisation culture.

The manager 'must be flexible but consistent, culturally diverse but recognisably an individual with his own identity. Therein lies the dilemma. Those ... who relapse into a culturally predominant style will find themselves rightly restricted to that part of the organisation where their culture prevails. Middle layers of organisations are often overcrowded with culturally rigid managers who have failed to deal with this cultural dilemma';

(b) the dilemma of time horizons. This is the problem of responsibility for both the present and the future at the same time, described above in paragraph 14(a);

(c) the trust-control dilemma. This is the problem of balance between management's wish to control the work for which they are responsible, and the necessity to delegate work to subordinates, thereby trusting them to do the work properly. The greater trust a manager places in subordinates, the less control he retains himself. Retaining control implies a lack of trust in subordinates. 'The managerial dilemma is always how to balance trust and control';

(d) the commando leader's dilemma. In many organisations, junior managers show a strong preference for working in project teams, with a clear task or objective, and working outside the normal bureaucratic structure of a large formal organisation. Unfortunately, there can be too many project groups (or 'commando groups') for the good of the total organisation, and a manager's dilemma is to decide how many project groups he should create to satisfy the needs of his subordinates, and how much bureaucratic organisation structure should be retained for the benefit of the total organisation despite the wishes of his subordinates.

19. <u>The manager as a person</u>. Management is developing into a 'semi-profession' and managers expect to be rewarded for their professional skills. The implications for individual managers are that 'increasingly it will come to be seen as the individual's responsibility to maintain, alter or boost his skills, to find the right market for his skills and to sell them to the appropriate buyer'. In other words, management must continue to develop their own professional skills and sell them to the best bidder.

20. The dilemmas of management help to explain why the process of managing might often seem easy in theory, but is more complex in 'real life'.

21. When a manager faces problems or dilemmas, his or her subordinates are bound to suffer too. In an article in the *'Administrator'* (Jan 1987), Sarah Rookledge describes the findings of an American report entitled: *'Working Well: Management for Health and High Performance'*.

    The report pointed out particular management traits which were held responsible by workshop interviewees for causing stress and health problems (eg high blood pressure - hyper-tension - insomnia, coronary heart disease and alcoholism). These included:

    (a) unpredictability. Staff work under constant threat of an outburst;
    (b) destruction of workers' self esteem - making them feel helpless and insecure;
    (c) setting up win/lose situations - turning work relationships into a battle for control;
    (d) providing too much - or too little - stimulation.

22. In British research, according to the same article, managers are criticised for:
    (a) not giving credit where it is due;
    (b) failing to communicate policy or involve staff in decisions;
    (c) supervising too closely; and
    (d) not defining duties clearly enough.

    The most 'harmful' style is said to be 'leave alone and zap' - where the employee (frequently young and inexperienced) is given a task, left without guidance, and then 'zapped' with a reprimand or punishment when mistakes are discovered. This simply creates a vicious circle of anxiety and guilt.

The functions of management: summary of theories

23. | In summary, the functions of management can be analysed (depending on your views) as planning, controlling, organising, commanding, motivating, staffing, communicating, acting as representative for the organisation, co-ordinating and developing people. |
    | --- |

24. Some theorists have suggested that managers can be efficient if they apply certain techniques or philosophies, and the scientific management school and the behavioural school of thinking were early contrasting approaches towards being an efficient and effective manager.

25. However, managing isn't so easy in practice, and at the end of this chapter some case studies will illustrate aspects of the problem.

● Managerial roles

26. Mintzburg suggests that, as well as performing certain functions, the manager also fulfils certain *roles* in an organisation. He identifies three types of role which a manager must play.

    (a) *Interpersonal* roles, which arise from the manager's formal authority, include:

        (i) the *figurehead* or ceremonial role: a large part of a Chief Executive's time is spent representing the company at dinners conferences etc.;

(ii) the *leader* role involves hiring, firing and training staff, motivating employees, and reconciling individual needs with the requirements of the organisation;

(iii) the *liaison* role, rarely mentioned in many management texts, is what managers perform when making contacts outside the vertical chain of command. Some managers spend up to half their meeting time with their peers rather than with their subordinates and as such are the ambassadors of the departments they control. They need to know what is happening in other departments to act accordingly. Senior managers may spend a great deal of time with people outside their organisation. Mintzburg says that the purpose of these contacts is to build up an informal information system, but at the same time they are a means of extending influence both within organisations and outside.

(b) *Informational* roles. As a leader, a manager has access to every member of staff, and is likely to have more external contacts than any of them. A manager's liaison contacts means that he or she is a channel of information from inside the department to outside and vice versa. Mintzburg, in an article published in the Harvard Business Review in 1975 states:

"The manager does not leave meetings or hang up the telephone in order to get back to work. In a large part communication *is* his work."

Mintzburg identifies three types of informational role.

(i) The manager *monitors* the environment, and receives information from subordinates or peers in other departments. Note that much of this information is of an informal nature, derived from his or her network of contacts. It might be gossip or speculation.

(ii) The manager *disseminates* information, which he or she has acquired both formally through the vertical chain of command and informally through the network of contacts, to subordinates in the department.

(iii) As a *spokesman* the manager provides information to interested parties, either within or outside the organisation.

(c) *Decisional* roles. The manager's formal authority and access to information means that no one else is in a position to take decisions relating to the work of the department.

(i) A manager acts as a sort of *entrepreneur* by initiating projects, quite possibly of a small scale, a number of which may be on the go at any one time, to improve the department or to help it react to a changed environment.

(ii) A manager has to respond to pressures over which the department has no control. A manager is therefore a *disturbance handler*, taking decisions in unusual situations which are impossible to predict.

(iii) A manager takes decisions relating to the *allocation of scarce resources*. The manager determines the department's direction, and authorises decisions taken by subordinates.

(iv) *Negotiation* both inside and outside the organisation takes up a great deal of management time, but is a vital component of managerial work.

27. Mintzburg was led to draw a number of conclusions about certain assumptions relating to managerial work.

    (a) The belief that a manager is a reflective and systematic planner is a myth. Managerial work is disjointed and discontinuous; planning is conducted on a day to day basis, in between more urgent tasks.

    (b) Another myth is that a manager has no regular or routine duties to perform, as these have been delegated to juniors. Mintzburg discovered that managers perform a number of routine duties, particularly of a ceremonial nature (eg receiving important guests).

    (c) It has often been assumed that managers need aggregated information which they can best obtain from a formal management information system. Mintzburg's research indicated that managers prefer *verbal* communication. Information conveyed by word of mouth in an informal way is likely to be more 'current' and also more concrete and thus easier to grasp.

    (d) Mintzburg says that management cannot be a science or even a profession, as "A science involves the enaction of systematic analytically determined procedures or programs. If we do not even know what procedures managers use, how can we describe them by scientific analysis? And how can we call management a profession when we cannot specify what managers are to learn?

28. Mintzburg states that general management is, in practice, a matter of judgement and intuition, gained from experience in particular situations rather than from abstract principles.

    "The manager is ... forced to do many tasks superficially. Brevity, fragmention and verbal communication characterise his work."

    His chief criticism of management science is that it has only concentrated on ideas that are easily susceptible to scientific analysis.

QUIZ

1. Outline the collective role of managers in an organisation.

   ● See para 1

2. What are the functions of management according to Henri Fayol?

   ● See para 7

3. Drucker saw the operations of management as being grouped into five categories. What are they?

   ● See para 9

4. According to Handy, how can managers solve problems to do with people, the work and its structure and the systems and procedures in an organisation?

   ● See para 17

5. What are the managerial roles as outlined by Mintzburg?

   ● See para 26

Chapter 16

ORGANISING

Topics covered in this chapter

- Organising
- Personal organisation and time management
- Organising others
    - Work planning and allocation
    - Follow-up systems
- Introduction to decision-making

Purpose of this chapter

To draw together various aspects of organising already mentioned in this text, with the addition of certain techniques for enhancing organisational efficiency.

To introduce decision-making as the basis of all management functions.

● Organising

1. This chapter draws together strands which have been covered elsewhere in this text.

"If *planning* is considered as providing the route map for the journey, then *organising* is the means by which you arrive at your chosen destination. Plans.... are statements of intent, of direction and of resourcing required. To put intentions into effect requires purposeful activity, and this is where the organising function of management comes in. Organising, above all, is concerned with activities."

Cole: *Management Theory and Practice*

---

2. Organising is not the same as 'organisation', which is the actual grouping or network of relationships, but is the *process* whereby organisation is formed and put into action. Organising involves:

    (a) identifying, grouping and giving structure to the activities the organisation needs to perform in pursuit of its objectives (forming functions, departments etc);

    (b) determining 'roles' which will be needed for the performance of those grouped activities (allocating responsibility for functional areas);

    (c) delegating authority and establishing accountability for performance; and

    (d) devising systems, procedures and rules for efficient working.

3.   We have already looked at:

- the grouping of tasks – that is, organisation structure: specialisation, centralisation or decentralisation, line and staff relationships etc (Chapters 2, 11)
- the structure of tasks (job design) (Chapter 11)
- the allocation of responsibility and accountability (Chapter 11)
- systems for organisation, eg communication, control etc (Chapters 12, 13)

4.   In this chapter we will look briefly at additional areas in which the manager can be more effective:

- *personal* organisation or time management; and
- work organisation.

5.   The emphasis of the revised 2.5B *'Effective Management'* paper is to focus on the role of the individual manager rather than dealing with management in general terms. In Chapter 13 we saw how managers plan and control performance, and in this chapter we shall look at how a good manager approaches his function of organising himself and the work and people for which he has responsibility.

• Personal organisation and time management

6.   A manager's use of his time is affected by a number of factors, such as:

    (a) the nature of his job;
    (b) his own personality; and
    (c) his work environment.

7.   *The nature of the job.* A manager's job involves regular contact with other people in the organisation. It is important to ensure that the inevitable interruptions which this causes are not allowed to encroach too much upon the supervisor's time. Keeping a detailed time diary is a common method of highlighting the amount of time taken up by interruptions and may suggest ways of reducing them.

8.   Typical causes of wasted time in a manager's job might be prolonged or unnecessary meetings with colleagues or the preparation of unnecessary paperwork (which could be replaced with a brief oral communication). Managers should be on their guard against this and should consider whether such meetings and paperwork can be dispensed with.

9.   *The personality of the manager.* In one respect this is linked with the previous heading; a manager whose personality is confident and assertive will be better able to resist interruptions than one who is diffident.

10. Other suggestions under this heading include:

   (a) Do work which is difficult and requires concentration at times when interruptions are least likely, perhaps very early in the morning or late in the afternoon. Some people find that they work better in the morning than in the evening, or vice versa, and this should also be taken into account.

   (b) Cultivate an organised and methodical approach, finishing one task before beginning on the next.

   (c) Set appropriate personal targets which will contribute to the goals of the organisation.

11. *The influence of colleagues.* Colleagues are defined as including superiors and subordinates as well as fellow managers.

   (a) Although communication skills are important in a manager's job, the need to avoid unnecessary and time-wasting communication (say in prolonged meetings) has already been mentioned.

   (b) A superior who interferes too much in the manager's job can be very disrupting. Tact in warding off such attention can be a valuable attribute.

12. *The work environment.*

   (a) The physical surroundings in which a person works may affect his use of time. Even if a manager does not have an office of his own, he should try to appropriate a reasonably quiet area where concentrated work can be carried out without interruptions.

   (b) Trips to the photocopier or to computer terminals should be minimised, particularly if they are housed in distant parts of the building.

   (c) Fixed procedures and red tape can be time-consuming. Managers should try to minimise the time they spend on merely complying with laid-down procedures, without cutting corners that might lead to lower quality of output.

Improving personal organisation

13. Ways in which managers can improve their own personal organisation include:

   (a) personal planning, in conjunction with detailed goal-planning or target setting;

   (b) willingness to delegate tasks to staff who are competent to perform them;

   (c) developing necessary skills in communication, gaining the co-operation of others, leadership (assertiveness) etc;

   (d) cutting down on time-wasting activities, eg unnecessary or lengthy meetings and paperwork, and interruptions.

14. Other pointers for improving personal efficiency include:

(a) *ensuring that resources are available*, in sufficient supply and good condition. This may involve setting up or adhering to procedures for stock control etc. (Do YOU know when your paper or ink is about to run out *before* it happens?);

(b) *ensuring that resources are to hand* (not buried under irrelevant files or items, litter etc. on a desk or work bench, nor 'somewhere else'). *Tidiness* is important for efficiency in the office as well as for the organisation's image: files and pieces of work should be easily locatable at all times (and should in any case never be left lying around, as a breach of security, fire hazard etc);

(c) *organising work in batches*, while relevant files are to hand, machines switched on etc. to save time spent in turning from one job to another;

(d) *working to plans, schedules, checklists etc.* This means:
   (i) not relying on memory alone for appointments, events and duties;
   (ii) working on one thing at a time, and finishing each task you start;
   (iii) not putting off large, difficult or unpleasant tasks simply because they are large, difficult or unpleasant. 'Never do today what you can put off till tomorrow' is *not* a good motto; today's routines will be tomorrow's emergencies, and today's emergencies will *still* be tomorrow's emergencies (and usually won't go away!);
   (iv) learning to anticipate and allow for work coming up; recognising and setting reasonable deadlines;

(e) *taking advantage of work patterns*. Self-discipline is aided by developing regular hours or days for certain tasks: getting into the habit of dealing with correspondence first thing, filing at the end of the day, (Christmas shopping in October?) etc. If you are able to plan your own schedules, you might also take into account your personal 'patterns' of energy, concentration, alertness etc. Large or complex tasks might be undertaken in the mornings before you get tired, or perhaps late at night with fewer distractions, while Friday afternoon is not usually a good time to start a demanding task in the office.

(f) *following up tasks* - seeing them through. Uncompleted work, necessary future action, expected results or feedback etc. should be scheduled for the appropriate time. Checklists are also useful for making sure an operation is completed, marking the stage reached in case it has to be handed over to someone else (because of illness, holiday etc.) or temporarily laid aside (because of higher priority interruptions).

● **Organising others**

15. As well as organising himself and his time so that his work gets done and he sets an example for his subordinates, the effective manager must also organise the work of others.

Work planning

16. 'Work planning', as the term implies, means planning how work should be done and establishing work methods and practices to ensure that predetermined objectives are efficiently met at all levels. Work planning provides a basis for:

(a) the scheduling and allocation of *routine* tasks - giving them to appropriate individuals and machines, for completion at appropriate times;

(b) the handling of *high priority* tasks and deadlines - working into the routine urgent tasks which interrupt the usual level of working;

(c) adapting to changes and unexpected demands - being prepared for emergencies, as far as possible;

(d) standards for working against which performance can be measured;

(e) the co-ordination of individual and combined efforts.

17. Basic steps in work planning include:

(a) the establishment of priorities (considering tasks in order of importance for the objective concerned);

(b) scheduling or timetabling tasks, and allocating them to different individuals within appropriate time scales. (For example, there will be continuous routine work, and arrangements for priority work with short-term deadlines);

(c) establishing checks and controls to ensure that:
   (i)   priority deadlines are being met and work is not 'falling behind';
   (ii) routine tasks are achieving their objectives;

(d) 'contingency plans' for unscheduled events. Nothing goes exactly according to plan, and one feature of good planning is to make arrangements for what should be done if a major upset were to occur, eg. if the company's computer were to break down, or if the major supplier of key raw materials were to go bust. The major upsets for which *contingency* plans might be made are events which, although unlikely, stand a not-impossible chance of actually happening.

18. 'Routine' priorities, such as regular peak times (the monthly issue of account statements, yearly tax returns etc.) can be planned ahead of time, and other tasks postponed or redistributed around them. 'Non-routine' priorities occur when unexpected demands are made: events 'crop up', perhaps at short notice, or errors are discovered and require corrective action. Thus planning of work should cover:

(a) routine: regular volumes of work achieved by established procedures to regular time scales;

(b) scheduled peaks: workloads will be higher at predictable 'busy periods' eg. for retailers at Christmas, for accountants at the end of each accounting period. Extra staff may be employed, work re-scheduled etc for these times;

(c) unscheduled peaks and emergencies: a special conference, product launch, marketing drive etc. are all outside the normal cycle of peaks and troughs in an organisation's activities, but plans could still be made to accommodate the extra work. Unexpected events, which cannot be planned for, may include machine breakdown, staff illness, or environmental factors (suppliers going bust, unanticipated action by competitors etc.). Backup plans for *likely* contingencies should be made (eg. contacts with temporary employment agencies and alternative suppliers, maintenance contracts on machinery).

Work allocation

19. It will be the job of those in authority - at organisational or departmental level - to divide duties and allocate them to available staff and machinery: departmental managers will have an overall understanding of the nature and volume of work to be accomplished, and the resources at their command.

20. Planning is essential in this division of labour, because although there are some obvious allocations eg. of specialist tasks to specialists (computer programmers, engineering draughtsmen etc), others may be more complicated.

    (a) Functions such as filing and reprography may not be centralised, and may not have the attention of a 'dedicated' employee. A small volume of filing may not require a 'filing clerk' for the department: who will do the work, and will it interfere with their other duties?

    (b) Peak periods in some tasks may necessitate re-distribution of staff to cope with the work load; there should be flexibility in who does, and is able to do, various non-specialist tasks. It is quite usual for staff to be pulled off one job and asked to help out somebody else who has a pile of work on his or her plate that needs clearing.

    (c) Status and staff attitudes must be considered. A hierarchical organisation structure with job grades and different levels of authority and seniority can work towards efficiency, providing close control, motivation etc. but it can also cause planning problems. Flexibility in reassigning people from one job to another or varying the work they do may be hampered by an employee's perception of his own status: 'helping out' or 'covering for' others may be out of the question: 'I'm a secretary, not a copy typist!' etc. Planning must take into account experience and seniority in allocating tasks, but it must also recognise that junior employees may desire and expect challenges and greater responsibility, and may leave if bored and frustrated.

    (d) Individual abilities and temperaments differ, and work should be allocated to the best person for the job. This may not be immediately obvious: some staff like routine work but crack under pressure, and vice versa; some are good with machines, some with people etc. Planning should allow for flexibility in the event of an employee proving unfit for a task, or more able than his present tasks indicate.

    (e) Efforts will have to be co-ordinated so that all those involved in a process (eg. sales orders) work together as a team. If the team is large, sub-groups may be formed (usually according to activity or skill eg. mail order and customer accounts, clerks and typists) for closer supervision and sense of unity. Work-sharing will also be more flexible for a unit with common skills and experience, so similar skills should be grouped together.

    (f) The hierarchy must function efficiently. There should be suitable team leaders, supervisors etc. to ensure control throughout the organisation, without an unmanageable span of control or waste of managerial time.

Follow-up systems

21. Control over work must be maintained to ensure that jobs do in fact reach completion, and if those jobs involve various tasks over varying periods, it will be necessary to keep track of future events, deadlines, results etc.

22. Systems which provide for this are also called 'bring forward' or 'bring up' systems: they can be operated in a diary, card index or file. Anything which needs action at a later date (and therefore may get forgotten) should be processed in this way:

(a) checking on progress of an operation;
(b) checking completion when the deadline is reached;
(c) checking payments when they fall due;
(d) action which may be delayed until more information has been gathered (eg. a report requested by management);
(e) retrieving files relevant to future discussions, meetings, correspondence.

Diary entries may be made on appropriate days eg.

'Production completed?'
'Payment received?'
'Bring forward file x'
'One week left for revision'

Alternatively, concertina files or file folders may be used for notes of action required, which are stored under the appropriate date, and retrieved as each day arrives.

A central file registry may use a card index system of 'bring forward slips' consulted each day for files to be brought forward.

● Introduction to decision-making

23. A decision may be defined as 'a formal judgement' or 'resolving to carry out a particular course of action'. In a business sense, a decision is usually the result of choosing between uncertainties. Often a decision is taken on the grounds of future projections and therefore is subject to uncertainty and risk. In this way it can be seen that the decision-making process is one involving value judgements and risk-taking.

24. The earliest management authors highlighted decision-making as one of the key differences between management and workers. Henri Fayol (1841-1925) included decision-making as one of the main functions of management. This remains true today in that decision-making is still the prerogative of management. Whether a manager is dealing with people, supervising production or quality or clerical staff, or whether he is involved in capital expenditure, it is inevitable that decision-making will be an important part of his job.

25.
> Managers are expected to act within their responsibilities and to take such decisions as necessary which fall within their scope of authority.

Therefore, only matters which cannot be adequately dealt with by a manager should be referred to more senior management. Thus, decisions taken at a higher level in a company should be of a senior character and broad in influence.

Principle of exception

26. The concept of making decisions within the manager's prescribed area of responsibilities is known as the *principle of exception*.

> This principle states that each manager carries out the duties allocated to him and will make such decisions as are necessary which fall within his scope of authority. Only when decisions are required which lie outside his authority would he be expected to call in higher authority. This is extended into the principle of *management by exception*, whereby a manager is informed when the results do not accord with the plan and some decision or corrective action is necessary. This means that a manager can concentrate on matters requiring attention and not duplicate the efforts of others on matters which are proceeding according to plan.

27. There are many theories of decision-making which have been proposed by management authors. Basically they fall into two main categories

    (a) *Scientific decision-making* depends on the quantitative techniques of management. In this way, attempts are made to measure and express all viable alternatives. This approach depends upon the view that full and complete information will lead to the 'ideal solution'. It is generally agreed that this is an over-simplification and ignores individual flair or 'hunch'. It should be recognised that many management decisions have to be taken in haste without the luxury of time in which to evaluate alternatives. If the manager were to postpone taking a decision until he obtained further information, he would be abdicating his responsibility. It is frequently necessary that a speedy decision be taken, otherwise events will continue to evolve and will enforce a decision which may not be the right one. Similarly, subordinates need decisions to be taken speedily or they will be unable to make progress in their areas.

    (b) *Reaction decisions theory* assumes that once policies and corporate plans are established, decisions that are required follow as a natural result of those plans. In this way, decision-making is regarded as an extension of the process of implementing corporate plans. Decisions therefore are partly predetermined by the detail of the plans.

28. In real life situations, both approaches are used, often in unison. Decisions are usually made on the basis of facts but individual judgement will also be a major ingredient.

Types of decision

29. Managers are employed to make decisions. There are different ways of categorising decisions. One useful analysis of decisions is into five categories.

    (a) *Routine planning decisions;* typically, budgeting and scheduling.

    (b) *Short-run problem decisions;* typically, decisions of a non-recurring nature. For example, a manager might have to deal with a staff problem, or give instructions to a subordinate about what to do next.

    (c) *Investment or disinvestment decisions.* For example, should an item of equipment be purchased? Should a department be shut down? Decisions of this nature often have long-term consequences.

    (d) *Longer-range decisions;* decisions made once and reviewed infrequently, but which are intended to provide a continuing solution to a continuing or recurring problem. Shillinglaw (1963) calls these 'quantitative policy decisions', and they include decisions about selling and distribution policies (eg. Should goods be sold through middlemen or direct to customers? What type of customer should the sales force attempt to attract? What should the company's discount policies be? Should a company employ its own delivery fleet, or should it hire contractors for distribution? Should a new product or service be launched? Should an additional shift be established in order to raise production levels to meet growing sales demand?).

(e) *Control decisions;* decisions about what to do when performance is disappointing and below expectation.

30. Decisions are needed to resolve problems, when there is a choice about what to do. Problems vary, not just according to what they are about, but also according to:

- how easy or complex they are to resolve;

- how frequently they arise;

- whether the problem can be quantified, or whether there are qualitative matters of judgement involved;

- how much information is available to help the manager to make the decision;

- how serious the consequences would be if a bad decision were made;

- whose job it is to make the decision about how to deal with it.

QUIZ

1. Distinguish between organising and organisation.

   ● See para 2

2. On what factors does the efficient use of managerial time depend, and how can efficiency be improved?

   ● See paras 6-14

3. What are the basic steps in work planning?

   ● See para 17

4. Name 3 types of follow-up system for work planning.

   ● See para 22

5. Briefly describe scientific and reaction decision-making.

   ● See para 27

Chapter 17

CO-ORDINATION

Topics covered in this chapter

- Co-ordination and integration
- Difficulties in achieving co-ordination
- Conflict
  - ○ Argument, competition and conflict
  - ○ Constructive and destructive conflict
  - ○ Causes and symptoms of conflict
  - ○ Managerial response to conflict
- Improving co-ordination
- Encouraging integration
- Conclusion on co-ordination and integration

Purpose of this chapter

To indicate the need for the co-ordination and integration of tasks, workflows, functions and structures, and to suggest how problems of co-ordination can be overcome.

● Co-ordination and integration

1. | Co-ordination is the process of integrating the work of different individuals, sections and departments in an organisation towards the effective achievement of the organisation's goals.

2. Co-ordination is vital so that:

   (a) the *timing* of activities is 'synchronised' for maximum usage of labour, machine hours and effort. If the buying of raw materials is 'behind' when Sales is creating huge demands for production, or if raw materials are coming in and the Production department is churning out products which Sales have no orders for, then frustration and wastage will occur. Scheduling is vital, as is anticipation of how long a procedure should take, and must be allowed to take (eg. Stock Control ensures that Purchasing fills a stock deficiency *before* the panic stage arrives; Production Control anticipates demand and gets things moving in advance so as to avoid alternating periods of bottlenecks and idle time);

(b) the *direction* of activities (allocation of human, money and material resources) is planned for maximum efficiency and effectiveness. Overall objectives should not be forgotten. Think back to the first things we noticed about organisations: they are a grouping together of individuals and their resources towards a common goal. If the efforts of individuals are not united, or are 'pulling' in different directions, those efforts will be wasted or even counter-productive: if the Marketing department is trying to 'sell' an 'upmarket' image of the company's products, while the production department is committed to increasing profit by cutting down on frills, packaging etc. and concentrating on cheap production, then efforts in both departments are counter-productive;

(c) service or staff functions (DP, Personnel, Office services etc.) provide the basis and backup for the line departments of production, marketing and finance, so that they can meet objectives. Legal proceedings, the processing of data for decision-making, recruitment of key employees, typing of documents, retrieval of a filed record - these are all 'service' activities that may affect speed, cost and quality of the production or marketing operations that are the main activity of the organisation;

(d) control procedures can be implemented for comparing actual with desired results: are all necessary tasks being performed in the most efficient and effective way?

● **Difficulties in co-ordination**

3. There are various reasons why co-ordination might be difficult to achieve.

(a) There might be poor communications both horizontally and vertically within the organisation.

(b) Different departments and managers may have varying views as to the plans for the organisation. They may be pursuing different objectives and have different priorities.

(c) Time pressures can vary between different parts of the organisation.

(d) Differences in leadership style can mean that two departments may have very different ways of doing things and very different time pressures to work under.

(e) Organisation structure may hinder co-ordination - particularly where there is a complex or matrix management structure.

(f) Interpersonal or interdepartmental jealousies and dislike can prevent co-ordination and cause conflict.

Signs of inadequate integration are
1. Persistent conflict between departments
2. Fudging integration issues through a proliferation of committees
3. Overloading top management with problems to resolve
4. The use of 'red tape' to try to ensure that integration does take place
5. Empire-building by co-ordinators
6. Complaints by clients, customers and other external parties (eg customers being told different things by different departments).

Reasons for lack of co-ordination
1. Poor communications
2. Inadequate system of planning and objective setting
3. Different groups work under different time pressures
4. Differences in leadership style
5. Weak organisation structure
6. Inter-departmental or inter-personal dislikes and rivalries - ie conflicts
7. Problems of integrating 'line' and 'staff' departments
8. Difficulties in creating an effective management team with people from different disciplines - eg a production management team must bring together people with technical skills (engineering, quality control), financial skills (budgetary control, cost reduction), personnel skills (recruitment and training) and planning skills (production planning).
9. In an organisation which must be innovative in response to environmental changes, there may be problems in promoting innovation - that is integrating innovation specialists into the mainstream of the organisation.

4. Let's now look at some of these reasons for lack of co-ordination in more detail. Some are discussed elsewhere in Chapter 2 on formal structure (eg the integration of line and staff), in Chapter 12 on communication (eg the need for communication, the use of committees as co-ordinating devices) and in Chapter 18 on leadership.

5. There might be *poor communications* both horizontally and vertically within the organisation:

(a) different departments might fail to communicate with each other properly;
(b) superiors and subordinates might communicate badly.

Poor communications are a symptom of conflict, as discussed later.

6. Management might *fail to provide a plan* for the organisation which is acceptable to everyone within the organisation. Different departments, for example, might have different views about how the goals of the organisation will best be achieved. The sales department might wish to satisfy customers by providing a wide range of products on time and adjusted to customer specifications, whereas the production department might seek economies of scale through standardisation of products, a limited production range and longer production run; the accounting department might emphasise the paramount importance of cost control etc. The goal of the sales department (high sales and customer satisfaction) the goal of the production department (lower unit costs) and the goal of the accounting department (keeping within budget) would then be difficult to reconcile.

7. It is difficult to co-ordinate the tasks and workflows of different departments and groups which work under *differing time pressures*.

   (a) The operational departments of a business have to produce output quickly and regularly. Decisions need to be taken for a speedy implementation. In contrast, a research and development department will carry out much of its work on projects which might take years to finish, so that the time pressures are not as great, planning and control might be very flexible, and the concern of the department will be for long-term profitability of the business rather than the short term.

   (b) Sometimes, it might be necessary to integrate the work of two groups which work to different time pressures. An example would be the implementation of a new computer system into an operational department, where the system has been designed by a project group over a number of years. The project group might be responsible for supervising the introduction of the system into operational working, and there might be problems of co-ordination because the project group will be used to working without severe time pressures, whereas the operational department will be concerned that the implementation of the system should not disrupt its work schedules and efficiency. Staff in the operational department might even claim that they do not have time, because of work pressure, to learn the new system adequately, and cannot afford to 'waste time' listening to members of the project group.

8. Co-ordination problems might be aggravated by *differences in leadership style*. If the manager of department X is strictly authoritarian, whereas the manager of department Y is democratic and encourages the interest and participation of subordinates in decision-making, it might be difficult for members of department X to co-operate efficiently with members of department Y. They will be used to different ways of doing things, and different timescales for getting a job done: these differences might well cause breakdowns in communication and therefore a failure to achieve a properly co-ordinated effort.

9. Moreover, leadership style may well determine the extent to which organisational goals and individual goals are perceived to be integrated. A manager adhering to McGregor's Theory Y achieves results by integrating the individual's needs and the organisation's requirements of him: 'Authority is an inappropriate means for obtaining commitment to objectives. Other forms of influence - help in achieving integration for example - are required for this purpose.'

10. Co-ordination also depends on the design of the *organisation structure*. It will be easier for section A to co-ordinate its efforts with section B if they are in the same department, with the same immediate superior. Where close organisational ties within the scalar chain of command are not practicable, methods of promoting co-ordination between different functional groups include:

    (a) a matrix management structure. For example, a product manager might be responsible for co-ordinating the efforts of functional groups dealing with development and design, production, manpower, purchasing, sales, marketing, distribution and warehousing;

    (b) the use of inter-disciplinary project teams - groups of staff drawn from different departments or regions;

    (c) the use of committees - representatives of the different departments whose efforts must be co-ordinated.

● Conflict

11. As a co-ordinator and integrator, a manager should be able to reconcile differences of opinion. Handy defined organisations as political systems where there are scarce resources and unequal influences. He identified three ways in which differences are expressed:

    (a) by *argument*: this is the constructive exchange of ideas with the positive intention of reaching an agreement;

    (b) by *competition*:

        (i) *constructive* competition between individuals or groups has the beneficial effect of:
            1   setting or improving standards of achievement;
            2   stimulating activities;
            3   sorting out the good, successful employees from the bad, unsuccessful ones;

        (ii) *harmful* competition occurs when one person or group can only do well at the expense of another; this is known as 'zero-sum' competition, because if one person gains, another loses an equal amount. Competition for resources, recognition and better results, if zero-sum, will degenerate into conflict;

    (c) by *conflict*.

Argument

12. *Argument* means resolving differences by discussion; this can encourage integration of a number of viewpoints into a better solution. Handy suggests that in order for argument to be effective:

    (a) the arguing group must have shared leadership, mutual trust, and a challenging task; and

    (b) the logic of the argument must be preserved - the issues under discussion must be classified, the discussion must concentrate on available information, and the values of the individuals must be expressed openly and taken into account.

    > Otherwise, argument will be frustrated. If this is so, or if the argument itself is merely the symptom of an underlying, unexpressed conflict, then conflict will be the result.

Competition

13. *Competition* can:
    (a) set standards, by establishing best performance through comparison;
    (b) motivate individuals to better efforts; and
    (c) sort out the 'sheep from the goats'.

14. In order to be fruitful, competition must be *open*, rather than *closed*; or, rather, must be *perceived* by the participants to be open, rather than closed.

    > 'Closed' competition is a win-lose (or 'zero-sum') situation, where one party's gain will be another party's loss. One party can only do well at the expense of another, in competition for resources, recognition etc. 'Open' competition exists where all participants can increase their gains - eg. productivity bargaining.

Conflict

15. The final, and often the most common, way in which differences are resolved in an organisation is by conflict. The first thing to remember is that conflict is not necessarily a 'bad thing'. We can see this by looking at three views of organisations and the conflict that exists in them – the 'happy family' view, the 'conflict' view and the 'evolutionary' view.

The 'happy family' view of organisations

16. This view presents organisations as:

    (a) co-operative structures, designed to achieve agreed common objectives, with no systematic conflict of interest; and

    (b) harmonious environments, where conflicts are exceptional and arise from:

        (i)   misunderstandings;
        (ii) personality factors;
        (iii) the expectations of inflexible employees; or
        (iv) factors outside the organisation and its control.

17. This kind of view is reasonably common in managerial literature, which attempts to come up with training and motivational techniques for dealing with conflicts which arise in what are potentially 'conflict-free' organisations.

18. Conflict is thus blamed on bad management, lack of leadership, poor communication, or 'bloody-mindedness' on the part of individuals or interest groups that impinge on the organisation. The theory is that a strong culture, good two-way communication, co-operation and motivational leadership will 'eliminate' conflict.

19. The 'happy family' view starts from a belief in 'social order' or 'industrial peace': conflict is a threat to stability, and must be avoided or eradicated.

The conflict view of organisation

20. In contrast, there is the view of organisations as inherently being arenas for conflict on individual and group levels. Members battle for limited resources, status, rewards, professional values etc. Organisational politics involve constant struggles for control, and choices of structure, technology and organisational goals are part of this process. Individual and organisational interests will not always coincide.

21. The extreme form of this perspective is the Marxist view, which is that:

    (a) organisations are one of the 'theatres of war' in which the class struggle is fought. Within an organisation, this war may have different 'fronts' - eg. industrial democracy, wages, equal opportunities, health and safety;

    (b) the organisation is the home of the bourgeoisie - opponents of the working class;

(c) organisational conflict is part of an inevitable struggle, as long as some own and control the means of production, and others do not.

22. This view still colours many people's perspective on trade unionism, big business, the worker/management divide etc. It starts from a belief that 'social order' or 'industrial peace' are themselves the problem: conflict is a way of instituting necessary revolutionary change.

> "The history of all hitherto society is the history of class struggles. Freeman and slave, patrician and plebeian, lord and serf, guildmaster and journeyman, in a word, oppressor and oppressed, stood in constant opposition to one another, carried on an uninterrupted, now hidden, now open fight ..."
> Marx and Engels. *The Communist Manifesto* (1888)

The evolutionary view of organisations

23. This view regards conflict as a means of maintaining the status quo, as a useful basis for evolutionary - rather than revolutionary - change. Conflict keeps the organisation sensitive to the need to change, while reinforcing its essential framework of control. The legitimate pursuit of competing interests can balance and preserve social and organisational arrangements.

> A flexible society benefits from conflict because such behaviour, by helping to create and modify norms, assumes the society's continuance under changed conditions.

24. This 'constructive conflict' view may perhaps be the most useful for managers of organisations, as it neither:

(a) attempts to dodge the issues of conflict, which is an observable fact of life in most organisations; nor

(b) seeks to pull down existing organisational structures altogether.

25. Ideology apart, managers have to get on with the job of managing, maintaining society as a going concern, and upholding organisational goals with the co-operation of other members. We will therefore look more closely at the idea of 'managing' conflict.

Constructive and destructive conflict

26. Given that conflict is inevitable, and assuming that organisational goals are broadly desirable, there are two aspects of conflict which are relevant in practice to the manager.

(a) Conflict can be highly desirable. It can energise relationships and clarify issues. Hunt suggests that conflict is constructive, when its effect is:

  (i)   to introduce different solutions to problems;
  (ii) to define power relationships more clearly;
  (iii) to encourage creativity, the testing of ideas;
  (iv) to focus attention on individual contributions;
  (v)   to bring emotions out into the open; or

(vi) to provide opportunity for catharsis - the release of hostile feelings etc that have been, or may be, repressed otherwise.

(b) Conflict can also be destructive, or negative (injurious to social systems, which the radical perspective regards as desirable). Hunt suggests that conflict of this kind may act in a group of individuals:

(i) to distract attention from the task;
(ii) to polarise views and 'dislocate' the group;
(iii) to subvert objectives in favour of secondary goals;
(iv) to encourage defensive or 'spoiling' behaviour;
(v) to result in disintegration of the group;
(vi) to stimulate emotional, win-lose conflicts, that is hostility.

Causes and symptoms of conflict

27. Conflict may be caused by lack of integration in the *objectives* of different groups or individuals. It is a function of management:

(a) to create a system of planning whereby individual or group objectives are formulated within the framework of a strategic plan. A poor planning structure leaves the door open for conflict to enter where formal objectives, roles, authority relationships etc overlap or are unclear; and also

(b) to provide leadership, and to encourage individuals to accept the goals of the organisation as being compatible with their personal goals. Poor leadership might also lead to conflict, with the goals of individuals of groups diverging and at odds with each other.

28. Conflict may also be caused by poor structural co-ordination in the shape of disputes about the *boundaries of authority*. For example:

(a) staff managers may attempt to encroach on the roles or 'territory' of line managers and usurp some of their authority;

(b) one department might start 'empire building' and try to take over the work previously done by another department.

29. According to Handy, the observable symptoms of conflict in an organisation will be:

(a) poor communications, in all 'directions';
(b) interpersonal friction;
(c) inter-group rivalry and jealousy;
(d) low morale and frustration; and
(d) proliferation of rules, norms and myths; especially widespread use of arbitration, appeals to higher authority, and inflexible attitudes towards change.

Managerial response to conflict

30. Hunt identifies five different management responses to the handling of conflict - not all of which are effective:

- *Denial/withdrawal*, or 'sweeping it under the carpet'. If the conflict is very trivial, it may indeed 'blow over' without an issue being made of it, but if the causes are not identified, the conflict may grow to unmanageable proportions.

- *Suppression* - 'smoothing over', to preserve working relationships despite minor conflicts. As Hunt remarks, however: "Some cracks cannot be papered over".

- *Dominance* - the application of power or influence to settle the conflict. The disadvantage of this is that it creates all the lingering resentment and hostility of 'win-lose' situations.

- *Compromise* - bargaining, negotiating, conciliating. To some extent, this will be inevitable in any organisation made up of different individuals. However, individuals tend to exaggerate their positions to allow for compromise, and compromise itself is seen to weaken the value of the decision, perhaps reducing commitment.

- *Integration/collaboration*. Emphasis must be put on the task, individuals must accept the need to modify their views for its sake, and group effort must be seen to be superior to individual effort. Not easy.

---

31. Handy suggests two types of strategy which may be used to turn conflict into competition or argument, or to manage it in some other acceptable way.

   (a) *Environmental ('ecological') strategies*. These involve creating conditions in which individuals may be better able to interact co-operatively with each other: they are wide-ranging, time-consuming, and unpredictable, because of the sheer range of human differences. Such strategies involve:

   (i) agreement of common objectives;
   (ii) reinforcing the group or 'team' nature of organisational life, via culture;
   (iii) providing feedback information on progress;
   (iv) providing adequate co-ordination and communication mechanisms;
   (v) sorting out territorial/role conflicts in the organisational structure.

   (b) *Regulation strategies*. These are directed to control conflict - though in fact they make it so much a part of the formal structure of the organisation that they tend to legitimise and even perpetuate it. Possible methods include:

   (i) the provision of arbitration to settle disputes;
   (ii) the establishment of detailed rules and procedures for conduct by employees;
   (iii) appointing a person to 'manage' the area of conflict - a liaison/co-ordination officer;
   (iv) using confrontation, or inter-group meetings, to hammer out differences, especially where territorial conflicts occur;
   (v) separating the conflicting individuals; and

(vi) ignoring the problem, if it is genuinely likely to 'go away', and there is no point in opening fresh wounds.

● **Improving co-ordination**

32. Co-ordination can be improved by the following methods.

(a) Good communication (formal and informal).

(b) Controlling conflict.

(c) An organisation structure which is designed so that where there will be a need for two departments to integrate their activities, a co-ordinating level of management exists to ensure that their work harmonises properly. By delegating responsibility for co-ordination, conflicts which escalate up to head of department or board level should be avoided.

(d) The organisation structure might provide for the appointment of *liaison* or *integration* officers. One example is the product manager in a matrix management structure, who co-ordinates the efforts of different departments so as to ensure the profitability and successful performance of the product or product range for which he is responsible.

(e) Co-ordination might be achieved through the appointment of:
 (i) committees, or
 (ii) project groups,
 which include representation from all departments whose work needs to be co-ordinated.

(f) Friendly, informal communication between managers of different departments should be built up. This might enable managers to co-ordinate their activities more effectively in the absence of any formal system or procedures for the integration of efforts.

(g) The system of planning and control within the organisation should recognise the need for integration of different departmental interests in the pursuit of organisational goals. In the preparation of a formal plan (eg a budget) managers should try to reach an understanding and agreement on how their efforts should be formally co-ordinated towards a common purpose.

● **Encouraging integration**

33. In *A behavioural theory of the firm* Richard M Cyert and James G March described their belief that a firm is a system adapting and responding to a variety of internal and external constraints. It is not monolithic. Its organisation is composed of a number of departments with diverse interests. The people concerned with the firm include managers, workers, shareholders, suppliers, customers, lawyers, auditors, tax collectors etc all of whom have differing interests. Decisions cannot be made without all their respective interests being taken into account, so *management must recognise the need to integrate the work and goal-directions of many different people and groups.*

34. It has already been suggested that management must act to provide an adequate communication system and to reduce conflict within the organisation. It is also possible to improve the co-ordination of efforts by the creation of *teams*.

(a) *Planning* within the organisation is more likely to be properly integrated if there is a long-term corporation plan. A corporate planning team acting in an advisory role, and as communicators, should help to co-ordinate this planning effort.

(b) *Innovation*: project teams (often inter-disciplinary) may be created to introduce changes into the organisation. Such teams should have a liaison manager (or several managers) whose job is to 'sell' the change to other members of the organisation and to act as a bridge between the team and the people who will be affected by the change.

A further feature of project teams may be that membership will vary throughout its life; new members will be brought in to lend temporary expertise, and released back to their department when their part of the task is done.

Some managers 'specialise' in change and new ideas - eg operational researchers, and systems analysts. These people should be trained to deal with the human aspect of innovation, and must be aware that their job includes the task of integration, so that their ideas are accepted by the people who must put them into practice.

(c) *Production*: a frequent problem for foremen is uncertainty about the authority of 'staff' experts, such as quality control managers, production planning and control management, work study engineers, the storekeeper, the management accountant etc. Many specialist functions are involved in production - production managers themselves, and also planning, finance and personnel departments. To co-ordinate the efforts of the different specialists, an organisation might use a production committee.

(d) *Professional services*: in local government, there are sometimes difficulties in co-ordinating the activities of different professional services, such as doctors, psychiatrists and social workers. A team or committee of professional experts might be established for the purpose of integrating their efforts.

35. Teams are covered in more detail in Chapter 23. Innovation is discussed further in Chapter 20.

Thompson and Galbraith

36. James Thompson *(Organisations in Action)* listed three types of integration:

(a) standardisation;
(b) plans and schedules; and
(c) mutual adjustment.

37. Standardisation, plans and schedules are used by bureaucracies. While policy and procedure manuals co-ordinate the day-to-day work of staff there is also a need for written communication of operating goals and objectives. The larger and better organised companies ensure that objectives and goals are clearly defined and quantified in respect of every manager in the organisation (eg in a system of management by objectives).

38. Mutual adjustment, which involves the exchange of information and a mutual response to these communications, is not commonly used, but Thompson argued that this method of integration is perhaps best for dealing with complex problems.

39. Thompson's ideas were supported by J Galbraith *(Designing Complex Organisations)* who argued that with the increasing complexity of organisations and management decisions, the systems of bureaucracy become less efficient. The choices open to management are:

   (a) to accept the reduction in efficiency, or to employ more staff;

   (b) to split up the organisation into autonomous divisions. This solution may be expensive because there will be some duplication of resources in each division;

   (c) to improve vertical communication up and down through the organisation, with improved (computerised) information systems;

   (d) to improve *lateral* (horizontal) communications by organising the interchange of ideas and co-operation of efforts between employees in different departments, but at the same level in the management hierarchy. This method of integration was preferred by Galbraith, as being likely to promote better decision-making at a lower cost.

Herbert Simon

40. It is interesting to compare the ideas of Thompson and Galbraith with those of Herbert Simon. In *The New Science of Management Decision* Simon stated that 'management' is equivalent to 'decision-making' and his major interest has been an analysis of how decisions are made and of how they might be more effective. He describes three stages of making a decision:

   (a) intelligence activity, finding occasions for making a decision;
   (b) design activity, finding possible courses of action;
   (c) choice activity, choosing the preferable option.

41. Simon considered that there is a range of decision types, from the highly repetitive routine to the new and most unusual (from *programmed* to *non-programmed*). An organisation should attempt to programme most decisions to reduce the areas of uncertainty. Different problem-solving techniques apply to programmed and to non-programmed types of decision.

42. Simon's arguments imply that a bureaucracy is capable of improving its decision-making, at least at lower levels in the organisation hierarchy, by programming (and computerisation). It is only at senior levels that complexities occur and where the problems of communication, integration and efficiency might therefore arise.

• Conclusions about co-ordination and integration

43. There is no easy solution to the problems of co-ordination and integration; indeed, it could be suggested that this entire text is concerned with aspects of improving integration and therefore the efficiency of an organisation. This chapter has merely focused on the problem, and suggested a few of the 'solutions' which can be attempted.

44. From earlier paragraphs in this chapter it might also be suggested that co-ordination and integration can only occur if communications are good between managers and subordinates and also laterally within the organisation. People should be willing to *co-operate*.

(a) Managers must develop a relationship of trust with their subordinates.

(b) Co-operation is a common cultural belief, and one that is basic to any economic system. In work organisations it is universally believed that co-operation is a Good Thing, and achieves greater productivity than lack of co-operation. For most tasks, this is proven by experience.

(c) Co-operation is a set of shared values, to the extent of submission of individual needs and differences to the needs of the 'team'.

(d) Co-operation has a rational appeal. It is demonstrable that a suitable number of people co-operating on a task will achieve a better result than one person doing the same task.

(e) Co-operation has an emotional appeal. It incorporates values about unity, teamwork, comradeship, insiders (versus outsiders).

(f) Methods of encouraging co-operation include reinforcing cultures, communication, team cohesiveness and the control of conflict. (Remember that co-operation itself may even involve a certain amount of argument or competition.)

QUIZ

1. What are the symptoms of inadequate integration?

   ● See para 3

2. What are the reasons for poor integration?

   ● See para 3

3. According to Handy how are differences of opinion reconciled in an organisation?

   ● See para 11

4. Describe briefly the 'happy family', 'conflict' and 'evolutionary' views of organisation.

   ● See paras 16, 20 and 23

5. What are the consequences of (a) constructive conflict and (b) destructive conflict?

   ● See para 26

6. What is the role of co-ordination in the control of conflict?

   ● See paras 27-28, 30-31

7. How might co-ordination be improved?

   ● See para 32

8. How can teams or committees aid co-ordination?

   ● See para 34

9. According to Galbraith, how should bureaucracies cope with the lack of co-ordination caused by increasing complexity?

   ● See para 39

10. How can co-operation aid co-ordination and integration?

    ● See para 44

Chapter 18

LEADERSHIP

Topics covered in this chapter

- The manager as leader
- Trait theories
  - o Ashridge studies
- Style theories
  - o Theory X and Theory Y
  - o Likert
  - o Blake's grid
- Direction and the management hierarchy
- Systems approach to leadership
- Contingency approach to leadership (Handy)

Purpose of this chapter

To consider the nature of leadership, and to look at the styles which managers use to direct and motivate others in more detail.

- **The manager as leader**

1. In Chapter 10 we looked at motivation in great detail and saw how a manager's style of management affects motivation. In turn we saw that management style was linked in with the theories held by the manager as to the motivation of his subordinates - McGregor's Theories X and Y.

2. In this chapter we will again be looking at the manager as 'leader' (and at subordinates as 'followers'). We shall concentrate on the ways in which leadership is a management function along with the other functions of planning, controlling, organising and co-ordinating (discussed in Chapters 13, 16 and 17).

   > Note that in the revised syllabus the term 'leadership' incorporates all the functions of 'management' as defined in this text - planning, controlling, organising, co-ordinating and directing. For the purposes of this chapter we have confined its meaning to that of *directing*.

18: LEADERSHIP

What is leadership?

3.
> Leadership is the process of influencing others to work willingly towards an organisation's goals, and to the best of their capabilities. ' The essence of leadership is followership. In other words it is the willingness of people to follow that makes a person a leader' (Koontz, O'Donnell, Weihrich).

4. Leadership comes about in a number of different ways:

   (a) a manager is appointed to a position of authority within the organisation. He relies mainly on the (legitimate) authority of that position. Leadership of his subordinates is a function of the position he holds;

   (b) some leaders (eg in politics or in trade unions) might be elected;

   (c) other leaders might emerge by popular choice and through their personal drive and qualities. Unofficial spokesmen for groups of people are leaders of this style.

> Our main concern, of course, is with managers who are appointed as leaders by virtue of their position in the organisation. Leaders are *given* their roles by their putative followers; their 'authority' may technically be removed if their followers cease to acknowledge them. The *personal, physical* or *expert* power of leaders is therefore more important than position power alone.

5. If a manager had indifferent or poor leadership 'qualities' or skills his subordinates would still do their job, but they would do it ineffectually or perhaps in a confused manner. By providing leadership, a manager should be able to use the capabilities of subordinates to better effect; leadership is the 'influential increment over and above mechanical compliance with the routine directives of the organisation' (Katz and Kahn *The Social Psychology of Organisations*).

> 'Since people tend to follow those whom they see as a means of satisfying their own personal goals, the more managers understand what motivates their subordinates and how these motivations operate, and the more they reflect this understanding in carrying out their managerial actions, the more effective leaders they are likely to be. '
>
> *Koontz, O'Donnell and Weihrich*

● **Trait theories of leadership**

6. Early theories suggested that there are certain qualities, personality characteristics or 'traits' which make a good leader. These might be aggressiveness, self-assurance, intelligence, initiative, energy, a drive for achievement or power, appearance, interpersonal skills, administrative ability, imagination, a certain upbringing and education, the 'helicopter factor' (the ability to rise above a situation and analyse it objectively) etc. Taylor believed the capacity to 'make others do what you want them to do' was an inherent characteristic.

7. This list is not exhaustive, and various writers attempted to show that their selected list of traits were the ones that provided the key to leadership. The full list of traits is so long that it appears to call for a man or woman of extraordinary, even superhuman, gifts to be a leader.

8. Ghiselli did show a significant correlation between leadership effectiveness and personal traits of intelligence, initiative, self-assurance and individuality. Hunt found a similar correlation between effectiveness and the 'helicopter factor'.

9. Jennings (1961) wrote that 'Research has produced such a variegated list of traits presumably to describe leadership, that for all practical purposes it describes nothing. Fifty years of study have failed to produce one personality trait or set of qualities that can be used to distinguish between leaders and non-leaders.'

> Trait theory, although superficially attractive, is now largely discredited. Although it may be possible to show that, without certain characteristics, it is difficult to be a good leader, it has proved impossible to show that all people with certain characteristics are good leaders.

10. Alternative approaches to leadership theory have been developed over the years, and some of these will be described under the headings of:

    (a) style theories, mainly of the 'behaviouralist' school of thought;
    (b) systems theory and leadership;
    (c) contingency theories of leadership.

● Style theories

11. In Chapter 10 we looked at McGregor's Theories X and Y, which are in fact style theories of leadership. Below we shall look at some other theories of management style.

Huneryager and Heckman

12. Four different types or styles of leadership were identified by Huneryager and Heckman (1967).

    (a) *Dictatorial style*: the manager forces subordinates to work by threatening punishment and penalties. The psychological contract between the subordinates and their organisation would be coercive. Dictatorial leadership might be rare in commerce and industry, but it is not uncommon in the style of government in some countries of the world, nor in the style of parenthood in many families.

    (b) *Autocratic style*: decision-making is centralised in the hands of the leader himself, who does not encourage participation by subordinates; indeed, subordinates' ideas might be actively discouraged and obedience to orders would be expected from them. The autocratic style is common in many organisations, and you will perhaps be able to identify examples from your own experience. Doctors, matrons and sisters in hospitals tend to practise an autocratic style; managers/directors who own their company also tend to expect things to be done their way.

(c) *Democratic style*: decision-making is decentralised, and shared by subordinates in participative group action. To be truly democratic, the subordinate must be willing to participate. The democratic style is described more fully later.

(d) *Laissez-faire style*: subordinates are given little or no direction at all, and are allowed to establish their own objectives and make all their own decisions. The leader of a research establishment might adopt a laissez-faire style, giving individual research workers freedom of choice to organise and conduct their research as they themselves want (within certain limits, such as budget spending limits).

13. These four divisions or 'compartments' of management style are really a simplification of a 'continuum' or range of styles, from the most dictatorial to the most laissez-faire.

Dicta-torial	*Autocratic*			*Democratic*				*Laissez-faire*
Manager makes decisions enforces them	Manager makes dec-isions and announces them	Manager 'sells' his decisions to subor-dinates	Manager suggests own ideas and asks for com-ments	Manager suggests his sketch ed ideas, asks for comments and amends his ideas as a result	Manager presents a problem, asks for ideas, makes a decision from the ideas	Manager presents a problem to his group of subor-dinates and asks them to solve it	Manager allows his subordinates to act as they wish within specified limits

This 'continuum' of leadership styles was first suggested by Tannenbaum and Schmidt (1958).

14.
> There are differing views as to which of these leadership styles (especially (a), (b) or (c)) is likely to be most effective. The probable truth is that the degree of effectiveness of a particular leadership style will depend on the work environment, the leader himself and his subordinates.

The Ashridge studies

15. A slightly different analysis of leadership styles, based on this continuum, was made by the Research Unit at Ashridge Management College, based on research in several industries in the UK (reported 1966). This research distinguished four different management styles.

(a) The autocratic or *'tells'* style. This is characterised by one-way communication between the manager and the subordinate, with the manager telling the subordinate what to do. The leader makes all the decisions and issues instructions, expecting them to be obeyed without question.

(b) The persuasive or *'sells'* style. The manager still makes all the decisions, but believes that subordinates need to be motivated to accept them before they will do what he wants them to. He therefore tries to explain his decisions in order to persuade them round to his point of view.

(c) The *consultative* style. This involves discussion between the manager and the subordinates involved in carrying out a decision, but the manager retains the right to make the decision himself. By conferring with his subordinates before making any decision, the manager will take account of their advice and feelings. Consultation is a form of limited participation in decision-making for subordinates, but there might be a tendency for a manager to appear to consult his subordinates when really he has made up his mind beforehand. Consultation will then be false and a facade for a 'sells' style of leadership whereby the manager hopes to win the acceptance of his decisions by subordinates by pretending to listen to their advice.

(d) The democratic or *'joins'* style. This is an approach whereby the leader joins his group of subordinates to make a decision on the basis of consensus or agreement. It is the most democratic style of leadership identified by the research study. Subordinates with the greatest knowledge of a problem will have greater influence over the decision. The 'joins' style is therefore most effective where all subordinates in the group have equal knowledge and can therefore contribute in equal measure to decisions.

16. The findings of the Ashridge studies included the following :

(a) There was a clear preference amongst the subordinates for the *consultative* style of leadership but managers were most commonly thought to be exercising the 'tells' or 'sells' style.

(b) The attitudes of subordinates towards their work varied according to the style of leadership they thought their boss exercised. The most favourable attitudes were found amongst those subordinates who perceived their boss to be exercising the *consultative style*.

(c) The least favourable attitudes were found amongst subordinates who were unable to perceive a consistent style of leadership in their boss. In other words, subordinates are unsettled by a boss who chops and changes between autocracy, persuasion, consultation and democracy. The conclusion from this finding of the study is that *consistency* in leadership style is important.

		Strengths		Weaknesses
● *Tells style*	(1)	Quick decisions can be made when speed is required	(1)	It does not encourage the subordinate to give his opinions when these might be useful.
	(2)	It is the most efficient type of leadership for highly-programmed routine work.	(2)	Communications between the manager and subordinate will be one-way and the manager will not know until afterwards whether his orders have been properly understood.
			(3)	It does not encourage initiaive and commitment from subordinates.
● *Sells style*	(1)	Employees are made aware of the reasons for decisions.	(1)	Communications are still largely one-way. Subordinates might not buy his decisions.
	(2)	Selling decisions to staff might make them more willing to co-operate.	(2)	It does not encourage initiative and commitment from subordinates
	(3)	Staff will have a better idea of what to do when unforeseen events arise in their work because the manager will have explained his intentions.		

• *Consultative style*	(1) Employees are involved in decisions before they are made. This encourages motivation through greater interest and involvement.	(1) It might take much longer to reach decisions.
	(2) An agreed consensus of opinion can be reached and for some decisions consensus can be an advantage rather than a weak compromise.	(2) Subordinates might be too inexperienced to formulate mature opinions and give practical advice.
	(3) Employees can contribute their knowledge and experience to help in solving more complex problems.	
• *Joins style*	(1) It can provide high motivation and commitment from employees.	(1) The authority of the manager might be undermined.
	(2) It shares the other advantages of the consultative style.	(2) Decision-making might become a very long process, and clear decisions might be difficult to reach.
		(3) Subordinates might lack enough experience.

Theory X and Theory Y

17. In Chapter 10 we discussed the work of Douglas McGregor on leadership style. We saw that leadership style may be affected by which theory of human nature the particular manager subscribes to:

   • *Theory X* - the average human being has an inherent dislike of work and will avoid it if he can, or

   • *Theory Y* - man's expenditure of physical and mental effort in work is as natural as play or rest.

18. Managers who consciously or unconsciously hold the view that most people belong, to different degrees, in the Theory X group will tend to adopt styles which are 'harder line' - the tells, dictatorial or autocratic end of the spectrum. Conversely, a manager who believes in Theory Y will be more participative and adopt a style closer to 'joins'.

19. Although Theories X and Y are extreme views, they do serve to define the two ends of a spectrum into which human attitudes towards work fall. Similarly, the strength of a manager's convictions about his subordinates' attitudes will define where his leadership style falls in the Ashridge or Tannenbaum and Schmidt continuum. Through the theories therefore we can see how a manager's leadership style links in with his attitudes to motivation - a Theory X autocrat wil probably believe that only attractive pay and coercion will get a job done, whilst a Theory Y democrat will acknowledge participation as a motivator.

Rensis Likert

20. Rensis Likert distinguished four styles of management:

- exploitive authoritative;
- benevolent authoritative;
- consultative authoritative;
- participative group management.

Managers, to be effective and to communicate, must adjust to the people they are managing.

21. Likert attempted to show that the effective manager is one who uses the participative style of management, although the ideal manager must be able to use the right leadership style for the right situation. Everyone in an organisation is interdependent with other people (as a manager is dependent upon his subordinates). Authority alone is insufficient to obtain good performance. It can only be effective in certain situations and with certain people. The complete manager is one who uses (normally) a supportive, participative approach but who can use any style effectively in the right situation.

22. In his books *New Patterns of Management* and *The Human Organisation* he attempted through research to answer the question 'what do effective managers have in common?' His research showed that four main elements are normally present in effective managers:

(a) *they expect high levels of performance.* Their standards and targets are high and apply overall, not only to their subordinates' performance, but also to other departments and their own personal performance;

(b) *they are employee-centred.* They spend time getting to know their workers and develop a situation of trust whereby their employees feel able to bring their problems to them. When necessary, their actions can be hard but fair, akin to the actions of a fond and responsible parent. Such managers are typified by their ability to face unpleasant facts in a constructive manner and help their staff to grow and develop a similar constructive attitude;

(c) *they do not practise close supervision.* The truly effective manager is aware of the performance levels that can be expected from each individual and he has helped them to define their own targets. Once this has been achieved, the manager judges results and does not closely supervise the actions of his staff. In this way he not only develops his people, he also frees himself to spend more time on other aspects of his work (for example, planning decisions, communications with other areas and personnel problems);

(d) *they operate the participative style of management as a natural style.* This means that if a job problem arises they do not impose a favoured solution. Instead, they pose the problem and ask the staff member involved to find the best solution. Having then agreed their solution the participative manager would assist his staff in implementing it.

23. Likert emphasises that all four features must be present for a manager to be truly effective. For example, if a manager is employee-centred, if he delegates and is participative, then he will have a happy working environment but he will not produce a high performance unless he also establishes high standards of performance. A manager's concern for people must be matched by his concern for achieving results. This linking of the human relations approach with scientific management targets will provide the recipe for real effective performance.

> It is important to remember that management techniques such as time and motion study, financial controls etc are used by high producing managers 'at least as completely as by the low producing managers, but in quite different ways.' The different application is caused by a better understanding of the motivations of human behaviour.

24. Likert's research showed that, on the whole:

(a) supervisors with the best performance were those who concentrated their main efforts on the human aspects of their staff's problems and attempted to build work groups with high performance standards.

(b) supervisors with poor performance spent more time in ensuring that their staff were busily employed in fulfilling specified stages of work.

(c) the participative, supportive supervisor who was transferred to a low-production unit was able to raise the performance at a fast rate.

> Likert's conclusion was that the style of supervision is more important in achieving better results than any more general factors such as job interest, loyalty towards the company etc.

Blake's grid

25. The writings of the human relations school (McGregor etc) tended to obscure the 'task' element of a manager's responsibilities. By emphasising style of direction and the importance of human relations, it is all too easy to forget that a manager is primarily responsible for ensuring that tasks are done efficiently and effectively.

26. Robert R Blake and Jane S Mouton designed the management grid (1964). It is based on two fundamental ingredients of managerial behaviour, namely:

(a) concern for production or the 'task'; and
(b) concern for people.

27. The results of their work were published under the heading of 'Ohio State Leadership Studies', but are now commonly referred to as Blake's grid.

18.1 Blake's grid

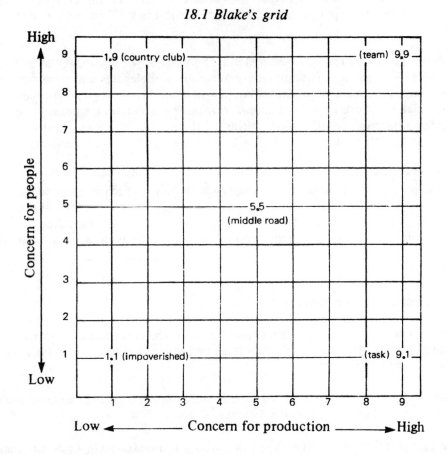

28. The extreme cases shown on the grid are defined by Blake as being:

    (a) 1.1 *impoverished*: manager is lazy, showing little effort or concern either for staff or work targets;

    (b) 1.9 *country club*: manager is attentive to staff needs and has developed satisfying relationships. However, there is little attention paid to achieving results;

    (c) 9.1 *task management*: almost total concentration on achieving results. People's needs are virtually ignored and conditions of work are so arranged that people cannot interfere to any significant extent;

    (d) 5.5 *middle of the road or the dampened pendulum*: adequate performance through balancing the necessity to get out work while maintaining morale of people at a satisfactory level;

    (e) 9.9 *team*: high performance manager who achieves high work accomplishment through 'leading' committed people who identify themselves with the organisational aims.

29. It is worth being clear in your own mind about the possible usefulness of Blake's grid. Its primary value is obtained from the appraisal of a manager's performance, either by the manager himself or by his superiors. The ideal manager is a 9.9 man or woman with high concern for both production and people. An individual manager can be placed on the grid, and his position on the

grid should help him to see how his performance as a leader and a manager can be improved. For example, a manager rated 3.8 has further to go in showing concern for the task itself than for developing the work of his subordinates.

30. You should also be aware that Blake's grid is based on the assumption that concern for production and concern for people are not incompatible with each other. In this respect, Blake and Mouton accept the Theory Y view of leadership style.

● **Direction and the management hierarchy**

31. A further consideration is whether the style of leadership should vary with the manager's level in the hierarchy. It could be argued, for instance, that shop-floor workers are likely to be less mature as individuals and therefore in need of Theory X supervision, whereas higher managers are more mature and worthy of a different leadership style from their superiors.

32. With certain reservations, the answer could possibly be that democratic leadership is preferable at all levels:

(a) *First line supervisors*: these do much technical work themselves, and are faced with more immediate, day-to-day problems of leadership. These managers must recognise the importance of co-operation, perhaps because they work in an area where it is most ignored.

Many managers vastly underrate the honesty, helpfulness and common sense of their fellow men as individuals because they do not realise that it is the social surrounding of the factory which largely makes them as they are. There is no behaviour on the part of the workers which is not copied exactly by management, eg questions of status, indulgence in restrictive practices, stealing and so on.

It is generally forgotten that in modern industry compulsion has to be replaced by co-operation, because the unco-operative worker is a danger in modern industry where sabotage may be catastrophic. Co-operation cannot be produced by force, and the factory manager is liable to forget that whilst, as the representative of formal authority in the factory, he may exert some control by reason of his power to hire or fire the workers, because of their informal authority, have the much greater power of accepting or rejecting co-operation with the formal hierarchy.

No agitator can organise a mass of well adjusted people into an aggressive movement but unrest caused by underlying frustrations which are already there can be utilised by a potential leader. Similarly, no leader can increase productivity, raise morale, or impose social conditions in the factory without the co-operation of others.

(b) *Middle managers*: 'Middle management is in a state of acute competition.' (Hunter). Managers on their way up the promotion ladder may feel under pressure from people they can see as rivals. This can make it difficult for them to take a cool, objective view of long-term results.

Because of this, they may become depressed, insecure and impetuous and some companies are trying to find a remedy for this by appraisal or development schemes which ensure a fair chance to all worthy of it.

Communication from below upwards is a major problem adding stresses to the 'man in between'. Perhaps it is in the area of the middle managers where the problems of leadership style are most acute.

● **A systems approach to leadership**

33. Systems theory is concerned with the complex inter-relationships between the many different parts of a system (organisation), and the effect of the environment on the system (and vice versa). Katz and Kahn have developed ideas on how leadership can contribute to the better functioning of a system.

34. Early research by Katz and Kahn (reported in 1951) into the effect of leadership style on productivity suggested that there were three aspects of leader behaviour which affected productivity:

   ● assumption of the leadership role;
   ● closeness of supervision; and
   ● degree of employee-orientation.

35. Comparisons were made between high-production and low-production groups and it was found that:

   (a) in the most efficient groups the supervisor assumed the leadership role and used his supervisory talents to get the best out of his group. He realised that the leader has special functions and cannot therefore behave as an ordinary group member (be 'one of the boys'). In large organisations the assumption of the supervisory role is often made easier by transferring staff on promotion so that they can make a fresh start among strangers;

   (b) supervision was closer in low-production than in high-production groups. Workers expect to have some control over the means by which they perform a set task, and they resent having means specified in too much detail. Supervisory behaviour was found to reflect management leadership styles, so the organisational context affects leadership;

   (c) studies of the attitudes held by supervisors towards their subordinates revealed that the men in charge of high-production groups were more employee-oriented (intent on promoting their welfare). In the research experiment, the attitudes of a manager were gauged by asking subordinates to rate bosses; results showed that the efficient bosses were seen by their subordinates to be more *considerate*.

36. Katz and Kahn have since developed their ideas and have suggested that the reason why the most effective managers show consideration and understanding towards their subordinates is because they supplement their formal position in the organisation and appreciate that their employees:

   (a) have interests and roles outside their job;
   (b) are subject to pressures and influences from their external environment;
   (c) need information to do their job with greater understanding; and
   (d) need to be guided in the dynamic, changing organisation, and to understand the significance of change.

37. Good leaders show a true awareness that organisations are 'open' systems, reacting to and changing with their environment, of which their subordinates are also a part. Leaders influence those aspects of their subordinates' interests, energies and drive which cannot be harnessed by simple organisation structure, job definitions, or more formal management techniques.

● **A contingency approach to leadership**

38. A contingency approach to leadership is one which argues that the ability of a manager to be a leader, and to influence his subordinate work group, depends on the particular situation, and will vary from case to case. Factors which vary in different situations are

   ● the personality of the leader
   ● his leadership style
   ● the nature of the group's tasks
   ● the nature and personality of the work group and its individual members
   ● conditions of work, and
   ● 'external environmental' factors.

Handy's 'best fit' approach

39. Charles Handy has suggested a contingency approach to leadership. The factors in any situation which contribute to a leader's effectiveness are:

   (a) the leader himself - his personality, character and preferred style of operating;
   (b) the subordinates - their individual and collective personalities, and their preference for a style of leadership;
   (c) the task - the objectives of the job, the technology of the job, methods of working etc; and
   (d) the environment.

40. Essentially, Handy argues that the most effective style of leadership in any particular situation is one which brings the first three factors - a leader, subordinates and task - into a 'best fit'. For each of the three factors, a spectrum can be drawn ranging from 'tight' to 'flexible'.

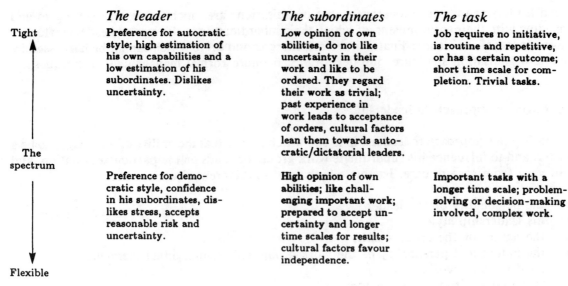

	The leader	*The subordinates*	*The task*
Tight	Preference for autocratic style; high estimation of his own capabilities and a low estimation of his subordinates. Dislikes uncertainty.	Low opinion of own abilities, do not like uncertainty in their work and like to be ordered. They regard their work as trivial; past experience in work leads to acceptance of orders, cultural factors lean them towards auto-cratic/dictatorial leaders.	Job requires no initiative, is routine and repetitive, or has a certain outcome; short time scale for com-pletion. Trivial tasks.
The spectrum			
	Preference for demo-cratic style, confidence in his subordinates, dis-likes stress, accepts reasonable risk and uncertainty.	High opinion of own abilities; like chall-enging important work; prepared to accept un-certainty and longer time scales for results; cultural factors favour independence.	Important tasks with a longer time scale; problem-solving or decision-making involved, complex work.
Flexible			

18.2 Handy's best fit approach

41. A best fit occurs when all three factors are on the same level in the spectrum. In practice, there is likely to be a misfit. Confronted with a lack of fit, the leader must decide which factor(s) should be changed to bring all three into line. The factor over which a leader has most influence is himself and his style; hence, Handy argues, the great emphasis on 'leadership style' in management literature. However, although the leader's style is theoretically the easiest to alter in the short term, there are often long-term benefits to be achieved from re-defining the task (eg job enlargement) or from developing the work group.

42. The fourth factor identified by Handy in the situational jig-saw is the *environment:*

   (a) *the position of 'power' held by the leader in the organisation and the relationship of the leader and his group.* Power might be a position of authority but it might also be the expertise or the charisma of the leader. A person with great power has a bigger capacity to set his own style of leadership, select his own subordinates and re-define the task of his work group;

   (b) *organisational 'norms' and the structure and technology of the organisation.* No manager can flout convention and act in a manner which is contrary to the customs and standards of the organisation. If the organisation has a history of autocratic leadership, it will be difficult to introduce a new style. If the formal organisation is highly centralised, there will be limits to how far a task can be re-structured by an individual manager. In mass-production industries where routine, repetitive work is in-built into the production technology, challenging tasks will be difficult to create, and leadership will tend, perforce, to be autocratic;

(c) *the variety of tasks and the variety of subordinates.* If the tasks of a work group are simple, few in number and repetitive, the best style of leadership will be different from a situation in which tasks are varied and difficult. In many groups, however, tasks vary from routine and simple, to complex 'one-off' problem-solving. Managing such work is complicated by this variety.

43. Similarly, the individuals in a work group might be widely different. One member of the group might seek participation and greater responsibility, whereas another might want to be told what to do. Furthermore, labour turnover may be frequent, and the individual persons who act as leaders or subordinates are constantly changing; such change is unsettling because the leadership style will have to be altered to suit the new situation each time a personnel change occurs.

44. The 'environment' can be improved for leaders within an organisation if top management acts to ensure that:

(a) leaders are given a clear role and 'power';
(b) organisational 'norms' can be broken;
(c) the organisational structure is not rigid and inflexible;
(d) subordinates in a work group are all of the same quality or type;
(e) labour turnover is reduced, especially by keeping managers in their job for a reasonably lengthy period of time.

QUIZ

1. Are there born leaders?

   ● See paras 6-9

2. Styles of leadership can be described in various ways. Name some of them.

   ● See paras 12, 15, 17, 20, 25

3. Explain Blake's grid.

   ● See paras 26-28

4. How does position in the management hierarchy affect leadership?

   ● See para 32

5. Describe the findings of Katz and Kahn and their systems approach to leadership.

   ● See paras 34-37

6. What is a contingency approach to leadership? Explain one such approach.

   ● See paras 38, or 39-42

Chapter 19

ORGANISATIONAL CULTURE

Topics covered in this chapter:

- The culture of organisations
- Culture and organisation structure
- Culture and change
  - The adaptive organisation
  - Organic and mechanistic organisations
  - Can a culture be changed?
- Organisation style
- Excellence

Purpose of this chapter:

To demonstrate how organisational culture and style affect management, and to describe the effects of pursuing excellence.

- **The culture of organisations**

1. > An organisation's culture may be defined as the complex body of shared values and beliefs of an organisation.

2. Peters and Waterman, in their study *(In Search of Excellence)* found that the 'dominance and coherence of culture' was an essential feature of the 'excellent' companies they observed. A 'handful of guiding values' was more powerful than manuals, rule books, norms and controls formally imposed (and resisted). They commented: 'If companies do not have strong notions of themselves, as reflected in their values, stories, myths and legends, people's only security comes from where they live on the organisation chart.'

3. Handy sums up 'culture' as 'that's the way we do things round here'. For Schein, it is 'the pattern of basic assumptions that a given group has invented, discovered, or developed, in learning to cope with its problems of external adaption and internal integration, and that have worked well enough to be considered valid and, therefore, to be taught to new members as the correct way to perceive, think and feel in relation to these problems.'

> 'I believe that the real difference between success and failure in a corporation can very often be traced to the question of how well the organisation brings out the great energies and talents of its people. What does it do to help these people find common cause with each other? And how can it sustain this common cause and sense of direction through the many changes which take place from one generation to another?...I think you will find that it owes its resiliency not to its form of organisation or administrative skills, but to the power of what we call *beliefs* and the appeal these beliefs have for its people.'
>
> Watson (IBM) quoted by
> Peters and Waterman

4. All organisations will generate their own cultures, whether spontaneously or under the guidance of positive managerial strategy. The culture will consist of the following.

(a) *Basic, underlying assumptions* which guide the behaviour of the individuals and groups in the organisation, e.g. customer orientation, or belief in quality, trust in the organisation to provide rewards, freedom to make decisions, freedom to make mistakes, the value of innovation and initiative at all levels etc.

(b) *Overt beliefs expressed by the organisation and its members*, which can be used to condition (a) above.

- These beliefs and values may emerge as sayings, slogans, mottos etc. such as 'we're getting there', 'the customer is always right', or 'the winning team'.

- They may emerge in a richer mythology - in jokes and stories about past successes, heroic failures or breakthroughs, legends about the 'early days', or about 'the time the boss...'. Organisations with strong cultures often centre themselves around almost legendary figures in their history.

Management can encourage this by 'selling' a sense of the corporate 'mission', or by promoting the company's 'image'; it can reward the 'right' attitudes and punish (or simply not employ) those who aren't prepared to commit themselves to the culture.

(c) *Visible artifacts* - the style of the offices or other premises, dress 'rules', display of 'trophies', the degree of informality between superiors and subordinates etc.

5. One way by which management can try to establish a culture is by drawing up a *mission statement*. A mission statement is a declaration of an organisation's aims, objectives and values. For example, J Sainsbury plc's mission statement states that the company's aim is:

"...to discharge the responsibility as leaders in our trade by acting with complete integrity, by carrying out our work to the highest standards and by contributing to the public good and quality of life." (*Financial Times*, 11/1/1989)

6. Such statements generate high levels of cynicism if they are at variance with reality, and so for a mission statement to mean anything at all, it must be an expression of a sense of mission already existing. When defining what an organisation's mission is, management needs to consider four issues:

    (a) the organisation's *purpose* (eg maximise shareholder value);

    (b) the organisation's *strategy* (ie the business it is in, its intentions for the future);

    (c) the *values* that determine the treatment of employees, suppliers, customers etc;

    (d) whether the organisation does in fact *behave* in accordance with its stated mission.

7.   It is not always clear to whom a mission statement is likely to be addressed, but mission statements are generally meant to encourage loyalty by giving employees motives for working other than pay and job security by providing a context of shared values.

8.   A culture takes shape and colour in wide variety of ways, such as:

    (a) the extent of formalisation of the structure;

    (b) whether decisions are made by committees or individuals;

    (c) the degree of freedom allowed to subordinates to show initiative and innovation (and the degree of freedom which subordinates expect to be given);

    (d) communication - eg whether junior employees feel free to talk to senior managers;

    (e) the formalisation of clothing and office layout;

    (f) the kind of people employed (eg their education, age, ambition);

    (g) the symbols and 'legends' that matter to people in the organisation, the beliefs and attitudes that become shared in the organisation;

    (h) management style;

    (i) the organisation's goals and attitudes to risk;

    (j) attitudes to training, team-building and personal aspirations;

    (k) commitment to quality; and

    (l) attitude to technology.

9.   Culture is unique to an organisation since it is made up of so many disparate elements. A supermarket has a different culture from a university, which in turn has a different culture from the armed services or a coal mine.

● **Culture and organisation structure**

10.   Analysis of an organisation's culture leads on to theories known as the cultures/structures approach. This states that the ideal organisation structure in any particular situation is dependent on the culture which exists within it.

11.   Charles Handy is one of the theorists who developed this approach. He discusses four cultures but it is first of all important to note that an organisation might have a structure which reflects a single culture; on the other hand, different structures reflecting different cultures

might exist in separate parts (or departments) of the organisation. (For example, the organisation structure of the field engineering division and the computer systems design department might differ, because the culture in the two departments are not the same.)

12. The four cultures proposed in Handy's descriptions are as follows.

   (a) *The power culture:* power and influence stem from a central source, perhaps the owner-directors. The degree of formalisation is limited, and there are not many rules and procedures. Important decisions are made by key people, and other employees tend to rely on precedent in the absence of other guidelines as to what to do. Other characteristics of the power culture are:

   (i) the organisation, since it is not rigidly structured, is capable of adapting quickly to meet change; however, success in adapting will depend on the luck or judgement of the key individuals who make the rapid decisions;

   (ii) personal influence decreases as the size of an organisation gets bigger. The power culture is therefore best suited to smaller organisations, where the leaders have direct communication with all employees.

   (b) *The role culture* or *bureaucracy.* These organisations have a formal structure, and operate by well-established rules and procedures. Job descriptions establish definite tasks for each person's job, and procedures are established for many work routines, communication between individuals and departments, and the settlement of disputes and appeals. The organisation structure defines authority and responsibility to individual managers, who enact the role expected of their position. Individuals are required to perform their job to the full, but not to overstep the boundaries of their authority. Line management will accept advice from specialist staff experts only when such advice seems necessary or appropriate. Since a wide variety of people of different personalities are capable of doing the same job, the efficiency of this organisation depends on the structuring of jobs and the design of communications and formal relationships, rather than on individual personalities. Individuals who work for such organisations tend to learn an expertise without experiencing risk; many do their job adequately, but are not over-ambitious.

   The bureaucratic style can be very efficient in a stable environment and when the organisation is of a large size. Thus the Civil Service, insurance companies and many large well-established companies with long-term products have been associated with bureaucratic organisations and the role culture. Unfortunately, bureaucracies are very slow to adapt to change and when severe change occurs (eg an economic depression) many run into financial difficulties or even bankruptcy (eg Rover and the British Steel Corporation in the late 70s).

   (c) *The task culture* as reflected in a matrix organisation or else in project teams and task forces. In such organisations, there is no dominant or clear leader. The principal concern in a task culture is to get the job done; therefore the individuals who are important are the experts with the ability to accomplish a particular aspect of the task. Each individual in the team considers he has more influence than he would have if the work were organised on a formal 'role culture' basis.

   Such organisations are flexible and constantly changing; for example, project teams are disbanded as soon as their task has been completed. Project teams and task forces are useful in helping an organisation adapt to change; for example, if a large department were to change from an existing method of working to a new, real-time computerised system of operations, a task force of data processing experts and departmental managers would probably be created to implement the change.

Since job satisfaction tends to be high owing to the degree of individual participation and group identity, 'behavioural' management theorists might recommend this type of organisation structure as being the most efficient available. Handy would argue that this type of structure might only be successful if the nature of the work is suited to matrix organisation or project work, and the employees of the organisation belong to the task culture and therefore want the work organised in this way.

(d) *The person culture*, formed in an organisation whose purpose is to serve the interests of a person or the individuals within it. These organisations are rare, although an example might be a partnership of a few individuals who do all the work of the organisation themselves (with perhaps a little secretarial or clerical assistance). It is quite common, however, for individuals to use an organisation to suit their own purposes - for example:

(i) studio artists look on their job as a means of expressing themselves artistically;
(ii) university lecturers might use their official position as a springboard from which to launch a wider career.

13. Cultures/structures theory clearly has implications for organisational design. In order to see how organisation design can 'mesh' culture with structure, we must begin by recognising the factors which help to determine, in any situation, what the predominant culture and therefore organisation structure will/should be.

(a) *Size:* large organisations are more likely to favour a bureaucracy (role culture) as a means of organising the complexity of work.

(b) *People:* some people like to be told what to do, and would favour an organisation structure based on power culture or role culture. Others enjoy the challenge of a complex job and 'ambiguity' and would therefore prefer (task-culture) project work. People with a strong need for security tend to prefer bureaucracies. Personal ambition is perhaps more associated with power culture and person culture, though it should be said that many bureaucracies are intensely 'political' with much energy spent on personal rivalry.

(c) *The age of the organisation:* many businesses and other organisations begin to grow through the efforts of a few individuals (eg owner-directors, or the founder of a political pressure group) and tend to be highly centralised (power culture). As the organisations get older, and the former leaders are replaced by a new 'generation' of managers, systems tend to formalise and bureaucracy develops.

(d) *The predominant goals or objectives of the organisation:* if the main purpose of an organisation is service to the community (eg hospitals, local government, railways, public utilities), a bureaucratic organisation will probably be most suitable for providing, monitoring and controlling the required level of service. If the predominant goal is growth or survival, an organisation based on power culture or task culture would be more efficient and successful.

(e) *The technology of the organisation:* an important school of thought best known through the works of Eric Trist and Joan Woodward suggests that the most efficient structure of an organisation will be one which is suited to the technological conditions of the work (ie the equipment, methods of working, the nature of automation etc).

(f) *The environment (economic, competitive, socio-cultural, legal, geographical etc):* examples of environmental influences are:

   (i) economic and market changes. Efficient organisations which adapt best are those structured according to a task culture or power culture;

   (ii) an organisation which is spread over a wide geographical area is likely to decentralise authority on a regional basis, so that different cultures might predominate in different regions;

   (iii) the appointment of worker-directors to the board of a company might betoken a change of attitudes towards decision-making within an organisation, from bureaucracy towards teamwork and group decisions (ie from a role culture to a task culture).

• Culture and change

14. Most organisations exist in a changing environment and must adapt in order to survive. Although formalisation and bureaucratic organisation help a small company to develop into a large one, they may be insufficient to enable the organisation to survive continuing environmental changes.

The adaptive organisation

15. Handy states that, depending on its culture and structure, an organisation adapts to change in one of three ways.

(a) *By deliberation:* the organisation 'seeks to reinforce the formal structure by more formal structures'. Companies or governments might establish committees with powers to investigate the state of affairs and recommend or even make decisions. Special project teams might be created, or new departments established (eg corporate planning department or economic advisory section).

(b) *By reproduction:* large national organisations might delegate authority ('decentralise') to regional headquarters. Unfortunately, decentralisation of this nature usually results in regional organisation structures which duplicate the former national structure. Bureaucracy remains in the same form, but on a smaller scale. Unless the environment is fairly stable, such organisational adaptation is likely to be inefficient.

(c) *By differentiation:* the organisation employs different structures with different cultures, in separate parts of the organisation, using a contingency approach - choosing the most suitable structure for each particular situation:

   (i) stable, routine work will be performed in a formalised bureaucratic manner (role culture);

   (ii) adaptation to change (development of new products and new markets, or meeting environmental 'threats') should be organised on a task basis;

   (iii) any sudden crisis might have to be dealt with by key individuals with emergency powers (power culture);

   (iv) overall policy decisions of the organisation should be set by a ruling body of key individuals (board of directors, the Cabinet of government ministers, or the supreme policy-making councils of other organisations) (power culture).

16. To be an adaptive organisation successfully, Handy found that 'One culture should not be allowed to swamp the organisation'.

17. However where differentiation, on a contingency basis, is applied in an organisation structure, there is a potential for conflict. Project teams might resent policy decisions of senior managers because they believe them to be inappropriate to the problems of the organisation; line managers might resent 'free-wheeling' 'undisciplined' members of project teams. The management of an organisation must be capable of reconciling differences and integrating the work of all employees towards a common aim.

Organic and mechanistic organisations

18. Burns and Stalker contributed significant ideas about managing organisation growth and change. They identified the need for a different organisation structure when the technology of the market is changing. They also found that innovation is crucial to the continuing success of any organisation operating in the market.

19. They recommended an *organic structure* (also called an 'organismic structure') which has the following characteristics.

   (a) There is a 'contributive nature' of specialised knowledge and experience to the common task of the organisation.

   (b) Each individual has a realistic task which can be understood in terms of the common task of the organisation.

   (c) There is a continual re-definition of an individual's task, through interaction between the individual and others.

   (d) There is a spread of commitment to the concern and its tasks.

   (e) There is a *network* structure of authority and communication.

   (f) Communication tends to be *lateral* rather than vertical.

   (g) Communication takes the form of information and advice rather than instructions and decisions.

20. Burns and Stalker contrasted the organic structure of management, which is more suitable to conditions of change, with a *mechanistic* system of management, which is more suited to stable conditions. A mechanistic structure has the following characteristics.

   (a) Authority is a hierarchical formal scalar chain.

   (b) Communication is *vertical* rather than lateral.

   (c) Individual tasks are not clearly related to the goals of the organisation, owing to specialisation of work.

   (d) Individuals regard their own tasks as something distinct and divorced from the organisation as a whole.

(e) There is a precise definition of duties in each individual job (eg rules, procedures, job definitions).

21. Mechanistic systems are unsuitable in conditions of change for three reasons:

(a) the *ambiguous figure system:* in dealing with unfamiliar problems authority lines are not clear, matters are referred 'higher-up' and the top of the organisation becomes over-burdened by decisions;

(b) *mechanistic jungle:* jobs and departments are created to deal with the new problems creating greater problems;

(c) *committee system:* committees are set up to cope with the problems. The committees can only be a temporary problem-solving device, but the situations which create the problems are not temporary.

Can a culture be changed?

22. Edwin Baker, in 1981, observed 12 corporations which developed unhealthy corporate cultures. He found a common pattern.

● The organisation flourished initially under its founder who created, usually without conscious effort, a cohesive group of employees who shared his beliefs and values.

● On the founder's retirement the organisation continued to flourish but many employees become rigid and insular in their thinking and behaviour.

● Concern for survival faded and, as a result, so did values regarding speed, flexibility, innovation and concern for the customer.

● Increased growth led to formalisation and the development of rules and procedures. Divisions occurred between employees and management because of specialisation. Communication and willingness to accept responsibility decreased.

● Employees identified with their departments, not with the organisation as a whole.

● Corrective action needed to challenge problems of mature products and markets met inertia. It was thwarted by the rigid culture.

23. In one case the rigidified culture led directly to bankruptcy. Baker warned that: "changing the distinctive culture of a large, old organisation is enormously difficult and may take years".

24. Ralph H Kilmann suggests the following steps for closing 'culture gaps':

(a) find out about what norms of behaviour are currently present (ie behaviour which is expected by a group of its members);

(b) decide the ways in which norms need to be changed;

(c) establish new norms;

(d)   identify culture gaps; and

(e)   close culture gaps.

25.   The sorts of norm which Kilmann is talking about relate to attitudes toward performance/ excellence, teamwork, communication, leadership, profitability, staff relations, customer relations, honesty and security, training and innovation. Positive norms of behaviour are those where individuals identify their own goals with those of the organisation. Negative norms are represented by insularity, slowness, complacence and hostility.

26.   The difficult task, obviously, is to establish new and positive norms of behaviour. A consistent approach is needed, requiring:

(a)   top management commitment;

(b)   modelling behaviour – management should be seen to be acting on the new norms themselves, not merely mouthing empty words about change;

(c)   support for positive behaviour and confrontation of negative behaviour;

(d)   consistency between the evaluation and reward system and positive behaviour (linking pay to acting on positive norms);

(e)   communication of desired norms;

(f)   recruitment and selection of the 'right' people;

(g)   induction programmes for new employees on the desired norms of behaviour; and

(h)   training and skills development.

27.   Most research has shown that, in a large organisation, shifting the value system or culture can take between three and eight years to bring about.

● Organisation style

28.
> The term 'organisation style' refers to the characteristics which distinguish one organisation from another. It refers to the internal environment or 'atmosphere', including the attitudes, behaviour, values and relationships of all who work within the organisation.

29.   The style or 'climate' of any organisation determines the context in which work takes place and therefore affects the quality of the psychological and social life of its members. Organisational style will be influenced by:

(a) *Economic conditions*
The organisational climate will be influenced by the surrounding environment. In prosperous times organisations will either be complacent or be adventurous - full of new ideas and initiatives. In recession organisations will prefer to consolidate, retaining existing custom rather than attracting new clients, and concentrate on cutting costs rather than increasing revenues. To a large extent the opportunities for individuals to advance and develop their careers will depend on economic conditions.

(b) *Nature of the business and its tasks*
The different types of technology used in different forms of business create the pace and priorities associated with different forms of work, eg the hustle and frantic conditions for people dealing in the international money markets for a bank compared with the quiet studious life of a bank's economic research officers.

(c) *Leadership style*
The approach used in exercising authority will determine the extent to which subordinates feel alienated and uninterested or involved and important.

(d) *Policies and practices*
Attitudes to the level of trust and understanding which exists between members of an organisation can often be seen in the way policies and objectives are achieved, eg the extent to which they are imposed by tight written rules and procedures or implied through custom and understanding.

(e) *Structure and culture*
The values and beliefs of the management in relation to the way in which work should be organised, authority exercised and people rewarded may be highly formalised and centralised or informal and decentralised.

(f) *Characteristics of the work force*
Organisation climate will be affected by the demographic nature of the workforce eg manual/clerical division, age, sex, length of service. Organisations which recruit a lot of school-leavers and graduates each year should have an atmosphere in which new ideas are welcomed and considered.

(g) *The stage reached in the life cycle of the company*
Like products, organisations go through cycles of expansion, consolidation and decline. The climate will change as the company moves from one stage to another. For example, ideas for change will be welcomed in 'young' companies, carefully considered in mature ones and ignored in decaying ones.

● **Corporate image**

30. In Chapter 14 we saw how many companies spend a great deal of time and money creating and enhancing a 'good' corporate image in the minds of customers.

31. The corporate image should be an extension of the organisation's culture and style, and bring out what it is that is unique about the organisation. This in turn can lead to changes or improvements in culture and style, particularly in terms of bringing the organisation 'up-to-date'.

● **The pursuit of excellence**

32. In 1982 Tom Peters and Robert Waterman published what became a seminal book in management theory, *"In Search of Excellence"*. By an anecdotal technique they set about describing and analysing what it was that made successful companies successful.

33. By 'excellent' companies Peters and Waterman mean companies which have achieved a certain kind of innovative performance:

   (a) they are usually good at producing commercially viable new products; *and*

   (b) they are especially adroit at continually responding to changes of any sort in their environment.

   > An excellent company is a continuously innovative big company.

34. By observing and analysing in depth about thirty highly successful American companies (in terms of growth, market value, return on capital etc), Peters and Waterman noted that excellent companies share certain common characteristics:

   (a) *thinking, wisdom* and *action* by managers were considered more important than tools, intellect and analysis;

   (b) they worked hard to keep things *simple* in a complex world;

   (c) they insisted on *top quality;*

   (d) they paid huge attention to *customer care;*

   (e) they listened to *employees* and treated them like adults;

   (f) they gave rein to *innovators;* and

   (g) they were prepared to put up with some *chaos* in return for quick action and experimentation.

35. These observed characteristics were analysed into eight key attributes of an excellent company and its culture.

   > 1.   A bias for action.
   > 2.   Closeness to the customer - quality, service and reliability.
   > 3.   Autonomy and entrepreneurship.
   > 4.   Productivity through people.
   > 5.   Hands-on management, driven by value.
   > 6.   'Stick to the knitting' - stick with what you know and can run.
   > 7.   Simple structures, small numbers of top-level staff.
   > 8.   Simultaneous loose-tight properties - they are at once centralised and decentralised. Autonomy is allowed on the shop-floor and in project teams but *all* parts of the organisation must adhere to core values.

Excellence and leadership

36. It is interesting to note that many of the 'excellent' companies showing these attributes were associated with very strong leaders who seemed to have a lot to do with making the company excellent in the first place. Provided this happened at an early stage in the company's life, the excellent value remained after the leader departed. The role of managers was to manage the *values* of the company.

37. A later work by Tom Peters with Nancy Austin, *A Passion for Excellence,* focusses on the importance of leadership and values. In particular, it advocates 'management by wandering about' (MBWA), by which it means that managers should keep in touch with what customers want, how products are produced and how employees are carrying out their work.

Excellence and the rational model of management

38. For many years the central theme of Western thinking on management was that managers make decisions in a rational way. Complex logical and mathematical methods were developed for the process: decision trees, critical path analysis etc.

39. However, behaviour in organisations is also about creativity, emotion, hunches, gut reactions, politics, enthusiasm and other unquantifiable human qualities that do not fit well into the rational model.

> "'Rational' has come to have a very narrow definition in business analysis. It is the 'right' answer, but it's missing all of that messy human stuff, such as good strategies that do not allow for persistent old habits, implementation barriers and simple human inconsistencies." *(Peters and Waterman)*

40. Peters and Waterman enumerate several shortcomings of the rational model of organisation, including the fact that:

   - the numerative analytical component has in-built conservative bias and stifles innovation;
   - it does not celebrate informality, internal competition and experimentation;
   - it denigrates the importance of values; culture is essentially irrational;
   - 'the rationalist approach takes the living element out of situations that should, above all, be alive'.

41. They suggest that the 'technology of reason' should be supplemented with a 'technology of foolishness': that sometimes, individuals should be free to act before they think. The right side of the brain - artistic and irrational - has its place in human behaviour. The decision making process should be like a 'garbage can': lots of ideas swirling around, mixing etc.

   (Note that these comments reflect the researchers' own attitudes as to what is desirable in an organisation to a large extent.)

42. Above all, Peters and Waterman find that the central problem with the rationalist view of organising people is that people are not very rational.

> "Logic, reason and analysis are necessary, but not sufficient for success. To ignore this is to confuse a part of the process with the whole. And such a confusion can lead to a state of corporate constipation known as 'analysis paralysis'."   *Ray Proctor*

Excellence and motivation

43. Peters and Waterman also discuss the central importance of positive reinforcement in any method of motivation. "Researchers studying motivation find that the prime factor is simply the self-perception among motivated subjects that they are in fact doing well ... Mere association with past personal success apparently leads to more persistence, higher motivation, or something that makes us do better."

44.
> At Mars Inc in America, Peters and Waterman observed that every employee - including the president - received a 10% pay bonus for each week in which he got to work on time every day. "That's an ... example of creating a setting in which virtually everybody wins regularly ... When the number of awards is high, it makes the perceived possibility of winning something high as well. And then the average man will stretch to achieve. *[cf expectancy]* Many companies do believe in special awards, but use them exclusively to honour the top few (who already are so highly motivated that they would probably have done their thing anyway)."

45. The observations of Peters and Waterman on the 'culture' and motivational environment of 'excellent' companies in the USA may seem slightly eccentric to British managers, but part of the writers' profile of an excellent company is that 'excellent companies require and demand extraordinary performance from the average man'.

46. Positive reinforcement - whether in the form of bonuses, prizes, 'reaffirming the heroic dimension' of the job itself, identifying workers with the company's success, or enhancing self-image in the workforce - is the method Peters and Waterman observed *succeeding*, although some research has shown that 'tough' managers, applying sanctions on undesirable behaviour, can also get improved performance out of their subordinates.

47. Peters and Waterman argue that employees can be 'switched on' to extraordinary loyalty and effort if:

(a)   the cause is perceived to be in some sense great - 'reaffirming the heroic dimension' of the work. Commitment comes from believing that a task is inherently worthwhile. Devotion to the *customer*, and his needs and wants, is an important motivator in this way.

> "Owing to good luck, or maybe even good sense, those companies that emphasise quality, reliability, and service have chosen the *only* area where it is readily possible to generate excitement in the average down-the-line employee. They give people pride in what they do. They make it possible to love the product."

Shared values and 'good news swapping' - a kind of folklore of past success and 'heroic' endeavour - create a climate where intrinsic motivation is a real driving force;

(b) they are treated as winners. "Label a man a loser and he'll start acting like one." Repressive control systems and negative reinforcement break down the employee's self-image. Positive reinforcement, 'good news swapping', attention from management etc enhance the employee's self-image and create positive attitudes to work and to the organisation;

(c) they can satisfy their dual needs:

(i) to be a conforming, secure part of a successful team; and
(ii) to be a 'star' in their own right.

48. This means applying control (through firm central direction, and shared values and beliefs) but also allowing maximum individual autonomy (at least, the *illusion* of control) and even competition between individual or groups within the organisation. Peters and Waterman call this 'loose-tight' management. Culture, peer pressure, a focus on action, customer-orientation etc are 'non-aversive' ways of exercising control over employees.

49. The implication of this for work behaviour affects the way in which individuals can be motivated and managed. As Peters and Waterman argue, a strong 'central faith', which binds the organisation together as a whole, should be combined with a strong emphasis on individual self-expression, contribution and success: individuals should be given at least the 'illusion of control' over their destinies, while still being given a sense of belonging and a secure, perceived meaningful framework in which to act.

Excellence and group behaviour

50. | Peters and Waterman *(In Search of Excellence)* outline the cultural attributes of successful *task force* teams. They should:

   ● be small - requiring the trust of those who are not involved;
   ● be of limited duration and working under the 'busy member theorem' - ie "get off the damned task force and back to work";
   ● be voluntary - which ensures that the business is 'real';
   ● have an informal structure and documentation - ie no bulky paperwork, and open communication;
   ● have swift follow-up - be *action* oriented.

Excellence and people

51. One of the prime attributes of 'excellent' companies identified by Peters and Waterman is what they call 'Productivity through People'.

   "We are not talking about mollycoddling. We are talking about tough-minded respect for the individual and the willingness to train him, to set reasonable and clear expectations for him, and to grant him practical autonomy to step out and contribute directly to his job." *In Search of Excellence.*

52. The emphasis is on *enabling contribution*. They quote IBM: "Our early emphasis on human relations was not motivated by altruism but by the simple belief that if we respected our people and helped them to respect themselves, the company would make the most profit."

53. 'Happy workers' are unlikely to be an end in themselves. A business organisation tries to get the best *out* of its people, not necessarily *for* them - unless the one cannot be achieved without the other.

54. We should also note that there are a great many other work and non-work variables in the equation. A 'happy' workforce will not *necessarily* make the organisation profitable (eg if the market is unfavourable): they will not necessarily be more productive (eg if the task itself is badly designed, or resources scarce) nor even more highly motivated. Nor is there a magic formula for making them happy by offering them opportunities suitable to their personality development (increased responsibility etc): their priorities may lie elsewhere, or they may be suffering frustration and failure in other areas of their lives that work cannot influence.

QUIZ

1. What is meant by organisational culture?

   ● See paras 1-4

2. What are the four cultures defined by Handy's cultures/structures approach?

   ● See para 12

3. According to Handy, how does an organisation adapt to change?

   ● See para 15

4. What are the characteristics of organic and mechanistic organisations?

   ● See paras 19-20

5. How should managers set about changing an organisation's culture?

   ● See paras 24-26

6. What are the influences on organisational style?

   ● See para 29

7. What common characteristics are shared by excellent companies?

   ● See paras 34-35

8. How do Peters and Waterman suggest that employees can be 'switched on' to loyalty and effort?

   ● See para 47

Chapter 20

BUSINESS DEVELOPMENT

Topics covered in this chapter

- Organisation development
- What does change mean?
- Innovation
- Entrepreneurship and intrapreneurship
- Encouraging innovation
  o Creativity and innovation
  o How to stifle innovation
- Management of growth and stability
- Motives for growth
- Management of contraction (divestment)
- Systematic approach to development

Purpose of this chapter

To consider why development is necessary, and the role of innovation and entrepreneurship/
i ntrapreneurship in change and its various aspects - growth, stability and contraction.

- **Organisation development**

1. It is important to have a good understanding of the term 'organisation development'. Two definitions may be seen in the following quotations:

   - 'Growth is defined as change in an organisation's size, when size is measured by the organisation's membership or employment; development is defined as change in an organisation's age.' (Starbuck 1965)

   - 'Development involves policy decisions that change organisational objectives. Growth, on the other hand, involves technical or administrative improvement by which it is possible more effectively to accomplish old objectives' (Hicks 1967)

   A better definition and one more appropriate to your examination is given by Bennis (1969). He says that organisation development 'is a complex educational strategy intended to change the beliefs, attitudes, values and structure of organisations so that they can better adapt to new technologies, markets and challenges and to the dizzying rate of change itself'.

2.   From the definition of Bennis, two important points must be emphasised:

(a)   organisation development is an *educative* process; and

(b)   it is based on the prescription that there is no ideal form of organisation design, but that organisations must be *adaptive* in order to survive.

3.   Bureaucracy and the formal structure of organisations offer security, familiarity and safety which continue to have strong appeal, but organisation theorists have begun to emphasise:

(a)   the importance of individuals in organisations. The problems of conflict between individuals or work groups, the psychological importance of the work group, the effect of different styles of leadership and the problems of motivation have all been researched;

(b)   the influence of the environment on an organisation and of the organisation on its environment (open systems theory);

(c)   the 'excellence' of companies which are continuously innovative.

4.   To adapt to the increasing complexities of modern business life, an organisation cannot afford to be a sluggish bureaucracy.

(a)   Individuals should be motivated to welcome change, and to co-operate with other members of an organisation in achieving change and adapting to it.

(b)   Management and leadership styles must be such as to make change and adaptation (development) possible.

(c)   All members of the organisation should be encouraged to innovate.

(d)   An organisation must react to its environment. 'A management which takes its environment as given and concentrates on organising internally is pursuing a dangerous course. This does not mean that top management should not be involved in internal problems, but that such involvement must be oriented to the environment opportunities and demands.'

Organisation development programmes

5.   The basic stages of an orchestrated organisation development programme might be as follows:

(a)   An organisation's management must first become aware of deficiencies and faults in its method of operations and take the decision to hire a consultant. An organisation development programme therefore begins with a recognition of a problem at work which 'scientific' methods of management (or techniques) cannot cure.

(b)   A full disclosure of the objectives of the programme must be given. It is vital that all employees should know the purpose of the exercise. It is also important that a mutual confidence should be quickly established between the consultant and the employees of the organisation with whom he will be dealing. At this stage (the 'entry' stage of the programme) the consultant must attempt to win over employees to his views on the relevance of individual attitudes, leadership styles and the environment etc.

(c) Having established the required mutual trust, the consultant may then proceed with a data gathering and diagnostic exercise, ie collecting the 'facts' and analysing them to discover the causes of deficiency or fault.

Data gathering can be time-consuming. Although it is possible to use questionnaires, it is common to collect data by interviewing individuals. The various methods of data gathering which can be used may be summarised as:

(i) collection of documented data (job descriptions, organisation charts, procedure manuals, personnel records eg for individual performance reports). Information which compares budgeted against actual performance, and records of the control action taken (and its effect) should also be gathered;

(ii) questionnaires (possibly as an initial step towards interviewing);

(iii) individual or group interviews. Group interviews may be used to save time or to resolve conflicting facts or opinions which emerged during personal interviews.

Diagnosis should be made by:

(i) encouraging individuals to say what they think is wrong and how it should be put right;

(ii) cross-checking and comparing all the collected data;

(iii) questioning and making suggestions about the causes of problems and deficiencies. In this way, the consultant may be able to lead employees to discover for themselves what is at fault. An awareness of motivation, inter-group conflicts etc, will be of particular importance here.

(d) The conclusions from the diagnostic exercise should be fed back to higher management in order that a strategy for organisation development may be agreed.

(e) The consultant should suggest a choice of objectives (what changes might be made) to senior management, and possibly to recommend the option he considers the most preferable. Once the objective has been agreed, the support and knowledge of the employees concerned must be secured.

(f) The consultant then has the task of formulating a strategy to enable the declared objective to be achieved. Implementing the changes will generally necessitate teaching employees to change their attitudes, and to overcome the difficulties of convincing individuals requires the expertise of the consultant.

(g) The implementation of any such change will require monitoring. The actual effects on the faults at work must be gauged to decide whether the aims of the programme have been achieved. It is also likely that new problems will emerge, and that these in turn will require diagnosis and educative, corrective action.

Benefits of using external consultants

1. They will use analytical techniques and specialist knowledge, in which internal staff do not have the training.

2. They bring experience from dealing with similar problems in other organisations.

3. They can help with the resolution of internal conflicts within the organisation, by acting as an 'independent referee'.

4. They are 'neutrals', outside departmental politics.

5. They are not tied by status or rank, and can discuss problems freely with the people involved, at all levels within the organisation.

6. They can look at problems objectively, and unlike internal managers don't have to worry about the consequences of their recommendations for their jobs or career prospects.

Disadvantages of using consultants

1. They might be seen as top management's 'poodles', or 'outside meddlers'.

2. They might show an inclination to bring a standard solution to a unique problems, and fail to resolve the problem properly.

3. They might be too academic, and lack experience in 'actual' management.

4. They will need time to learn about an organisation, and 'acclimatise' themselves. The client organisation will have to pay consultancy fees for this learning process!

---

6. The process of constructing a development programme could be quickened up if the organisation was continuously innovative.

● **What does change mean?**

7. Change, in the context of organisation and management, could relate to any of the following.

(a) *Changes in the 'environment'*
These could be changes in what competitors are doing, what customers are buying, how they spend their money, changes in the law, changes in social behaviour and attitudes, economic changes, and so on.

(b) *Changes in the products the organisation makes, or the services it provides*

These are made in response to changes in customer demands, competitors' actions, new technology, and so on.

(c) *Changes in how products are made, or who makes them. Changes in working methods.*

These changes are also in response to environmental change - eg new technology, new laws on safety at work etc.

(d) *Changes in management and working relationships*

For example, changes in leadership style, and in the way that employees are encouraged to work together. Also changes in training and development.

(e) *Changes in organisation structure or size (growth)*

These might involve creating new departments and divisions, greater delegation of authority or more centralisation, changes in the way that plans are made, management information is provided and control is exercised, and so on. Organisation re-structuring will be made in response to changes in (a),(b),(c) or (d) above.

8. Buckley and Perkins (1984) made a distinction between:

(a) change, which is gradual and small; and
(b) transformation, which is change on a significant scale.

20.1 Transformation

TRANSFORMATION

Organisational	*In the way the system operates*	*In employee consciousness*
major changes in job definitions, reporting lines (lines of authority) etc	major changes in communication patterns, working relationships and processes	major changes in the way that things are viewed, involving shifts in attitudes, beliefs and myths

● **Innovation**

9. *Innovation* is a term that is often associated with change. Innovation, quite simply, is something completely new. Some changes might result in going back to something that was done before: change doesn't necessarily mean doing something entirely new. Innovation creates change, but change isn't always innovative.

10. The rate of change might be fast or slow, depending on the organisation's circumstances, and the environment in which it operates.

> Organisations which operate in a rapidly-changing environment need to be innovative, and responsive to change, if they are to survive and grow (cf. Burns and Stalker's ideas about organic and mechanistic structures, mentioned in Chapter 19).

11. Very few organisations operate in a static environment. You might argue that Western society is geared up for change, and all organisations within such a society must innovate continually just to survive.

> "Organisations must breathe new life into procedures and management styles; if not, established organisations will lose ground to more vibrant, smaller or newer enterprises. For innovation to succeed, corporate culture - the missing link in moving forward in today's world - must be managed, and all the strategies for managing complex organisations implemented."
> Tom Attwood,
> *Management Accounting*, January 1990

12. To encourage innovation the objective for management should be to create a more outward-looking organisation.

   ● Emphasis should be placed on self-reliance and vigorous initiative.

   ● People should be encouraged to look for new products, markets, processes, designs. People should seek ways to improve productivity.

13. Tom Attwood suggests the following steps for creating an innovative culture from one which has previously existed in a cosy, unthreatening world:

   (a) ensure management and staff know what innovation is and how it happens;
   (b) ensure that senior managers welcome, and are seen to welcome, changes for the better;
   (c) stimulate and motivate management and staff to think and act innovatively;
   (d) understand people in the organisation and their needs; and
   (e) recognise and encourage potential 'intrapreneurs' (see below).

The value of innovation

14. The chief object of being innovative is to ensure the organisation's survival and success in a changing world. It can also have the following advantages:

   (a) improvements in quality of product and service;

   (b) a leaner structure - layers of management or administration may be done away with, and the need for specialist support may be reduced;

   (c) prompt and imaginative solutions to problems (through use of project teams);

   (d) less formality in structure and style - leading to better communication; and

   (e) greater confidence inside and outside the organisation in its ability to cope with change.

15. One of the necessary corollarys of innovation is increased delegation. Part of the creed is to give subordinates more authority so they can 'have their head' and act on creative ideas. In itself delegation has great value - morale and performance are improved, top management is freed for strategic planning and decisions are made by those 'on the ground' and therefore more 'in the know'. Most importantly the organisation benefits from the imagination and thinking of its highflyers.

16. Warning bells ring, however, when delegation is confused with lack of control.

> "The line between efficient corporate performance through delegation and anarchy resulting from a loss of total control is a very fine one."
> *Alec Reed*
> MD, Reed Accounting

17. The logical consequence of being continuously innovative and involving all personnel in initiative-taking amidst consistent change would indeed seem to be anarchy and chaos. Chaos is seen as a positive thing by Tom Peters in his 1987 book, *Thriving on Chaos*. He suggests that a company which reacts proactively with chaos will thrive; it is 'a source of market advantage, not a problem to be got round'.

18. The dilemma then is between the need to be innovative so as to deal with a chaotic environment and the need to retain control over employees so as to prevent anarchy. This can be done simply by giving employees and managers parameters within which discretion can be exercised, and by ensuring that they know they are accountable for their actions.

● **Entrepreneurship and intrapreneurship**

19. Koontz, O'Donnell and Weihrich mention the 'entrepreneurial' aspects of managing as comprising:

   ● profit maximisation
   ● innovation, and
   ● risk-taking.

> We usually think of an entrepreneur as existing only in business - as a person who sees a business opportunity, obtains the needed capital, knows how to put together an operation successfully, and has the willingness to take a personal risk of success or failure. But in a real sense we see entrepreneurial ability also as an important input in most non-business operations.'
> *Koontz et al*

20. Charles Garfield (*Peak performers: the new heroes in business*) writes of the change in ethos which now celebrates innovation and adaptability, opportunism and flair - the attributes of the entrepreneur.

> "Entrepreneurs and intrapreneurs (the internal entrepreneurs who pull together diverse strengths within their organisations to promote innovation) are the new stars."

21. Garfield quotes the example of 3M (Minnesota Mining and Manufacturing) in America (a favourite of Peters and Waterman too). "It is company policy to measure the results of innovation, and actually to *require* it. At least 25 percent of sales in every 3M division each year must come from products introduced within the last five years. Toward that end, employees can spend 15 percent of their office time on independent projects."

22. Peters and Waterman, in their influential anecdotal study of successful American companies - *"In Search of Excellence"* - define 'excellent' as *'continually innovative'*. They, too, note that the promotion of exploration, experimentation, willingness to change, opportunism and internal competition create an entrepreneurial 'culture' or 'climate' in organisations that keeps them adaptive to their environment and enables consistent success.

Intrapreneurial groups

23. In 1982 Macrae developed the idea that a company should consider several different ways of doing the same thing by creating separate intrapreneurial groups consisting of a small number of people, each group being in competition with the others. Together each group would seek the best way of doing something to maximise productivity.

24. Macrae used the example of a small typing pool as an intrapreneurial group within a large pool, each person being paid for what he or she produced rather than merely for turning up at work. Each group was autonomous in its organisation. He identified great differences in the groups' operations compared with classical structures.

20.2 Macrae's intrapreneurial groups

	Role (Classic) organisation	Intrapreneurial organisation
Emphasis	Bureaucracy	Enterprise
Control	Exercised by managers down	Internal within group by members
Size orientation	Single large unit	Many small units
Inter-unit relation	Co-ordination	Competition
Relationship to centre	Strictly controlled	Independent
Work flexibility	Low	High
Sphere of operation	Company	Company but can also take on outside work
Leadership	Appointed by management	Group's choice of leader accepted by management
Work design	Done by experts and managers	Done by group members themselves

• Encouraging innovation

25. An innovation strategy calls for a management policy of giving encouragement to innovative ideas. This will require:

   (a) giving financial backing to innovation, by spending on R & D and market research and risking capital on new ideas;

   (b) giving employees the opportunity to work in an environment where the exchange of ideas for innovation can take place. Management style and organisation structure can help here:

       (i) management can actively encourage employees and customers to put forward new ideas. Participation by subordinates in development decisions might encourage employees to become more involved with development projects and committed to their success;

       (ii) development teams can be set up and an organisation built up on project team-work;

   (c) where appropriate, recruitment policy should be directed towards appointing employees with the necessary skills for doing innovative work. Employees should be trained and kept up to date;

   (d) certain managers should be made responsible for obtaining information from outside the organisation about innovative ideas, and for communicating this information throughout the organisation;

   (e) strategic planning should result in targets being set for innovation, and successful achievements by employees should if possible be rewarded.

Creativity and innovation

26. Creative ideas can come from anywhere and at any time, but if management wish to foster innovation they should try to provide an organisation structure in which innovative ideas are encouraged to emerge.

   (a) Innovation requires creativity. Creativity may be encouraged in an individual or group by establishing a climate in which free expression of abilities is allowed. 'Hot water thought sessions' (brainstorming etc) could be used. The *role of the R & D department* will be significant in many organisations.

   (b) Creative ideas must then be rationally analysed (in 'cold water thought sessions') to decide whether they provide a viable (commercial etc) proposition.

   (c) A system of organisation must exist whereby a viable creative idea is converted into action through effective control procedures.

27. One example of a formal structure for encouraging innovation is the *quality circle*. Quality circles seem to have emerged first in the United States, but it was in Japan that they were adopted most enthusiastically. The modern success story of Japanese industry has prompted Western countries to imitate many of the Japanese working methods, with the result that quality circles are now re-appearing in American and West European companies. We looked at quality circles in more detail in Chapter 7.

How to stifle innovation

28. The Financial Times of 25 June 1986 reported the ideas of Rosabeth Moss Kanter on leadership styles. Moss Kanter is a business consultant whose services are much in demand. She criticises excessively authoritarian and non-participative management on the ground that it stifles innovation and entrepreneurship.

29. Her list of 'Rules for stifling innovation' is a critique of 'management by terror'.

---

1. Regard any new idea from below with suspicion.
2. Insist that people who need your approval first go through several other levels of management.
3. Get departments/individuals to challenge each other's proposals.
4. Express criticism freely, withhold praise, instil job insecurity.
5. Treat identification of problems as signs of failure.
6. Control everything carefully. Count everything in sight - frequently.
7. Make decisions in secret, and spring them on people.
8. Do not hand out information to managers freely.
9. Get lower-level managers to implement your threatening decisions.
10. Above all, never forget that you, the higher-ups, already know everything important about the business.

● Management of growth and stability

30. An organisation will usually seek to grow by increasing its range of products and markets, its sales turnover and its profits. At the least, it will seek stability with a secure and stable level of sales turnover and profits.

> Companies might seek to grow organically, by developing their own internal resources, or else to grow by merger and acquisition (in takeover). Many companies seek growth through a combination of the two strategies.

Innovation and growth

31. If a company operates in a market with a good prospect for growth, it can grow organically either by exploiting existing product-market opportunities or by diversifying. However, because existing products have a finite life, a strategy of organic growth must include plans for *innovation* - developing new products.

32. Kotler wrote (1972):

> 'Business firms are increasingly recognising that the key to their survival and growth lies in the continuous development of new and improved products. Gone is the confidence that established products will maintain strong market positions indefinitely. There are too many competitors with fast-moving research laboratories, sophisticated marketing strategies and large budgets standing ready to woo away customers'.

Innovation and stability

33. Stability calls for innovation too. An organisation cannot rely on its existing products and markets for ever, because products have a finite life, and customer demands change. An organisation which wants to maintain its sales and profits must therefore develop new or improved products, or new markets, to replace the old ones in decline. It is a case of having to keep on running just to stand still.

34. Product development involves:

    (a) expenditure on R & D. Even if a company chooses to copy the products already developed by competitors, and so never be first in the market with a new product, it must be prepared to follow the innovations of others. Innovation is crucial to organic growth in the long term;

    (b) often, heavy capital expenditure to set up a new product or new market operation.

35. An innovation strategy should take a broad view of what sort of innovations should be sought. A product might be completely new, or just a different quality version of an existing product. A new product is not necessarily much different from existing products; rather, the essential characteristic is that it should be distinguishable from its predecessors in the eyes of its customers.

> The car industry provides a very good example of the different types of product innovation. Some years ago, the hatchback was a fairly major innovation. Different quality versions of basically the same model are now a common feature of the car market. Modifications to existing models are made regularly, to keep consumers interested and wanting to buy.

Examples of organic growth/innovation strategy: Courtaulds

36. Courtaulds is one of the world's largest textiles-to-clothing businesses, but competition from low cost producers in the Far East and Eastern Europe ate into its market for 'run of the mill' commodity fibres, so that Courtaulds' output was nearly halved within a few years in the 1980s.

37. All fibre producers in the Western world such as Courtaulds, ICI, duPont and Hoechst etc have reacted by changing their strategy, and looking for new high quality fibres. These have the advantage of selling at prices that give a higher added-value than commodity fibres.

38. This change of strategy has meant:

    (a) Relying on innovation through R & D to develop new high quality fibres. Courtaulds developed a new generation of cellulose fibre, under the project name Genesis.

    (b) Combining R&D with a switch in marketing effort, from the Third World markets and other 'long distance' markets to the economically sophisticated markets of Western Europe. Courtaulds, which used to sell 50% of its output outside Western Europe, now sells 90% of its output inside Western Europe.

Leaders and followers

39. Some firms lead the way with technological innovation, and actively seek new products for their markets. Other firms react to what the leaders do – they 'follow-my-leader'. Either approach can be a successful strategy for innovation. Imitation might even be a more successful approach than leadership in innovation, because the leader will make mistakes that the followers can learn from and avoid.

New product strategies

40. Innovation can mean creating new markets as well as new products – creating extra demand from existing customers in a 'strengthened' market, or creating new demand from new customers. A matrix of new product strategies and new market strategies can be set out as follows. (The analysis was first presented by Johnson and Jones in 1957.)

20.3 New product and market strategies

Product

	No technological change	*Improved technology*	*New technology*
Market unchanged	-	*Reformulation* A new balance between price/ quality has to be formulated	*Replacement* The new technology replaces the old
Market strengthened (new demand from same customers)	*Remerchandising* The product is sold in a new way – eg by re-packaging	*Improved product* Sales growth to existing customers sought on the strength of product improve-ents	*Product line extension* The new product is added to the existing product line to increase total demand
New market	*New use* By finding a new use for the existing product, new customers are found	*Market extension* New customers sought on the strength of product improvements	*Diversification*

● **The management of contraction (divestment)**

41. Development might involve a *contraction* of the organisation and its business, rather than growth.

> Divestment means getting rid of something. In strategic planning terms, it means selling off a part of a firm's operations, or pulling out of certain product-market areas (such as closing down a product line).

42. One reason for divestment is de-growth (shrinkage). A more common reason is to rationalise a business as a result of a strategic appraisal. A company might decide:

(a) to concentrate on its 'core' businesses and sell off fringe activities (it wants to 'get back to its knitting' in Peters and Waterman's phraseology)
(b) to sell off subsidiaries where performance is poor, or where growth prospects are not good.

Examples: Beecham and Cadbury Schweppes

43. From 1982 to 1985 the profits of Beecham, the pharmaceuticals and consumer products company, had been fairly constant, with little or no growth. A diversification by the group into the home improvements business in 1983 failed to have the desired effect on growth and profits. Rumours began to circulate in financial and investment circles that Beecham might be prey for a takeover bid by a predator. In a strategy review in 1986, Beecham's board of directors announced its intention of restoring growth into the group by means of selling off 'non-core' businesses, and concentrating on the 'core' businesses of health and personal care. Proposed sell-offs included:

   (a)   the home improvements division;
   (b)   the Findlater, Mackie Todd wines and spirits business; and
   (c)   Germaine Monteil, the US cosmetics company.

> These divestments, it was announced, would be the first Beecham had made in *20 years* - an indication of the radical re-think in strategic planning that the group had made with its new policy of divestment.

44. Cadbury Schweppes provides another example of a company that decided to divest itself of some non-core businesses in order to concentrate on core businesses as a strategy for improving profitability. The Chairman's statement in the company's 1985 accounts commented:

   'In 1985 Cadbury Schweppes took a number of strategic decisions .... Cadbury Schweppes is concentrating its efforts behind its strengths in its international confectionery and soft drinks businesses and your Board is confident that the 1986 results will confirm that the right strategic course has been taken ....

   With the objective of concentrating on our core international health businesses, we have sold the Health & Hygiene Division and announced the sale of the Beverages & Foods Division. The sale of these companies at a premium over their asset value will free resources for investment in the Group's mainstream businesses, which earn a higher rate of return on capital employed. Your Board continues to monitor the changing structure of the food industry in its major markets and to look for opportunities to strengthen the Group's presence in them, in line with the strategic objectives ....'

45.

Growth, stability and contraction: summary

Many companies pursue a growth objective - growth in turnover, profit, EPS (earnings per share), share price and market capitalisation (total market value).

Growth can be achieved

(a)   organically (internally), or
(b)   by means of a merger or takeover.

Growth can be pursued in existing markets and products, or by *diversifying* into new products and new market areas, depending on the product-market strategy selected.

Some companies do not pursue a growth strategy, but instead

(a)   opt to divest some of their operations, perhaps to concentrate on core products in which they have a major competitive advantage;

(b)   in some cases, decide simply to survive or remain stable. Survival and stability, like growth, call for continual innovation and change.

● **A systematic approach to development**

46. For an organisation to be innovative, and continually responsive to the need for change, a systematic approach can still be established, for planning and implementing changes.

47. A step-by-step model for development is shown below.

Step

1   Determine need or desire for change in a particular area.

2   Prepare a tentative plan.
- Brainstorming sessions a good idea, since alternatives for change should be considered *(Lippitt 1981)*

3   Analyse probable reactions to the change

4   Make a final decision from the choice of alternative options
- Decision taken either by group problem-solving (participative) or by manager on his own (coercive)

5   Establish a timetable for change

- 'Coerced' changes can probably be implemented faster, without time for discussions.

- Speed of implementation that is achievable will depend on the likely reactions of the people affected (all in favour, half in favour, all against etc).

- Identify those in favour of the change, and perhaps set up a pilot programme involving them. Talk with the others who resist the change.

6   Communicate the plan for change
- This is really a continuous process, beginning at Step 1 and going through to Step 7.

7   Implement the change. Review the change.
- Continuous evaluation and modifications

---

48. Management must make sure that:

(a) they have the resources to make the change:

     (i)   they have the money to buy the new equipment or premises or other assets they will need;

     (ii)   they have the staff, properly *trained in advance*, to deal with the new systems;

(b) the change is worth doing. The major test of whether a change is worthwhile is a cost-benefit analysis. The benefits from the change - which might be non-money benefits as well as money-benefits - must justify the costs of making the change. The costs of change include the time and effort it takes, as well as the money cost.

QUIZ

1. What are the advantages and disadvantages of using external consultants to help with organisational change or development?

    ● See para 5 (box)

2. What are the various types of organisational change?

    ● See para 7

3. How might innovative ideas and creative ideas be encouraged and assessed?

    ● See paras 12-13, 25-27

4. What are the qualities of entrepreneurship and how do they contribute to the development and growth of an organisation?

    ● See paras 19-22

5. What strategy should be adopted if an organisation finds that demand has strengthened and it has new technology available to make the product demanded?

    ● See para 40

6. What are the steps in a model for planning change?

    ● See para 47

Chapter 21

PERSONNEL MANAGEMENT: MANPOWER RESOURCING

Topics covered in this chapter

- Personnel management
- Manpower planning
  - o Supply and demand forecasting
- Recruitment and selection
  - o Job description
  - o Personnel specification
  - o Advertising vacancies
  - o Application forms
  - o Interviews
  - o Testing
  - o Group selection methods
- Induction

Purpose of this chapter

To show how organisations determine their manpower needs, and how they go about obtaining
the human resources they require.

- **Personnel management**

1. Staffing or 'personnel management' is the managerial function of recruiting, selecting,
    appraising, training and developing people to carry out jobs or roles in the organisational
    structure. Staffing is therefore closely related to organising. Organising involves creating a
    formal structure of departments and positions: staffing involves filling the positions with
    people.

2. Staffing is important both to the organisation and to the people it employs.

    (a) Employees are human assets of an organisation, and as such they have a value to the
         organisation. An employee's value will be higher if he has more basic abilities, and it
         will grow higher as he gains experience. When an organisation loses an employee, it loses

the experience and abilities of that person, and these might be difficult or costly to replace. The costs of high labour turnover, for example, in terms of recruitment and training costs and lost production etc can be very high.

An organisation should try to apply a staffing policy which provides:
(i) recruitment of the right numbers of people;
(ii) selection of people of the required basic abilities;
(iii) training and development of people to fill senior vacancies when these arise.

(b) Employees often have career ambitions, and might be motivated by:
(i) concern for their career development (through an appraisal scheme or training and development programme);
(ii) the prospects of promotion.

It is therefore important to employees that their organisation should have a policy of filling vacancies in more senior positions, to some extent at least, by internal promotions instead of recruiting staff on the external job market whenever a vacancy arises.

● Manpower planning

3. Labour is one of the resources of an organisation which management must plan and control. Compared to machines, materials and money, labour is a relatively unpredictable and uncontrollable resource because:

(a) environmental factors such a government decisions or the state of the markets create uncertainties in the demand for labour, whereas other factors (such as education or the demands of competitors for labour) create uncertainties in the supply of labour;

(b) employees as individuals may have their own personal goals, and make their own decisions about, for example, whether to leave the organisation, whether to co-operate with management strategies and whether to undertake further training. When large numbers of individuals are involved, the pattern of behaviour which emerges in response to any change in strategy may be hard to predict for reasons such as local culture and attitudes and industrial relations in the local area or plant;

Management and employees may be capable of adapting to change by accepting changes in job content, work organisation or retraining. However, it may be necessary to negotiate rather than impose changes and to accept the consequences of changes for labour turnover and employee motivation;

(c) legislation as well as social and ethical values constrain the ways in which labour may be used, the controls which may be placed over labour, the ease with which labour may be replaced, the criteria which may be used in recruitment or promotion and, in some cases, the rate of pay.

4. The purpose of manpower planning in both the short and the long term is therefore:

(a) to estimate the (uncertain) demand for each grade and skill of employee;
(b) to estimate the (uncertain) supply of labour for the appropriate grades and skills;
(c) where there is a discrepancy between demand and supply, to take measures which will reduce demand or improve supply. Attention must be given to pay, productivity, labour turnover, training, career structure, job enrichment etc.

> This purpose can perhaps be stated more simply as being the objective of having the right people in the right jobs at the right time.

5.   The process of manpower planning may be described in general terms as follows:

(a)   obtaining information on current manpower analysed by grades, skills, ages and retention rates, on which to base estimates of future manpower;

(b)   forecasting manpower requirements, by grades and skills, to meet the long term and short term needs of the organisation;

(c)   devising a strategy to meet the projected manpower requirements by grades and skills;

(d)   acquiring manpower and controlling its 'flow' through the organisation; these are the personnel functions of conditions of employment, pay, training, welfare, recruitment, promotion etc;

(e)   developing the skills of individuals so that with experience, they will become more productive and effective (eg management development);

(f)   attempting to persuade employees to adapt to changes in technology, organisation structure, the social habits of co-workers etc;

(g)   attending to the human relations factor so that corporate goals are achieved in a manner acceptable to and approved by the workforce.

Manpower planning as supply and demand forecasting

> 'The general aim of corporate manpower planning is to reduce the risk of either surplus or shortage of particular kinds of manpower, because any imbalance between personnel and other resources or corporate needs is likely to involve waste.' (Smith 1971)

6.   The demand for labour must be forecast by considering:

(a)   the objectives of the organisation, and the long and short term plans in operation to achieve those objectives. Where plans are changed, the effect of the change must be estimated;

(b)   manpower utilisation - how much labour will be required, given the expected *productivity* or work load of different types of employee. Improvements in productivity might be estimated on the assumption that concessions will be made on pay to the employees concerned.

7. Planning future manpower requires accurate forecasts of turnover and productivity. Suppose, for example, a company employing 3,000 people (of whom 20 are mechanics) estimates that in five years time turnover will be doubled and productivity increased by 50%. Thirty mechanics would therefore be needed to meet the requirement in five years time. In fact, turnover may be three times greater and labour productivity unchanged so that the calculations will be inaccurate, and sixty mechanics would really be needed.

8. The supply of labour will be forecast by considering:

   (a) forecasts of wastage (turnover through resignations, retirement etc), promotion and absentee and productivity levels etc;

   (b) the existing work force structure (age distribution, grades, location, sex, skills, hours of work and rates of pay);

   (c) the potential supply of new labour with the relevant skills from the 'environment', that is the labour market.

9. Demand and supply must be compared in a review we could call a *manpower position survey*. Forecasts of discrepancies between them in the numbers required/available, their grade, skills or location can be removed through the application of an integrated manpower strategy. Short-term adjustments of manpower to requirements may be made and consultation concerning the long-term strategy continued.

Closing the manpower gap between demand and supply

10. Manpower strategy requires the integration of *policies* for:

   - pay and conditions of employment;
   - promotion;
   - recruitment;
   - training;
   - industrial relations.

11. Because all these factors are inter-related, an integrated approach is necessary. For example:

   (a) job/rate evaluation should be carried out in large companies to avoid unfairness; a serious problem is the narrow pay differential in the UK between skilled and unskilled workers, and between middle management and other workers;

   (b) the costs of recruitment include intensive training if personnel move quickly between companies and labour turnover is high;

   (c) for management development, a strong policy is required to ensure that junior management is given sufficient training for senior management positions. If this is not implemented there will be a vacuum when senior managers retire or resign;

   (d) in industrial relations, problems may occur because of a lack of communication between unions and management. Schemes of employee participation which have occasionally proved successful in Europe may also eventually be effective in Britain following EEC measures aimed at increasing employee participation.

12. *Tactical plans* can then be made, within this integrated framework, for:

> - pay and productivity bargaining;
> - physical conditions of employment;
> - management and technical development and career development;
> - organisation and job specifications;
> - recruitment and redundancies;
> - training and retraining;
> - manpower costs.

13. Shortages or surpluses of labour which emerge in the process of formulating the position survey may be dealt with in various ways.

    (a) a *deficiency* may be met through:

        (i)   internal transfers and promotions, training etc;
        (ii)   external recruitment;
        (iii) reducing labour turnover, by reviewing possible causes.

    (b) A *surplus* may be met by:

        (i)   running down manning levels by natural wastage;
        (ii)   restricting recruitment;
        (iii) redundancies - as a last resort, and with careful planning (as discussed in the next chapter).

Control over manpower

14. Once a manpower plan has been established, regular control reports should be produced.

    (a) Actual numbers recruited, leaving and being promoted should be compared with planned numbers. If actual levels seem too high, action can be taken by stopping recruitment temporarily. If levels seem too low recruitment, promotions or retraining activity should be stepped up.

    (b) Actual pay, conditions of employment and training should be compared with assumptions in the manpower plan. Do divergences explain any excessive staff turnover?

    (c) Periodically the manpower plan itself should be reviewed and brought up to date.

> **The manpower plan**
>
> The manpower plan is prepared on the basis of the analysis of manpower requirements, and the implications for productivity and costs. The plan may consist of:
>
> - *The recruitment plan:* numbers, types of people, when required; recruitment programme.
>
> - *The training plan:* numbers of trainees required and/or existing staff needing training; training programme.
>
> - *The redevelopment plan:* programmes for transferring, retraining employees.
>
> - *The productivity plan:* programmes for improving productivity, or reducing manpower costs; setting productivity targets.
>
> - *The redundancy plan:* where and when redundancies are to occur; policies for selection and declaration of redundancies; re-development, re-training or re-location of redundant employees; policy on redundancy payments, union consultation etc.
>
> - *The retention plan:* actions to reduce avoidable labour wastage.
>
> The plan should include budgets, targets and standards. It should allocate responsibilities for implementation and control (reporting, monitoring achievement against plan).

• Recruitment and selection

15. Note that there is an important distinction between recruitment and selection.

> - *Recruitment* is the part of the process concerned with finding the applicants: it is a 'positive' action by management, going out into the labour market, communicating opportunities and information, generating interest.
>
> - *Selection* is the part of the employee recruiting process which involves choosing between applicants for jobs: it is largely a 'negative' process, eliminating unsuitable applicants.

16. A systematic approach to recruitment and selection will therefore embrace:

   (a) detailed manpower planning;

   (b) job analysis, so that for any given job there is:

      (i) a statement of the component tasks, duties, objectives and standards (*a job description*);

      (ii) a specification of the skills, knowledge and qualities required to perform the job (*a job specification*); and

      (iii) a reworking of the job specification in terms of the kind of person needed to perform the job (*a person specification*);

(c) an identification of vacancies, by way of the manpower plan (if vacancies are created by demand for new labour) or requisitions for replacement staff by a department which has 'lost' a current job-holder;

(d) evaluation of the sources of labour, again by way of the manpower plan, which should outline manpower supply and availability, at macro- and micro-levels. Internal and external sources, and media for reaching both, will be considered;

(e) preparation and publication of information, which will:
    (i)   attract the attention and interest of potentially suitable candidates;
    (ii) give a favourable (but accurate) impression of the job and the organisation; and
    (iii) equip those interested to make an attractive and relevant application (how and to whom to apply, desired skills, qualifications etc);

(f) processing applications, assessing the relative merits of broadly suitable candidates;

(g) notifying applicants of the results of the selection process;

(h) preparing employment contracts, induction, training programmes etc.

17. Once the total numbers for recruitment or selection have been decided in keeping with the manpower plan there are two methods of setting about the task of deciding what sort of people are needed to fill the jobs. These methods will both be used together, and are:

(a) the preparation of a job description;
(b) the preparation of a personnel specification.

Job description

18. A *job description* is a broad statement of the purpose, scope, duties and responsibilities of a particular 'job'. It is used to determine and specify:

(a) the content of a job; and

(b) its relative importance in comparison with other jobs. (This does not mean necessarily that the job is evaluated quantitatively, although job evaluation can be carried out when a job description is prepared).

19. The first step is to prepare a *job analysis*. This is "the determination of the essential characteristics of a job" (British Standards Institution) - that is, the process of examining a job to identify its component parts and the circumstances in which it is performed. The product of the analysis is usually a *job specification* - a detailed statement of the activities (mental and physical) involved in the job, and other relevant factors in the social and physical environment.

20. Information which should be elicited from a job analysis is both task-oriented information and worker-oriented information, including:

    (a) *initial requirements* of the employee: aptitudes, qualifications, experience, training required etc;

    (b) *duties and responsibilities:* physical aspects; mental effort; routine or requiring initiative; difficult and/or disagreeable features; consequences of failure; responsibilities for staff, materials, equipment or cash etc;

    (c) *environment and conditions:* physical surroundings, with particular features - eg temperature or noise; hazards; remuneration; other conditions such as hours, shifts, benefits, holidays; career prospects; provision of employee services - canteens, protective clothing etc;

    (d) *social factors:* size of the department; teamwork or isolation; sort of people dealt with - senior management, the public etc; amount of supervision; job status.

21. The fact that a job analysis is being carried out may cause some concern among employees: fear of standards being raised, rates cut, redundancy etc. The job analyst will need to gain their confidence by:

    (a) communicating: explaining the process, methods and purpose of the appraisal;

    (b) being thorough and competent in carrying out the analysis;

    (c) respecting the work flow of the department, which should not be disrupted; and

    (d) giving feedback on the results of the appraisal, and the achievement of its objectives. If staff are asked to co-operate in developing a framework for office training - and then "never hear anything" - they are unlikely to be responsive on a later occasion.

22. The job description is prepared from the job analysis and will list:

    (a) job title;
    (b) location of the job (department, place);
    (c) the relationship of the job to other positions (especially to a senior manager and to subordinate employees, ie to whom is the job holder responsible and who are the job-holder's subordinates)?
    (d) the main duties of the job;
    (e) the responsibilities of the job holder;
    (f) the limits to the job holder's authority;
    (g) major tasks to be accomplished by the job holder;
    (h) any equipment for which the job holder is responsible.

    Some job descriptions include objectives and expected results, whilst others might also describe terms and conditions of employment.

23. A job description can then be used:

    (a) to decide what skills (technical, human, conceptual, design etc) and qualifications are required of the job holder. When interviewing an applicant for the job, the interviewer can use the job description to match the candidate against the job.

    (b) to ensure that the job:
        (i)   will be a full time job for the job holder and will not under-utilise him by not giving him enough to do;

        (ii) provides a sufficient challenge to the job holder - job content is a factor in the motivation of individuals;

    (c) to determine a rate of pay which is fair for the job, if this has not already been decided by some other means eg a separate job evaluation exercise;

    (d) to provide information from which particular job vacancies can be advertised.

Personnel specification

24. A job description is best suited to individual jobs, but for generalised recruitment of young people into junior grades, a *personnel specification* will be more important. Even so, both job descriptions and personnel specifications will be used in the recruitment process.

> A personnel specification identifies the type of person the organisation should be trying to recruit - their character, aptitudes, educational or other qualifications, aspirations in their career etc. It is an interpretation of the job specification in terms of the kind of person suitable for the job.

25. You might well be wondering why a job description does not do this. After all, if we know what a job consists of, we can work out what type of person is needed to fill it. Surely we don't need a personnel specification as well? Here are some reasons why a personnel specification is valuable.

    (a) A job description refers to one sort of job. In generalised recruitment of a large number of people, the recruits may be required for a number of different sorts of job, so that there might be no single job description, but several.

    (b) In a large organisation, junior recruits are taken on with the intention that many of them should eventually become technical and supervisory staff, and some of them managers. If recruits are taken on for a lifetime career, it is not just their ability to do their first job that matters - their potential to progress should be considered as well. A job description for a junior clerical job would therefore not be enough (although it would be of some value, both to the interviewer and the applicant) and a personnel specification would serve more purpose.

21.1 Recruitment process

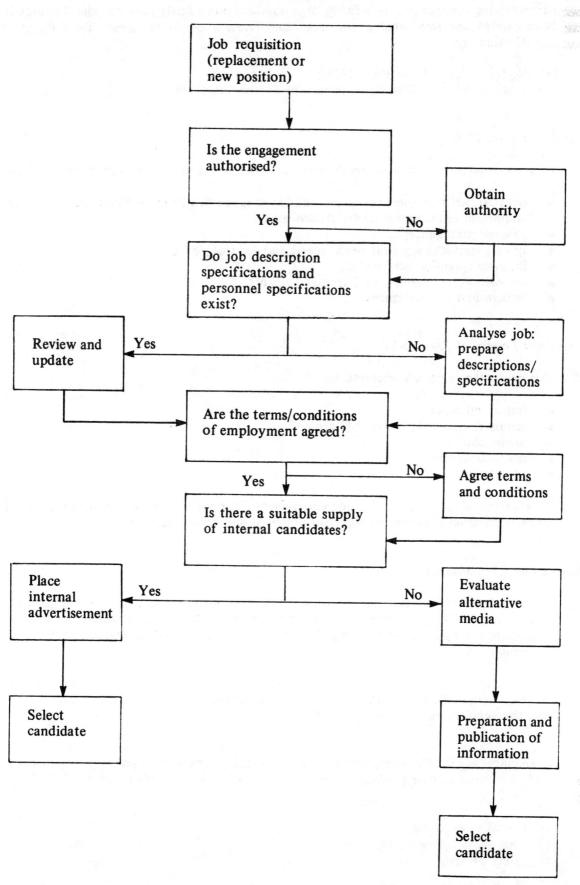

26. A personnel specification is therefore often used as an all-purpose selection assessment plan for recruiting younger people in fairly large numbers into a fairly junior grade. Research has been carried out into what a personnel specification ought to assess. Two designs of specification are:

(a) Rodger's Seven Point Plan (1951);
(b) J Munro Fraser's Five Point Pattern of Personality (1966).

The Seven Point Plan

27. This personnel specification draws the selector's attention to seven points about the candidate:

- physical attributes (neat appearance, ability to speak clearly and without impediment etc);
- attainment (educational qualifications etc);
- general intelligence;
- special aptitudes (eg neat work, speed and accuracy etc);
- interests (practical and social);
- disposition (or manner, eg friendly, helpful);
- background circumstances.

Five Point Pattern of Personality

28. This draws the selector's attention to:

- impact on others;
- acquired knowledge or qualifications;*
- innate ability;
- motivation; and
- adjustment.

*Most personnel specifications include achievements in education, because there appears to be a strong correlation between management potential and higher education.

Advertising job vacancies

29. After a job description and a personnel specification have been prepared, the organisation should advertise the job vacancy (or vacancies). In many large organisations, the personnel department arranges the advertising, deals with applications and arranges interviews with applicants.

30. The job description and personnel specification can be used as guidelines for the wording of any advertisement or careers prospectus pamphlet.

31. An employer must not automatically think he will be doing someone a favour by giving him or her a job. Anyone answering an advertisement will want to know a bit about the job first, in particular:

(a) the salary or wage;
(b) what the job consists of;
(c) career prospects;

(d) qualifications required for the job;

(e) who is to apply for the job.

32. The way in which a job is advertised will depend on the type of organisation and the type of job. A factory is likely to advertise a vacancy for an unskilled worker in a different way to a bank advertising vacancies for clerical staff.

33. The choice of advertising medium will depend on:

(a) the cost of advertising. It is more expensive to advertise in a national newspaper than on local radio, and more expensive to advertise on local radio than in a local newspaper etc;

(b) the frequency with which the organisation wants to advertise the job vacancy. A monthly magazine or weekly newspaper are probably only useful for advertising a vacancy once. This is probably sufficient for a senior management position, since managers who are interested in changing their jobs will be on the look-out for vacancies advertised in certain magazines or newspapers.

34. On the other hand, when the job vacancy is for a grade of staff where suitable applicants are unlikely to be looking in a certain newspaper on a given day, a more continuous advertising message is required. This can be provided by job centres, recruitment agencies, schools careers officers or university careers offices.

35. The common methods or media for advertising jobs are as follows:

(a) *In-house magazines.* An organisation might advertise vacancies for particular jobs through its own in-house magazine or journal, inviting applications from employees who would like a transfer or a promotion to the particular vacancy advertised.

(b) *Professional newspapers or magazines*, such as *Campaign* for advertising executives, *Computer Weekly* for data processing staff, *Accountancy Age* for accountants.

(c) *National newspapers*, especially for senior management jobs or vacancies for skilled workers, where potential applicants will not necessarily be found through local advertising.

(d) *Local newspapers*, for jobs where applicants are sought from the local area.

(e) *Local radio.*

(f) *Job centres.* On the whole, vacancies for unskilled work (rather than skilled work or management jobs) are advertised through local job centres, although in theory any type of job can be advertised here.

(g) *Recruitment agencies.* An organisation might leave the task of advertising a vacancy and selecting candidates for interview to a recruitment agency.

(h) *Schools careers officers.* When an organisation recruits school leavers for long term careers, it would be advisable to advertise vacancies through the careers officers of schools. School leavers are able to find out about the job and career from the careers officer; and suitable advertising material (eg brochures) should be made available. Ideally, the manager responsible for recruitment in an area should try to maintain a close liaison with careers officers.

(i) *University careers officers.* Similarly, an organisation which wants graduates for long-term careers could make use of university careers officers.

(k) *Careers/job fairs.* If an organisation has a large number of vacancies for graduates or other young people, it may choose to attend a fair organised specifically for employers to recruit such persons. Although full attendance may be costly in terms of money and time, the fairs are an increasingly successful way of filling vacancies and the organisation may lose out to its rivals for young people if it fails to attend.

Application forms

36. Applicants who reply to job advertisements are usually asked to fill in a job application form, or to send a letter giving details about themselves and their previous job experience (their CV or *curriculum vitae*) and explaining why they think they are qualified to do the job.

37. An application form should be used to find out relevant information about the applicant, in order to decide:

(a) whether the applicant is obviously unsuitable for the job; or
(b) whether the applicant might be of the right calibre, and worth inviting to an interview.

38. The application form should therefore help the selection officer(s) to sift through the applicants, and to reject some at once so as to avoid the time and costs of unnecessary interviews. If the form is to be useful in the sifting process, it should be designed carefully so as to:

(a) ask questions which will elicit information about the applicant and which can be compared with the requirements for the job. For example, if the personnel specification requires a minimum of 2 'A' level passes the application form should ask for details of the applicant's educational qualifications. Similarly, if practical and social interests are thought to be relevant, the application form should ask for details of the applicant's hobbies and pastimes, membership of societies and sporting clubs or teams etc. If a job description indicates that the successful candidate will be a person aged 30-35 with at least 4 years' experience in a certain type of job and with experience of supervising staff, the application form should ask, amongst other things, for details of age, job experience, and experience in supervising staff;

(b) give the applicant the opportunity to write about himself (or herself), his career ambitions or why he wants the job. By allowing the applicant to write in his own words at length, it might be possible to obtain some information about his:
    (i) neatness;
    (ii) intelligence;
    (iii) ability to express himself in writing;
    (iv) motivation; and
    (v) character (possibly).

21.2 Selection process

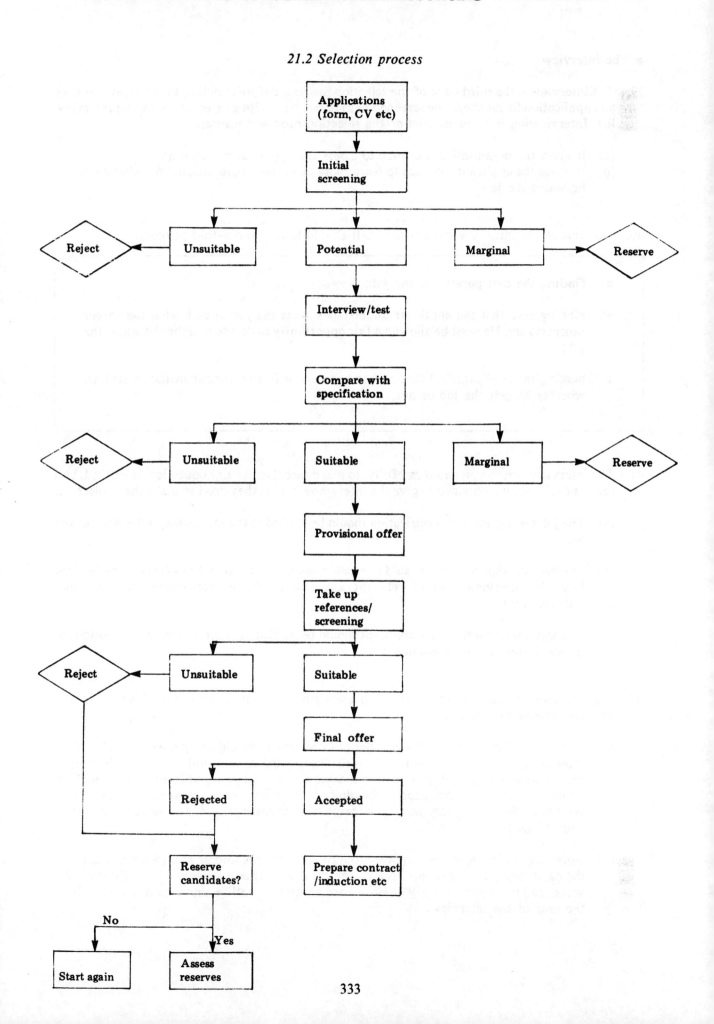

● **The interview**

39. The interview is the third stage of the selection process. Before deciding to interview the CVs and application forms should be screened so as to come up with a reject, reserve and interview list. Interviewing is a crucial part of the selection process because:

    (a) it gives the organisation a chance to assess the applicant directly; and
    (b) it gives the applicant a chance to learn more about the organisation, and whether or not he wants the job.

40. The aim of the interview must be clear. It should have a three-fold purpose:

● finding the best person for the job;

● making sure that the applicant understands what the job is and what the career prospects are. He must be allowed a fair opportunity to decide whether he wants the job;

● making the applicant feel that he has been given fair treatment in the interview, whether he gets the job or not.

---

41. The interview must be prepared carefully, to make sure that the right questions are asked, and relevant information obtained to give the interviewers what they need to make their selection.

    (a) The job description and specification should be studied to review the major demands of the job.

    (b) The personnel specification should be studied and questions should be planned which might help the interviewer make relevant assessments of the applicant's character and qualifications.

    (c) The application form of each applicant should be studied in order to decide on questions or question areas for each applicant.

42. The interview should be conducted in such a way that the information required is successfully obtained during the interview.

    (a) The layout of the room and the number of interviewers should be planned carefully. Most interviewers wish to put candidates at their ease, and so it would be inadvisable to put the candidate in a 'hot seat' across a table from a large number of hostile-looking interviewers. On the other hand, some interviewers might want to observe the candidate's reaction under severe pressure, and deliberately make the layout of the room uncomfortable and off-putting.

    (b) Normally, however, the interviewers do want to put the candidate at his ease, and to make the candidate feel able to talk freely. The manner of the interviewers, the tone of their voice, and the way their early questions are phrased can all be significant in establishing the tone of the interview.

(c) Questions should be put carefully. The interviewers should not be trying to confuse the candidate, but should be trying to obtain the information about him that they need.

(d) The best way to find out about a candidate is to encourage him to talk. It is necessary to ask relevant questions, but the time of the interview should be taken up mostly with the candidate talking, and not with the interviewers asking questions. Questions should therefore discourage short answers. The more a candidate talks, the easier it should be to assess his suitability for the job.

(e) The candidate should be given the opportunity to ask questions. Indeed, a well-prepared candidate should go into an interview knowing what questions he may want to ask. His choice of questions might well have some influence on how the interviewers finally assess him.

43. As a result of the evaluation process a decision will be taken whether or not:

    (a) to offer the candidate the job, subject to:
        (i)   taking up the references which the candidate was asked to supply in his job application;
        (ii)   obtaining any evidence required of educational and professional qualifications;
        (iii) in some cases, a medical examination;

    (b) to invite the candidate to a second interview. Some organisations have a two-stage interview process, whereby first-stage interview candidates are reduced to a short-list for a second stage interview. The second stage of the interview might well be based on a group selection method (see below).

The limitations of interviews

44. Interviews have often been criticised because they fail to select suitable people for job vacancies. The criticisms occur because recruits turn out to be unsuitable for the job, and questions are asked about how it could happen that they should be employed at all in the first place. The main criticisms of interviews are:

(a) unreliable assessments. The opinion of one interviewer may differ from the opinion of another. They cannot both be right, but because of their different opinions, a suitable candidate might be rejected or an unsuitable candidate offered a job;

(b) they fail to provide accurate predictions of how a person will perform in the job;

(c) the interviewers are likely to make errors of judgement even when they agree about a candidate. These might be:

    (i)   a halo effect - this is a tendency for interviewers to make a general judgement about a person based on one single attribute, which will colour the interviewers' opinions and make them mark the person up or down on every other factor in their assessment;

    (ii)   contagious bias - this is a process whereby an interviewer changes the behaviour of the applicant by suggestions. The applicant might be led by the wording of questions or non-verbal clues from the interviewer and change what he is doing or saying in response to the signals he is getting. The consequence would be that the applicant would start to tell the interviewers more of what they wanted to hear, and this would not provide an accurate assessment of the applicant. For example, questions which begin: 'Don't you think that....?' are an obvious way in which applicants might be led by the interview;

    (iii)   a possible inclination by interviewers to stereotype candidates on the basis of insufficient evidence, eg on the basis of dress, hair style, accent of voice etc;

    (iv)   incorrect assessment of qualitative factors such as motivation, honesty or integrity. Abstract qualities are very difficult to assess in an interview;

    (v)   logical error - in other words, an interviewer might draw conclusions about a candidate from what he says or does when there is no logical justification for those conclusions. For example, an interviewer might decide that a person who talks a lot in a confident voice must be intelligent, when this is not the case;

    (vi)   incorrectly used rating scales. For example, if interviewers are required to rate a candidate on a scale of 1-5 for a number of different attributes, there might be a tendency to:
        (1) mark candidates in the middle range when they are not sure what opinion they have obtained;
        (2) mark candidates consistently above or below average for every attribute, because a general impression about the candidate clouds the interviewer's assessment of particular attributes.

45.   It might be apparent from the list of limitations above that a major problem with interviews is the skill and experience of the interviewers themselves. Any interviewer is prone to bias, but a person can learn to reduce this problem through training and experience. The problems with inexperienced interviewers are not only bias, but also:

    (a)   inability to evaluate properly information about a candidate;

    (b)   inability to compare a candidate against the requirements for a job or a personnel specification;

    (c)   badly planned interviews;

    (d)   a tendency to talk too much in interviews, and to ask questions which call for a short answer;

    (e)   a tendency to act as an inquisitor and make candidates feel uneasy.

46.   Interviewers should be trained to conduct and assess interviews. However, although some interviewers might be experts from the personnel department of the organisation it is usually thought desirable to include managers from other departments in the interview team. These managers cannot be full-time interviewers, obviously: they have their other work to do. No matter how much training they are given in interview techniques, they might be poor interviewers through lack of experience and a failure to give interviewing as much thought or interest as they should. They might think that interviewing is an unwelcome chore which drags them away from more important work.

Testing

47. In some job selection procedures, an interview is supplemented by some form of selection test. The interviewers must be certain that the results of such tests are reliable, and that a candidate who scores well in a test will be more likely to succeed in the job. The test will have no value unless there is a direct relationship between ability in the test and ability in the job.

Psychological testing

48. Psychological tests may be used:

    (a) in the initial selection of new recruits;
    (b) in the allocation of new entrants to different branches of work; and
    (c) as part of the process of transfer or promotion.

49. There are four types of test commonly used in practice:

    ● intelligence tests;
    ● aptitude tests;
    ● proficiency tests;
    ● personality tests.

Sometimes applicants are required to attempt several tests (a *test battery*) aimed at giving a more rounded picture than would be available from a single test.

50. *Intelligence tests* aim to measure the applicant's general intellectual ability. They may test the applicant's memory, his ability to think quickly and logically and his skill at solving problems.

51. *Proficiency tests* are perhaps the most closely related to an assessor's objectives, because they measure ability to do the work involved. An applicant for an audio typist's job, for example, might be given a dictation tape and asked to type from it.

52. *Personality tests* may measure a variety of characteristics, such as an applicant's skill in dealing with other people, his ambition and motivation or his emotional stability. They usually consist of questionnaires asking respondents to state their interest in or preference for jobs, leisure activities etc. To a trained psychologist, such questionnaires may give clues about the dominant qualities or characteristics of the individuals tested, but wide experience is needed to make good use of the results.

Aptitude tests

53. In some job selection procedures, an interview is supplemented with an aptitude test. The test must be able to provide information about the candidate's abilities which will be relevant to deciding whether he is suitable for the job or not.

Aptitude tests can test mental ability (IQ tests, tests in mathematics, general knowledge or use of English) and physical dexterity.

54. The selectors/interviewers must be certain that the results of the tests are reliable, and that a candidate who scores well in a test will be more likely to succeed in the job. If a direct relationship between ability in the test and ability in the job does not exist, the test will have little or no value.

When group selection methods are used, the selectors will probably use tests as well as interviews as part of their selection process.

Group selection methods

55. Group selection methods might be used by an organisation as the final stage of a selection process for management jobs. They consist of a series of tests, interviews and group situations over a period of 2 days or so, involving a small number of candidates for a job. Typically, 6 or 8 candidates will be invited to the organisation's premises for 2 days.

After an introductory chat to make the candidates feel at home, they will be given one or two tests, one or two individual interviews, and several group situations in which the candidates are invited to discuss problems together and arrive at solutions as a management team.

56. Applicants for a job might be expected to submit an application form and be called to a first interview before they are invited to a group selection gathering. These gatherings might be thought useful because:

    (a) they give the organisation's selectors a longer opportunity to study the candidates;

    (b) they reveal more than application forms, interviews and tests alone about the ability of candidates to persuade others, to negotiate with others, to explain ideas to others and to investigate problems efficiently. These are typical management skills;

    (c) they reveal more about the candidates' personalities - eg stamina, interests, social interaction with others (ability to co-operate and compete etc) intelligence, energy, self-confidence etc.

57. Since they are most suitable for selection of potential managers who have:

    (a) little or no previous experience; and
    (b) two days to spare for interviews etc;

    group selection methods are most commonly used for selecting university graduates for management trainee jobs.

58. The drawbacks to group selection methods are:

    (a) the time and cost;
    (b) the lack of experience of interviewers/selectors;
    (c) the rather false and unreal nature of the group situations in which candidates are expected to participate. Candidates might behave differently in a contrived situation than they would given a real-life problem.

• Induction

59. When an applicant for a job is offered the job and accepts it, he will have to be introduced to the job. This is the process of induction.

> If you are examined about the induction process, you should be able to draw on your own experience on first starting work.

60. From his first day in a job, a new recruit should be helped to find his bearings. There are limits to what any person can pick up in a short time, so that the process of getting one's feet under the table will be a gradual one.

61. On the first day, a senior person should welcome new recruits. The seniority of this manager is likely to vary according to the size of the organisation, and the size of the office etc where the recruits will be working. In smaller organisations recruits are more likely to see a manager in a more senior position than in larger organisations. The manager might discuss in broad terms what he requires from people at work, working conditions, pay and benefits, training opportunities and career opportunities. He should then introduce the new recruits to the person who will be their immediate supervisor.

62. The immediate supervisor should then take over the on-going process of induction. He should:

(a) pinpoint the areas that the recruits will have to learn about in order to start their jobs. Some things (eg. detailed technical knowledge) may be identified as areas for later study or training, while others (eg. some of the office procedures and systems with which the recruits will have to deal) will have to be explained immediately. A list of learning priorities should be drawn up, so that the recruits, and the supervisor, are clear about the rate and direction of progress required;

(b) explain first of all the nature of the recruits' jobs and of the department as a whole. The goals of each task should be explained. This will help the recruits to work to specific targets and to understand how their tasks relate to the overall objectives of the department - or even the organisation as a whole;

(c) explain about hours of work and stress the importance of time-keeping. If flexitime is operated, he should explain how it works;

(d) explain the structure of the department - to whom the recruits will report, to whom they can go with complaints or queries etc;

(e) introduce the recruits to the people in the office. They should meet all the members of the immediate work team and perhaps be given the opportunity to get to know them informally, over lunch in the canteen etc. They should also be introduced to the departmental manager; they ought to identify who he is, and he may wish to welcome them. One particular colleague may be assigned to each recruit as a mentor for their first few days - to keep an eye on them, answer routine queries, 'show them the ropes' etc. The layout of the office, procedures for lunch hours or holidays, rules about smoking or eating in the office etc. will then be 'taught' informally;

(f) plan and implement an appropriate training programme for whatever technical or practical knowledge is required. Again, the programme should have a clear schedule and set of goals so that the recruits have a sense of purpose, and so that the programme can be efficiently organised to fit in with the activities of the department;

(g) coach and/or train the recruits; check regularly on their progress, as demonstrated by performance, as reported by the recruits' mentor, and as perceived by the recruits themselves. Feedback information on how they are doing will be essential to the learning process, correcting any faults at an early stage and building the confidence of the recruits;

(h) integrate the recruits into the 'culture' of the office. Much of this may be done informally - they will pick up the prevailing norms of dress, degree of formality in the office, attitude to customers etc. However, the supervisor should try to 'sell' the values and 'style' of the office - its 'mission statement' (if any) - and should reinforce commitment to those values by rewarding evidence of loyalty, hard work, desired behaviour etc.

63. There might be a supervisor or manager who is specifically responsible for the induction of new recruits. He should introduce himself to the new recruit, and may wish to deal with any paperwork on the first day, such as giving the recruit his contract of employment. He should repeat the information already given about training opportunities, hours of work, pay and conditions etc. He might also arrange to introduce the new recruit to other recruits in other sections.

He can also provide information about the staff canteen, sports and social clubs, travel facilities to and from work, details about local shops etc.

He should encourage the recruit to come to him with any worries and problems he might have later which he cannot really discuss with his direct supervisor.

64. Note that induction is a continuing process which might last for several months or even longer.

(a) The supervisor must arrange for the recruit's training programme to start.

(b) The recruit will only gradually learn his job through continued on-the-job training.

(c) The person responsible for induction should keep checking up on the new recruit, to make sure that he is settling in well and is learning the ropes.

(d) The senior manager should check on the recruit from time to time (in particular, find out how his training is progressing).

65. After three months, six months or one year, the performance of a new recruit should be formally appraised and discussed with him. Indeed when the process of induction has been finished, a recruit should continue to receive periodic appraisals, just like every other employee in the organisation. (Appraisal will be discussed in the following chapter.)

QUIZ

1. Describe the process of manpower planning, and indicate the component plans that might be drawn up as part of the management programme.

   ● See paras 5, 14 (box)

2. What is the difference between recruitment and selection? Outline a systematic approach to both.

   ● See paras 15, 16

3. What is the purpose of (a) job analysis, (b) a job description and (b) a personnel specification?

   ● See paras 19, 23, 25-26

4. What factors will influence the choice of advertising media for job vacancies?

   ● See paras 32-33

5. What are the problems of using interviews in selection?

   ● See paras 44-45

6. Outline an induction programme for new recruits.

   ● See paras 61-63.

Chapter 22

PERSONNEL MANAGEMENT: TRAINING, APPRAISAL AND TERMINATION

Topics covered in this chapter

- Purposes of training
- Formal and on-the-job training
- Technical training
- Group training
- Staff appraisal
- Promotion
- Resignation
- Prevention of high turnover
- Termination
  - o Unfair dismissal
  - o Redundancy
  - o Wrongful dismissal
- Employee records

Purpose of this chapter

To show how the human resources of the organisation can be developed, by training, appraisal and promotion. To describe the termination of the employment contract by either party.

● The purposes of training

1. As we saw in the previous chapter, providing the organisation with the most suitable human resources for the task and environment is an on-going process. It involves not only recruitment and selection, but the training and development of employees - prior to employment, or at any time during their employment, in order to help them meet the requirements of their current, and potential future job.

2. Both selection and training are concerned with:

   (a) fitting people to the requirements of the job;
   (b) securing better occupational adjustment; and
   (c) in methodological terms, setting and achieving targets, defining performance criteria against which the success of the process can be monitored.

> "Training is to some extent a management reaction to change, eg changes in equipment and design, methods of work, new tools and machines, control systems, or in response to changes dictated by new products, services, or markets. On the other hand, training also induces change. A capable workforce will bring about new initiatives, developments and improvements - in an organic way, and of its own accord. Training is both a cause and an effect of change."
>
> Brian Livy:*Corporate Personnel Management*

3. Education and training may be divided into three basic types:
   (a) formal training (internal and external), or studying for a professional qualification;
   (b) on-the-job training; and
   (c) occasionally, group learning.

● **Formal training**

4. Internal courses are run by the organisation's training department. External courses vary, and may involve:

   (a) day-release, which means that the employee works in the organisation and on one day per week attends a local college for theoretical teaching;

   (b) evening classes, which make demands on the individual's time outside work; this is commonly used, for example, by typists wishing to develop or 'refresh' shorthand skills;

   (c) revision courses for examinations of professional bodies;

   (d) block release courses which may involve four weeks at a college followed by a period back at work;

   (e) sandwich courses, usually involving 6 months at college then 6 months at work, in rotation, for 2 or 3 years;

   (f) a sponsored full-time course at a university or polytechnic for 1 or 2 years.

5. The disadvantages of formal training might be that:

   (a) an individual will not benefit from formal training unless he/she *wants* to learn. The individual's superior may need to provide encouragement in this respect;

   (b) if the subject matter of the training course does not relate to an individual's job, the learning will quickly be forgotten. Many training managers provide internal courses without relating their content to the needs of individuals attending them. Equally, professional and other examinations often include subjects in which individuals have no job experience, and these are usually difficult to learn and are quickly forgotten afterwards;

   (c) individuals may not be able to accept that what they learn on a course applies in the context of their own particular job. For example, a manager may attend an internal course on man-management which suggests a participatory style of leadership, but on returning to his job he may consider that what he has learned is not relevant in his case, because his subordinates are 'too young' or 'too inexperienced'.

On-the-job training or coaching

6. On-the-job training is very common, especially when the work involved is not complex. Trainee managers require more coaching, and may be given assignments or projects as part of a planned programme to develop their experience. Unfortunately, this type of training will be unsuccessful if:

    (a) the assignments do not have a specific purpose from which the trainee can learn and gain experience; or

    (b) the organisation is intolerant of any mistakes which the trainee makes. Mistakes are an inevitable part of on-the-job learning.

7. Experienced supervisors and managers, either promoted from within the organisation or recruited from outside, will need a period of orientation in their new job. It takes time to settle down, and learn the way the 'system' operates. There must be tolerance of mistakes during this orientation period, because it is a form of on-the-job training.

8. Different methods of on-the-job training include:

    (a) *coaching:* the trainee is put under the guidance of an experienced employee who shows the trainee how to do the job. The length of the coaching period will depend on the complexity of the job and the previous experience of the trainee;

    (b) *job rotation:* the trainee is given several jobs in succession, to gain experience of a wide range of activities. (Even experienced managers may rotate their jobs, to gain wider experience; this philosophy of job education is commonly applied in the Civil Service, where an employee may expect to move on to another job after a few years);

    (c) *temporary promotion:* an individual is promoted into his/her superior's position whilst the superior is absent due to illness. This gives the individual a chance to experience the demands of a more senior position;

    (d) *'assistant to' positions:* a junior manager with good potential may be appointed as assistant to the managing director or another executive director. In this way, the individual gains experience of how the organisation is managed 'at the top';

    (e) *committees:* trainees might be included in the membership of committees, in order to obtain an understanding of inter-departmental relationships.

9. Essential steps in the training/coaching process are:

    ● *Establish learning targets.* The areas to be learnt should be identified, and specific, realistic goals stated. These will refer not only to the 'timetable' for acquiring necessary skills and knowledge, but to standards of performance to be attained, which should if possible be formulated by agreement with the trainee.

    ● *Plan a systematic learning and development programme.* This will ensure regular progress, appropriate stages for consolidation and practice. It will ensure that all stages of learning are relevant to the trainee and the task he will be asked to perform.

- *Identify opportunities for broadening the trainee's knowledge and experience* - eg. by involving him in new projects, encouraging him to serve on interdepartmental committees, giving him new contacts, or simply extending his job, giving him more tasks, greater responsibility etc.

- *Take into account the strengths and limitations of the trainee*, and take advantage of learning opportunities that suit his ability, preferred style and goals. A trainee from an academic background may learn best through research-based learning - eg. fact-finding for a committee, off-the-job study etc; those who learn best by 'doing' may profit from project work, hands-on training etc.

- *Exchange feedback*. The supervisor will want to know how the trainee sees his progress and his future. He will also need performance information in order to monitor the trainee's progress, adjust the learning programme if necessary, identify further needs which may emerge and plan future development for the trainee.

All the above will require the commitment of the organisation, and the department manager in particular, to the learning programme. They must 'believe' in training and developing employees, so that they are prepared to devote money, opportunity and the time of all people concerned. The manager will largely dictate the department's attitude to these things. His own time and support will be required to give praise and constructive criticism, to show an interest etc.

• Technical training

10. Technical training is concerned with teaching a person how to do a particular job, or how to do it better.

11. A systematic approach to technical training involves identification of technical work which will lend itself to training, the design of a training scheme, implementation of the scheme and subsequent review to decide whether or not it has succeeded in achieving its purpose at a reasonable cost. The stages in a systematic approach of this kind may be listed as follows.

    (a) Identify areas where training will be beneficial.
    (b) Set training objectives.
    (c) Decide on the training method.
    (d) Compare the costs and benefits of the proposed course.
    (e) Introduce a pilot or test scheme.
    (f) Implement the scheme in full.
    (g) Monitor the results to check that:
        (i)   training works and
        (ii) benefits exceed costs.

22.1 Technical training plan

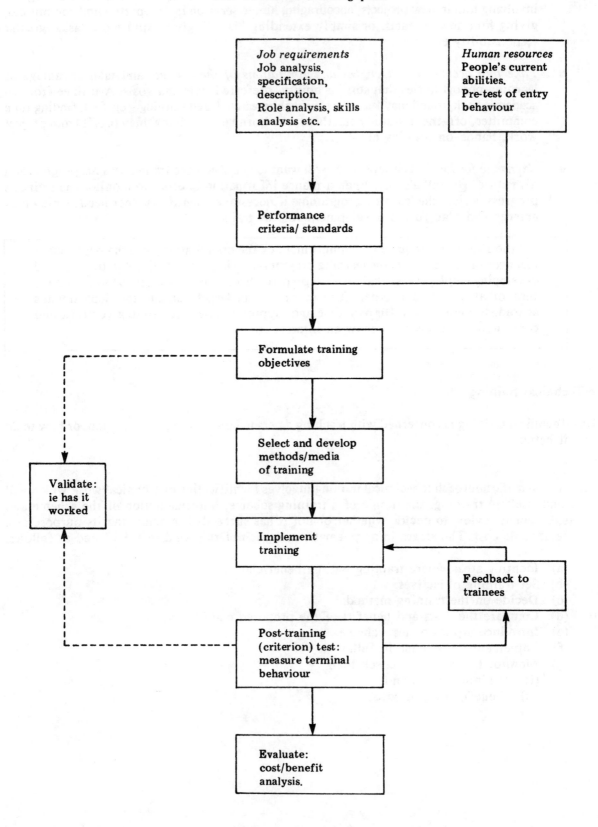

12. Operational managers should suggest to the training department areas of work where they think that training would be beneficial. Alternatively, the training department itself may look for areas of work where training might be provided.

> *Training needs* can be identified by considering the gap between:
>
> - job requirements, as determined by job analysis, job description etc; and
> - the ability of the job holder, as determined by testing or observation and appraisal.

13. The training department's management should make an initial investigation of the problem. (If there were no problem, there would be no call for training.) Even if work is not done as well as it could be, training is not necessarily the right answer. Poor working standards might be caused by:

    (a) poor motivation amongst staff;
    (b) a distracting or uncomfortable working environment (eg a busy office where telephones are continually ringing might distract people from their work);
    (c) badly designed jobs or technology.

14. If the training department concludes that the provision of training *could* improve work performance, it must analyse the work in detail in order to decide what the requirements of a training programme should be. In particular, there should be a training objective or objectives. These are tangible, observable targets which trainees should be capable of reaching at the end of the course.

15. The training objectives should be clear, specific and measurable, for example: 'at the end of a course a trainee must be able to describe...., or identify...., or list...., or state...., or distinguish x from y.... etc'.

    It is insufficient to state as an objective of a course 'to give trainees a grounding in ....' or 'to give trainees a better appreciation of....'. These objectives are too woolly, and actual achievements cannot be measured (quantifiably) against them.

16. Having decided what must be learned and to what standard of achievement, the next stage is to decide what method of training should be used. Training methods include:

    (a) residential courses;
    (b) day courses or lectures;
    (c) programmed learning;
    (d) computer assisted learning. This is where a training programme is provided on a computer. The trainee learns on a computer terminal. (For example, computer-assisted training programmes exist to teach trainees how to use a computer terminal in the first place).

17. *Programmed learning* can be provided on a computer terminal, but it is still sometimes associated with printed booklets which provide information in easy-to-learn steps. From time to time, the booklet then asks simple questions which the trainee must answer. If they are answered

correctly, the trainee is instructed to carry on with more learning. If the questions are answered wrongly, the booklet gives an alternative set of instructions to go back and learn again. The advantages of programmed learning are that:

(a) a trainee can work through the course in simple stages and continually checks whether he is going wrong. Misunderstandings are quickly put right;

(b) a trainee is kept actively involved in the learning process because he must keep answering questions put to him in the booklet;

(c) giving correct answers immediately reinforces the learning process. It is easier for a learner to remember what he knows he has got right;

(d) the trainee can work at his own pace and can take the time he needs. In classroom learning, this is not possible.

18. The training course should only go ahead if the likely benefits are expected to exceed the costs of designing and then running the course. The problem here is not so much in estimating costs, but in estimating the potential benefits.

(a) Costs will be the costs of the training establishment, training materials, the salaries of the staff attending training courses, their travelling expenses, the salaries of training staff etc.

(b) Benefits might be measured in terms of:
   (i) quicker working and therefore reductions in overtime or staff numbers;
   (ii) greater accuracy of work;
   (iii) more extensive skills.

As you will appreciate, the benefits are more easily stated in general terms than quantified in money terms.

19. When the training course has been designed, it may be decided to have a pilot test of the course. The purpose of the test would be to find out whether the training scheme appears to achieve what it has set out to do, or whether some revisions are necessary. After the pilot test, the scheme can be implemented in full.

20. Implementation of the training scheme is not the end of the story. The scheme should be validated and evaluated.

(a) Validation means observing the results of the course, and measuring whether the training objective has been achieved.

(b) Evaluation means comparing the actual costs of the scheme against the assessed benefits which are being obtained. If the costs exceed the benefits, the scheme will need to be re-designed or withdrawn.

21. There are various ways of monitoring a training scheme. These are:

   (a) asking the trainee whether they thought the training programme was relevant to their work, and whether they found it useful. This form of monitoring is rather inexact and it does not allow the training department to measure results for comparison against the training objective;

   (b) measuring what the trainees have learned on the course, perhaps by means of a 'test' at the end of the course;

   (c) studying the subsequent behaviour of the trainees in their jobs to measure how the training scheme has altered the way they do their work. This is possible where the purpose of the course was to learn a particular skill;

   (d) finding out whether the training has affected the work or behaviour of other employees not on the course - eg seeing whether there has been a general change in attitudes arising from a new course in, say, computer terminal work. This form of monitoring would probably be reserved for senior managers in the training department;

   (e) seeing whether the training (all training schemes collectively) has contributed to the overall objectives of the organisation. This too is a form of monitoring reserved for senior managers and would perhaps be discussed at board level in the organisation.

● **Group learning: 'T' groups**

22. Group learning is not common in industry but is common in organisations such as social services departments of local government authorities. The purpose of group learning is:

   (a) to give each individual in a training group (or T group) a greater insight into his own behaviour;

   (b) to teach an individual how he 'appears' to other people, as a result of responses from other members of the group;

   (c) to teach an understanding of intra-group processes, or how people inter-relate;

   (d) to develop an individual's skills in taking action to control such intra-group processes.

   'Encounter groups' for therapy are a development of the T-group principle.

23. Group learning may be of educational value to individuals whose job is dealing with other people. This process must have the full co-operation of all participants in the group if the training is to provide positive educational results.

24. The underlying concept of T-groups is that groups will study their own behaviour with the help of an experienced trainer. They will meet in sessions of about 1½ -2 hours each, and will be left to decide for themselves how to organise their time and what to talk about. The purpose of T-groups training in management would be:

   (a) to give individuals more awareness of being part of a group of people;

(b) to help individuals to understand their attitudes to other people, and to improve these attitudes when they are harmful;

(c) to make individuals more sensitive to the opinions of other people;

(d) to learn how to help others;

(e) to learn how to let other people become the leader in a situation where that other person emerges as the most natural leader for the situation. (This in turn might help a manager to delegate work more freely).

25. T-groups can therefore be used to develop human relations skills. 'Participation in any group activity probably enhances a person's sensitivity to how others see him and his skill in assessing the behaviour of others and the reasons for it.' However, it can be argued that membership of committees can also be a useful aid to development without the intense pressures that may arise in T-groups.

● Staff appraisal

26. Staff appraisal is the process of:

(a) looking at the past performance of an employee, and assessing his strengths and weaknesses;

(b) considering the suitability of the employee for promotion (ideally, by considering his potential to do a more senior job well);

(c) considering how the performance of the employee can be improved (or developed) by training, moving to another job to obtain more experience or counselling about his faults and how to overcome them.

In many organisations, a formal appraisal is carried out once each year, and an annual report on the employee prepared for personnel records.

Appraisal schemes

27. The purpose of formal appraisal schemes is:

(a) to gather information about the skills and potential of existing employees;

(b) to assess the performance of employees, so as to reward them (eg with the promise of promotion);

(c) to let the employee know how well he or she has performed, and give an assessment of his/her strengths and weaknesses;

(d) to allow the person being appraised and his/her superior to discuss how they should plan to achieve the objectives of both the person and his/her job.

28. Appraisal schemes are therefore means of rewarding, criticising, encouraging and counselling. The superior of the person appraised is meant to be both critic and counsellor, but in practice these twin roles tend to be incompatible.

29. The 'traditional' method of individual appraisal in bureaucracies (that is for office workers) is *trait* appraisal. The individual's superior (and perhaps the superior's boss) will be asked to complete an appraisal report on the individual, grading him/her with regard to certain characteristics or traits, such as intelligence, initiative, enthusiasm, skill, punctuality, appearance etc. A report might be designed as follows:

22.2 Trait appraisal report

APPRAISAL REPORT							
Name: Position: Department:	Time in position: Period of review: Age:						
	A	B	C	D	E	Comment	
Overall assessment Job knowledge Effective output Co-operation Initiative Time-keeping Other relevant factors (specify)							
A = Outstanding B = Above standard C = To required standard D = Short of standard in some respects E = Not up to required standard							
Potential	A	B	C	D	E	Comment	
A = Overdue for promotion B = Ready for promotion C = Potential for promotion D = No evidence of promotion potential at present E = Has not worked long enough with me for judgement							
Training, if any, required							
Assessment discussed with employee? Yes ☐ No ☐							
Signed: Date: Confirmed: Date:							

where the grading system ranges from excellent (grade A) to very weak (grade E)
The report may then be discussed in an interview between the individual and his superior.

30. Various other appraisal techniques have been formulated, including the following.

(a) *Overall assessment*. This is the most simple method, requiring the manager to write in narrative form his judgement about the appraisee, possibly with a checklist of personality characteristics and performance targets to work from. There will be no guaranteed consistency of the criteria and areas of assessment, however, and managers may not be able to convey clear, effective judgements in writing.

(b) *Guided assessment*. Assessors are required to comment on a number of specified characteristics and performance elements, with guidelines as to how the terms (eg 'application', 'integrity', 'adaptability') are to be interpreted in the work context. This is a more precise, but still rather vague method.

(c) *Grading*. Grading adds a comparative frame of reference to the general guidelines, whereby managers are asked to select one of a number of levels or degrees to which the individual in question displays the given characteristic. These are also known as *rating scales*, and are much used in standard appraisal forms. Their effectiveness depends to a large extent on:

   (i) the relevance of the factors chosen for assessment. These may be nebulous personality traits, for example, or clearly defined job factors, eg job knowledge, performance against targets, decision-making etc;

   (ii) the definition of the agreed standards of assessment. Grades A–D might simply be labelled 'Outstanding – Satisfactory – Fair – Poor', in which case assessments are subject to much variation and subjectivity. They may, on the other hand, be more closely related to work priorities and standards, using definitions such as 'Performance is broadly acceptable, but employee needs training in several major areas and/or motivation is lacking.'

Numerical values may be added to ratings to give rating 'scores'. Alternatively a less precise *graphic scale* may be used to indicate general position on a plus/minus scale, eg:

Factor: job knowledge

High ⊢————————✓————⊣ Average ⊢————————————⊣ Low

(d) *Behavioural incident methods*. These concentrate on employee behaviour, measured against definitions of 'typical' behaviour in each job, which are based on common 'critical incidents' of successful and unsuccessful job behaviour reported by managers. Time and effort are required to collect and analyse reports and to develop the scheme, and it only really applies to large groups of people in broadly similar jobs. However, it is firmly rooted in observation of 'real-life' job behaviour, and the important aspects of the job.

(e) *Results-orientated schemes*. The above techniques may be used with more or less results-orientated criteria for assessment - but are commonly based on trait or behavioural appraisal. A wholly results-orientated approach (eg Management by Objectives) sets out to review performance against specific targets and standards of performance agreed in advance by manager and subordinate together. The advantages of this are that:

   (i) the subordinate is more involved in appraisal of his own performance, because he is able to evaluate his success or progress in achieving specific, jointly-agreed targets;

(ii)   the manager is therefore relieved, to an extent, of his role as critic, and becomes a 'counsellor';

(iii)   learning and motivation theories suggest that clear and known targets are instrumental in modifying and determining behaviour.

> The effectiveness of the scheme will still, however, depend on the targets set (are they clearly defined? realistic?) and the commitment of both parties to make it work. The measurement of success or failure is only part of the picture: reasons for failure and opportunities arising from success must be evaluated.

31.   In theory, such appraisal schemes may seem very 'fair' to the individual, but in practice, the system often goes wrong because:

(a)   appraisal interviews are often defensive on the part of the subordinate, who believes that any criticism will lessen the rewards for his/her performance (eg promotion will be missed);

(b)   interviews are also often defensive on the part of the superior, who cannot reconcile the role of judge and critic with the 'human relations' aspect of the interview. The superior may therefore misrepresent the extent of the criticism of the subordinate which is contained in the report;

(c)   the superior might show bias in his report (in the same way that an interviewer might show incorrect judgement in the interview process);

(d)   reports from one department's managers might be more favourable or lenient than reports from another department. However, when a standard appraisal report is used throughout the organisation, there is a reasonable prospect that reporting will be fairly consistent in all areas and in all departments.

32.   Criticism can only be beneficial if it is constructive, and if the threat of withholding rewards such as promotion or better pay is not present (or at least does not dominate the counselling interview). A mutual trust and respect must exist between the superior and the subordinate, and in practice, this is all too rare. In other words, it is easy to write appraisal reports, but it is not so easy to use them in counselling interviews. Criticism is easily taken the wrong way by subordinates and sometimes given harshly by superiors!

33.   Various ideas have been put forward to suggest how appraisal can be made more effective.

(a)   Its purpose should be constructive, which means that the superior and subordinate in a counselling interview should agree on goals for the subordinate to achieve. The interview should preferably take place at the instigation of the subordinate, who is ready to be given more goal-direction by the superior.

(b)   Instead of trait appraisal, the individual might be judged on his/her success in achieving stated objectives. The drawback to this idea, however, is that the individual may expect to be in a job for only 2 or 3 years, so that he/she will not be concerned with longer-term objectives. There will also be a tendency to suppress any trouble until promotion is secured - to keep the lid on a problem and leave it to blow up in the face of the individual's successor in the job.

(c) The link between past performance and future reward should be broken unless the organisation clearly intends a connection to exist. In many formal organisations:
   (i)   promotion tends to depend on seniority, not performance; and
   (ii) there is a rigid pay structure. Employees and their trade unions believe in equity of pay so that there is a clearly defined pay structure for employees in different grades. The pay of an individual is not related to his performance.

   Unless the connection between performance and reward is a very real one, it is damaging to the system of appraisal of employees to believe that the connection exists.

(d) When a person is promoted, he or she will move into a job which calls for a different mixture of skills. It is widely agreed that as managers move up an organisation's hierarchy, they do less technical work and more human relations work. Senior managers spend most of their time on strategic planning - that is design work.

22.3 Time spent in the hierarchy

The argument can be made that if an individual is assessed on the basis of past performance, the assessment will not properly show whether the individual will be capable of handling a more senior job with a demand for different abilities. (Indeed, by using past performance as a guide to promotion prospects, the organisation is likely to promote managers to their level of incompetence - the Peter principle.)

Appraisal for promotion might therefore be based on an assessment, not of an individual's traits or past performance, but in terms of his/her *potential* skills as a manager; the individual can be graded on his known ability to plan, to be a controller and make decisions, on his skills in human relations and leadership, on his ability to organise, gather, analyse and communicate information and on his ability to innovate.

34. An alternative approach to individual appraisal (which also removes the link between past performance and reward) is *peer rating* in which an individual is judged and counselled, not by his/her superior, but by people in the same level in the organisation hierarchy - by workmates or colleagues. It has been argued that peer rating will be devoid of mistrust and fear of missing promotion and will therefore be more honest and constructive, thus aiding the individual to develop in his job.

35. The criteria for assessment of an appraisal scheme may be broadly classified as follows:

(a) *Relevance*

    (i)   Does the system have a useful purpose? - eg. to assess the skills and potential of employees, to reward them appropriately, to give feedback information for their development, to allow the appraisee to co-operate with his/her superior in planning the future.

    (ii)   Is the purpose clearly expressed and widely understood by all concerned, both appraisers and appraisees? (Otherwise, resentment and/or insecurity may result from the perceived 'threat' of appraisal.)

    (iii)   Are the appraisal criteria relevant to the purposes of the system? If the purpose is to assess performance, the appraiser should not focus on personality issues, his own feelings about the appraisee, the appraisee's life outside etc.

(b) *Fairness*

    (i)   Is there reasonable standardisation throughout the organisation - are employees of one branch being assessed by the same criteria and against the same standards as those of another?

    (ii)   Is there reasonable objectivity? There should be controls to ensure that personal bias does not colour the appraisal. The appraiser's style and attitude should be assessed from time to time. There should be some machinery for appeal to higher levels, in the event of alleged unfairness.

(c) *Genuineness* - is the system taken seriously by the organisation and by the individuals involved?

    (i)   Are the managers concerned committed to the system - or is it just something the personnel department thrusts upon them?

    (ii)   Who does the interviewing, and are they properly trained in interviewing and assessment techniques?

    (iii)   Is reasonable time and attention given to the interviews - or is it a question of 'getting them over with'?

    (iv)   Is there a genuine demonstrable link between performance and reward? If there isn't, the appraisals may be perceived as useless.

(d) *Co-operation*

    (i)   Is the appraisal a joint activity of appraiser and appraisee? - is it regarded as a co-operative problem-solving opportunity, or merely as a tool of management control?

    (ii)   Is the appraisee given time and encouragement to prepare for the appraisal, so that he/she can make a constructive contribution?

    (iii)   Does a jointly-agreed, concrete conclusion emerge from the interview? - in the form of a written summary or statement.

      (iv)   Are appraisals held at the appraisee's instigation or do management have to force them on employees? Are they held regularly - or once in a blue moon?

(e) *Efficiency*

      (i)   Does the system seem overly time-consuming compared to the value of its outcome?

      (ii)   Is it difficult and costly to administer? - are there efficient systems for the gathering, storage and retrieval of the performance information required, secretarial support for summaries etc. arising from appraisals, schedules for holding appraisal interviews etc?

> A positive answer to the above questions will indicate a healthy, effective appraisal system.

● Promotion

36. Promotion is not only useful from the firm's point of view - in establishing a management succession, filling more senior position with proven, experienced and loyal employees. It is also one of the main forms of reward the organisation can offer to its employees, especially where, in the pursuit of 'equity', employees are paid a rate for the job rather than for performance: pay ceases to be a prime incentive. In order to be a motivator, promotion must be seen to be available, and fair. It can also cause political and structural problems in the organisation if it is not carefully planned.

37. A coherent policy for promotion is needed. This may vary to include provisions such as:

(a) all promotions, as far as possible, are to be made from within the firm; this is particularly important with reference to senior positions if junior ranks are not to be discouraged and de-motivated;

(b) merit and ability (systematically appraised) should be the principal basis of promotion, rather than seniority (years of service). Loyalty and experience will obviously be considered but should not be the sole criterion. Management will have to demonstrate to staff and unions, however, that their system of appraisal and merit rating is fair and fairly applied if the bases for promotion are to be trusted and accepted;

(c) vacancies should be advertised and open to all employees;

(d) there should be full opportunities for all employees to be promoted to highest grades;

(e) personnel and appraisal records should be kept and up-dated regularly;

(f) training should be offered to encourage and develop employees of ability and ambition in advance of promotion;

(g) scales of pay, areas of responsibility, duties and privileges of each post etc should be clearly communicated so that employees know what promotion means - what they are being promoted *to*.

38.

> It is worth bearing in mind a principle first propounded by Laurence J Peter (and known as the *Peter Principle*): that people are promoted to the level of their incompetence: that is people are promoted on the basis of performance at a lower level – not necessarily on potential for success at the higher level (and they only cease to rise up the ladder when they have – possibly disastrously – proved themselves unable to cope in their current position).

39. The decision of whether to promote from within or fill a position from outside will hinge on many factors. If there is simply no-one available on the current staff with the expertise or ability required (eg. if the company is venturing into new areas of activity, or changing its methods by computerisation etc), the recruitment manager will obviously have to seek qualified people outside. If there is time, a person of particular potential in the organisation could be trained in the necessary skills, but that will require an analysis of the costs as compared to the possible (and probably less quantifiable) benefits of promoting an insider.

40. Where the company has the choice, it should consider the following points:

(a) Management will 'know' the promotee: there will be detailed merit-rating and appraisal information available from the employee records. The outside recruit will to a greater extent be an 'unknown quantity' – and the organisation will be taking a greater risk of an unacceptable personality emerging later.

(b) A promotee has already worked within the organisation and will be familiar with its:
   (i)   culture, or philosophy; informal rules and norms as well as stated policy etc;
   (ii) politics; power-structures and relationships;
   (iii) systems and procedures;
   (iv) objectives;
   (v)   other personnel (who will likewise be familiar with him).

(c) Promotion of insiders is visible proof of the organisation's willingness to develop the careers of employees. This may well have an encouraging and motivating effect. Outsiders may well invite resentment.

(d) On the other hand, an organisation must retain its ability to adapt, grow and change, and this may well require 'new blood' – wider views, fresh ideas etc. Insiders may be too socialised into the prevailing culture to see faults or to be willing to 'upset the apple-cart' where necessary.

● **Resignation**

41. Employees may resign for any number of reasons, personal or occupational. Some or all of these reasons may well be a reflection on the structure, management style, culture or personnel policies of the organisation itself. When an employee announces his intention to leave, verbally and/or by letter, it is important for management to find the real reasons why he is leaving, in an *exit interview*. This may lead to a review of the existing policies on pay, training, promotion, the work environment, the quality and style of supervision etc.

42. The principal aspect of any policy formulated to deal with resignations must be the length to which the organisation will go to try and dissuade a person from leaving. In some cases, the organisation may decide to simply let the person go, but when an employee has been trained at considerable cost to the firm, or is particularly well qualified and experienced (no employee is irreplaceable - but some are more replaceable than others...), or has knowledge of information or methods that should not fall into the hands of competitors, the organisation may try to keep him.

43. Particular problems the employee has been experiencing may be solvable, though not always in the short term. It may be that the organisation will try to match or improve on a salary offer made to the individual by a prospective new employer. In that case, however, there may well be a problem of pay differentials and the individual's colleagues, doing the same work, may have to be given similar increases: can so large a cost be justified?

44. Various arrangements will have to be made when an employee decides to leave. There will have to be co-operation and full exchange of information between the personnel function, departmental heads and the office manager (if he has responsibility overall for clerical staff) so that procedures can be commenced upon notification of an intending departure.

    (a) If attempts (if any) to make the employee stay have been unsuccessful, the exit interview will have to be arranged.

    (b) The period of notice required for the employee to leave should be set out in his contract of employment, but some leeway may be negotiated on this. The time needed for recruitment and induction of a replacement may dictate that the leaving employee work out his full period of notice, and perhaps even longer if he is willing. On the other hand, if it is felt that he can be easily replaced, and that his continuing presence maybe destructive of morale (or possibly of advantage to competitors, as he continues to glean information), it may be possible to persuade him to accept pay in lieu of notice and leave immediately.

    (c) Details of the departure will have to be notified to the wages clerk, pension fund officer, social secretary, security officer etc. so that the appropriate paperwork and other procedures can be completed by his date of leaving.

    (d) The departmental head and/or supervisor should complete a leaving report form: an overall assessment of the employee's performance in the organisation. This can then be used to provide references to his future employer(s). NB - there is no obligation to give a reference to a former employee but if one is given, care should be taken in the wording. If it can be proved that the employer acted maliciously, there may be a case for defamation of character.

● **The prevention of high labour turnover**

45. A systematic investigation into the causes of turnover will have to be made, using:

    (a) information given in *exit interviews* with leaving staff, which should be the first step after an employee announces his intention to leave. It must be recognised, however, that the reasons given for leaving may not be complete, true, or those that would be most useful to the organisation. The interviewer should be trained in interview techniques, and should be perceived to be 'safe' to talk to and objective in his appraisal of the situation (rather than being the supervisor against whom the resigning employee has a complaint, the manager who is going to write a reference etc);

(b) information gleaned from interviews with leavers, in their homes, shortly after they have gone. This is an occasionally-used practice, intended to encourage greater objectivity and frankness, but one which requires tact and diplomacy if it is not to be resented by the subject;

(c) attitude surveys, to gauge the general climate of the organisation, and the response of the workforce as a whole to working conditions, management style etc.

46. Some reasons for leaving will be genuine and largely unavoidable, or unforeseeable, eg:

- illness or accident, although transfer to lighter duties, excusing the employee from shiftwork etc might be possible;
- a move from the locality for domestic reasons, transport or housing difficulties;
- marriage or pregnancy. Many women still give up working when their family situation changes;
- retirement;
- career change.

---

47. Other 'environmental' factors should, however, be considered. It may be possible to reduce labour turnover by attending to what Frederick Herzberg considered to be 'hygiene' factors in the environment (these are sources of worker dissatisfaction - as opposed to sources of positive satisfaction, or 'motivation' factors).

(a) The organisation will have to offer satisfactory (or at least competitive) wages and benefits, with fair differentials, and incentives. If it can also offer job security, through sound corporate planning, this is also an advantage.

(b) It will have to ensure that hours and conditions of work are in compliance with legal standards and best practice. Health and safety at least should be a priority.

(c) Jobs should be designed to offer, as far as possible, variety and discretion to those who desire them.

(d) Recruitment and selection procedures should ensure that the right calibre of worker is put into any given job. Some workers will be able to handle monotony, pressure, responsibility, lack of discretion etc better than others. The organisation should also ensure that its recruitment material does not make claims which will not be confirmed by the recruits' experience.

(e) Induction should be creatively used to introduce employees to the organisation. Training should be systematically planned to be on-going, effective and motivating. Career progression should be open to all employees, and clearly planned and communicated.

(f) Supervision and management style should be effective and appropriate to the nature of the task, the technology, the environment and the individuals concerned. If the leader is inadequate, lacks informal authority, is 'psychologically distant' from his team or over-autocratic, employees may be dissatisfied. In particular, management should ensure that plans, progress, and other feedback information is regularly communicated to employees.

● **Termination**

48. Employment may be terminated by:

> ● *lay-off*. This is a temporary measure when there is insufficient work - eg. in seasonal activities such as building, peak sales periods etc. When work becomes available, workers are recalled;
>
> ● *suspension*. This is usually temporary action by the employer, imposed for breaking rules or regulations. There should be a disciplinary policy fixing periods of suspension for particular offences;
>
> ● *dismissal*. Workers are protected by legislation against arbitrary discharge. The *Employment Protection (Consolidation) Act 1978* sets out various provisions (discussed below); or
>
> ● *redundancy*, where the employee is dismissed because the employer has ceased to operate, or because the employee's work itself is no longer needed.

49. An employee who has been continuously employed (for at least 16 hours a week) for any period between 4 weeks and 2 years is entitled to not less than 1 week's notice, with an additional entitlement of 1 week for each following year's continuous employment up to 12 years (that is 12 weeks' notice). Longer periods may be written into the employee's contract, at the organisation's discretion.

Unfair dismissal

50. An employee who has been continuously employed for at least 2 years and who considers himself to have been unfairly dismissed may bring a claim before the Industrial Tribunal. 'Dismissal' in this context includes not only termination of an employment contract, but also:
   (a) the ending of a fixed term contract without renewal on the same terms; and
   (b) termination by the employee himself where the employer's conduct makes him entitled to do so ('constructive dismissal').

51. The employee first has to prove that he has been dismissed. The onus is then on the employer to prove that the dismissal was *fair*, although it is no longer automatically presumed to be unfair. This is not entirely a matter of breach of contract: even if correct notice is given, according to contract, 'unfair' dismissal may still be claimed.

52. Under the 1978 Act, dismissal is fair and justified if the reason for it was:
   (a) redundancy (provided that the selection for redundancy was fair);
   (b) legal impediment - the employee could not continue to work in his present position without breaking a legal duty or restriction (provided the employee was offered any suitable alternative employment);
   (c) non-capability (provided adequate training and warnings had been given);
   (d) misconduct (provided warnings suitable to the offence have been given); or
   (e) some other 'substantial' reason.

An employee who has been dismissed is entitled to a written statement from his employer, within 14 days of request, of the reasons for his dismissal.

53. The procedures used for disciplining and dismissing employees are vitally important because even if a fair reason for dismissal has been proved, the employer must be shown to have *acted reasonably* in treating it as a reason for dismissal. There are guidelines on disciplinary practices and procedures in employment issued by ACAS (the Advisory, Conciliation and Arbitration Service), including the following.

(a) The employer should issue a copy of rules on disciplinary procedures to all employees. Rules should state clearly the employees to whom they are relevant, and the range of disciplinary action that may be taken.

(b) Employees should be informed of any complaints made against them, and should be given an opportunity to state their case. They should have the right to be accompanied by a trade union representative or colleague of their choice.

(c) No action should be taken prior to full investigation of the case. Immediate superiors should not have authority to dismiss an employee without reference to more senior management.

(d) Except in cases of gross misconduct, a first breach of discipline should not be punished with dismissal. Other than summary dismissal, disciplinary action should be notified: by formal oral warning by the supervisor in the case of minor offences, and written warning in more serious cases.

(e) Employees should have any penalties imposed on them explained and there should be procedures for appeal.

54. Special situations in which dismissal can be claimed as automatically unfair include:
(a) unfair selection for redundancy;
(b) dismissal because of membership and involvement in the activities of an independent trade union (an 'inadmissible reason' - the 2 year employment record does not count here). If, on the other hand, there is a practice in accordance with a union membership agreement (closed shop) requiring all employees to belong to a specified union, and the employee refuses to join (other than for conscientious or religious reasons) he may be fairly dismissed;
(c) dismissal because of pregnancy.

55. The Tribunal may order various remedies including:
(a) re-instatement - giving the employee his old job back;
(b) re-engagement - giving him a job comparable to his old one;
(c) compensation. This may consist of:
(i) the basic award, payable in all cases; and
(ii) the compensatory award, if the employee has suffered financial loss.

Redundancy

56. Redundancy is defined by the Act as dismissal where:
(a) the employer has ceased to carry on the business;
(b) the employer has ceased to carry on the business in the place where the employee was employed; or

   (c)   the requirements of the business for employees to carry out work of a particular kind have ceased or diminished or are expected to.

57. Redundant employees are entitled to compensation:

   (a) for loss of security; and
   (b) to encourage employees to accept redundancy without damage to industrial relations. (Voluntary redundancy may be offered to workers, with a financial incentive, thus avoiding the need for selection.)

58. The employee is not entitled to compensation if the employer has made a 'suitable' offer of alternative employment and the employee has unreasonably rejected it. The 'suitability' of the offer will have to be examined in each case. If he has accepted an offer the employee is entitled to a trial period of at least 4 weeks, during which time he may decide that the job is unsuitable and can still claim a redundancy payment. Employees of pension age and over, and those with less than 2 years' continuous employment, are *not* eligible to claim.

59. The employer planning on making redundancies must:

   (a) consult appropriate trade unions about their implementation;
   (b) note and reply to any representations made;
   (c) notify the Secretary of State for Employment if planned redundancies affect more than 10 workers over a one month period.

If unions are not consulted, they can apply to an industrial tribunal for a protective award, which requires the employer to maintain the pay of affected employees for a specified period.

Wrongful dismissal

60. An employee who is dismissed without the required period of notice (summary dismissal) may seek to claim damages from the employer for wrongful dismissal. It is important therefore that employees should not be summarily dismissed without justification - the employee must be seriously at fault. The following circumstances *may* justify summary dismissal:

- wilful disobedience of a proper order
- serious misconduct within or (rarely) outside the business
- dishonesty
- incompetence
- neglect
- gross negligence
- immorality (very rarely)
- drunkenness at work (on repeated occasions)

61. Unless the circumstance is very grave - such as discovering an employee red-handed in the till - the employer should be careful not to dismiss summarily for an isolated incident.

Employee Records

- the employee's original job application form, interview record and letters of reference

- the employee's contract of employment, giving details such as period of notice required etc

- 'standing' details about the employee such as:
  - (i)   age;
  - (ii) home address;
  - (iii) current position/grade in the organisation;
  - (iv) details of pay;
  - (v)   details of holiday entitlement;
  - (vi) date of birth;
  - (vii) date of commencement of employment

- 'accumulated' details such as:
  - (i)   holidays taken;
  - (ii)   training;
  - (iii) professional qualifications acquired;
  - (iv)   positions held previously in the organisation;
  - (v)   medical history;
  - (vi)   appraisal forms;
  - (vii) dates of salary reviews;
  - (viii) results of any proficiency tests;
  - (ix)   details of any disciplinary measures taken against the employee

---

QUIZ

1. What are the purposes of training?

    ● See para 2

2. What are the potential problems with formal training?

    ● See para 5

3. List the steps for a manager drawing up a training programme.

    ● See paras 9, 11

4. How may a training scheme be monitored?

    ● See para 21

5. List the various methods of appraisal.

    ● See paras 28, 29

5. If you had to assess the appraisal scheme of your organisation, what criteria might you use?

    ● See para 35

6. Outline possible points of a promotion policy.

    ● See para 37

7. In what circumstances is dismissal fair and justified? When is it unfair or wrongful?

    ● See paras 52, 54, 60

Chapter 23

PERSONNEL MANAGEMENT: DEVELOPING TEAMWORK

Topics covered in this chapter

- Attributes of teams
- Function of teams
- The formation of teams
- Group norms
- Team cohesion and competition
- 'Group think'
- Creating an effective work team
- A contingency theory of team leadership
- The characteristics of effective and ineffective work teams
- Case study

Purpose of this chapter

To indicate the importance of work groups or 'teams' and suggest how effective teams can be created and managed.

● **Attributes of teams**

1. Handy in *Understanding Organizations* defines a group as 'any collection of people who perceive themselves to be a group'. The point of this definition is the distinction it implies between a random collection of individuals and a 'group' of individuals who share a common sense of identity and belonging.

2. A group has certain attributes that a random 'crowd' does not possess. For example:

    (a) *a sense of identity.* Whether the group is formal or informal, its existence is recognised by its members: there are acknowledged boundaries to the group which define who is 'in' and who is 'out', who is 'us' and who is 'them'. People generally need to feel that they 'belong', that they share something with others and are of value to others;

    (b) loyalty to the group, and acceptance within the group. This generally expresses itself as *conformity* or the acceptance of the 'norms' of behaviour and attitude that bind the group together and exclude others from it;

(c) *purpose and leadership*. Most groups have an expressed purpose, aim or set of objectives, whatever field they are in: most will, spontaneously or formally, choose individuals or sub-groups to lead them towards the fulfilment of those goals.

3.   People in organisations will be drawn together into groups by:

(a)   a preference for small groups, where closer relationships can develop;
(b)   the need to belong and to make a contribution that will be noticed and appreciated;
(c)   familiarity: a shared office, canteen etc;
(d)   common rank, specialisms, objectives and interests;
(e)   the attractiveness of a particular group activity (eg. joining an interesting club);
(f)   resources offered to groups (eg. sports facilities);
(g)   'power' greater than the individuals alone could muster (eg. trade union, pressure group).

4.   *Formal* groups will have a formal structure; they will be consciously organised for a function allotted to them by the organisation, and for which they are held responsible - they are task oriented, and become *teams*.

●   *Permanent* formal groups include standing committees, management teams (eg the board of directors) or specialist services (eg information technology support).

●   *Temporary* formal groups include task forces, designed to work on a particular project, ad hoc committees etc.

● **Functions of teams**

5.   From the organisation's standpoint the functions of groups or teams include:

(a)   performing tasks which require the collective skills of more than one person;
(b)   creating a formal organisation by which management can control work, by defining responsibilities and delegating as appropriate;
(c)   testing and ratifying decisions made outside the group;
(d)   consulting or negotiating, especially to resolve disputes within the organisation;
(e)   creating ideas (acting as a 'think tank');
(f)   exchanging ideas, collecting and transmitting information;
(g)   co-ordinating the work of different individuals or other groups;
(h)   enquiring into what has happened in the past;
(i)   motivating individuals to devote more energy and effort into achieving the organisation's goals.

6.   There may be no strict division between these different functions. They will inevitably overlap in practice. But the effectiveness with which a group acts is likely to be greater if they are not attempting to cope with different functions simultaneously.

7.   From the individual's standpoint teams also perform some important functions.

(a)   They satisfy social needs for friendship and belonging.

(b)   They help individuals in developing images of themselves (eg a person may need to see himself as a member of the corporate planning department or of the works snooker team).

(c) They enable individuals to help each other in matters which are not necessarily connected with the organisation's purpose (eg people at work may organise a baby-sitting circle).

(d) They enable individuals to share the burdens of any responsibility they may have in their work.

● **The formation of teams**

8. Groups are not static. They mature and develop. Four stages in this development are commonly identified:

    ● forming
    ● storming
    ● norming and
    ● performing.

9. During the first stage (*forming*) the team is just coming together, and may still be seen as a collection of individuals. Each individual wishes to impress his personality on the group, while its purpose, composition, and organisation are being established. The individuals will be trying to find out about each other, and about the aims and norms of the team. There will at this stage probably be a wariness about introducing new ideas. The objectives being pursued may as yet be unclear and a leader may not yet have emerged.

    This settling down period is essential, but may be time wasting: the team as a unit will not be used to being autonomous, and will probably not be an efficient agent in the planning of its activities or the activities of others. It may resort to complex bureaucratic procedures to ensure that what it is doing is at least something which will not get its members into trouble.

10. The second stage is called '*storming*' because it frequently involves more or less open conflict between team members. There may be changes agreed in the original objectives, procedures and norms established for the group. If the team is developing successfully this may be a fruitful phase as more realistic targets are set and trust between the group members increases.

11. The third stage (*norming*) is a period of settling down. There will be agreements about work sharing, individual requirements and expectations of output. The enthusiasm and brain-storming of the second stage may be less apparent, but norms and procedures may evolve which enable methodical working to be introduced and maintained.

12. Once the fourth stage (*performing*) has been reached the team sets to work to execute its task. Even at earlier stages some performance will have been achieved but the fourth stage marks the point where the difficulties of growth and development no longer hinder the group's objectives.

13. It would be misleading to suggest that these four stages always follow in a clearly-defined progression, or that the development of a group must be a slow and complicated process. Particularly where the task to be performed is urgent, or where team members are highly motivated, the fourth stage will be reached very quickly while the earlier stages will be hard to distinguish.

● **Group norms**

14. A work group establishes 'norms' or acceptable levels and methods of behaviour, to which all members of the group are expected to conform. This team attitude will have a negative effect on an organisation if it sets unreasonably low production norms (anyone producing more is made the social outcast of the group).

---

15. The general nature of group pressure is to require the individual to share in the team's identity, and individuals may react to group norms, customs etc with:

   ● compliance - 'toeing the line' without real commitment;
   ● internalisation - full acceptance and identification; or
   ● counter-conformity - rejecting the group and/or its norms.

16. Pressure is strongest on the individual when:

   ● the issue is not clear-cut;
   ● he lacks support for his own attitude or behaviour; and
   ● he is exposed to other members of the group for a length of time.

---

17. This 'consensus' power is often demonstrated in the ways in which work teams 'manipulate' output.

   Roethlisberger and Dickson quote employees who were told by their colleagues that if an operation turned out more than x units in a day "they'll just raise the rate and ask you to do more for the same money". The same discouragement was offered an individual who had a suggestion to improve work methods.

18. From the findings that an individual's opinions can be changed or swayed by group consensus, it may be argued that it would be more effective, and probably also easier in practice, to change group norms than to change individual norms. Motivation should therefore involve the work group as a whole, because changes agreed by a group are likely to be more effective and longer-lasting.

● **Team cohesion and competition**

19. In an experiment reported by Deutsch (1949), psychology students were given puzzles and human relation problems to work at in discussion groups. Some groups ('co-operative' ones) were told that the grade each individual got at the end of the course would depend on the performance of his group. Other groups ('competitive' ones) were told that each student would receive a grade according to his own contributions.

20. No significant differences were found between the two kinds of group in the amount of interest and involvement in the tasks, or in the amount of learning. But the co-operative groups, compared with the competitive ones, had greater productivity per unit time, better quality of product and discussion, greater co-ordination of effort and sub-division of activity, more diversity in amount of contribution per member, more attentiveness to fellow members and more friendliness during discussion.

Sherif and Sherif

21. Another experiment, conducted in 1949 by Sherif and Sherif, set out to investigate how groups are formed, and how relationships between groups are created. The experimenters also tried to create friction between their teams of schoolboys. The results suggested that *inter-group competition may have a positive effect on team cohesion and performance.*

22. Within each competing group:

    (a) members close ranks, and submerge their differences; loyalty and conformity are demanded;
    (b) the 'climate' changes from informal and social to work and task-oriented; individual needs are subordinated to achievement;
    (c) leadership moves from democratic to autocratic, with the group's acceptance;
    (d) the group tends to become more structured and organised.

23. Between competing groups:
    (a) the other group begins to be perceived as 'the enemy'; and
    (b) inter-group communication decreases.

24. The 'winning' team, if there is one, will:

    (a) retain its cohesion;
    (b) relax into a complacent, playful state ('fat and happy');
    (c) return to group maintenance, concern for members' needs etc; and
    (d) be confirmed in its group 'self-concept' with little re-evaluation.

25. The losing group will:

    (a) deny defeat if possible, or place the blame on the management, the system etc;
    (b) lose its cohesion and splinter into conflict, as 'blame' is apportioned;
    (c) be keyed-up, fighting mad ('lean and hungry');
    (d) turn towards work-orientation to regroup - rather than members' needs, group maintenance etc;
    (e) tend to learn by revaluating its perceptions of itself and the other group. It is more likely to become a cohesive and effective unit once the 'loss' has been accepted.

26.
    > All members of a team will act in unison if the group's existence or patterns of behaviour are threatened from outside. Cohesion is naturally assumed to be the result of communication, agreement and mutual trust - but in the face of a 'common enemy' (competition, crisis or emergency) cohesion and productivity benefit.

27. In an ideal functioning team:

   (a) each individual gets the support of the team, a sense of identity and belonging which encourages loyalty and hard work on the group's behalf;
   (b) skills, information and ideas are 'pooled' or shared, so that the team's capabilities are greater than those of the individuals;
   (c) new ideas can be tested, reactions taken into account and persuasive skills brought into play in group discussion for decision-making and problem-solving;
   (d) each individual is encouraged to participate and contribute and thus becomes personally involved in and committed to the team's activities;
   (e) goodwill, trust and respect can be built up between individuals, so that communication is encouraged and potential problems more easily overcome.

28. Unfortunately, team working is rarely such an undiluted success. There are certain constraints involved in working with others:

   (a) awareness of group norms and the desire to be acceptable to the group may restrict individual personality and flair. This may perhaps create pressure or a sense of 'schizophrenia' for the individual concerned who can't 'be himself' in a team situation;

   (b) conflicting roles and relationships (where an individual is a member of more than one group) can cause difficulties in communicating effectively, especially if sub-groups or cliques are formed in conflict with others;

   (c) the effective functioning of the team is dependent upon each of its members, and will suffer if one member:

   - dislikes or distrusts another;
   - is so dominant that others cannot participate; or
   - is so timid that the value of his ideas is lost; or
   - is so negative in attitude that constructive communication is rendered impossible;

   (d) rigid leadership and procedures may strangle initiative and creativity in individuals;

   (e) differences of opinion and political conflicts of interest are always likely and if all policies and decisions are to be determined by consultation and agreement within the team, decisions may never be reached and action never taken.

- **'Group think'**

29. It is possible for groups to be *too* cohesive, too all-absorbing. Handy notes that "ultra-cohesive groups can be dangerous because in the organisational context the group must serve the organisation, not itself."

   If a group is completely absorbed with its own maintenance, members and priorities, it can become dangerously blinkered to what is going on around it, and may confidently forge ahead in a completely wrong direction. I L Janis describes this as 'group think'.

30. The cosy consensus of the group prevents consideration of alternatives, constructive criticism or conflict. Symptoms of 'group think' include:

   (a) sense of invulnerability – blindness to the risk involved in 'pet' strategies;
   (b) rationalisations for inconsistent facts;
   (c) moral blindness – 'might is right';
   (d) tendency to stereotype 'outsiders' and 'enemies';
   (e) strong group pressure to quell dissent;
   (f) self-censorship by members – not 'rocking the boat';
   (g) perception of unanimity – filtering out divergent views;
   (h) mutual support and solidarity to 'guard' the decision.

31. Victims of 'group think' – which is rife at the top and centre of organisations – take great risks in their decisions, fail to recognise failure, and are highly resistant to unpalatable information. Such groups must:

   (a) actively encourage self-criticism;
   (b) welcome outside ideas and evaluation; and
   (c) respond positively to conflicting evidence.

● **Creating an effective team**

32. The management problem is how to create an effective, efficient work team. If managers can motivate groups (and individuals) to work harder and better to achieve organisational goals, the sense of pride in their own competence might create job satisfaction through belonging to the team and performing its tasks.

33. Handy takes a contingency approach to the problem of team effectiveness which, he argues, iss constructed as follows:

23.1 Handy's approach to groups

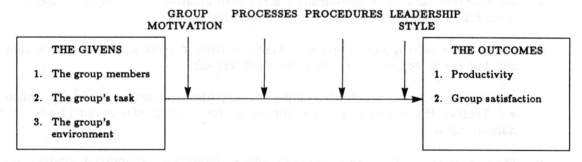

These factors are important, and are worth learning carefully. Management can operate on both 'givens' and 'intervening factors' to affect the 'outcomes'.

Group members

34. The personalities and characteristics of the individual members of the team, and the personal goals of these members, will help to determine the group's personality and goals. An individual is likely to be influenced more strongly by a small group than by a large group in which he may feel like a small fish in a large pond, and therefore unable to participate effectively in team decisions.

35. It has been suggested that the effectiveness of a team depends on the blend of the individual skills and abilities of its members. A project team might be most effective if it contains:

    (a) a person of originality and ideas;
    (b) a 'get-up-and-go' person with considerable energy, enthusiasm and drive;
    (c) a quiet, logical thinker, who ponders carefully and criticises the ideas of others;
    (d) a plodder, who is happy to do the humdrum routine work;
    (e) a conciliator, who is adept at negotiating compromises or a consensus of thought between other members of the group.

36. Belbin, in a study of business-game teams at Carnegie Institute of Technology in 1981, discovered that a differentiation of influence among team members (agreement that some members were more influential than others) resulted in higher morale and better performance. Belbin's picture (which many managers have found a useful guide to team working) of the most effective character-mix in a team involves eight necessary roles which should ideally be balanced and evenly 'spread' in the team:

    ● the *chairman* - presides and co-ordinates; balanced, disciplined, good at working through others;

    ● the *shaper* - highly strung, dominant, extrovert, passionate about the task itself, a spur to action;

    ● the *plant* - introverted, but intellectually dominant and imaginative; source of ideas and proposals but with disadvantages of introversion;

    ● the *monitor-evaluator* - analytically (rather than creatively) intelligent; dissects ideas, spots flaws; possibly aloof, tactless - but necessary;

    ● the *resource-investigator* - popular, sociable, extrovert, relaxed; source of new contacts etc. but not an originator; needs to be made use of;

    ● the *company worker* - practical organiser, turning ideas into tasks - scheduling, planning etc. Trustworthy and efficient - but not excited (or exciting, often); not a leader, but an administrator;

    ● the *team worker* - most concerned with team maintenance - supportive, understanding, diplomatic; popular but uncompetitive - noticed only in absence;

    ● the *finisher* - chivvies the team to meet deadlines, attend to details etc; urgency and follow-through important, though not always popular.

The group's task

37. The nature of the task must have some bearing on how a group should be managed. If a job must be done urgently, it is often necessary to dictate how things should be done, rather than to encourage a participatory style of working. Jobs which are routine, unimportant and undemanding will be insufficient to motivate either individuals or the group as a whole. If individuals in the team want authoritarian leadership, they are also likely to want clearly defined targets.

Environment

38. The team's environment relates to factors such as the physical surroundings at work and to inter-group relations. An open-plan office, in which the members of the group are closely situated, is more conducive to cohesion than a situation in which individuals are partitioned into separate offices, or geographically distant from each other. Team attitudes will also be affected, as described previously, by the relationship with other teams, which may be friendly, neutral or hostile.

Intervening factors

39. Of the 'intervening factors', motivation and leadership have already been discussed in separate chapters of this text. With regard to processes and procedures, research indicates that a team which tackles its work systematically will be more effective than one which lives from hand to mouth, and muddles through.

Outcomes

40. High productivity may be achieved if work is so arranged that satisfaction of individuals' needs coincides with high output. Where teams are, for example, allowed to set their own improvement goals and methods and to measure their own progress towards those goals, it has been observed (by Peters and Waterman among others) that they regularly *exceed* their targets.

41. Individuals may bring their own 'hidden agendas' to groups for satisfaction - goals which may have nothing to do with the declared aims of the team - such as protection of a sub-group, impressing the boss, inter-personal rivalry etc.

42. Refer back to Chapter 19 for the outline by Peters and Waterman *(In Search of Excellence)* of the cultural attributes of successful *task force* teams.

● A contingency theory of team leadership

43. Perhaps the leading advocate of contingency theory is F E Fiedler. In an early work (1960) he studied the relationship between style of leadership and the effectiveness of the work group. Two styles of leadership were identified:

    (a) *psychologically distant managers* (PDMs) who maintain distance from their subordinates by:

        (i) formalising the roles and relationships between themselves and their superiors and subordinates;

      (ii)   being withdrawn and reserved in their inter-personal relationships within the organisation;

      (iii)   preferring formal consultation methods rather than seeking opinions of their staff informally;

  (b) *psychologically close managers* (PCMs) who:

      (i)   do not seek to formalise roles and relationships with superiors and subordinates;

      (ii)   are more concerned to maintain good human relationships at work than to ensure that tasks are carried out efficiently;

      (iii)   prefer informal contacts to regular formal staff meetings.

44. It is perhaps not surprising that in his 1960 study Fiedler concluded that the most effective work groups were led by psychologically distant managers and not by psychologically close managers. The explanation for this appeared to be that a manager cannot properly control and discipline subordinates if he is too close to them emotionally. Moreover, PDMs were observed to be primarily task-oriented.

45. Fiedler went on to develop his contingency theory in *A Theory of Leadership Effectiveness*. He suggested that the effectiveness of a work team depended basically on two factors:

  (a) the relationship between the leader and his group; and

  (b) the nature of the work or tasks done by the group.

46. He concluded that:

  (a) a structured (or psychologically distant) style works best when the 'situation' is either very favourable, or very unfavourable to the leader;

  (b) a supportive (or psychologically close) style works best when the 'situation' is moderately favourable to the leader.

A situation is 'favourable' to the leader when:
(a) the leader is liked and trusted by the team;
(b) the tasks of the team are clearly defined;
(c) the power of the leader to reward and punish with organisation backing is high.

---

47. Fiedler's analysis can be described by a 3-dimensional cube:

  (a) the first dimension represents the level of respect and trust for the leader amongst subordinates;

  (b) a second dimension is the degree to which the tasks of the group are clearly defined; and

  (c) a third dimension is the degree to which the leader has power and authority to reward or punish subordinates.

23.2 Friedler's contingency analysis of groups

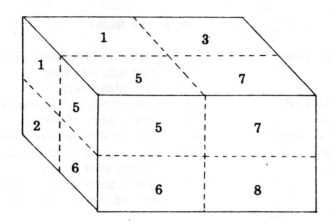

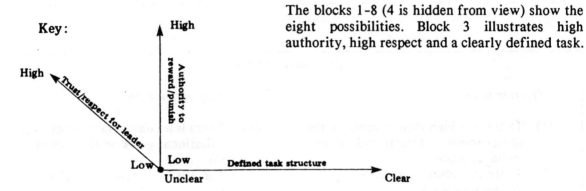

The blocks 1–8 (4 is hidden from view) show the eight possibilities. Block 3 illustrates high authority, high respect and a clearly defined task.

(a) When the situation is very favourable for the leader, he can afford to concentrate on the task, and be a task-orientated, psychologically distant manager. The leader of a research team might be in this position.

(b) When the situation is only moderately favourable for the leader, he will need to show more concern for people – be a psychologically close manager.

(c) When the situation is unfavourable for the leader, he will need to be task-orientated, and a psychologically distant autocrat.

(d) Concern for task and concern for people should be balanced according to the needs of the situation, and the degree to which it favours the leader.

● **The characteristics of effective and ineffective work teams**

48. If a manager is to try to improve the effectiveness of his work team he must be able to identify the different characteristics of an effective and an ineffective group.

Quantifiable factors

Effective teams

(1) Low rate of labour turnover
(2) Low accident rate
(3) Low absenteeism
(4) High output and productivity
(5) Good quality of output
(6) Individual targets are achieved
(7) There are few stoppages and interruptions to work

Ineffective teams

(1) High rate of labour turnover
(2) High accident rate
(3) High absenteeism
(4) Low output and productivity
(5) Poor quality of output
(6) Individual targets are not achieved
(7) Much time is wasted owing to disruption of work flow
(8) Time is lost owing to disagreements between superior and subordinates

---

Qualitative factors

Effective teams

(1) There is a high commitment to the achievement of targets and organisational goals
(2) There is a clear understanding of the group's work
(3) There is a clear understanding of the role of each person within the group
(4) There is free and open communication between members of the group and trust between members
(5) There is idea sharing
(6) The group is good at generating new ideas
(7) Group members try to help each other out by offering constructive criticisms and suggestions
(8) There is group problem-solving which gets to the root causes of the work problem
(9) There is an active interest in work decisions
(10) Group members seek a united consensus of opinion
(11) The members of the group want to develop their abilities in their work
(12) The group is sufficiently motivated to be able to carry on working in the absence of its leader

Ineffective teams

(1) There is no understanding of organisational goals or the role of the group
(2) There is a low commitment to targets
(3) There is confusion and uncertainty about the role of each person within the group
(4) There is mistrust between group members and suspicion of group's leader
(5) There is little idea sharing
(6) The group does not generate any good new ideas
(7) Group members make negative and hostile criticisms about each other's work
(8) Work problems are dealt with superficially, with attention paid to the symptoms but not the cause
(9) Decisions about work are accepted passively
(10) Group members hold strongly opposed views
(11) Group members find work boring and do it reluctantly
(12) The group needs its leader there to get work done

49. It will be helpful if you try to make a distinction in your mind between:

    (a) what work teams can be organised to do (perform a task, control work, make decisions, ratify decisions, create ideas, exchange ideas and co-ordinate work etc); and

    (b) the implication for management that since some groups develop certain characteristics and norms, it would be advisable to give some attention to the leadership of teams and to making norms and attitudes work in the organisation's favour (perhaps through participation in decision-making etc).

Disadvantages of groups as work units

50. It is worth noting, too, that for all its opportunities for exchanged ideas and knowledge, immediate feedback, 'brainstorming' etc, the 'group' as a work unit is not necessarily superior to the individual in terms of performance in all situations.

    (a) Decision-making may be a cumbersome process where consensus has to be reached. However, it has been shown (rather surprisingly) that teams take *riskier* decisions than the individuals comprising them - perhaps because of the sense of shared responsibility.

    (b) Group norms may work to lower the standard rate of unit production - though, again, individuals need groups psychologically; isolation can produce stress and hostile behaviour, and can impair performance just as surely as 'rate fixing'.

    (c) Group cohesion may provide a position of strength - solidarity - from which to behave in hostile or deviant (from the organisation's point of view) ways.

    (d) Groups have been shown to produce less ideas - though better evaluated - than the individuals of the group working separately. A group *will* often produce a better solution to a quiz than its best individual, since 'missing pieces' can be added to his performance.

● Case study

51. | George Gillespie is a team leader. Sometimes he makes decisions unilaterally. At other times he will not decide unless he has the consensus of his entire team. It is never clear on which basis he decides to act. As a result, the members of his team are often confused and demoralised. How would you help him?

Discussion

52. First of all, we must diagnose the problem and its causes. The problem concerns George Gillespie's approach to decision making. It also suggests that his leadership style should be investigated since the warning signs of confusion and demoralisation of his team indicate that they don't know what to expect from him, and he lacks consistency.

53. The factors causing the problems may include the following:

    (a) George might never have had any formal training as regards decision-making or participation. As a result he is continually changing from one management style to another in order to find the one which feels best, ignoring the fact that no one style can be correct for all the various types of decisions he had to make.

(b) He might not have a clear idea of the relative importance of the decisions he has to make. Some will be his sole preserve, others could be given to subordinates, others might involve consulting the whole section for a consensus opinion.

(c) George may be having difficulty in reconciling the need to be seen to be in charge of his team and a desire to involve his group in the decision-making process.

(d) George may not be suited to leadership.

54. To find out which factor (or factors) is the main cause of the problem, we would need to obtain the following information:

(a) the nature of the work allocated to the team;
(b) the importance of the decisions that have to be made by George and his team;
(c) the quality of his staff.

55. George should be given a counselling interview and asked to discuss his approach to decision-making. It should be explained to him that he must learn to distinguish between decisions that he must take unilaterally and decisions which should be made by the group or by subordinates. The factors relevant to this distinction are:

(a) the importance of the decision. The cost of making a mistake should be considered and evaluated. Important decisions should be taken by George himself;

(b) the subject matter of the decision. Sometimes delegation or sharing is not possible because of either company policy in relation to confidentiality or the technical and complex nature of the decision;

(c) the amount of time available and the ability of his team to deal with such situations;

(d) the importance of his team's acceptance of the decision. With some decisions such acceptance is vital to successful implementation, and so the decisions should either involve or be taken by the team as a whole;

(e) the quality of the members of the team and George's confidence in them;

(f) George's own preference for leadership style. He might prefer to be autocratic or democratic, a Theory X, Y or Z manager and so on, but he should be *consistent* whatever style he chooses to adopt.

56. George may well benefit from a training course in the art of decision-making and teamwork. He would be told that the choice is not a simple one between unilateral decision or group consensus. The department can be involved in the process by:

(a) obtaining information for George so that he will be better equipped to make the right decision;

(b) offering opinions either as individuals or as a team for George to consider, although he would not be bound to follow any suggested course of action;

(c) making decisions George feels can be safely delegated. This should improve morale as employees feel more regularly involved;

(d) reaching a decision by consensus which George then endorses.

The situation should be reviewed after a period to see if a more consistent pattern of decision-making had evolved and staff morale improved while an acceptable standard of work had been maintained. If the problem persists, further training may be necessary.

QUIZ

1.   List the possible functions of a team.

   ● See paras 5 and 7

2.   Describe the four stages of team formation.

   ● See paras 9-12

3.   What are the implications for management of the existence of group norms?

   ● See paras 17-18

4.   Describe some of the constraints which may affect team work.

   ● See paras 28, 29, 33

5.   List the roles required in an ideal team.

   ● See paras 35-36

6.   What can a team leader do to improve the effectiveness of his team?

   ● See paras 21, 37-40, 42, 47

7.   List the characteristics of an effective work team.

   ● See para 48 (box)

Chapter 24

MANAGEMENT COMMUNICATION SKILLS

Topics covered in this chapter

- Information
- Written communication
- Reports
- Report writing
- Writing style
- The business letter
- The memorandum

Purpose of this chapter

In Chapter 12 we analysed the purpose and importance of communication, barriers to communication and communication methods. Our purpose in this chapter is to expand on the personal skills of written communication and report-writing which should be possessed by effective managers.

- **Information**

1. The objective of communication by a manager is to exchange, impart or receive *information*. This does not mean that unedited or uncollated data should be transmitted to all and sundry. Management communication skills, particularly in written form, have the objective of communicating *good* information.

2. Good information will:

    - be relevant to a user's needs.

      For the communicator, this means:

      -   *Identifying the user*. Information must be suited and sent to the right person, ie. one who needs it to do his job, make a decision etc.

      -   *Getting the purpose right*. Information is effective only when it helps a user to act or make a decision. If you ask someone the way to the nearest train station, you do not expect or need to be told that the weather is fine, or even that there is a very interesting train station in another town some miles away.

- *Getting the volume right*. Information must be complete for its purpose, ie. not omitting any necessary item: it should also be no *more* in volume that the user will find helpful or be able to take in.

● be accurate within the user's needs. Information should be 'accurate' in the sense of 'correct': downright falsehood and error are fatal to effective communication of any sort. It may, however, be impossible - or at least time-consuming and expensive - to gather, process and assimilate information that is minutely detailed. An approximation or an average figure is often sufficient to our needs. If you asked: 'Is it hot in Brighton in August?' because you were planning a holiday, you would be happy to hear that it 'averaged 78°F': you would not waste time and effort poring through a sheet of daily temperature readings for the last five years.

● inspire the user's confidence. Information should not give the user reason to mistrust, disbelieve or ignore it, eg. because it is out-of-date, badly presented or from an unreliable source.

It should be *verifiable* by reference, or by application (which risks finding out the hard way, if the information is incorrect). If you are told that a cement mix suitable for pointing stonework consists of one part of cement, four parts of sand and one part of lime, you may be utterly convinced, or you may think that this is the wrong mix. You can then look it up in a book, ask another expert, or take a risk and test the information by making up the cement and applying it to a wall.

● be timely. Information must be readily available within the time period which makes it useful: ie. it must be in the right place at the right time. A beautifully researched and presented report will be of no value if it arrives on a manager's desk too late to influence his decision on the matter in hand.

● be appropriately communicated. Information will lose its value if it is not clearly communicated to the user in a suitable format and through a suitable medium. For example, your words and symbols should be familiar or at least explained to the user; the layout of text and graphics should be easy to read; a telephone call may not be appropriate for complex or confidential matters, or those requiring written records (eg. legal documents).

● be cost-effective. Good information should not cost more than it is worth. Gathering, storing, retrieving and communicating an item of information may require expense of time, energy and resources: if the expense is greater than the potential value of the item, re-consider whether the information is necessary to such a degree of accuracy, completeness etc - or even necessary at all.

● **Written communications**

3. Although verbal communication is the most common form of day-to-day communication, by its nature it is transitory and is often informal. Hence a verbal agreement is commonly supplemented by written confirmation - the written communication serves as a permanent formal record of what passed in what might have been a relatively informal manner (eg in a telephone conversation).

4. The advantages of written messages include the following.

(a) They provide a permanent record of a transaction or agreement, for confirmation and recollection of details. Evidence may also be necessary in legal affairs.

(b) They provide confirmation and clarification of verbal messages, again in case evidence should be needed, but also as an aid to memory.

(c) They are easily duplicated and sent out to numerous recipients: this ensures that information, operating instructions etc. will be consistent.

(d) They are capable of relaying complex ideas, aided by suitable layout and the permanence of the record which allows the recipient to pore over it at length if necessary.

(e) They can be stored and later retrieved for reference and analysis as required.

5. Disadvantages of written messages involve:

(a) *time*. A written message can take time to produce, and to send (eg. by post), if expensive technology is beyond the user's reach. Instant feedback is not available, and so errors in interpretation may not be corrected immediately. Because of the time factor, swift 'interactive' exchanges of opinion, attitude etc. are impossible;

(b) *inflexibility*. Once sent, the message cannot immediately be altered or amended, even though circumstances change, errors are discovered etc. Written communication also tends to come across as formal and impersonal, so in situations requiring greater sensitivity or persuasion, the personal presence or voice of the sender may be more effective.

● **Reports**

6. 'Report' is a general term and one that may suggest a wide range of formats. If you give someone a verbal account, or write him a message in a letter or memorandum informing him of facts, events, actions you have taken or suggestions you wish to make as a result of an investigation, you are 'reporting'. In this sense the word means simply 'telling' or 'relating', and we shall later see reports of this kind in memorandum form.

7. There will be variety in the format and style of a report, according to whether it is:

(a) *formal or informal*. Reports can be huge documents with sections, subsections, paras, subparas, indices, appendices etc. A single sheet ordinary memorandum may be sufficient in many contexts. Emphasis should always be placed on the content of the report and its *organisation* - a simple report should not have a complex structure, and *vice versa*.

(b) *routine* (produced at regular intervals eg. budgetary control reports, sales reports or progress reports), *occasional* (eg. an accident report or disciplinary report) or specially commissioned for *'one-off'* planning and decision-making (eg. a market research report, report on a proposed merger or particular issue);

(c) *professional*, or for a *wider audience* of laymen. A report prepared for a fellow specialist (eg on issues in accounting), will require a different tone and vocabulary to an article for a club magazine with a non-specialist readership.

8. Reports are meant to be *useful*. There should be no such thing as 'information for information's sake' in an efficient organisation: information is stored in files and retrieved for a purpose. The information contained in a business report might be used:

   (a) as a permanent record and source of reference; or

   (b) as a management tool – a source of information prepared in order to assist in management decision-making. Often more junior managers do the 'legwork' in obtaining information on a matter and then prepare a report for more senior managers to consider. This saves senior managers' time and ensures that the information on which they base their decision is more objective than if it had all been gathered and used by one person only.

9. Depending on its ultimate purpose, a report may consist of:

   (a) information, retrieved from files or other sources as a basis for management activity;

   (b) narrative or description, eg of one-off events or procedures, such as a takeover target or the installation of new equipment;

   (c) analysis, ie a further processing of data and information to render it more useful; or

   (d) evaluation and recommendation, directly assisting in the decision-making process.

10. Different types of information may be presented in a report:

   - *descriptive or factual information*. This consists of a description of facts and is objective: inferences can be drawn from the facts, but they must be logical and unbiased;

   - *instructive information*. This is information that tells the report user how to do something, or what to do. A recommendation in a report is a form of advice, and is therefore instructive information;

   - *dialectical information*. This consists of opinions and ideas, based on an objective assessment of the facts and with reasons for why these opinions and ideas have been reached.

11. The value of recognising these different types of information is that it can help to make clear what a report writer is trying to say:

   - these are the facts *(factual)*;
   - this is what the facts seem to suggest is happening, has happened or will happen *(dialectical)*; and
   - this is what should be done about matters to sort out the situation *(instructive)*.

The reporter and the report user

12. A business report is usually made by someone who is instructed by a superior. Whether the report is 'one-off' or routine, there is an obligation on the part of the manager calling for the report to state the use to which the report will be put. In other words the purpose of the report must be clear to both the report writer and the report user.

13. In the case of routine reports, their purpose and how they should be used ought to be specified in a procedures manual. 'One-offs' will require 'terms of reference', explaining the purpose of the report and any restrictions on its scope. For example, the terms of reference of a management accounting report might be to investigate the short-term profit prospects for a particular product, with a view to recommending either the closure of the product line or its continuation. These terms of reference would exclude considerations of long-term prospects for the product, and so place a limitation on the scope and purpose of the report.

14. There is also an obligation on the part of the report writer to communicate information in an unbiased way. The report writer knows more about the subject matter of the report than the report user (otherwise there would be no need for the report in the first place). It is important that this information should be communicated impartially, so that the report user can make his own judgements. This means that:

   • any assumptions, evaluations and recommendations by the report writer should be clearly 'signalled' as such;

   • points should not be over-weighted (or omitted as irrelevant) without honest evaluation of the objectivity of the selection;

   • facts and findings should be balanced against each other; and

   • a firm conclusion should, if possible, be reached. It should be clear *how* and *why* it was reached.

15. The needs and abilities of the report user should be recognised by the report writer:

   (a) jargon, technical terms and specialist knowledge should be kept at the level of the user's comprehension;

   (b) simple vocabulary, sentence and paragraph structures should be used for clarity (although the user should not thereby be patronised);

   (c) the type and level of detail should be kept to what is relevant for the user.

● **Report writing**

16. The above considerations naturally inform the whole process of report writing. This process involves the following steps, which we shall discuss in turn:

   (a) planning the report;
   (b) formating the report; and
   (c) report style.

Planning the report

17. Only people with *extremely* ordered minds should attempt to prepare a report without planning it first. Without planning the information will not be put together and communicated effectively, and so the purpose of the report will be confounded.

18. The factors to be considered when planning a report are:

    - who is the user?
    - what type of report will be most useful to him/her?
    - what exactly does he/she need to know, and for what purpose?
    - how much information is required, how quickly and at what cost?
    - do judgements, recommendations etc need to be given, or just information?

19. The report plan should indicate the following matters.

    (a) The basic objective of the report - providing the required information in the necessary way.

    (b) The reasoning required in the report - particularly if the report is to contain analysis of facts, the line of reasoning should be clear and any assumptions should be stated.

    (c) The sources of information and techniques used.

    (d) The type of conclusion required - 'more information needed', 'we can do this, this or this' or 'we must do this'.

    (e) The structure of the report - including headings, subheadings, appendices etc.

Formating formal and informal reports

20. When a formal request is made by a superior for a report to be prepared, eg. in a formally worded memorandum or letter, the format and style of the report will obviously have to be formal as well: it will be strictly schematic, using impersonal constructions and avoiding emotive or colloquial expressions.

21. An informal request for a report - 'Can you jot down a few ideas for me about...' or 'Let me know what happens, will you?' - will result in an informal report, in which the structure will be less rigid, and the style slightly more personal (depending on the relationship perceived to exist between the writer and user).

The long formal report

22. Large-scale formal reports are extensive and high-level. They may run to hundreds of pages, and will therefore require: a list of contents and index; summary of findings (to give the reader an initial idea); strict sectionalisation and referencing (to help the reader to 'dip in' to particular points as necessary); supporting appendices and list of sources (carrying subsidiary material, in order to keep the body of the report as brief as possible) etc.

The short formal report

23. The short formal report is used in formal contexts eg. middle management reporting to senior. It should be laid out according to certain basic guidelines. It will be split into logical sections, each referenced and headed appropriately:

TITLE

I TERMS OF REFERENCE (or INTRODUCTION)
II PROCEDURE (or METHOD)
III FINDINGS
    1 Section heading
    2 Section heading   if required
    (a) sub heading
      (i) sub point
IV CONCLUSIONS
V RECOMMENDATIONS   if asked for

SHORT FORMAL REPORT

TITLE   At the top of every report (or on a title page, for lengthy ones) should be the *title* of the report (ie. its subject), *who* has prepared it, *for whom* it is intended, the *date* of completion, and the *status* of the report (ie. 'Confidential' or 'Urgent').

I TERMS OF REFERENCE
Here is laid out the scope and purpose of the report: what is to be investigated, what kind of information is required, whether recommendations are to be made etc. This section may more simply be called **'Introduction'**, and may include the details set above under 'Title'. The title itself would then give only the subject of the report.

II PROCEDURE or METHOD
This outlines the steps taken to make an investigation, collect data, put events in motion etc. Telephone calls or visits made, documents or computer files consulted, computations or analyses made etc. should be briefly described, with the names of other people involved.

III FINDINGS
In this section the information itself is set out, with appropriate headings and sub-headings, if the report covers more than one topic. The content should be complete, but concise, and clearly structured in chronological order, order of importance, or any other *logical* relationship.

IV CONCLUSIONS
This section allows for a summary of main findings (if the report is complex and lengthy). For a simpler report it may include **action taken** or decisions reached (if any) as a result of the investigation, or an expression of the overall 'message' of the report.

V RECOMMENDATIONS
Here, if asked to do so in the terms of reference, the writer of the report may suggest a solution to the problem investigated so that the recipient will be able to make a decision if necessary.

The short informal report

24. The short informal report is used for less complex and lower level information. You might be asked to prepare such a report for your own direct boss.

25. The structure of the informal report is less developed: it will be shorter and less complex in any case, so will not require elaborate referencing and layout. There will be three main sections, each of which may be headed *in any way appropriate to the context* in which the report is written.

TITLE

1. BACKGROUND/INTRODUCTION/SITUATION

2. FINDINGS/ANALYSIS OF SITUATION

3. ACTION/SOLUTION/CONCLUSION

SHORT INFORMAL REPORT

Title   Again, the subject title, 'to', 'from', 'date' and 'reference' (if necessary) should be provided.

1.   Background or Introduction or Situation
This sets the context of the report. Include anything that will help the reader to understand the rest of the report: the reason why it was requested, the current situation, and any other background information on people and things that will be mentioned in the following detailed section. This section may also contain the equivalent of 'terms of reference' and 'procedure' ('method').

2.   Findings or Analysis of the situation
Here is set out the detailed information gathered, narrative of events or other substance of the report as required by the user. This section may or may not require subheadings: concise prose paragraphs may be sufficient.

3.   Action or Solution or Conclusions
The main thrust of the findings may be summarised in this section and conclusions drawn, together with a note of the outcome of events, or action required, or recommendations as to how a problem might be solved.

The memorandum report

26. In informal reporting situations within an organisation, the 'short informal report' may well be presented in A4 *memorandum* format, which incorporates title headings and can thereafter be laid out at the writer's discretion. An ordinary memorandum may be used for flexible, informal reports: aside from the convenient title headings, there are no particular requirements for structure, headings or layout. The writer may consider whatever is logical, convenient and attractive for the reader. For an example, see the memorandum on the following page.

MEMORANDUM

To: M Ployer, Office Manager   Date: 17 September 19XX
From: M Ployee, Supervisor   Ref: MP/XX/913

Subject: ABUSE OF TELEPHONE PROCEDURES

In view of the rising costs of maintaining current telephone equipment and procedures, and as requested by you, I have investigated the situation with regard to abuse of facilities.

I have identified three main causes of the rise in costs over the last quarter.

1.   There are more telephones in the office than are necessary for efficient communication.

2.   Staff have become accustomed to making personal calls on office apparatus.

3.   Many calls are made at expensive charge rates and are of unnecessary length.

I outline below a number of courses of action which could be taken to prevent further abuses.

1.   **Remove superfluous equipment**
Several extensions are un-allocated or little used for business purposes, and are therefore not only unnecessary but open to abuse. These could be immediately disconnected.

2.   **Circularise all staff and Department Heads**
This might discourage personal and unnecessarily lengthy calls on office apparatus, and encourage staff to be more conscious of economy when telephoning at more expensive rates.

3.   **Monitor the length and cost of calls**
Small single-line devices are currently available at an approximate cost of £50. Such devices are capable of displaying the value of units used on domestic calls and logging long-distance calls.

4.   **Route all calls through the central switchboard**
This would provide control over the use of the apparatus, each call having to be verified. The risk of congestion at the switchboard and the inconvenience to the operator, however, might make this a less acceptable long-term option.

5.   **Provide alternative telephone facilities to staff**
The installation of pay telephones at generally accessible locations within the building would allow staff to continue to make personal calls, thereby preserving good working relations in the office.

Report style

27. There are certain stylistic requirements in the writing of reports, formal or informal.

(a) *Objectivity and balance.* Even in a report designed to persuade as well as inform, subjective value-judgements and emotions should be kept out of the content and style as far as possible: bias, if recognised, can undermine the credibility of the report and its recommendations.

    (i) Emotional or otherwise loaded words should be avoided.

    (ii) In more formal reports, *impersonal constructions* should be used, rather than 'I', 'we' etc., which carry personal and possibly subjective associations. In other words, first person subjects should be replaced with third person:

> It became clear that...
> I/we found that... (Your name) found that...
> Investigation revealed that...

    (iii) Colloquialisms and abbreviated forms should be avoided in formal written English. 'I've', 'don't' etc should be replaced by 'I have' and 'do not'. You would not use expressions like 'blew his top' when what you meant was 'showed considerable irritation'.

(b) *Ease of understanding.*

    (i) This will involve avoiding technical language and complex sentence structures for non-technical users.

    (ii) The material will have to be logically organised, especially if it is leading up to a conclusion or recommendation.

    (iii) Relevant themes should be signalled by appropriate headings or highlighted for easy scanning.

    (iv) The layout of the report should display data clearly and attractively. Figures and diagrams should be used with discretion, and it might be helpful to highlight key figures which appear within large tables of numbers.

28. Various display techniques may be used to make the content of a report easy to identify and digest. For example, the relative importance of points should be signalled, each point may be referenced, and the body of text should be broken up to be easy on the eye. These things may be achieved as follows.

- *Headings.*

    Spaced out or enlarged **CAPITALS** may be used for the main title.

    Important headings, eg. of sections of the report, may be in CAPITALS.

    Underlining or *Italics* may be used for subheadings.

- *References.*

  Each section or point in a formal report should have a code for easy identification and reference.

  I,II,III,IV,V etc.   may be used to reference main section headings.
  A,B,C,D,E etc.

  1,2,3,4,5 etc.   may be used to reference subsections.

  (a), (b), (c) etc.   may be used to reference points and
  (i), (ii), (iii) etc.   subpoints, with appropriate indentation.

  Alternatively a 'decimal' system may be used:

1	Heading 1
1.1	Subheading 1
1.1.1	Point 1
1.1.2	Point 2
1.2	Subheading 2
1.2.1	Point 1 etc.
2	Heading 2

- *Spacing.*
  Intelligent use of spacing separates headings from the body of the text for easy scanning, and also makes a large block more attractive and 'digestible'.

29. The following check list for report writing indicates many of the factors that should be considered in planning content, layout and style.

    - *Purpose or terms of reference*
      - What is the report being written about?
      - Why is it needed?
      - Who are the report users? How much do they know already?
      - What is wanted – a definite recommendation or less specific advice or information?

    - *Information in the report*
      - What is the source of each item of information in the report?
      - What period or range does the report cover – a single event, a month, a year etc?
      - How can the accuracy of the information be checked and verified? To what extent might it be subject to error?

    - *Preparing the report*
      - Who is responsible for preparing the report?
      - How long will it take to prepare?
      - How is the information in the report put together (eg. computations or analysis necessary)?
      - How many copies of the report should be prepared and to whom should they be sent?

    - *Usefulness of the report*
      - What action is it intended to trigger?
      - How will each recipient use it for his or her own purposes?
      - Does the report meet the requirements of the terms of reference?

● **Writing style**

30. 'Style' is a vital part of any written communication. It is often defined as 'getting the best words in the best order' in order to get the desired result from messages.

31. As with report planning and formatting, writing style is dictated to a large degree by the reason why the report or other document is being written and by the person to whom it is addressed.

- ● *Reason*
  What is to be accomplished and what response is required? To demonstrate how this affects style, consider the following three cases (they concern letters, but the principle is the same):

  - o If you are applying for a job, for example, your style will need to demonstrate good formal language skills; you will need to sound quietly confident, but not arrogant; willing, even eager, but not desperate; polite and intelligent.

  - o If you are writing an advertising or selling letter, your style will need to be informal and friendly without being too familiar; persuasive without being obviously pushy; attention-grabbing but not hysterical; confident and honest.

  - o If you are writing a letter of complaint, and you do want action (not just a chance to moan), you will write in a style that is clear, uncompromising; polite but firm. You would then expect a reply that is equally clear, apologetic and conciliatory without false humility.

- ● *Recipient*
  What type of person is the report aimed at and what is their reaction likely to be if the message if expressed in a certain way?

  - o An information leaflet or circular letter to the general public has an undefinable audience. The document's written style should be simple and free from jargon, assumptions etc, yet remain convincing and informative.

  - o An open letter to employees for a notice board or general circulation has a known audience. The styles, depending on the document's purpose, could be more 'friendly' and contain jargon or abbreviations commonly used in the organisation etc.

32. Specific factors about the recipient which need to be taken into account are as follows.

   (a) *Age*. People's attitudes vary with age and experience. They may become less flexible with the years: a young person writing to a senior will have to be respectful and persuasive. The feelings of an older person overtaken in the promotion race by a younger one should be considered. From the opposite angle, beware of talking 'over the head' of younger and less experienced people, and also of 'talking down' to them in a patronising way.

   (b) *Culture*. The personal and corporate background and culture of the recipient may have to be taken into account. Different language may be needed in reports to, say, a colleague in the same city and building as the sender and to a person in a small overseas branch of the organisation which has a different language and has a different cultural and religious context.

(c) *Education.* Differences in practical, technical and academic education will mean that communication should be expressed as simply and clearly as possible without patronising the recipient.

(d) *Work environment.* People whose jobs are highly specialised - in finance, as much as in medicine or science - often have a language of their own. It is important to recognise when technical language or 'jargon' is being used which the recipient is unlikely to know. An overly simple general vocabulary, however, may be irritating to someone who would understand more specialist terms. The position and authority of the recipient should also be remembered: there is usually a well-defined hierarchy in any office and a senior manager will not take kindly to being browbeaten by, say, a supervisor.

(e) *Context in which document is received.* Obviously the sender has no control over the situation prevailing when the document is received, but as far as possible it should be taken into account. When writing or reporting to a senior, busy person the language and level of detail should be kept as minimal as possible so that the content is absorbed and understood quickly. Context also has an impact on the level of formality of the document.

(f) *Relationship.* The vocabulary and tone will vary depending on the relationship between sender and recipient - they may be distant acquaintances, trusted colleagues, good friends etc. The degree of warmth and familiarity will depend on this - in a communication between superior and subordinate there will be more formality and distance than in one between two colleagues at the same level.

33. From the above analysis, you will see that in written English, style involves conscious choices about:

- *vocabulary:* which words should be used?
- *syntax:* what kind of sentence should be constructed? and
- *tone:* what reaction is wanted?

Aspects of style: vocabulary

34. Each individual has a stock of words from which to select the expressions that will have the desired effect. This stock is called the *'vocabulary'.* English is very rich in the selection of different words and expressions it offers, with various shadings of tone and meaning: synonyms abound (see *Roget's Thesaurus,* which supplies them), as do colloquial expressions influenced by the diverse cultures and contexts in which English is spoken and written. Elements of Australian, American and Caribbean English, for example, can be almost unrecognisable to the average English person, as can the specialised vocabularies of 'legalese', 'officialese' or 'techno-speak'. [You might like to consider how many of the words and expressions you use would be readily accessible to people outside the world of business and accounting ...] The language is also drawn from many other sources: if you have learnt Greek, Latin, French or German you might recognise the roots of many English words.

35. Each word used may:

(a) be familiar and understandable, or unfamiliar and baffling to the recipient;
(b) be clear and specific, or vague and ambiguous;
(c) be factual and objective, or emotional and subjective;
(d) carry underlying meanings that might have an adverse effect on the recipient;

(e) carry the right tone (friendly, encouraging, tactful) or the wrong tone (insincere, indifferent, antagonistic, patronising) to elicit the desired response.

> In other words the effectiveness of vocabulary depends on:
>
> - how well the recipient will be able to understand it, and
>
> - the associations it has for him or her (which will condition his or her reaction)

36. In business communications, words used should generally:

    (a) be short, direct and English rather than long, ambiguous and foreign;
    (b) be rational and objective to *inform*, or be *discreetly* emotive and subjective to *persuade*;
    (c) be formal unless friendliness/persuasiveness requires familiarity and colloquialism;
    (d) be kept to a minimum - circumlocution and needless verbosity should be avoided.

Aspects of style: syntax

37. 'Syntax' broadly means sentence (or language) structure. It is the order in which words and groups of words are placed so as to achieve a complete and orderly unit of sense or meaning.

    - Sentence structures should be simple, rather than complex. A very long sentence full of subordinate clauses can get completely out of hand, and never reach the point it was intended to make.

    - A string of very short simple sentences, however, can be boring, irritatingly abrupt and immature (suitable for a young reading age, which doesn't flatter an adult reader).

    - A controlled complex sentence has greater fluency or 'flow'.

    - Varying sentence structure adds interest and impact.

> *Example*
> Consider the following passage in a letter.
>
> "The goods were delivered to your factory in March. We sent you an invoice at the end of last month. You have not paid the invoice yet. The credit terms state that payment is due after 30 days. We expect payment in the next 10 days. We shall take legal action if this is not forthcoming."
>
> This comes across as extremely abrupt and threatening. This is partly because the sentences are so short, but also because they all have the same basic structure - subject noun + verb etc. It is rewritten below.
>
> "During March deliveries to your factory were made by us of goods for which we invoiced you at the month-end. Although our credit terms state that payment should be made within 30 days, the invoices do not appear to have been paid yet. We regret to inform you that unless payment is received in the next 10 days, we shall have to take legal action for recovery."

- Ideas can be linked together and their relationship indicated using conjunctions. Eg: X 'because' Y, X 'despite' Y, X 'and' Y etc.

- Balance or 'poise' can be achieved by using two main clauses divided by a semi-colon, or paired constructions such as '(n)either. . . (n)or. . .', 'not only. . . but also. . .' etc.

- Emphasis. Starting a sentence with a dependent clause creates suspense, and places emphasis on the main clause following: 'Although the decision was not an easy one to make, we have decided to offer you the job.' Putting the dependent clause last, however, tends to let the sentence tail off in anticlimax: 'We have decided to offer you the job, although the decision was not an easy one to make.'

Aspects of style: tone

38. The total effect on the reader of vocabulary and sentence structure, as well as the message's content, may be called 'tone'. The writer must aim consciously for a warm, friendly, firm or honest tone, lest he unwittingly offend the reader or fail to elicit a positive response: the 'tone' of the message is judged by the reader's reaction to it, 'how he takes it'.

39. There are various ways in which a writer can show his own attitude to what he is expressing, whether he consciously intends to do so or not. Some points to look out for include the following.

    (a) *Positive and negative sentence constructions*. Things can always be expressed in a positive or in a negative way: people respond more favourably to the positive. Eg: compare your reaction to: 'I haven't finished my assignment today' and 'I will finish my assignment tomorrow.'

    (b) *'Mood'*. There are three moods in English: the indicative (for statements and questions); the imperative (for commands and requests); and the subjunctive (for wishes, doubts, probabilities and possibilities). For example, the imperative 'Shut that door' or even 'Shut that door, please' may not be suitable in situations where courtesy and respect are necessary. The indicative question 'Will you shut that door, please?' would be preferable, as would the even more polite subjunctive 'Would you shut that door, please?'

    (c) *Personal and impersonal*. Note the distancing effect of the impersonal 'It + passive verb', similar to that of indirect speech. It might be appropriate in a formal report, or where a writer deliberately wants to distance himself from his message. In a more personal context the air of indifference might be offensive: 'it is considered by the President that closure of the branch may be necessary' and 'It was agreed that you should be made redundant.'

• The business letter

40. The letter is a very flexible and versatile medium of communication. It can be used to:

    (a) request, supply and confirm information and instructions;
    (b) offer and accept goods and services;
    (c) convey and acknowledge satisfaction and dissatisfaction;
    (d) request and insist on payment, compliance;
    (e) apply for or resign from a job.

41. The letter is also a 'high profile' medium of communication. It is in many cases the first – or *only* – contact between organisations or the individuals who represent them. The content and style of the message must be finely tuned to get the desired result (action or acknowledgement from the recipient). The appearance of the letter will be no less important: paper and print quality, layout and letterhead all project to the outside world an image of the organisation responsible. It must consider its reputation, as well as the 'success' of a particular message.

> Successful management letter-writing therefore depends on style and tone (discussed above) and correct layout or 'display'.

Layout

42. The example on the following page is a fairly standard way of setting out a business letter.

Notes:

1. Having a *subject heading* on a business letter (eg "Sales contract for Sudso washing machines" in a letter between manufacturer and wholesaler) allows the recipient to identify quickly the main subject-matter of the letter.

2. The *complimentary close* is usually 'yours sincerely' unless the recipient is an unknown person in an organisation (in which case it starts 'Dear Sir' and ends 'yours faithfully') or is well-known (something like 'kind regards' could be used).

Structuring the content

43. Basically, a letter should have a beginning, a middle and an end.

The reader will have a very general idea of the letter's contents already. The letterhead will have told him something about the sender: he may also have glanced first at the signature, name and designation at the foot of the letter. The subject heading will prepare him and direct his thoughts to the topic in hand. However, you can 'lose' your reader very quickly if you do not at each stage make it clear:
- why you are writing;
- what it is that you are trying to say, and
- what you think he or she can do for you.

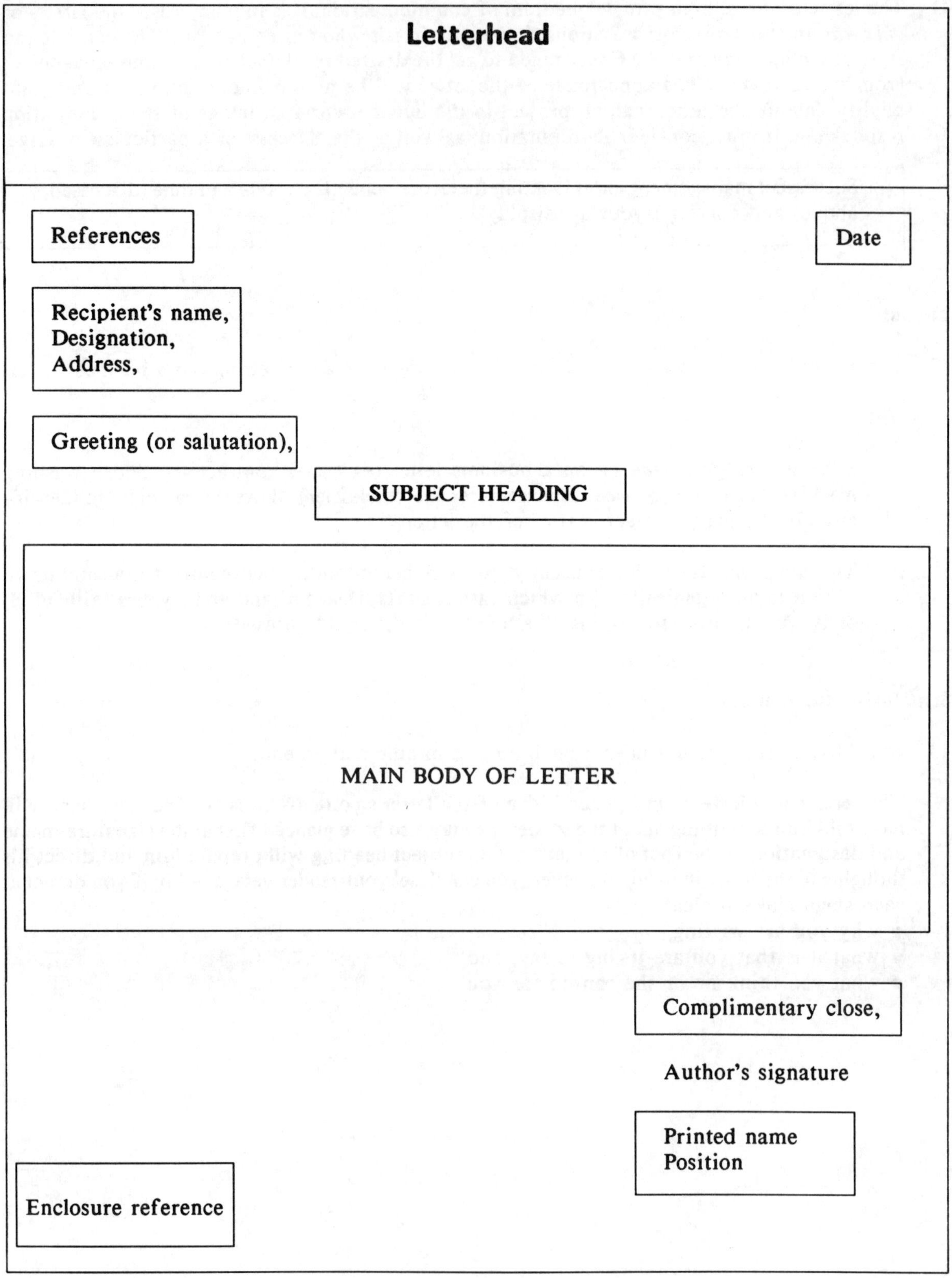

Letterhead

References

Date

Recipient's name,
Designation,
Address,

Greeting (or salutation),

SUBJECT HEADING

MAIN BODY OF LETTER

Complimentary close,

Author's signature

Printed name
Position

Enclosure reference

Dear Mr Bloggs,

SUBJECT HEADING

1. The opening paragraph. Don't dive straight in with the detailed point of your message, since the reader will not be as familiar with its context as you are. Tell him what the context of the message is: response to a previous communication from him (eg. continuing a sequence of letters); response to other events (eg. if you are complaining about something); initiation of contact or action (eg. if you are introducing yourself, or advertising goods). You would usually put in your opening: ● Straightforward (brief) explanation of why you are writing. ● Acknowledgement of receipt of any previous correspondence, together with its date and nature. ● Important details of the circumstances leading to the letter (names, dates).

2. Development of the message. The middle paragraph(s) should then be used to set out the letter's message, which will elaborate or move forward from the introductory paragraph. Here will be: the substance of your response to a previous message; details of the matter in hand; or the information you wish to communicate.

If you are making several points, start a new paragraph with each, so that the reader can 'digest' each part of your message in turn. You should organise your material so that points are in logical order, not just as they spill out of your brain. Eg:
- (a) chronological order, for narrating/explaining a sequence of actions or events; X happened <u>and then</u> Y happened...;
- (b) cause and effect. X happened (cause) <u>and so</u> Y happened (effect);
- (c) topical order. Keep together points which are related to the same topic;
- (d) order of importance. This can involve a choice: putting the most important first gains attention, lesser details following: putting the major point last has more persuasive impact.

3. The closing paragraph. Your letter will not be effective unless it has the desired result of creating understanding or initiating action. Unless your message has been very brief and simple, it is a good idea to draw together the points you have made in a brief summary which will recall and put into perspective your main ideas. If you are not just writing to inform, but want some action or response from the reader, this is also the place to make clear exactly what you expect from him. The conclusion is the last item, apart from the complimentary close, that the reader will take in: it will be clearest in his mind when the letter is finished.

Yours sincerely,

A. COUNTANT
Finance Director

● **The memorandum**

44. The memorandum is a very flexible form used within an organisation for communication at all levels and for many different reasons. It performs *internally* the same function as a letter does in *external* communication by an organisation.

45. A 'memo', as it is known, may be used to:

(a) transmit suggestions, requests and instructions from superior to subordinate;
(b) motivate, encourage or discipline subordinates;
(c) convey policy changes, decisions and information about the company to staff;
(d) transmit unsolicited suggestions, ideas or complaints from subordinate to superior;
(e) aid co-operation between departments: requests for information, advice or assistance;
(f) aid co-ordination: copies of a memo may be circulated to keep interested personnel informed of developments in which they may not be actively involved;
(g) provide accurate written confirmation of the details of an oral communication;
(h) seek and provide information, confirmation or assistance generally.

Note that a memorandum may be sent 'upwards', 'downwards' or 'sideways' in the organisation's hierarchy. It may be sent from one individual to another, from one department to another or from one individual to a department or a larger body of staff. Some of these people will have to take action on receiving the memo, others will simply absorb the information contained in it whilst others still will file it away for confirmation and future reference.

Format of a memo

46. Memorandum format will vary slightly according to the degree of formality required and the organisation's policy on filing, authorisation of memoranda by their writer etc. When answering an exam question it is probably best to follow the conventions of 'house style' in your own organisation.

Organisation's name (optional)
'MEMORANDUM' heading

'To:' (recipient's name or designation)   'Ref:' (for filing)

'From:' (author's name or designation)   'Date:'(in full)

'Subject:' (main theme of message)

The message of the memorandum is set out like that of a letter: good English in spaced paragraphs. Note that no inside address, salutation or complimentary close are required.

'Copies to:' (recipient(s) of copies)   'Signed:'   (optional)
                                               author signs/initials

'Enc.:' to indicate accompanying material

Content of a memo

47. As its name suggests, a memorandum is an aid to the memory of its reader. As such, it will mainly be used for brief messages, providing a confirmation and record of the various plans, decisions and activities of the company.

This is not to say that a memorandum can only be of the one-idea type. A5 memos will necessarily be brief, perhaps only one sentence, but A4 several-page memoranda may be used for making informal reports, or outlining new policies etc.

48. The structure and style of the memo will vary according to its nature, the number of people it is addressed to, and who those people are (what position they occupy etc.). The flexibility of the medium means that some memos will be able to be less formal than others: the same guidelines will apply as with a letter.

● If you are reporting to, or making a suggestion to, someone higher in the hierarchy than yourself, your tone will have to be appropriately formal, businesslike and tactful.

● If you are dashing off a handwritten note on a memo pad to a colleague with whom you enjoy an informal working relationship, you can be as direct, familiar and friendly as you like.

● If you are instructing or disciplining junior personnel, you will have to retain a certain formality for the sake of authority; a more persuasive and less formal tone might be appropriate if you are congratulating, motivating or making a request.

QUIZ

1. What are the qualities of good information?

    - See para 2

2. What are the advantages and disadvantages of written messages?

    - See paras 4 and 5

3. What types of information might a report contain?

    - See paras 8–10

4. What are the three essential steps in writing a report?

    - See para 16

5. What are the basic stylistic requirements for report writing?

    - See para 27

6. What choices need to be made when deciding on English style?

    - See para 33

7. In what ways would you hope to affect the syntax and tone of a letter?

    - See paras 37 and 39

8. What are the purposes of a subject heading and a complimentary close on a business letter?

    - See para 42

Chapter 25

THE MANAGEMENT OF PROFESSIONALLY QUALIFIED STAFF

Topics covered in this chapter

- The management of managers
- Management education, training and development
- Management education
- Management training
  - An approach to skills training
  - A programme for education and training
- Management development
- The transition from functional to general management: problems and recommendations
- Case study

Purpose of this chapter

To look at management education, training and development, as a process of grooming professionally qualified individuals for management jobs.

● The management of managers

1. In previous chapters, we have looked at the function of managers to provide leadership, direction and motivation to employees and subordinates. The subordinates of middle-ranking and senior managers are managers themselves, and so the principles and policies described apply to the management of other managers and professionally qualified individuals, as well as to the management of rank-and-file 'workers'.

2. Policies for the organisation's management of its professionally qualified staff should focus on the functions of management - that is, to plan, organise, coordinate, direct and control.

Planning

3. The planning required vis-à-vis professionally qualified staff should be in terms of overall manpower planning, from recruitment and training to how to plan for staff turnover and retirement.

4. A manpower plan should be constructed for the organisation to denote present and future manpower needs, given any planned changes such as growth, divestment, diversification etc. It will dictate how many staff should be recruited and how they should be trained, taking into account how long it is expected that training to become professionally qualified should take and what the likely dropout rate will be.

5. Planning for training is also important because without carefully constructed individual development programmes professionally qualified staff are likely to become out-of-date and/or to leave. Training and the promotion which goes with it are important motivational factors for staff whose qualification is a hard-won and rare commodity. If these are not provided it is likely that staff turnover will be relatively high, which must therefore also be taken into account.

6. Although professionally qualified staff are neither more nor less likely to retire early, the organisation must plan for staff losses through retirement. If it wants to be more sure of retaining staff then it is wise to have an attractive pension policy to entice them to stay.

7. These plans become even more vital if the organisation depends on the development of teamwork and long-term commitment from qualified staff - say in the aerospace industry where planning horizons are broad and technical expertise vital.

Organising

8. As with any other staff the work of professionally qualified managers must be organised so that organisational objectives are met. However, organising can prove problematic since in effect such people have two roles - as professionals and as managers. They may see a dichotomy between *working* - implementing their own technical skills - and *attending* - watching over others using their skills (ie managing). Broadly speaking, the balance must be right.

    (a) *Flexibility.* Although workflow must be organised so that individual and departmental task and job objectives and allocation are integrated, such organisation must be flexible enough to allow the professionally qualified staff to feel that they have some autonomy and are achieving a balance of professional and managerial work.

    (b) *Training and development,* as we have seen, must be built into the organisation of staff so that both organisational and individual objectives are met.

    (c) *Delegation* of authority can be problematic because, although managerial authority may be delegated, professional ethics often state that professional authority cannot be implemented by another person. This may mean that every professional in the hierarchy feels that he must minutely analyse the work of his subordinates to ensure that it meets his own professional standards. This can be time-consuming.

    (d) *Responsibility,* in a professional and in a management sense, may mean two different things (linked with (c) above). In order to ensure professional standards it may be necessary to organise a review body which assesses whether the line professional staff have performed their work properly.

Coordinating

9. Both within a professionally qualified manager's job and within the organisation as a whole there must be coordination between the functional context - getting the job done - and the professional context - doing the job properly. This will require formal communication channels as well as, possibly, elements of a matrix structure.

Directing

10. Professionally qualified staff, as with any other type, need to be motivated to produce satisfactory work and to remain with the organisation. They may be motivated by:

    (a) having responsibility and discretion;
    (b) being included in decision-making (consultation or participation);
    (c) a clear promotion policy and good continuing training;
    (d) good remuneration and terms and conditions of work;
    (e) being treated as intelligent, self-starting and conscientious staff (a management style based on Theory X would alienate them);
    (f) being clearly and fairly directed in accordance with stated policies. (Inconsistent management styles are likely to be as counter-productive with professionally-qualified staff as they are with others.)

11. Because it is probable that professionally qualified staff will be directed by other qualified staff, it is important that there should be mutual respect. Hence the leader should ideally be better-qualified (say by being a fellow of the relevant institute rather than an associate), more highly-skilled and capable of doing all those tasks which subordinates are called upon to do.

Controlling

12. The output of professionally qualified staff needs to be reviewed and controlled in the light of original plans as much as any employee's work, but there can be difficulties if control is too tight and impinges on their professional integrity. They expect to be trusted to exercise self-direction and, to some extent, self-supervision.

13. This dilemma can be met by operating an agreed and defined staff appraisal system whose objectives are stated clearly. Although this may be viewed as a vehicle of control, it is also a useful way to identify training and other development needs of the professional staff and, linked to a job evaluation scheme, should be seen as an integral part of promotion planning.

14. With senior professional staff it may be preferable to exercise control more informally. This will allow the professionals to feel that they 'own' their own careers and are free to seek further training if they feel they need it.

15. It is possible to have across-the-board control of all professional staff by ensuring that each and every one of them attend technical updating training. This will mean that none is allowed to become out of date whilst, at the same time, none feels that he or she has been singled out.

16. The degree of control can depend on the context in which the organisation is operating. During a period of change it may be necessary to exert more control than at a time when operations are just 'ticking over'.

17. In the managerial framework, control procedures should be implemented with professionally qualified staff as with non-qualified people. In particular responsibility for a budget cannot be differentiated between the two types of employee.

The broad features of the management of managers might be summarised as follows:

Function	How it might be done
1. Plan and control the activities of other managers.	(a) Corporate planning (b) Budgeting, budgetary control (c) Performance measurement/appraisal (d) Accountability.
2. Direct and motivate other managers. *Note.* Motivating subordinate managers is necessary if their own subordinates in turn are to stand much chance of being motivated. Managers set an example for their staff.	(a) Delegation of authority or centralisation of decision-making authority. (b) Allowing subordinate managers decision-making discretion.
3. Organise the work of other managers. Co-ordinate their work.	(a) Suitable organisation structure (b) Good communication.
4. Fill managerial vacancies. Staff, recruit, guide and develop managers.	(a) Selection procedures (b) Management development and appraisal programmes (c) Training and education.

---

18. In the rest of this chapter, we shall concentrate on item (4). An organisation should have:

   (a) a capable management team, with a suitable blend of abilities and experience; and
   (b) a system for filling management positions when vacancies arise, either through:
      (i) promotion from within; or
      (ii) appointments of managers from 'outside'; or
      (iii) a mixture of (i) and (ii).

● Management education, training and development

19. You might subscribe to the trait theory of leadership, that some individuals are 'born' with the personal qualities to be a good manager, and others aren't. There might be some bits of truth in this view but very few individuals, if any, can walk into a management job and do it well without some guidance, experience or training.

20. In every organisation, there should be some arrangements or system whereby:

   (a) managers gain *experience*, which will enable them to do another more senior job in due course of time;

   (b) subordinate managers are given *guidance* and *counselling* by their bosses;

   (c) managers are given suitable *training* and *education* to develop their skills and knowledge.

   If there is a planned programme for developing managers, it is called a *management development programme.*

The difference between management education, training and development

21. A useful distinction between management education, training and development was given in the report *'The Making of British Managers'*, prepared for the BIM and CBI in 1987 by Constable and McCormick. The report gave the following definitions.

- '*Education* is that process which results in formal qualifications up to and including post-graduate degrees.'

- *Training* is 'the formal learning activities which may not lead to qualifications, and which may be received at any time in a working career.'

- '*Development* is broader again: job experience and learning from other managers, particularly one's immediate superior, are integral parts of the development process.'

   Development will include features such as:
   (i) career planning for individual managers;
   (ii) job rotation;
   (iii) standing in for the boss while he is away on holiday;
   (iv) on-the-job training;
   (v) counselling, perhaps by means of regular appraisal reports;
   (vi) guidance from superiors or colleagues; and
   (vii) education and training.

---

22. Education is therefore an element of training, which is an aspect of development.

25.1 The relationship of education, training and development

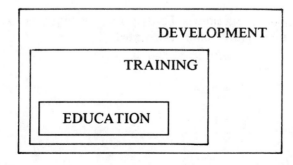

23. It is worth getting clear in your mind at the beginning why management education, training and development are needed.

   (a) Without training and development, managers are unlikely to be ready for promotion when the time comes, and they will not do their new job well until they have learnt by mistakes.

   (b) The selection of individuals for promotion is unlikely to be reliable, and the 'wrong people' might be selected for senior jobs. Individuals will rise to their level of incompetence!

   (c) Vacancies will often have to be filled by recruitment from outside the organisation, because not enough 'in-house' managers will be good enough or sufficiently ready for promotion.

   (d) An organisation should show an interest in the career development of its staff, so as to motivate them and encourage them to stay with the firm. Management development programmes are an important feature of being a good employer.

● **Management education**

24. Education, for successful students, leads on to a formal qualification. For managers in the UK, these qualifications include:

   (a) undergraduate business and management degrees;

   (b) undergraduate degrees in related subjects such and Economics and Accountancy;

   (c) postgraduate business and management degrees (MBA course);

   (d) the postgraduate Diploma in Management Studies (DMS);

   (e) qualifications from professional institutes. Accountancy qualifications (ACCA, ACA, ACMA) are the most common professional qualifications in the UK.

● **Management training**

25. Formal training which does *not* lead on to a qualification consists mainly of:
   (a) post-experience management courses, provided by training companies or colleges and polytechnics;

   (b) in-company management training, using the company's own training staff and/or consultants brought in from outside.

26. In-company management training ranges from:

   (a) basic training for those without any formal education and training, such as induction courses for new recruits into junior management posts; to

   (b) continuing internal development programmes, for managers as they progress through their careers and up the seniority scale; to

   (c) senior general management programmes. Fairly senior managers need training too, to help their development to even more senior positions!

27. The report by Constable and McCormick, referred to earlier, found from a survey of UK employers that:

- most employers regard innate ability and experience as the two key ingredients of an effective manager. But education and training help, *especially in broadening the outlook of managers with only functional experience previously, and without experience of general management;*

- there was agreement that it would be both inappropriate and impossible to make management a controlled profession similar to accountancy and law. However, making a managerial career more similar to the professions and *having managers require specific competences appropriate to each stage of their career* were seen as beneficial.

An approach to skills training

28. Skills training is concerned with teaching a person how to do a particular job, or how to do it better. Functional managers, especially supervisors and junior managers, should be given skills training to help them to do their job better.

29. In addition to skills training, an organisation should provide training to potential managers or existing managers in management techniques and skills. It has already been suggested that employees might want promotion, but cannot be offered it yet, either because there are not enough vacancies and they must wait their turn, or because they are not yet good enough, or even because they might never be good enough for further advancement. Large organisations have the problem of:

   (a) motivating their existing staff and keeping them where they might be expected to wait for further promotion; and

   (b) providing training to ensure that sufficient staff are available to fill management positions capably when vacancies do arise. (In this respect, management training and development should be planned within the framework of the manpower plan).

30. Training follows on from recruitment and selection, and also appraisal of performance.

   (a) Potential managers can be given training in management skills, either on internal courses or on courses with external organisations such as business schools.

   (b) Existing managers can be given training in new skills required for their existing job (eg the technological changes in organisations and the development of computer usage suggest the need for training in computer applications and software for management work).

   (c) Existing managers can be given training in the skills required for higher, general management (eg with discussions of organisation policy, and lectures given by directors).

A programme for education and training

31. A successful programme for management education and training should involve both senior management and the individual managers who should expect to receive training.

Recommendations

Senior management	*Individual managers*
1. Create an atmosphere within the organisation where continuing management training and development is the norm.	1. Actively want and seek training and development. 'Own' their own career.
2. Utilise appraisal procedures which encourage management training and development.	2. Recognise what new skills they require, and seek them out positively.
3. Encourage individual managers, especially by *making time available* for training.	3. Where appropriate, join a professional institute and seek to qualify as a professional member.
4. Provide support to local educational institutes (eg. colleges) to provide management education and training.	
5. Integrate in-house training courses into a wider system of management education and training. *Make the subject matter of in-house courses relevant to managers' needs.* Work closely with academic institutions and professional institutions to ensure that the 'right' programmes are provided.	

32. Designing appropriate in-house courses and encouraging some managers to obtain a professional qualification should be two key features of an education and training programme for managers.

33. The time given to managers for education could be provided by:
    (a) a full year off to study for a qualification, say;
    (b) block release to attend study courses or revision courses;
    (c) day release, perhaps to attend courses at a local college;
    (d) reducing the workload on individuals, so that they don't have to work long hours and overtime, to give them time to attend evening classes or study at home.

Time off for studying should be paid for by the employer, who might also contribute towards the cost of text books and courses for professional examinations.

● **Management development**

34. Management development is the process of improving the effectiveness of an individual manager by training him/her in the necessary skills and understanding of organisational goals. Although management development is in some respects a natural process, the term is generally used to refer to a conscious policy within an organisation to provide a programme of individual development. The techniques of management development include:

    (a) formal education and training;
    (b) on-the-job training;
    (c) group learning sessions;
    (d) conferences; and
    (e) counselling.

35. The principle behind management development is that by giving an individual time to study the techniques of being a good manager, and by counselling him about his achievements in these respects, the individual will realise his full potential. The time required to bring a manager to this potential is *possibly* fairly short.

36. It is important to emphasise the planned nature of management development programmes. Consider the following as an illustration:

25.2 Management development programme

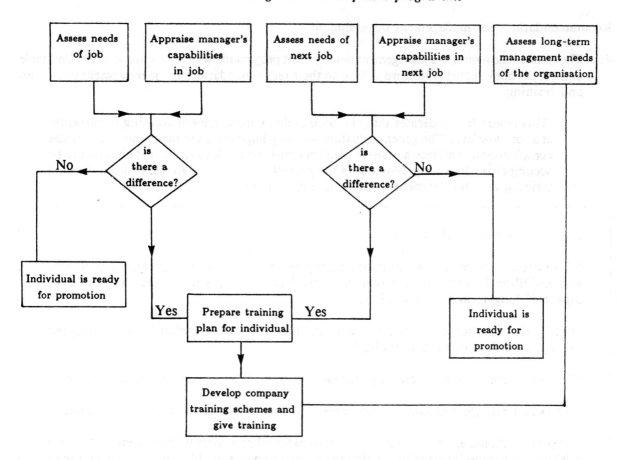

37. This diagram brings out the importance of *appraisal* in a system of development. Although we have been discussing the development of managers, staff appraisal is important for all grades of employees.

Footnote: the plateaued manager

38. One particular problem of staff development has recently been discussed in the Harvard Business Review by Jay W Lorsch and Haruo Takagi.

39. Lorsch and Takagi looked at the problem of the *plateaued manager*. Long-serving managers may reach a plateau in an organisation, beyond which they recognise that they are unlikely to make progress. They may be faced with a further ten or fifteen years before retirement during which they will feel uncommitted and frustrated.

40. Lorsch and Takagi argue that this common problem can be converted into a benefit both for the organisation and for the manager concerned. Experienced executives who have spent a number of challenging 'mainstream' years in an organisation will identify with it and will care about the development of its next generation of professionals and managers. If they participate in the training of newer management staff they will benefit from a renewed sense of importance; meanwhile, the new generation will benefit from their experience and advice.

Recommendations for management development

41. The recommendations for a management development programme which were made in the Constable and McCormick report (1987) are similar to their recommendations for management education and training.

> 'This research ... indicates that the total scale of management training is currently at a very low level. The general situation will only improve when many more companies conscientiously embrace a positive plan for management development. This needs to be accompanied by strong demand on the part of individual managers for continuing training and development throughout their careers.'

Recommendations in the report

'Chief executives should see continuing management development as a major area of their responsibility. It should be a regular item for boardroom discussion and an important aspect of long-term corporate plans.'

'The implementation of strategic initiatives should be accompanied by well-designed management development activities.'

'Employers should seek to create personal development programmes for all managers.'

'Individual managers should be encouraged to 'own' their development programme.'

'Employers should establish strong links with external providers of management training with a view to both influencing the design of programmes and obtaining maximum use of expertise.'

---

42. It should also be added that a senior manager in the organisation - perhaps the personnel director - should be given the responsibility for implementing a planned management development programme, and the issue of management development within the organisation should be regularly discussed at board level.

● **Transition from functional to general management**

43. There is one particular aspect of management development and training that organisations should look at closely - *the transition from functional to general management*. At some stage in his or her career, a manager will be promoted from a job which is concentrated mainly on functional expertise (eg. knowledge of production techniques, personnel techniques, accountancy skills, marketing skills) into a job where the requirement is for broader and more general management skills - eg. organising, staffing, controlling, dealing with other departments or organisations, long-term planning and so on.

44. The change in a manager's work caused by moving from a functional to a general management position can be seen by highlighting some of the important differences in the two types of role.

	Functional manager	*General manager*
Orientation	● task orientated - focus on the functional tasks in hand	● goal orientated - focus on achievement of organisational (and divisional) goals and objectives
Role	● organiser	● facilitator - co-ordinating interdepartmental activities; obtaining and allocating resources
Information	● defined sources ● usually through formal channels	● poorly defined sources ● often acquired by informal contacts
Goals	● short term	● long term

45. The transition from functional to general manager is usually accompanied by promotion to a more senior position in the management hierarchy and therefore the contrast in roles between functional and general management is also found between junior and middle/senior management. But this comparison must not be overstated; much depends on the structure of the organisation concerned. The traditional, functional structure tends to keep managers in functional roles until they reach very senior levels and sometimes for their entire careers.

46. A *divisional structure*, however, gives relatively junior managers experience of general management roles, usually as the chief executive of small business units. Organisational structure can therefore have a significant impact on the age and seniority of managers making the transition from functional to general management and therefore the extent of the difficulties it may create.

47. Recent research has brought to light the difficulties which managers face in changing from one role to another and these are often particularly acute when the change involves moving from a functional to a general management position. In addition to the normal problems of switching jobs, the manager taking up a general management post has to deal with an abrupt change in the skills needed to perform his role effectively.

25.3 Skills required of managers

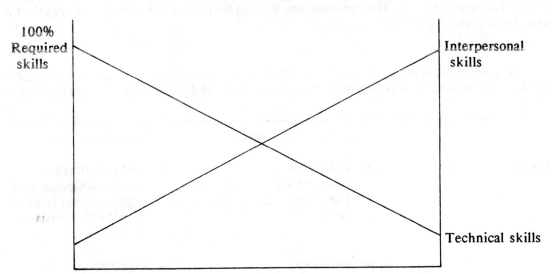

48. Technical skills are concerned with an ability to cope with large quantities of data and information and to select the appropriate key points to form the basis for decision-taking. Interpersonal skills involve inspiring, motivating, leading and controlling people to achieve goals which are often poorly defined. For the general manager, the latter are more important.

The transition curve

49. The transition from functional to general manager is a complex process and the time taken to complete the 'learning curve' varies depending on the degree of perceived change. Since a move from functional to general management is often, and correctly, viewed as a major change, transitions of this sort take longer than average to complete. The diagram below shows a typical transition curve.

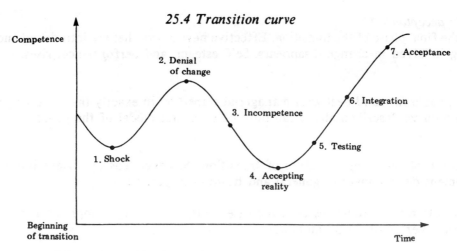

25.4 Transition curve

50. *Stage 1: immobilisation or shock*
A sense of feeling overwhelmed. This occurs because the reality of the new job does not match the person's expectations. The individual stops and tries to understand what is happening. Typical attitudes at this stage are "did I really want this job?" and "this isn't the job I expected".

51. *Stage 2: denial of change*
There is a reversion to previously successful behaviour. This can be useful if it is temporary, but becomes a handicap if it goes on too long and inappropriate behaviour becomes dominant. Sometimes individuals do remain at this point on the curve indefinitely and this is what is described as the *Peter Principle* (promoted to the level of their incompetence). They perform badly because their behaviour is based on their past activities rather than their current ones.

52. *Stage 3: incompetence*
Awareness that change is necessary accompanied by frustration because the individual finds it difficult to cope with the new situation or relationships. A fall in performance level is common but, despite this, the phase is very important in the transition process since, without the realisation of change, people can never develop new attitudes and patterns of behaviour. Organisations which adopt a "sink or swim" approach to transition actually hinder the process in that this phase is commonly regarded as the start of "sinking". Consequently, individuals are reluctant to share their current experience with others.

53. *Stage 4: accepting reality*
The reality of the new situation is accepted for the first time. Up to this point managers have been concerned with hanging on to past values, attitudes and behaviours. There is now a preparedness and willingness to experiment with change.

54. *Stage 5: testing*
Testing new behaviour and approaches. There is a lot of activity and energy as the testing progresses and mistakes are liable to be made. But the experimentation needs to be encouraged since only by doing this can effective approaches be found.

55. *Stage 6: integration*
This is a reflective period, in which individuals search for meaning in an attempt to understand all the activity, anger and frustration that went before.

56. *Stage 7: acceptance*
    This is the final phase of the transition. Effective new approaches are introduced and the sense of being involved in change disappears. Self-esteem, and performance, rises.

57. No two people face and deal with managerial transition in exactly the same way and so the transition curve described above can only be a general model of the process.

58. Recognition of the complex nature of transition, however, has important implications for management development in general and training in particular.

    (a) Transition takes time; research indicates that, on average, people feel in control only after a period of 24-30 months.

    (b) Changes which involve considerable adaptation, such as moving from a functional to a general management position, take longer than the average.

    (c) Because transition is often a lengthy process, management should avoid moving people from position to position too frequently.

    (d) For succession planning and training to be successful, it needs to go beyond the point of entry to the new job.

    (e) People in transition often have more severe entry problems than newcomers, since they are frequently not given a "breathing space" before being expected to perform adequately. This increases the pressures on them and may ultimately reduce their performance and that of the organisation as a whole.

59. To help with the transition from technical to general management, an organisation should have a *planned management development programme.*

    (a) Individuals should be encouraged to acquire suitable educational qualifications for senior management. 'High-fliers' for example might be encouraged to study for an MBA or a DMS early on in their career. Top finance managers (eg. the finance director) ought to have an accountancy or similar qualification.

    (b) Provide in-house training programmes for senior managers and individuals who are being groomed for senior management. Formal training in general management skills can be very helpful.

    (c) Careful promotion procedures. Only managers with the potential to be a good senior manager should be promoted into a senior management position.

    (d) A system of regular performance appraisal, in which individuals are interviewed by their boss (or their boss's boss) and counselled about:
        (i)   what they have done well;
        (ii)   what they have not done so well;
        (iii) how to improve their performance in their current job;
        (iv)   how to develop their skills for a more senior job.

    (e) Provide suitable experience to managers for more senior positions. This can be done, as mentioned earlier, by means of:
        (i)   allowing subordinates to stand in for their boss whenever the boss is away;

    (ii)   using 'staff officer' positions to groom future 'high fliers'. More is said about these jobs later;

    (iii)   job rotation;

    (iv)   using a divisionalised organisation structure to delegate general management responsibilities further down the management hierarchy. Divisional organisation can give managers experience of general management at a fairly early stage in their careers.

• Case study

60. Let's look now at a simple case study on **management training and development**.

You have recently been made responsible for training in your company's head office. This morning six young graduates, all of whom are on a two-year management programme, have complained about the quality of the training they have been receiving. Departmental heads seem to be unclear as to what sort of training they are supposed to provide for the graduates. The graduates are given dull routine work which they could master in five days, but they are kept at it for a month at a time. They are not told whether they are doing well or badly. They are bored and dispirited.

> Required:
> (a)   What is wrong with the management training programme?
> (b)   What action should you take to improve the training of the graduates?

61. *Discussion.* The graduates' complaint relates to the dull work they are given to do. It is assumed therefore that the problem relates entirely to on-the-job training and not to formal tutorial training.

62. *Deficiencies in the management training programme*

    (a)   Highly-qualified management trainees should be capable of mastering new techniques and work procedures very quickly. Department heads seem to be under-estimating the graduates' ability to do so. Graduates are being assigned for a whole month to routine work which they can master in a week. Department heads may have failed to realise the difference in learning speeds between recruits of school-leaving age and graduates specially selected for accelerated management training programmes.

    (b)   The graduates are poorly motivated because they are bored and do not experience any challenge in their work. Department heads are said to be 'unclear as to what sort of training they are supposed to provide'. They apparently do not realise that the purpose of a management training programme should be to introduce graduates as quickly as possible to *managerial* work, rather than the routine work they are doing now.

    (c)   There seems to be no system of appraisal and feedback. The trainees are not told whether they are doing well or badly. As well as being poor for morale, this is inefficient in that the graduates will not be able to improve their performance if they are not told where improvements are needed.

63. *Suggestions for improvement*

   ● Job rotation. The purpose of this is to broaden the knowledge and experience of the trainees. They can be shifted to a variety of posts, not all of them necessarily including supervisory duties. But the results may be unsatisfactory if insufficient time is allowed in each position.

   ● Use of 'assistant to' positions. Acting managers, preferably those with talent and experience as teachers, are assisted in their jobs by trainees. The trainees are able to observe the managers in the exercise of their normal duties, as well as carrying out useful work themselves.

   ● Temporary promotions. If managers are ill or on holiday trainees can be appointed as 'acting managers' in their absence. This can be a convenience for the organisation as well as an element in staff development. Obviously the trainees may need assistance in carrying out their duties and they should be encouraged to discuss any difficulties with their superiors.

   ● Committees. Trainees might be included in the membership of committees in order to gain an understanding of inter-departmental relationships.

   ● Establishing objectives. The graduates are likely to find their work more satisfying if targets are set for them. As it is, they appear not to know what is expected of them and cannot understand why they spend long periods on work which they have already mastered.

   ● Appraisal reports. A formal system of feedback should achieve improvements in staff performance as well as being a good motivator.

64. Formal education and training should back up on-the-job training. Each graduate should be encouraged to take an *active* interest in his or her own education, training and development.

QUIZ

Here are some examination-style problems. Jot down some ideas that you think are relevant to answering them.

1. Outline a development programme for managers taking account of the need to be adaptable and flexible with a particular concern for clients or markets.

2. What would you define as the main management development needs of a functional manager identified for promotion to general management?

3. What are the advantages and problems of a policy of "promotion from within an organisation"?

25: THE MANAGEMENT OF PROFESSIONALLY QUALIFIED STAFF

Discussion points

Question 1
Points to cover would include:
(i)   a *planned* programme;
(ii)   putting a senior manager (eg. personnel director) in charge of the programme;
(iii)   education;
(iv)   careful recruitment;
(v)   skills training;
(vi)   continuous in-house training;
(vii)   general management training;
(viii) on-the-job training with job rotation, delegation, 'assistant to' positions etc;
(ix)   formal and regular appraisal and counselling;
(x)   guidance from superiors for subordinates;
(xi)   planned transition from functional to general management;
(xii)   planning for succession into senior management positions.

The question emphasises the need to be adaptable and flexible, with particular concern for clients and markets. Flexibility and change are likely to be encouraged by involving as many managers as possible in the process of adapting and innovation. Delegation of authority would be advisable. In particular, a divisionalised organisation structure based on products or markets would seem particularly suitable.

Question 2
Here, the need is for a gradual introduction to the skills of general management. The differences between functional and general management should be pinpointed (paragraph 44) and recommendations for helping transition described (paragraph 58).

Question 3

Advantages	*Disadvantages*
1. Career opportunities for employers.	1. Appointees from outside likely to be more innovative, bringing fresh ideas.
2. Appointees understand the corporate values.	2. Possibly better people available outside.
3. Individuals can be *trained* and *developed* for promotion.	3. Organisation might lack a good management development programme.
4. Makes a career with the organisation more attractive, and reduces staff turnover.	4. Outside appointees should have broader experience.
5. Likely to be greater continuity.	
6. Appointees likely to have a better technical understanding of the business.	

Chapter 26

BUSINESS PLANNING: OBJECTIVES

Topics covered in this chapter

- Objectives
- The prime corporate objective
- The hierarchy of objectives
- Management by objectives (MBO)

Purpose of this chapter

To consider what objectives might be set for an organisation and for individual managers within it as a part of the business planning process.

● Objectives

1. The effectiveness of an organisation and its management can be monitored by checking whether objectives have been achieved. Objectives should be set for the organisation as a whole, where possible expressed as quantitative targets (eg target return on investment of x% pa). Objectives could also be set for individual managers, throughout the management hierarchy, within a system of 'management by objectives' or MBO. Once objectives are set plans can be made to achieve them at strategic, tactical and operational levels.

2. Drucker suggested that objectives should be identified and quantified under eight headings;

    - *market standing*. This must be measured against the total market potential, and the market standing of competitors. The goals which should then be established are:

        (i)   the desired standing of existing products in existing markets (£ turnover and % market share);

        (ii) the desired standing of existing products in new markets;

        (iii) the products which should be abandoned because they will no longer be profitable enough;

(iv) the number of new products required in existing markets, their necessary characteristics, and their desired standing;

(v) the number of new products (and their desired market standing) in new markets;

(vi) the distribution organisation needed to accomplish these marketing goals, and the pricing policy required;

(vii) a customer service objective (a measure of how well the customer should be supplied with 'value for money');

- *innovation*. Innovation objectives should attempt to forecast future technological developments, and how the organisation should adapt:

(i) its products and services; or
(ii) its methods of working;

to the changes. However, innovation in products or services are necessary even in industries where technological change is not significant. Changes in consumer demand will render many existing products and services obsolete, and create marketing opportunities for new ones;

- *productivity and added value*. Productivity targets are a measure of the desired efficiency with which resources should be utilised (eg. output per man hour, output per metre of cloth, output per machine hour). Added value is the difference between the revenue from a product and the material costs of production and sales. Targets for performance might therefore be that:

(i) the company should earn added value of £x per employee;
(ii) employees should earn in total wages or salaries equal to y% of added value;

- *physical and financial resources*. Every business uses physical resources and money, and it must be sure of its supply. Objectives should be set for obtaining sufficient resources to enable the business to achieve its goals for market standing and innovation;

- *profitability*. Profitability targets must be set. These may be 'satisficing' profit targets; however, Drucker argued that they should be *minimum* profit targets that will ensure survival and the provision of funds for re-investment in future innovation for expansion;

- *manager performance and development*. These objectives are considered below, with regard to management by objectives;

- *worker performance and attitudes*. Objectives should be set for worker performance and should not be left in the initiative of trade unions. However there is the problem that there is no clear link between workers' attitudes and their performance. Setting objectives for absenteeism, labour turnover, safety, grievances or attitudes will not necessarily ensure that worker performance is at all satisfactory;

- *public responsibility*. It is management's job to cover the demands placed on an organisation by public opinion and attitudes, and legal and political pressures, into opportunities for future growth and innovation.

3. 'Objectives are needed in every area where performance and results directly and vitally affect the survival and prosperity of the business' (*Drucker*).

Objectives in these key areas should enable management:

- to organise and explain the purpose and direction of the business in a small number of general statements about goals;

o to test the validity of these goals as a means of achieving the organisation's purpose;

- to predict behaviour;

- to appraise the validity of decisions about strategies and budgets (by assessing whether these are sufficient to achieve the stated objectives); and

- to assess and control actual performance.

● **The prime corporate objective**

4. It is generally accepted that there is a *hierarchy* of objectives, with one supreme corporate objective (restricted by certain constraints on corporate activity) and a series of subordinate strategic objectives which should combine to ensure the achievement of the overall objective.

5. There has been considerable disagreement about the choice of the overall corporate objective, although it is often agreed that for a *company* it will be a financial objective, such as:

(a) profitability;
(b) return on capital employed (ROCE);
(c) survival;
(d) (growth in) earnings per share (EPS);
(e) (growth in) dividends to shareholders;
(f) a target price earnings (P/E) ratio;
(g) return on shareholders' capital with an allowance for the element of risk.

These objectives all differ in some respects, although it is perhaps sufficient to note that they are all concerned with financial achievements (even (c) - survival - since it predicates the avoidance of making continual losses).

6. In many organisations, especially large ones, managers do not operate on the principle of *maximising* profits. They are content to achieve a level of profits or return on capital which will appear acceptable and realistic to all managers in the organisation, shareholders, employees, government and public opinion! In other words, they will seek a satisfactory or *satisficing* level of profits.

7. Although many writers agree that there should be an overall financial objective, expressed as a quantified target, they acknowledge that there are certain social or ethical obligations which a company must fulfil, as discussed in Chapter 14 on boundary management. In many companies, this is now taking the form of a mission statement which, as we have seen, also serves to motivate staff and tie the company in to a marketing orientation.

● **Hierarchy of objectives**

8. After the overall financial objective has been identified and quantified as a target and, similarly, after the mission statement has been identified, it is necessary to identify objectives for sub-divisions of the company:

26.1 Hierarchy of objectives

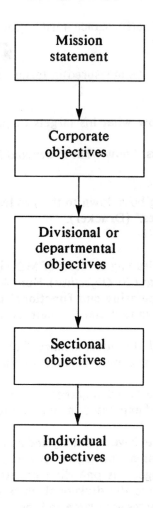

● **Management by objectives**

9. Management by objectives (MBO) is a 'comprehensive' approach to setting objectives, targets and plans. MBO is a scheme of planning and control which provides:

    (a) co-ordination of short-term plans with longer-term plans and goals;
    (b) co-ordination of the plans (and commitment) of junior with senior management; and
    (c) co-ordination of the efforts of different departments.

'Management by objectives requires effort and special instruments. For in the business enterprise managers are not automatically directed towards a common goal. On the contrary business, by its very nature, contains three powerful factors of misdirection: in the specialised work of most managers; in the hierarchical structure of management; and in the difference in vision and work and the resultant insulation of various levels of management'. *(Drucker)*.

10. Successful achievement of organisational goals requires that:

(a) each job is directed towards the same organisational goals. Each managerial job must be focused on the success of the business as a whole, not just on one part of it;

(b) each manager's targeted performance must be derived from targets of achievement for the organisation as a whole;

(c) a manager's results must be measured in terms of their contribution to the business as a whole;

(d) each manager must know what his targets of performance are;

(e) a manager's superior must know what to demand from the manager, and how to judge his performance.

'Each manager, from the big boss down to the production foreman or the chief clerk, needs clearly spelled-out objectives.' (Drucker).

11. Another writer who became a leading advocate of MBO in the 1960s is John Humble (in *Improving Business Results* and *Management By Objectives*). Humble argues that against a background of long-term corporate plans, the operating and functional units of a company (branches, regions, marketing department etc.) should clarify their own objectives:

(a) Both team objectives and individual managers' objectives must be identified; therefore key tasks must be analysed and performance standards agreed.

(b) These key tasks will be fused together into individual plans, prepared each year by divisional managers, and expressed in strategic terms rather than in short-term budgets.

(c) The divisional plans are reviewed centrally and amended by company or group headquarters, in consultation with divisional managers. Any imbalance between divisional objectives can be adjusted at this stage - is one division attempting to do too much and another attempting too little? Are the divisional plans consistent with each other, or is there sub-optimality? If resources are scarce and the demand by divisions for resources exceeds the supply, how should a fair allocation be made between them?

(d) Having agreed annual plans for each division, with key tasks identified and performance indicators established for each team and individual manager within the division, managers identify:

(i) *policies*: guides to making decisions which are in keeping with corporate objectives;

      (ii) *financial budgets*: a statement in money terms of a plan to achieve certain objectives. Financial budgets *are not the objectives themselves*.

      Humble said that each of these three devices (policies, procedures and financial budgets) were necessary to sound management control.

(e) Each division should make a monthly operating report, measuring actual results against key performance indicators. There should also be similar quarterly and annual reviews, after which new divisional plans would be prepared.

12. One of the most difficult problems for top management is finding the right balance between the conflicting claims of long-term and short-term results. Shareholders expect dividends every year, and may not be content to wait for the long term to receive their returns. On the other hand, large capital-intensive companies are forced to take the long view because they do not have the flexibility to change plans and direction quickly:

    (a) 'since any attempt to interlock different levels of objectives in detail is bound to fail, great concentration must be made on selecting a limited number of priorities which *must* be linked from top to bottom of the business' (Humble);

    (b) interlocking these key objectives must be not only vertical, but horizontal; the objectives of the production function must be linked with those of sales, warehousing, purchasing, R & D etc;

    (c) short-term objectives can be regarded as intermediate 'staging-posts' on the road towards long-term objectives.

    short-term ———————▶ short-term ———————▶ short-term ———————▶ long-term
    objective   objective   objective   objective

13. The hierarchy of objectives which emerges is as follows:

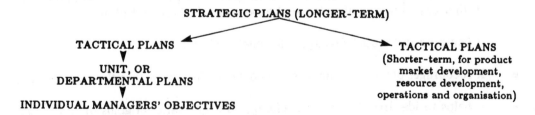

STRATEGIC PLANS (LONGER-TERM)

TACTICAL PLANS   TACTICAL PLANS
                                          (Shorter-term, for product
UNIT, OR   market development,
DEPARTMENTAL PLANS   resource development,
                                       operations and organisation)
INDIVIDUAL MANAGERS' OBJECTIVES

14. There are two approaches to establishing this hierarchy of objectives:

    (a) Senior managers (perhaps the managing director himself) can tell managers what to do and set up control procedures. Humble comments that 'this apparently sensible and logical approach often misses the spark of vitality, challenge and involvement on which the real use of human beings depends'. It is 'top-down' management.

    (b) Develop the contribution and motivation of each manager in the business by involving him in the planning process. This approach, which Humble called 'improving management performance', introduces an element of 'bottom-up' management, organised within the framework of corporate objectives and strategic plans.

15. Advocates of MBO (Drucker, Humble etc) argue that managers will only be committed to their objectives if they are allowed to assume responsibility for setting their own objectives for their unit of the business. Higher management should:

   (a) reserve the right to approve or disapprove the manager's objectives set by himself;

   (b) help the manager to set his objectives by communicating to him the goals and broad strategies of the organisation over the business planning period.

   > Management development is a key feature of MBO and it will only be successful if managers are given the responsibility for setting their own objectives (in consultation perhaps with their superiors).

16. Each manager should be given the information he needs to control his own performance, as soon as the information can be made available (economically) for him to use. The control information should go directly to him, and not to his boss. Control should not be seen to come down from above, because this will reduce managers' commitment to their objectives.

Advantages and disadvantages of MBO

17. The advantages of MBO may be summarised briefly as follows:

   > - better managing through better planning and control;
   >
   > - clarification of organisational goals within the framework of a long-term plan;
   >
   > - it is a scheme for converting strategic plans into management action plans and budgets;
   >
   > - there is co-ordination of individual management targets into the overall scheme, so that each individual manager knows what is expected of him;
   >
   > - it commits individual managers to meet their targets;
   >
   > - it encourages better communication and co-ordination within the organisation;
   >
   > - it helps to identify the need for change in organisational goals or individual managers and provides a system for making such changes.

18. The disadvantages of MBO are, briefly:

- it is not as effective as it should be if strategic plans have not been properly established; MBO should be used within the structure of an overall corporate planning system;

- some targets may be long-term whereas managers may prefer short-term targets and tangible results. If a person expects to be transferred to a different job after, say, 2 years, he will not be satisfied with targets for a 3 or 4 year period;

- there is a danger of inflexibility - individual objectives, once set, are not changed because the overall plan is rigidly adhered to. There must be flexibility and a willingness to accept amended objectives in the light of changing circumstances;

- it can be a time-consuming exercise which might not justify the benefit achieved;

- it might call for a significant change in the attitudes of senior managers, the style of leadership and the organisation structure if it is to function effectively as a system;

- it requires considerable inter-personal skills by managers throughout the organisation (in setting objectives and in reviewing performance with subordinates);

- it might overstress the need for individual achievements at the expense of teamwork.

QUIZ

1. List categories of possible organisational objectives.

   - See para 2

2. What is the purpose of objective-setting?

   - See para 3

3. List possible financial objectives that might be the prime objective of an organisation.

   - See para 5

4. What is the reasoning behind MBO?

   - See paras 10-11

Chapter 27

BUSINESS PLANNING:
STRATEGIC MANAGEMENT

Topics covered in this chapter

- Business planning
- Should business planning be a formal or informal process?
- Strategic management
- Strategic planning
- SWOT analysis
  - o Internal appraisal of strengths and weaknesses
  - o External appraisal of opportunities and threats
- Strategy selection and evaluation
- Corporate planning: a summary

Purpose of this chapter

To describe the business planning process, and to outline the role of strategic management.

- **Business planning**

1. Every business enterprise must plan ahead to survive. Plans must be made for the longer term as well as for the immediate future. Some businesses do not have an organised planning system and so tend to carry out their planning and control decisions in a disorganised and haphazard manner. However, in businesses where the scale and complexity of operations is large and diverse, business (or corporate) planning can be an invaluable aid to management.

2. Business planning and strategic planning are two terms which can be taken to mean the same thing.

3. Corporate planning has been variously described as follows:

- 'Corporate planning is a comprehensive, future oriented, continuous process of management which is implemented within a formal framework. It is responsive to relevant changes in the external environment. It is concerned with both strategic and operational planning and, through the participation of relevant members of the organisation, develops plans and actions at the appropriate levels in the organisation. It incorporates monitoring and control mechanisms and is concerned with both the short and the long term.'

- It is 'a systematic and disciplined study designed to help identify the objective of any organisation or corporate body, determine an appropriate target, decide upon suitable constraints, and devise a practical plan by which the objective may be achieved.'   *(Argenti 1968)*

---

4. Prof. John Higgins (University of Bradford Management Centre) has defined *strategic planning* as 'comprehending the environment, and ensuring that the organisation adapts to that environment.'

5. Strategic planning is a complex process, which involves taking a view of the organisation, and the future that it is likely to encounter, and then attempting to organise the structure and resources of the organisation accordingly. To that end, strategic planning includes both strategy and policy formulation, and the development of a set of plans.

6. Higgins describes the strategic planning process as embracing:

    (a) setting the corporate/strategic *objectives* which need to be expressed in quantitative terms with any *constraints* identified;

    (b) from (a), establishing the corporate performance required;

    (c) internal appraisal, by means of assessing the organisation's current state in terms of resources and performance;

    (d) external appraisal, by means of a survey and analysis of the organisation's environment;

    (e) forecasting future performance based on the information obtained from (c) and (d), initially as purely passive extrapolations into the future of past and current achievements;

    (f) analysing the *gap* between the results of (b) and (e);

    (g) identifying and evaluating various strategies to reduce this 'performance gap' in order to meet strategic objectives;

    (h) choosing between alternative strategies;

(i)   preparing the final corporate plan, with divisions between short term and long term as appropriate;

(j)   evaluating actual performance against the corporate plan.

● **Strategic planning as a discipline: formal or informal planning?**

7.   There are two different approaches to strategic planning:

(a)   one approach is that strategic planning must be a disciplined, structured and continuous planning exercise;

(b)   alternatively, there is the view that strategic planning should be an 'ad hoc' exercise - planning should be done at the corporate level only when opportunities arise for implementing a new business strategy.

Formal planning

8.   The large majority of writers favour a disciplined approach, for many reasons.

(a)   Many organisations are large, have a complex structure and operate in many different markets. Conglomerates and multinationals are among the most complex. Without discipline, planning would be unmanageable and in the case of multinationals or conglomerates, a failure to impose the discipline of strategic planning would result in the fragmentation of the organisation into separate unco-ordinated parts.

(b)   The rate of change in production, technologies and markets is very fast. A manager must be able not only to deal with change when it occurs, but to be able to foresee changes before they happen in order to be better prepared to meet them. Unless planning is disciplined, managers will think in the short term and not far enough into the future.

(c)   Because of the complexity of many business decisions, there is need for an information system which provides information of a sufficient quality to enable better decisions to be made. A formal information system, drawing from external sources as well as internal feedback, should be linked to a formal system for corporate planning and control.

(d)   There is still a growing tendency for managers to be less authoritarian in style and to allow subordinates a greater scope of authority. Management objectives to subordinates have therefore, in many instances, become more generalised and longer term.

(e)   If there is discipline in budgeting, we should expect to find discipline at the higher level of strategic planning. Planning itself is a discipline which focuses attention on significant issues which might otherwise be ignored.

(f)   A disciplined approach to strategic planning should ensure that:
   (i)   all the stages in the planning process are carried out;
   (ii) it is a continuous system, not an occasional 'one-off' exercise, so that there is a monitoring and review process;
   (iii) the entire organisation is co-ordinated, from the decisions of top managers to those of factory foremen and other front-line supervisors.

Informal planning

9. The second approach to strategic planning is to operate a system whereby opportunities are exploited as they arise; they are judged on their individual merits and not within the rigid structure of an overall corporate strategy. This approach contrasts with the generally accepted principles of disciplined strategic planning and is called *freewheeling opportunism*.

10. The advantages of this approach are that:

    (a) opportunities can be seized when they arise, whereas a rigid planning framework might impose restrictions so that the opportunities are lost;

    (b) it is flexible and adaptable. A formal corporate plan might take a long time to prepare and is fully documented. Any sudden, unexpected change (eg. a very steep rise in the price of a key commodity) might cause serious disruption, so that the process of preparing a new components plan would be slow. A freewheeling opportunistic approach would adapt to the change more quickly;

    (c) it might encourage a more flexible, innovative attitude among lower-level managers, whereas the procedures of formal planning might not.

11. Professor Bernard Taylor in his paper '*New Dimensions in Corporate Planning*' reiterates the fact that the way strategic planning is practised will vary with circumstances. Fitting the planning 'mode' to the situation will require a good deal of skill and experience.

    (a) In a large bureaucratic organisation, this will probably require the introduction of a formal planning system.

    (b) In circumstances where growth or innovation are required, it will be important to organise for new projects.

    (c) In an uncertain situation with many interest groups involved, it may be advisable to use an organisational 'learning' process - to improve mutual understanding, to explore the problem, and possibly to evolve a consensus.

    (d) If it is necessary to influence decisions in other organisations there may be a need for special arrangements to improve formal and informal contacts, eg. through joint committees, liaison officers etc.

    (e) Where there is a 'crisis of identity' in the organisation (eg. if it is not thought to be socially valuable or if the future of the enterprise is tied up with the creation of a new technology with important social implications) it may be particularly important to re-examine the future role of the enterprise in society.

• Strategic management

12. Rosemary Stewart stated that there are four major influences on organisation structures:

    (a) *the rapidity of change*: this has increased significantly in the last decade, leaving many traditional types of activity behind whilst generating new ones. Management's ability to respond to such changes is the ultimate determinant of its ability to survive;

(b) *shareholder attitudes*: the growth of institutional investors and the increasing sophistication of private investors mean that the general body of investors is more sensitive to long-term trends and the need to protect real values. The large, old, below-average-growth company (often a 'blue-chip') shows declining values relative to other investments. Frequently, it has become institutionalised and wedded to outmoded ideas;

(c) *grow or perish*: a company which does not adapt to change and achieve the expectations of investors will either quietly die or, if it is one of the type of companies mentioned in (b), will be the target of a takeover by more aggressive entrepreneurial managements closely attuned to the investors' need for a steady growth in earnings per share;

(d) *two types of management*: the response to this need for dynamism should be the recognition that two types of management are required within the company if the challenge of change is to be squarely faced. The functions of operating management are unchanged, but extraneous to this should be a strategic management whose objective is the achievement of at least average growth in earnings per share. The functions of strategic management are keeping the company's business mix healthy by 'positioning' the company - that is, by entering new areas of opportunity and by establishing corporate policy on force feeding the 'pullers' and correcting the 'draggers' in the present business mix.

13. The growth in earnings per share that is required is the ultimate responsibility of top management and will be contributed to by both operating and strategic management, with the latter probably playing the preponderant role. This it will achieve by the continuous positioning of the company in the best product mix.

14. Strategic management is therefore seen as having three specific tasks:

(a) to see that the product mix provides the optimum return on investment and stability commensurate with the company's strengths and weaknesses, through new product selection. For existing products, the identification of areas of high return so that research effort, capital resources etc can be deployed to win the maximum benefit, and of low return areas for correction or withdrawal of resources;

(b) to maximise share values through establishing a quality of earnings providing attractive future growth and ensuring that this earnings pattern is converted into investor assessment of the price/earnings ratio for the company's shares;

(c) to ensure that management skills are not excessively diluted by trying to do too much at once. It is better to do a few things well than many badly. The range of activities chosen for the future should be within the capacity of management, either existing or potential, and will of course be selected on a basis of mutual compatibility.

15. Strategic management continuously evaluates change and its opportunities in terms of established criteria. Rather than specific definitions of products or services, these will comprise a statement of corporate purpose and product rationale; the growth forces upon which to build; the growth markets to serve and the growth technologies from which to benefit.

16. In the past, and indeed at the present time, management has been heavily operations-oriented, with the relative places of each in the organisation something like that shown in Figure 27.1. Once the business was launched upon a course of action, operational management made nearly all the decisions, often including even non-recurring decisions.

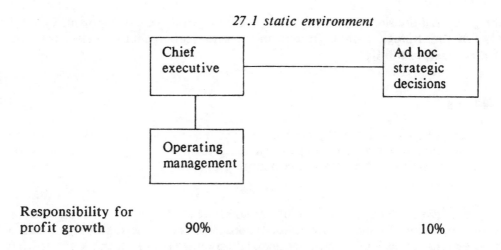

27.1 static environment

Responsibility for
profit growth   90%   10%

17. The advent of corporate or long-range planning groups in a business recognises that corporate development is a specialised function. In many cases, separate departments have been set up, often with direct access to top management. Often, however, such departments have functioned in an advisory or staff role manned by staff with no operating responsibilities as shown in Figure 27.2. While operating management has participated in strategic planning, it has been rare for strategic management to have any direct or major responsibility for producing an increased level of earnings per share.

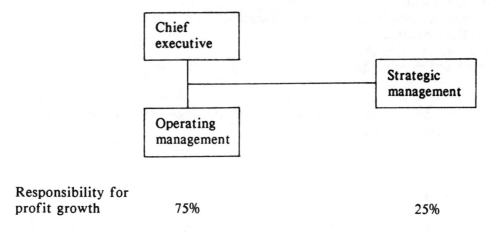

27.2 slow change in environment

Responsibility for
profit growth   75%   25%

18. Successful corporate development is the result of separating the functions and responsibilities of operating and strategic management. The functions of the chief executive are to organise and staff the subordinate positions; to ensure that individual actions conform to long-term objectives and policies; and to act as a link with investors and external agencies. Subordinate levels of management would be allocated to the function that accords the closest with their talents and interests.

19. In the organisation structure outline, strategic management is no longer performing a purely staff function but is charged with the direct responsibility for producing increased earnings per share. At the same time there is a decentralisation of activities subject to the usual financial and other constraints, with top management concerned with stimulating drive on the

part of the group and divisional operating heads, including strategic development. The standing of the head of the strategic planning group in the organisation should reflect this changed status of direct responsibility.

● **Strategic planning**

20. The process of setting corporate objectives, and expressing these objectives as targets for achievement within a designated time span, was described in Chapter 26. Setting an overall objective is the first step in the corporate planning process.

21. The next aim of the planning process should be to select strategies which should enable the organisation to achieve its main objectives. In order to select these strategies, and to set strategic objectives for each of them, the organisation must first of all think about what it is good at, and what it is bad at, and about what dangers and opportunities it is likely to face in the future.

Position audit (situation audit)

22. A starting point for developing strategies is a position (or situation) audit. This examines the organisation's present position in terms of

- products and markets
- production facilities
- resources - people, fixed assets and finance
- internal organisation
- current results being obtained
- shareholders' expectations

> A position audit works on the basis that if you want to know how to get somewhere, you need to know where you're starting from.

23. Key parts of the position audit are as follows.

(a) *Marketing audit* - a review of the organisation's products and markets, the marketing environment and its marketing systems and operation. The profitability of each product and market should be assessed, and the costs of marketing activities established. Information should be obtained on:

   (i)   size of the customer base;
   (ii)   size of individual orders;
   (iii) sales revenue and profitability;
   (iv)   split between export and domestic markets;
   (v)   market shares by product groups; and
   (vi)   sales and contribution growth over the previous periods.

(b) *Resource audit* - a review of the organisation's resources, being:

    (i)   physical resources;
    (ii)   human resources;
    (iii) systems;
    (iv) financial resources; and
    (v)   intangible resources (goodwill, patents etc).

Business planning models

24. Business planning models allow the organisation to develop forecasts for the business.

Forecasting what will happen in the future calls for data about the organisation itself and its resources, that is internal data and also external environmental data. Large quantities of data are needed to make reasonably reliable forecasts, and the value of computer databases might seem obvious in this context.

Scenario building

25. Scenario building is another name for strategic or long-range planning. It can be described as the process of identifying alternative futures, constructing a number of distinct possible futures permitting deductions to be made about future developments of markets, products and technology. Such models include simple surprise-free extrapolations, creative thinking such as brainstorming, systems models such as the MIT World Model, and the Delphi model.

26. From a more general standpoint, McNamee has outlined a seven point approach to scenario building.

(a) *Develop a data base.* Any modelling must have access to a sufficient database. Let it suffice to say here that it should include data about both the organisation itself and the environment.

(b) *Develop a strategic profile of the organisation* - establish its culture and style of leadership etc. Strengths and weaknesses analysis may be an element of this exercise. Much of the data will be highly quantitative; financial values, physical resources in terms of raw materials, skilled headcount, market share, cash and potential for increased gearing etc.

(c) *Develop a profile for the environment.* The Delphi technique is one way of doing this. Much of the UK public sector has been faced with greater competition from private sector organisations, against a background of government policy that has been alien to traditional public sector thinking and culture. Privatisation has emerged as a strategy for many public sector organisations to develop.

(d) *Test the impact of the environmental element upon the organisational element.* Essentially this means bringing the environmental factors and internal strengths and weaknesses together in order to assess strategies that are under review.

(e) *Analyse further the elements revealed by the analysis in step (d).* For example, a power supply company in a sunshine state of the USA may identify the growth of the population in its territory. This may need further analysis as to the population's profile, and what its requirements might be. Population growth may just be the result of older people migrating towards the sunshine on retirement, or else it might be part of a more general population movement towards the sunshine states, bringing with it a growth in commercial and industrial customers. The nature of the population growth would have implications for the power supply company in terms of planning capacity, eg. how long can the company continue to use imported power from a neighbouring state? When is the latest time to take decisions about capacity expansion? Most important, how may this capacity expansion be undertaken bearing in mind the environmental lobby groups and possible resistance to the use of coal (sulphur emissions) and nuclear power.

(f) *Repeated testing of the information revealed by the first analysis.* Plans are rarely finalised at the first attempt, and it is not unreasonable to assume that this process may have to be repeated several times.

(g) *Select the final strategy*, subject to the constraints of suitability, acceptability and feasibility.

• SWOT analysis - corporate appraisal

27. The internal appraisal of the organisation's strengths and weaknesses, and external appraisal of the opportunities and threats facing it, is known as SWOT analysis.

```
S  -  strengths
W  -  weaknesses
O  -  opportunities
T  -  threats
```

Internal appraisal: strengths and weaknesses

28. The purpose of a strengths-and-weaknesses analysis is to express, quantitatively or qualitatively:

(a) which areas of the business have strengths that should be exploited by suitable strategies;

(b) which areas of the business have weaknesses for which strategies should be developed to improve them.

29. The strengths and weaknesses analysis is internal to the company and intended to shape its approach to the external world. For instance, the identification of shortcomings in skills or resources could lead to a planned acquisition programme or staff recruitment and training.

The strengths and weaknesses part of the SWOT analysis involves looking at the findings of the position audit.

30. Typically, the SWOT analysis would consider information in the following areas.

(a) *Marketing*
(i) Fate of new product launches - have these a good success record or not, and so is the organisation developing new products successfully?

    (ii)   Success or failure of advertising campaigns - is the organisation using advertising to good effect?

    (iii)   Market shares and market sizes - is the organisation in a strong or weak position?

    (iv)   Company's standing in growth markets - is the organisation well-placed in growth markets, or does it rely on mature or declining markets?

    (v)   Skills of the sales force and selling techniques used - how good is the success rate of the sales team in winning orders?

(b) *Products*
    (i)   Analysis of sales by market, area, product groups, outlets etc.

    (ii)   Profit margin and overall profit contribution - are profits for each product good or not?

    (iii)   Age and future life of products - does the company have a good balance between old and new products, and between rising, mature and declining products?

    (iv)   Price elasticity of demand of products - is demand price-sensitive, and so are prospects for putting up prices poor?

(c) *Distribution*
    (i)   Delivery service standards - what are delivery lead times, and how do they compare?

    (ii)   Warehouse delivery fleet facilities - can the delivery fleet cope with demand?

    (iii)   Geographical availability of products - is the distribution network poor/adequate/excellent?

(d) *Research and development*
    (i)   Are R & D projects relevant to future marketing plans?

    (ii)   The costs of R & D - is R & D spending too little/too much?

    (iii)   Benefits of R & D in new products/variations on existing products - how good has R & D been?

    (iv)   R & D workload and schedules. Will we beat our competitors to the new launch?

(e) *Finance*
    (i)   Availability of short term and long term funds, cash flow - is the organisation in a strong or weak position for further borrowing or cash flow?

    (ii)   Contribution of each product - how is each product contributing to cash flow?

    (iii)   Returns on investment.

    (iv)   Accounting ratios - ratio analysis should help to identify areas of strength or weakness in performance (eg. asset turnover ratios, liquidity ratios etc).

(f) *Plant and equipment and other facilities*
    (i)   Age, value, production capacity and suitability of plant and equipment.

    (ii)   Valuation of all assets.

    (iii)   Location of land and buildings, their value, area, use, length of lease, current book value.

Are assets inadequate? too old? well kept? technologically advanced? Does the organisation have freehold or long leasehold property? If not, does renting or holding short leases on property indicate a potential danger/weakness?

(g) *Management and staff*
    (i)   Age spread, succession plans.

    (ii)   Skills and attitudes.

    (iii)   State of industrial relations, morale and labour turnover.

    (iv)   Training and recruitment facilities.

    (v)   Manpower utilisation.

In general, is the management team strong or weak, and in what ways?

(h) *Business management: organisation*
   (i)   Organisation structure - is this properly suited to the organisation's needs? Is the organisation based on functional divisions (eg. production, marketing, finance etc) or product/market profit centres?
   (ii) Management style and philosophy - does the management style seem well-suited to the businesses the organisation operates in?
   (iii) Communication links - are these adequate?

(i) *Raw material and finished goods stocks*
   (i)   The sources of supply - is there a single supplier or can supplies be obtained from numerous sources?
   (ii) Number and description of items.
   (iii) Turnover periods - long or short?
   (iv) Storage capacity - adequate? Is there spare capacity?
   (v)   Obsolescence and deterioration.
   (vi) Pilfering.

31. The purpose of the analysis is to express, qualitatively or quantitatively, which areas of the business have strengths to exploit, and which areas have weaknesses which must be improved. Although every area of the business should be investigated, only the areas of significant strength or weakness should warrant further attention.

32. A strengths and weaknesses analysis might come up with the following results:

- *Strengths:*

   (i)   marketing, products and markets:
         - products A, B and C are market leaders;
         - product D, new product launch, high profit potential;
         - good brand images;
         - good relations with suppliers and dealers;
         - good packaging and advertising appeal;

   (ii) production:
         - new factory in North West, fully operational for next year;
         - thorough quality inspection standards;

   (iii) finance:
         - £0.5 million cash available from internal resources;
         - further £2.0 million overdraft facility, so far unused;

   (iv) management and staff:
         - high skills in marketing areas of packaging, sales promotion, advertising and sales generally;
         - good labour relations, except at Plant Q which has low productivity.

- *Weaknesses:*

   (i)   marketing:
         - products X, Y and Z make no contribution to fixed costs;
         - products P, Q and R are declining and will lose profitability in 3 years;

- sales of product D are dependent upon a high level of sales of complementary products (eg. razor blades and razor);
- no new products, except for D, have been successfully launched in the last two years;

(ii) research and development:
- no major new products have been derived from R & D for two years. Becoming too dependent on acquisition for additions to product range;
- little control over R & D budget;

(iii) production:
- plant at most factories has an average age of 8.7 years;
- new developments could threaten ability to compete;
- high level of spoiled goods on lines 3, 7, 9 at Plant M;
- low productivity on all lines at Plant Q;

(iv) management and staff:
- poor labour relations at Plant Q with low productivity;
- senior executives approaching retirement with no clearly recognisable successors;
- success of the organisation too dependent on senior executive charisma.

External appraisal: opportunities and threats

33. The internal appraisal highlights areas within the company which are strong and which might therefore be exploited more fully, and weaknesses where some 'defensive' planning might be required to protect the company from poor results. Strengths and weaknesses show up inherent *potential*.

34. An external appraisal is required to identify profit-making opportunities which can be exploited by the company's strengths and also to anticipate environmental threats (a declining economy, competitors' actions, government legislation, industrial unrest etc) against which the company must protect itself. The external appraisal is the opportunities and threats analysis part of SWOT analysis.

35. For *opportunities* it is necessary to decide:

(a) what opportunities exist in the business environment;

(b) what is their inherent profit-making potential;

(c) what are the internal strengths/weaknesses of the organisation, and is it capable of exploiting the worthwhile opportunities and still achieve its social and ethical objectives;

(d) what is the comparative capability profile of competitors and are these competitors better placed to exploit these opportunities;

(e) what is the company's comparative performance potential in this field of opportunity.

The opportunities might involve product development, market development, market penetration or diversification. No realistic opportunity should be ignored.

36. For *threats* it is necessary to decide:

    (a) what threats might arise, to the company or its business environment;

    (b) how competitors will be affected by threats;

    (c) how the company will be affected. Does it have strengths to deal with the threats or do weaknesses need to be corrected so as to survive? Are contingency strategies required?

37. The opportunities and threats which might be identified include the following.

    ● *Economic:* at a local or national level, threats and opportunities would relate to unemployment, the level of wages and salaries, the level of interest rates and their effect on consumer spending, increases in local government rates and fuel costs, the expected total market behaviour for products, total customer demand, the growth and decline of industries and suppliers, general investment levels etc. At an international level, world production and the volume of international trade, demand, recessions and exchange controls must be considered.

    ● *Government:* legislation may affect a company's prospects through the threats/ opportunities of pollution control or a ban on certain products. A law to ban lead in petrol would be a threat to petrol producers and car makers, but at the same time an opportunity for selling lead-free petrol and making cars that use it. Pollution controls offer opportunities for companies that make equipment to prevent or limit pollution. Taxation incentives, rent-free factory buildings, or investment grants might be available for exploitation or under threat of withdrawal. Government policy may be to increase expenditure on housing, defence, schools and hospitals or roads and transport by joint funding by private companies and the relevant government organisations. Political attitudes may threaten the nationalisation of companies' assets, or nationalised industries may face the threats/opportunities of privatisation. Political upheaval might damage market and investment prospects, especially overseas.

    ● *Competitors:*

        (i) Possible competitors' actions in the future must be considered and their comparative strengths and weaknesses evaluated. In Britain, it is especially important to identify where competitors are weak in export markets, and where foreign competitors might threaten the industry with cheaper or better imports. British industry in fairly recent years has called at some time or another for protection against Japanese cars, foreign textiles and imported fish, having been unable to meet the external threat successfully and therefore requiring external assistance from the government. In contrast, manufacturers of lawn-mowers successfully identified a threat from Japanese importers and developed competitive new products of their own.

        (ii) The company must decide whether it is under threat of a takeover bid by any other company. A comparison of internal strength and weakness and potential buyers is needed.

    ● *Technology:* technological changes must be forecast so as to identify the possibility of new products appearing, or cheaper means of production or distribution being introduced. The potential of the microchip has far-reaching effects for producers (eg. the use of robots), service industries (eg. the communications and information services), and markets (eg. the new products that will be made available for consumers).

● *Social:*Social attitudes will have a significant effect on customer demand and employee attitudes.

(i) Attitudes to work are changing, and employees are increasingly unwilling to work in 'dirty' jobs or menial work. Hours of work are shortening, holidays getting longer, and the age of retirement may be lowered. Voluntary early retirement has been a feature in recent years.

(ii) Inflation in the 1970s and the availability of credit in the 1980s appear to have encouraged a switch of attitudes to 'spend now, pay later'. This important shift in social attitudes explains the growing interest by many companies in exploiting the leisure and health industry - eg. golf clubs and driving ranges, squash, home computers, gambling, holiday items, fitness centres etc.

(iii) Society is applying pressure to improve the environment, and to reduce noise and pollution.

(iv) The government in Britain is making efforts to protect the employment rights of women and encourage racial equality

(v) Population trends must be considered. Britain currently has an ageing population so that, in future, an increased market will exist among retired people, some of whom have considerable spending power. Sheltered housing and tours for the Over 60s are growth areas in the UK. There is growth in the personal pensions market facilitated by recent legislation.

(vi) Permanently high unemployment figures will influence the available total spending power of consumers, especially in some of the more depressed regions of the UK.

Example: opportunities and threats analysis

38. Some years ago, an analysis of opportunities and threats in its industrial environment would have been of some value to strategic planners in the UK paint industry. From 1980, four pressures built up on the industry:

(a) the economic recession;
(b) rising costs of production and marketing;
(c) fragmentation of the markets for paint products;
(d) new technology.

39. As raw material costs rose, paint prices were kept down by intense competition between paint manufacturers, so that profit margins were squeezed. New market segments combined with new technology have forced paint manufacturers to spend heavily on product development - paints for plastics, paints for painting steel coils or aluminium coils on automated production lines, one-coat paints, non-drip paints, and all-weather woodstains are examples of product changes based on new technology. With low profit margins, companies need to have a 15% - 20% share of a market segment to be profitable, but there are still about 10 big paint manufacturers in the UK.

40. The threats and opportunities in the environment might suggest that:

(a) there are threats of being taken over by a UK or foreign competitor or opportunities to take over a rival;

(b) some manufacturers should plan to 'divest' and get out of certain segments of the market. Indeed, ICI, the overall market leader, pulled out of the market for heavy duty paints for agricultural, construction and earth-moving equipment, leaving Macpherson as the dominant market leader in this market segment.

The changes in the paint industry are no doubt still far from over.

● **Strategy selection and evaluation**

41. The internal and external appraisals will be brought together, and perhaps shown in cruciform chart, so that potential strategies can be identified.

42. A cruciform chart is simply a table listing the significant strengths and weaknesses, and opportunities and threats. For example:

STRENGTHS	*WEAKNESSES*
£10 million of capital available	Heavy reliance on a small number of customers
Production expertise and appropriate marketing skills	Limited product range, with no new products and expected market decline. Small marketing organisation.
THREATS	*OPPORTUNITIES*
A major competitor has already entered the new market	Government tax incentives for new investment.
	Growing demand in the new market, although customers so far relatively small in number.

43. In this example, it might be possible to identify that the company is in imminent danger of losing its existing markets and must diversify its products, or its products and markets. The new market opportunity exists to be exploited, and since the number of customers is currently small, the relatively small size of the existing marketing force would not be an immediate hindrance. A strategic plan could be developed to buy new equipment and use existing production and marketing to enter the new market, with a view to rapid expansion. Careful planning of manpower, equipment, facilities, research and development would be required and there would be an objective to meet the threat of competition so as to obtain a substantial share of a growing market. The cost of entry at this early stage of market development should not be unacceptably high.

44. In this example, one individual strategy has been identified from our simplified cruciform chart. In practice, a combination of individual strategies will be required with regard to product development, market development, diversification, resource planning, risk reduction etc.

45. Once a company has defined its business and analysed strengths and weaknesses, taking regard of external factors, it is in a position to develop its strategy and define a range of strategic objectives. To define the range of objectives does not, of itself, bring about their attainment. The company will need to identify opportunities for growth and profit improvement that will enable it to achieve its objectives.

46. Drucker tells us that 'successful planning is always based on maximising opportunities' and he cites the example of Marks and Spencer who are consistently asking themselves - 'which are the opportunities where doing something new and different is likely to have the greatest economic results?' Drucker goes on to outline (*Management for results*) three main approaches to improving business effectiveness:

   ● The executive can define 'the ideal business' which would produce best results from the available market knowledge and opportunities.

   ● He can try to maximise opportunities by focusing the available resources on the most attractive possibilities to obtain greatest results.

   ● He can maximise resources so that those opportunities are found - if not created - that give the available resources the greatest possible impact.

47. The following diagram shows how a company progresses through the sequence of defining its business, assessing external factors, analysing its strengths and assessing weaknesses, and formulating objectives through to evaluation of alternative courses of action.

27.3 Sequence for selecting strategies

● **Corporate planning: a summary**

48. The task of selecting a suitable 'portfolio of strategies' is a very complex one because of the wide variety of options available.

49. The choice is so complex that Argenti recommends that the corporate plan should exclude as much detail as possible, and provide only a 'coarse-grained' strategic structure for the long-term future, leaving the detail of new product selection, new markets, diversification opportunities (in detail), R & D projects, resource management etc. in the hands of executive managers. He wrote:

> 'A corporate plan, then, will specify both the strategic structure towards which the company is to move and the individual strategic actions that will bring it about. The depth of detail required in the corporate plan should be sufficient to allow the management to judge their confidence in it; if more than this depth of detail is present then the scope for opportunism and initiative by individual managers may be needlessly curtailed. Deciding how much to decide is an important part of all planning.'

50. The major obstacles to corporate planning can be listed as follows:

   (a) senior management might fail to specify clear objectives and goals for the organisation on which to base realistic strategic plans. This in turn means that divisions and departments cannot set clear goals and objectives for themselves;

   (b) if a business exists in a rapidly-changing environment, planning becomes extremely difficult because there are so many unforeseen or unpredictable events which might quickly invalidate plans. It has been suggested, for example, that the current state of technological change in the banking industry makes it extremely difficult to foresee what new competition might enter the banking market, and what customer demand for 'new-technology' services (eg. electronic funds transfer at the point of sale, cash management systems, home banking) might be;

   (c) time scale. The longer a (corporate) planning period is, the greater will be the likelihood of unforeseen events occurring, which will make the plan invalid. This factor and also (b) above inevitably discourage managers from attempting detailed long-term plans;

   (d) lack of information. An organisation's information system might be inadequate and unable to provide the information from the business environment which is necessary for long-term planning;

   (e) inflexibility. Management might fail to provide for periodic reviews of the corporate plan, and for adapting it to changing circumstances as they arise or as they are foreseen. An inflexible corporate plan will quickly become out-of-date;

   (f) it is difficult to reconcile all the long-term and short-term, financial and non-financial interests of an organisation. This is a problem which has several adverse consequences:

      (i) it might be difficult to obtain the agreement of all managers in the organisation to a set of objectives and strategies in the corporate plan;

(ii)   strategic plans might be too generalised so that sub-units of the organisation are unable to convert these plans into action plans;

(iii)   corporate planning objectives are long-term as well as short-term, so that it might be difficult to communicate them to lower levels of management in such a way that they are not soon forgotten. Commitment to the objectives is necessary, and a system of continual reminders or performance appraisal will be necessary;

(iv)   managers not involved in preparing the corporate plan might be hostile to or unenthusiastic about it.

(g)   Managers will only be committed to a set of objectives if their performance is measured against a set of quantified targets for achievement. It is a failure of many long-term plans that they do not provide quantified targets. It is more convenient to judge management performance against a budget and, all too often, budget targets are concerned with achieving revenue or profit targets, or keeping within budget cost limits. Non-profit factors (such as public responsibility and employee welfare) are not often budgeted for.

Furthermore, if budgets are prepared independently of the corporate plan, and are not treated as a short-term part of it, management will be working towards budget goals which are not necessarily consistent with the corporate plan. In other words, there might be a problem of co-ordinating the corporate plan with budgets.

(h)   Corporate planning can be an expensive exercise. Large organisations might even have a corporate planning department advising the board of directors. The benefits from corporate planning must exceed the costs if the exercise is to be justified.

(i)   Corporate planning might be a paper exercise. Senior management might pay lip service to certain objectives, but in practice their actual behaviour might belie their intentions and interests. For example, objectives about public responsibilities and employee welfare might soon be forgotten when profit margins are tight. Similarly, plans for innovation through research and development might be the first to suffer in a round of budget cuts.

51.   The problems in corporate planning can be overcome if management organises its planning processes correctly.

Factors to consider in corporate planning
A checklist

1. Establishing the main objective of the organisation.

2. Establishing ethical 'constraints' which the organisation should be bound by.

3. How formal should the planning process be?

4. How can the planning process be co-ordinated and made effective?

5. There is likely to be a need to encourage innovative thinking. How can this be achieved?

6. Should corporate planning involve departmental and functional management? Should planning be confined to a small corporate planning team at central HQ? In a divisionalised organisation, should divisions prepare their own corporate plans, subject to approval by central HQ? A key issue is getting the *commitment* of all management to the plans.

7. What information is needed for planning - is a position audit required? Where will the information come from? Who will provide it? How good will it be?

8. What forecasting methods should be used?

9. To what extent will forecasts be reliable, and how much uncertainty is there in the future?

10. What areas of the organisation and its environment should be investigated in SWOT analysis? Nothing of potential significance should be overlooked.

11. Will there be any constraints on the development of strategies for the future (eg a shortage of finance, or a shortage of key resources, such as skilled labour?)

12. How often should plans be reviewed to assess whether they are still valid?

13. How can objectives be set for management for which they can be made responsible and accountable? Control through performance appraisal is essential in corporate planning, just as in other systems of planning and control.

14. It is always important to keep *change* in mind when planning for the longer term future - eg changes in technology.

QUIZ

1. What are the steps in corporate planning?

   ● See para 6

2. What are the arguments for and against formal and informal planning?

   ● See paras 8 and 10

3. What are the three specific tasks of strategic management?

   ● See para 14

4. What areas does a position audit examine?

   ● See paras 22–23

5. What is SWOT analysis? What areas of manufacturing business should it cover?

   ● See paras 27,30

6. Suggest what opportunities and threats might face an organisation in the future.

   ● See para 37

7. List the major obstacles to corporate planning.

   ● See para 50

8. What factors should be considered in corporate planning?

   ● See checklist above

Chapter 28

THE INTERNATIONAL PERSPECTIVE

Topics covered in this chapter

- Management principles and the global context
- Comparative management
- Farmer–Richman and KOW models
- International management
- Cultural differences and management

Purpose of this chapter

To illustrate the problem of comparing organisations by challenging the universality of management principles.

To introduce the environment of organisations in the particular context of international organisations. Managers must think globally but manage locally.

- **Management principles and the global context**

1. *Comparative management* is concerned with analysing the job of managing in different environments (eg different countries) and the reasons why enterprises show different results in different environments.

2. *International management* is concerned with the way in which local conditions affect the operation of management in multinational and international organisations.

3. In this text we have tried to illustrate general principles of management, and our assumption has been that such principles have universal validity. This chapter examines some of the limitations in that assumption. The need to question the assumption arises primarily from the fact that nearly all research into management and organisation has taken place in societies which are economically and culturally advanced, and which have a strong basis of private enterprise. This inherent bias may lead to distortion if research is used as the basis of general conclusions. Furthermore, for UK managers the Single European Market of 1992 means that they must increasingly think globally - but continue to manage locally as well.

● **Comparative management**

4. Two American writers, Gonzalez and McMillan, suggested that 'American management experience abroad provides evidence that the uniquely American philosophy of management is not universally applicable but is a rather special case . . . That aspect of management which lacks universality has to do with interpersonal relationships, including those between management and workers, management and suppliers, management and the customer, the community, competition and government'. This conclusion was based on a two-year study of management in Brazil.

5. This suggests that no general conclusions on management principles can be arrived at, and that different principles will apply in different cultures. It even opens up the possibility that general management principles may not be applicable throughout a large country such as the United States because of the variety of sub-cultures that may exist.

6. Despite this, Gonzalez and McMillan believe that the export of managerial know-how from the United Stages has benefited other countries. American ideas (such as innovation etc) may at first be greeted with scepticism, but eventually the objective and systematic approach is welcomed.

7. Koontz, O'Donnell and Weihrich (KOW) have argued that apparent differences between management *principles* in different countries are actually differences of *application*, and that this distinction has been blurred by careless use of terminology. Their idea is that certain universal *fundamentals* of management exist, which may be applied in different ways depending on the local culture.

● **The Farmer-Richman and KOW models**

8. R N Farmer and B M Richman emphasise the importance of the external environment in which an organisation operates. They developed a model to illustrate the distinction between the management process and the environment of managing.

28.1 The Farmer-Richman model

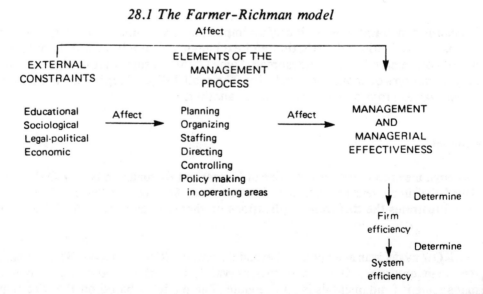

9. Farmer and Richman elaborate on the four categories of external constraints identified in the model.

10. *Educational* constraints include the level of literacy in the environment (country) and the availability of secondary education, vocational training and higher education. Poor educational facilities will inevitably result in poor management.

11. *Sociological* constraints are the most numerous category. For example, one country may have a tradition of antagonism between trade unions and management whereas another might have a history of mutual trust and co-operation. In some societies there may be an inflexible class structure which prevents some members of society from entering management. One country might have a conservative outlook and incline to resist change, whereas the society of another country might favour radical change. In some countries there might exist a prejudice against careers in commerce, so that educated people would prefer professional careers. Different societies might take different views on the desirability of wealth and material gain.

12. *Legal and political* constraints are analysed by Farmer and Richman under six headings:

    (a) the 'rules of the game', including legislation on prices and competitions, health and safety, contracts, taxation, hours and conditions of work;

    (b) defence policy and national security. This often has a considerable effect on the allocation of labour and resources;

    (c) foreign policy, including tariffs and quotas, protection of local trade, exchange controls and restrictions on foreign ownership and investment;

    (d) political stability. Political uncertainty in a country may affect management's ability to carry out its planning functions;

    (e) political organisation, including the degree to which a country's government is federal or centralised;

    (f) the flexibility of law, ie the ease with which legal charges are brought about in a society.

13. *Economic* constraints are obviously an important environmental factor. In some countries the means of production, distribution and exchange are largely in public ownership; in others, private ownership is more widespread. Some countries suffer from high rates of inflation and other symptoms of economic instability. The availability of capital is another important factor which varies from one environment to another.

KOW model

14. Although they accept the broad outline of Farmer and Richman's model, KOW continue to maintain their belief in universal management fundamentals. They believe that the Farmer–Richman model only illustrates the different applications of these fundamentals in different environments.

15. The KOW model is an attempt to go beyond the Farmer-Richman model. While accepting the Farmer-Richman environmental constraints as valid, it tries to show that a belief in universal management fundamentals is still tenable. The model is based on the idea that management knowledge is only a part of the total knowledge utilised in an enterprise. Enterprise activities fall into the two categories of managerial and non-managerial.

28.2 The KOW model

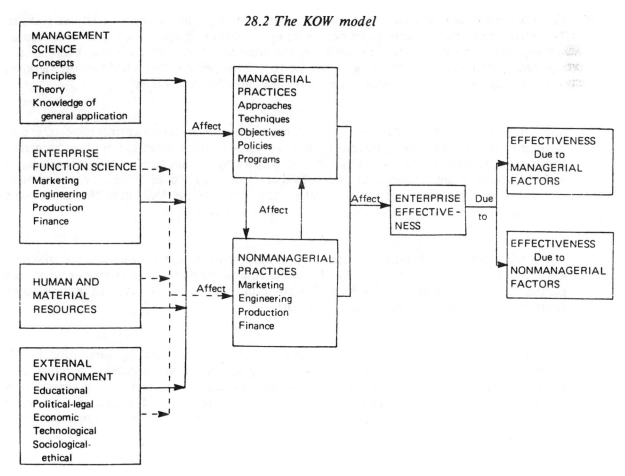

16. Kow prefer to talk of environmental factors not as constraints, but as *variables* which may constitute constraints or opportunities.

17. One example of comparative management might help to illustrate the effect of environmental factors on managerial practices. In Japan, social and cultural conditions have led to a situation in which large companies attempt to look after their employees and provide lifelong employment. Authority is based on seniority and respect for age, although employees at lower levels are positively encouraged to contribute to the process of making planning decisions. In return companies expect complete loyalty to the firm from all employees. This socio-cultural background therefore affects the management tasks of planning (consultation), organising (seniority), staffing (lifelong employment) and leadership (loyalty to the firm, respect for age).

● **International management**

18. *Multinational companies* are groups of companies with a head office and parent company in one country, and subsidiaries in other countries. (An *international company* might be based in one country, but sell goods to other countries. It would not then be a multinational.)

19. There is a continuing growth in the development of multinationals, for a variety of reasons. There are economies of scale to be obtained, even when a company operates with foreign subsidiaries. Distribution of production saves transport costs. In addition, there is the advantage to suppliers in achieving a monopolist or oligopolist status within world markets, because they can then set higher prices and earn supernormal profits.

20. International trade is made uncertain by the threat of government action against imports, and so large producers in one country might choose to set up domestic production in other countries. Many multinationals operate with subsidiaries in which a significant number of senior managers and shareholders are nationals of the subsidiary's country, so as to satisfy government requirements about employment and ownership. As an example, the decision of Nissan to build a car plant in the UK was influenced by the import restrictions of the EEC.

21. The world's capital markets are efficient and capital is mobile. A large international company has access to sources of substantial funds, and is able to invest them in countries where the greatest cost efficiencies can be achieved. Many multinationals have invested in developing countries where labour is still relatively cheap.

22. The increase in multinationals may be seen as a consequence of expanding international trade (despite temporary recessions) and the cost advantages of large-scale production, together with action by firms to create or preserve monopolies (creating barriers to entry against new competitors, perhaps by means of price discrimination), mobility of capital to take better advantage of labour markets, and defensive measures against protectionism by foreign governments.

Disadvantages of multinationals

23. Although multinationals can exploit a number of advantages over smaller firms (eg economies of scale, access to capital markets worldwide, ability to manufacture and produce in countries where material and labour resources are cheap), they also suffer from a number of specific managerial disadvantages. These will be examined by looking in turn at the management function of planning, organising, staffing, leading and controlling.

24. *Planning*. The environmental variables within which an organisation operates make planning difficult even in local terms. But a multinational faces problems of forecasting environmental variables over many countries, possibly throughout the world. Plans which look promising in the local environment may founder abroad.

25. *Organising*. The possible structures of an organisation have been discussed in earlier chapters. Multinationals face the problem that no one structure can meet the needs of the many different environments in which they operate.

26. *Staffing*. The basic problem here is whether managers should be chosen from the home country or selected locally. Home-grown managers may be familiar with headquarters philosophy, but may find it difficult to get on with local staff from a different background. Differences in language are an obvious problem. On the other hand, use of locally-selected managers may lead to a lack of homogeneity in the multinational's trading efforts.

27. *Leading*. In Western countries a participative style of management is generally practised, or at least aimed at. But this may be difficult to transfer to other countries where there is a tradition of autocratic rule. Again, the problem of different languages is relevant: effective leadership is hardly possible without good communication.

28. *Controlling*. Effective controlling depends on accurate measurement of performance. When many aspects of performance are measured in monetary terms this means that currency differences are a serious obstacle to control. In addition, accounting practices, financial reporting and taxation may all vary from country to country. Inflation rates may be different, and exchange rates will exacerbate the problem. The sheer size and geographical dispersion of multinationals mean that delays elapse between the measurement of performance and the taking of corrective action.

29. Finally, it is worth noting one particular political difficulty. Since many multinationals are American, a situation has arisen where the US government has imposed restrictions on US multinationals which in turn have affected sales between firms in other countries; UK government opposition to high technology sales to the USSR resulted in legislation whereby US multinationals were forbidden to sell certain goods to foreign companies, even through their foreign subsidiaries, if those customers would in turn manufacture goods for the USSR.

● **Cultural differences and management**

30. The social or environmental 'climate' or 'culture' of a country may be defined as 'all the social factors that affect the way people behave' (Rosemary Stewart) or the sum of all its environmental influences; ie the class structure, economy, political structure, legal framework, employee representation structure, education, culture, lifestyle, level of technology etc created by the socio-political and economic trends in the country's history.

31. Four features of this climate that may affect the attitudes and practices of managers in different countries include:

    (a) *class structure*. The class structure of a nation is likely to influence the way in which management and workforce perceive each other, and the way in which both regard their work. It is an accepted fact that in Britain there is a greater perceived social distance between manager and worker, leading to greater formality in interpersonal relations and a greater stress in management attitudes on the traditional hierarchical aspects of organisation than is evident in Japan or America, where informality and worker participation in management are far more developed. According to Rosemary Stewart, 'the gap, or social distance, that exists between different levels in the organisation reflects both the class structure in the society as a whole and management's place in it';

    (b) *the labour relations climate* - including governmental influences (ie employment law), regulation and the structure of worker representation/trade unionism. The attitudes of management to labour is reflected in how authority is exercised and how conditions of work and employee services are regarded. Governmental intervention may shape management policy in these areas: in Latin America, the government is a vital intermediary in industrial relations, and in the early days of industrialisation in Britain, many factory owners had to be forced by the Factory Acts to provide minimum conditions, pay and welfare for their employees, to stop child labour etc. There are other influences: a paternalistic approach to the employment relationship might grow out of a feudal social structure (as in Japan) or out of a strong traditional class/family structure (as in Italy). A history of industrial disputes in a country may reinforce managerial stereotypes of the militant worker etc;

(c) *the dominant values of the society.* Whether they arise from history, religion, politics or any other source, there will be certain mainstream cultural characteristics which will affect the manager himself and the conditions within which he operates. Where materialistic values are uppermost, eg in countries like America, the manager will have high status, which will be reflected in his attitudes to his work and to his subordinates. Japanese cultural values, such as concern for the individual, respect for seniority and the concept of 'wa' or 'harmony', are closely bound up with the managerial practices of consensus decision-making, paternalism, 'nenko' or lifetime employment etc;

(d) *technological advancement.* The extent to which technology is an accepted part of the social structure will influence managers' attitudes to its implementation and advancement in the workplace, and possibly to change in general. Managerial attitudes to work patterns, eg pace of work, and place of work - with networking eroding the supremacy of the office as the administrative heart of the organisation - have to take into account the level of technology available, employed by the competition etc. Workers with new technology are considered to be 'knowledge' workers with necessary skills and experience: administrative staff in countries where information technology is less advanced are likely to be less highly regarded, and the few who may have gathered technology-based skills elevated;

(e) *the occupational/professional structure.* This will depend on how organised and how highly-regarded the occupations and professions are in a country. The medical and teaching professions may be very highly prized in some cultures, whereas in more materialistic cultures, financial professions have the highest status. This will affect managers' attitudes to their own position in their society, and to their importance in the organisation. Accountants may run companies in Britain, where engineers or production designers are in senior positions in Germany etc.

QUIZ

1. What is the difference between comparative and international management?

   - See paras 1-2

2. What are the four external constraints on an international business identified by Farmer and Richman?

   - See paras 10-13

3. Why have multinationals grown as a form of business organisation?

   - See para 22

4. What are the managerial disadvantages suffered by multinationals?

   - See paras 24-29

ILLUSTRATIVE
QUESTIONS AND SOLUTIONS

Business organisation

1. Types of organisation
2. Centralisation and decentralisation
3. Line and staff

Business functions

4. Production planning
5. The marketing concept

Principles of management

6. Japanese firms
7. Delegation
8. Communication
9. Social responsibility

Functions of management

10. Effective work teams
11. Case study: poor organisation
12. Selection
13. Notes: job satisfaction, job description, appraisal
14. Corporate planning

ILLUSTRATIVE QUESTIONS

1. The mixed economies of industrialised and less developed countries have large commercial enterprises that are either partly (semi-state) or fully (nationalised) state owned.

   What policy, planning and operating difficulties may be faced by nationalised or semi-state business enterprises (in any mixed economy) when they are instructed to act in a more profit-orientated and market-sensitive manner than hitherto?

2. What factors will have influenced the extent to which an organisation is centralised or decentralised? Support each factor with a reason.

3. (a) Identify two fundamentally different jobs or positions, one in a manufacturing company and the other in a commercial bank, which you would classify as being 'staff' in character.
   (b) Why should they be so clearly classified as staff positions?
   (c) In what ways do they differ from line jobs or positions to be found in the same organisation?
   (d) What are the limitations on the use of staff specialists?

4. The production process is one by which goods and services are brought into existence. Write a brief account of the planning and operating decisions which the production manager is likely to encounter in a business which manufactures toy motor cars.

5. What is the 'marketing concept'? Comment on its relationship to other business orientations.

6. Outline and comment on those organisational and cultural characteristics, with specific reference to the employment relationship, which you consider to be unique to large Japanese business concerns?

7. What factors would influence your decision to delegate work to a subordinate? What are the major barriers to delegation?

8. The efficiency of your department is being impaired because two members of your staff seem to be unable to communicate properly with each other. What are the barriers to effective personal communication that you would investigate, and the remedies you would seek to apply in an attempt to solve the problem?

9. (a) How would an understanding of the economic and social history of the surrounding community be relevant to the organisation and management of a commercial enterprise?

   (b) The senior management of your company has expressed the opinion that there should be a social responsibility of managers. What do you understand by this and could you expect this view to be translated into policies and procedures within the organisation?

10. What are the characteristics of an effective work team? Describe briefly one training method by which an effective team can be developed.

11. One of your supervisors is consistently in trouble with his manager because his department always seems to be in a state of confusion. Work appears to be allocated on a haphazard basis; some people are overloaded, others have little to do. He does not produce information when required and he appears to be consistently harassed and pre-occupied in trying to solve the latest crisis. What steps can be taken to help him?

12. (a) Examine the role of tests in the employee selection process.
    (b) Briefly identify the type of tests which might be appropriate for selecting a bank cashier. Refer to the limitations of the tests you identify.
    (c) Describe the limitations of interviews in the selection process.

13. Write brief notes on *two* of the following:
    (a) job satisfaction;
    (b) job description;
    (c) periodic appraisal.

14. What is corporate planning, and why is it carried out? Describe and show the relationship between its different components at strategic, tactical and operational levels.

1.

> *Tutorial note.* This question is obviously trying to be 'topical' in the context of the UK in the late 1980s and early 1990s. The policy, planning and operating difficulties of state-owned enterprises have been well publicised over the past few years! Try to make a distinction between policy making, planning and operating, although the distinctions you make will inevitably be blurred.

Suggested solution

The UK government in the 1980s attempted to make nationalised industries act in a more profit-orientated and market-sensitive manner than in the past. This shift in requirement created a variety of policy, planning and operating difficulties, which would presumably be experienced in any other country where the government tried to achieve a similar change.

Policy

In a nationalised industry, where profitability is not a prime consideration, the objectives and policies of the organisation will usually be directed towards:

(a) providing a certain level of service to everyone who wants it, especially in key industries such as transport, electricity, postal deliveries and, in the past in the UK, gas supplies, water supply and telephone services;

(b) supporting other government policies, for example, on employment and regional development, by providing jobs in economically-depressed regions of the country.

Profit orientation and market sensitivity undermine the predominance of public service considerations, and a difficulty that arises for the nationalised industry's management is to reassess the industry's objectives and policies.

(a) The overall objective of the industry might now be any of the following: profit maximisation, or profit maximisation subject to certain minimum service requirements, or providing a service but with certain minimum requirements about efficiency of resource utilisation (as is the case with the National Health Service).

(b) The industry's management might be uncertain about whether the ultimate objective of the government is privatisation. Where privatisation is planned, the industry will need to be *more* market-sensitive than might otherwise be necessary.

(c) The industry's policy towards employment and regional development might be required to change. In the coal industry, for example, greater profit-awareness in the 1980s resulted in widespread pit closures, even though this created (and continues to create) high unemployment levels in economically depressed areas.

(d) Difficulties arise with employment policy, as suggested above, because the nationalised industry will be required to reassess its manning levels, recruitment and promotion policies. Employees should expect market rates of pay for working in a profit-orientated industry, but at the same time security of employment and 'carrying' weak staff might no longer be acceptable.

(e) Policy decisions about the quality of service provided, or the range of services, become more complex, because the industry's management will have to reassess the standards of service it is currently providing. In the case of the public transport industry, for example, management might have to assess its policy for maintaining certain routes or lines. Profit orientation might dictate significant closures.

Planning
Policy difficulties lead on to planning difficulties, and the problems for planning cover areas such as capital investment decisions, disinvestment, pricing and manpower.

(a) Most nationalised industries make large-scale capital investments, on which the return might be earned over a long time-scale. Greater profit-orientation will probably result in pressure for a quicker payback, higher returns and risk-avoidance. Schemes which would have been financially acceptable when profit-orientation was less strong might be doubtful investments if the need to earn a good return is paramount. When returns are uncertain and 'risky', a profit-orientated approach would be more likely to result in decisions not to invest. A difficulty that this creates is that the consequence of decisions *not* to invest now might not become apparent until much later, and the adverse effects on service of profit-orientated decision-making might not yet be apparent in the UK.

(b) Planning decisions by nationalised industries cannot be taken without making allowances for government wishes and public pressure. Although a government might pay lip service to 'the market', it might also impose certain requirements on nationalised industries that prevent it from taking market orientated decisions. Public pressure is also likely to be much stronger in the case of planning decisions by a nationalised industry than in the case of a private company. Decisions to build a nuclear power station, construct a tunnel link, develop an open-cast coal mine and so on almost always meet strong time-consuming public resistance.

(c) Pricing decisions might be restricted by monopolies legislation or public resistance to price rises from a monopoly industry. If the industry's prices are currently 'too low', it could be difficult to raise them for this reason.

(d) Planning to withdraw services, reduce service levels or disinvest, as mentioned earlier, will be difficult to make because of public expectations.

(e) Manpower planning will be plagued by difficulties of trying to establish a profit-orientated management. 'Old' managers might have to give way to younger managers, many recruited externally, but pay levels will have to be high enough to attract staff of a suitable calibre.

Operating
Many planning difficulties also become operating difficulties.

(a) Manpower and employee relations will be a particularly difficult problem. Trade unions and employees might be reluctant to accept the new profit-orientated approach, with the result that there might be trade union opposition or employee resistance to changes. It will also be difficult to introduce performance-related pay structures, which are often associated with market-orientation.

(b) To improve profit-orientation, there must be a better management information and control system. The task of creating a management accounting system and the other information systems that are needed could be complex and lengthy.

(c) Change is difficult to implement. It is one thing to pay lip service to profits but it is more difficult to put intentions into practice. Attitudes and ways of doing things have to be altered, and changes might be slow.

2.　In any organisation, there are pressures for uniformity and pressures for diversity. Uniformity is best achieved by means of a centralised authority, whereas diversity implies greater decentralisation for efficiency.

Factors affecting the extent of decentralisation are as follows:

(a)　*the requirement for uniform practices, products or policy.* In government, for example, there are certain aspects of services to the general public which need to be applied equitably. A person in one part of the country will expect treatment according to the same rules, in terms of, say, income support as a person in another part. Laws should ideally originate from one source and government policies need to be co-ordinated from the centre to provide a 'balanced' strategy.

(b)　*the need for control and the cost of mistakes which may occur.* If central management needs to keep a firm control over results in the organisation, especially in the situation where a mistake will be very costly, there will be greater centralisation of authority;

(c)　*the savings which might be made from a centralised system.* If centralisation involves the duplication of efforts and tasks, it will be more costly, whereas a centralised system might provide economies of scale;

(d)　*technology.* It has been suggested (eg by Joan Woodward) that the technology of an industry will affect the extent of decentralisation. In a survey of 100 manufacturing firms in Essex, she found that decentralisation of authority seems well-suited to mass-production enterprises (middle range technology) whereas decentralisation is more appropriate to jobbing industries (less advanced technology) and also continuous processing industries (more advanced technology). Computerisation of information systems at one time implied greater centralisation, because of the size and cost of mainframe computers, but the recent growth of micro-technology and on-line systems has meant that computer technology is no longer a hindrance to decentralisation;

(e)　*specialisation.* When an organisation needs specialised services which would be uneconomic to have duplicated in decentralised units, there will be specialist 'staff' departments under the control of 'head office'. For example, an organisation may have a central legal department, data processing department, or economics section;

(f)　*the diversity of the market.* Where an organisation deals with a widely-diversified market, decisions at the top by the senior management are likely to be uninformed, with an ignorance about 'local' conditions and special circumstances. Greater delegation and decentralisation of decision-making is likely to result in better decisions;

(g)　for a similar reason, *geographical dispersion* of the organisation is likely to create pressure for decentralisation with junior managers using their 'local' knowledge to make better decisions;

(h)　*the quality of middle and junior managers and the trust of senior managers in their subordinates.* If a senior manager does not trust the judgement of his subordinates, or the skill and ability of junior and middle managers, he will prefer to make decisions himself - to centralise authority. If middle and junior managers are experienced, or well-educated and with ability, they will want authority to be delegated and their superiors will be more prepared to allow such decentralisation to occur;

(i)　*the rate of change in the organisation.* Burns and Stalker, for example, argue that a formal organisation structure is not suited to conditions of change, when an 'organic' organisation structure, involving greater decentralisation of authority, would be more efficient;

(j) *different goals*. Lawrence and Lorsch have argued that an efficient organisation in a rapidly changing environment will be differentiated. Planning, for example, will be based on both long-term and short-term considerations. An R & D manager will look to the long-term and the introduction of new equipment and new products in the next four years, and a sales manager perhaps to the immediate problem of generating sufficient sales this year. Given a wide variety of problems and goals (long and short-term) there must be greater decentralisation of authority, with different managers concentrating on different goals;

(k) *the age and history of the organisation*. It has been suggested that a small organisation, if it grows, will go through a phase of entrepreneurial, centralised control, before a formal centralised structure will be created. As time progresses, there will be greater decentralisation of authority. When an organisation becomes very large, it may split up into a multi-structure organisation with many separate, autonomous divisions (eg a conglomerate group with many independent subsidiary companies);

(l) *the environment of the organisation, which may be legal and political, economic or social and cultural*. For example, there may be a general view in society as a whole that one organisation should be decentralised, whereas a different type of organisation should have centralised control. In the UK, for example, there is a 'cultural' view that subordinates should be given sufficient authority to do a worthwhile job, although central control should be maintained in some organisations such as the army.

3. (a) Quality control manager or product design engineer in a manufacturing company. Accounts staff, personnel department staff and marketing management in a commercial bank. (Note: most jobs in the branches of large clearing banks are 'line' rather than 'staff'.)

(b) A staff position is one where technical authority dominates. Staff positions are advisory and independent. A quality control manager cannot direct operations upon the shop floor, but if operations management does not heed his instructions, the consequences could be serious. The staff position always reports to senior management in such a way that it cannot be influenced or pressured by operations management. (In the same way, a production design engineer advises on new products, but does not have line responsibility for active production.)

(c) Staff positions differ because of their relationship and authority. An operations manager is not compelled to consult staff experts, nor to heed their advice. Equally, however, they are not accountable to the operations manager if things go wrong either as a result of the advice or as a result of ignoring it. Staff positions are independent. In a manufacturing environment, if quality control personnel reported to the production operations manager and were paid by him, there would be scope for manipulation of output performance at the expense of quality. To ensure that they always are consulted and their advice appreciated, they must be demonstratively good at their particular expertise.

(d) The basic limitations on the use of staff specialists are that they cannot enforce authority. A quality control expert or design specialist cannot insist that he is consulted, nor that his advice, if asked for, is followed.

Their advice may appear to conflict with the objectives of an organisation as seen by line managers. An operations production manager is always under pressure for output albeit within the parameters of the agreed quality control standards. The quality control area may increase the number of rejects or reworked items, creating the problem of under achieved production targets and loss of possible bonuses. Similarly, if a personnel manager asks for staff to be sent on training courses, their absence would put more workload on to the remaining line staff.

Staff specialists are often viewed as people who only see the world in black and white, and fail to see that the reality of the operations management is a world of kaleidoscopic grey. Conversely, in certain areas, such as taxation and legal counselling, the staff specialist will know that the answer may not be as clear cut as line management might like, with the result that they may have an image of being indecisive.

Culturally, staff functions are made up of a small group of specialists who work as a team of virtual equals. Line functions are very much a master and servant operation requiring skilful man-management. Staff managers often lack the man-management skills in that their pontificating frequently overlooks behavioural implications.

4. The basic features of management decision-making are the same, no matter whether a manager specialises in production, selling, purchasing or any other operating function. Similarly, the decisions of a production manager in a toy car manufacturing business are the same as the decisions of a production manager in a different type of manufacturing business.

If we assume that the production manager is fairly senior in the management hierarchy, but that a business manufacturing toy cars will be a fairly small organisation, it could be presumed that the production manager would be involved in strategic decision-making, budgeting and weekly or daily production planning and control.

Strategic planning decisions which the production manager might be involved with are:

(a) planning new products. Product research and design might be a specific responsibility of an 'engineering' manager, but the production manager would need to be consulted about operational considerations involving new product development and manufacture. Similarly, he would be involved in decisions to develop existing products, promotion methods, and the timing and duration of advertising or promotion campaigns.

(b) deciding capital expenditure plans. The production manager will make recommendations about capital expenditure on production fixed assets. Such decisions would include re-siting the production plant, introducing new production technology (eg to make a new range of toy cars, such as cars with microtechnology in their remote control system) or replacing worn-out existing plant.

(c) The quality of products is a key factor in the marketing mix. When a strategic decision is taken about the target market position for the organisation's toy cars, the choice of balance between quality and price will have to be made, and the production manager will be involved in this decision because he should be able to advise on what quality of output can be achieved with given production resources.

(d) Decisions to shut down a plant, or to 'rationalise' production so as to achieve lower costs or greater efficiency, are either strategic or 'budgeting' decisions. During the economic recession of the early 1980's, toy manufacturers suffered a sharp fall in sales and profits; survival might have depended on the success of management in pruning their production capacity and at the same time increasing productivity.

The production manager will be involved in production budgeting decisions. The production budget will be a plan of how many of each product should be made, what resources will be required to make them, and how much they will cost.

The resource utilisation budget will state the planned requirement for materials, labour and machine time. To determine these requirements, a decision must be made about standard rates of efficiency for material usage, labour productivity and machine operations. (Standard rates might be renegotiated annually with the work force as part of a pay and productivity arrangement.) A decision might be needed on second shift working, or overtime. The production manager might also be involved in deciding the appropriate levels of raw materials inventories, and the optimal size of batches, if the toy models are made by a batch production method.

Methods of working might be reviewed periodically, and improvements agreed by the production manager in consultation with trade union representatives.

Where limiting factors exist whereby some production resources place a constraint on what the business can make and sell, the production manager might need to decide whether to pay extra to overcome the production constraints (eg by suggesting that some work could be subcontracted, if this is technically feasible).

Within the framework of the budget, the production manager will be involved with weekly and day-to-day operating decisions. These will include production scheduling (deciding on output quotas, the allocation of different jobs to different groups, assigning priorities to jobs etc).

Operating decisions consist of putting plans into effect and control decisions. Control decisions might involve some strategic control (monitoring the success or failure of the organisation in achieving its strategic plans) but most control decisions will be at a 'tactical' (budgetary) or operational (day-to-day) level.

Budgetary control involves a comparison of actual results against the budget plan, and the highlighting of excessive variances which might indicate that control action is required. Control might then involve decisions about improving efficiency and labour productivity, controlling expenditure levels, postponing expenditure, reducing idle time improving capacity-utilisation of the plant, or quality control. Similar comparisons of actual results against production schedules might be carried out daily or weekly, involving control decisions by the production manager.

5. The marketing concept has been defined as a 'management orientation or outlook that accepts that the key task of the organisation is to determine the needs, wants and values of a target market and to adapt the organisation to delivering the desired satisfaction more effectively and efficiently than its competitors'.

In other words, customer needs are considered of paramount importance. Since technology, markets, the economy, social attitudes, fashions, the law etc. are all constantly changing, customer needs are likely to change too. The marketing concept is that changing needs must be identified, and products or services adapted and developed to satisfy them. Only in this way can a supplier hope to operate successfully and profitably (if the supplier of the goods or service is a profit-making organisation).

Some firms may be *product oriented* and others *sales oriented*, although a firm should be *marketing oriented* to be successful in the longer term.

(a) A product oriented firm is one which believes that if it can make a good quality product at a reasonable price, then customers will inevitably buy it with a minimum of marketing effort by the firm. The firm will probably concentrate on product developments and improvements, and production efficiencies to cut costs. If there is a lack of competition in the market, or a shortage of goods to meet a basic demand, then product orientation should be successful. However, if there is competition and over-supply of a product, demand must be stimulated, and a product-oriented firm will resort to the 'hard-sell' or 'product push' to 'convince' the customer of what he wants.

(b) A sales oriented firm is one which believes that in order to achieve cost efficiencies through large volumes of output, it must invest heavily in sales promotion. This attitude implies a belief that potential customers are by nature sales-resistant and have to be persuaded to buy (or buy more), so that the task of the firm is to develop a strong sales department, with well-trained salesmen. The popular image of a used car salesman or a door-to-door salesman would suggest that sales orientation is unlikely to achieve any long-term satisfaction of customer needs.

The marketing concept should be applied by management because it is the most practical philosophy for achieving any organisation's objective. A profit-making company's objective might be to achieve a growth in profits, earnings per share or return on shareholder funds. By applying the marketing concept to product design etc the company might hope to make more attractive products, hence to achieve sustained sales growth and so make higher profits etc.

Another implication of the marketing concept is that an organisation's management should continually be asking 'What business are we in?' This is a question which is fundamental to strategic planning too, and the importance of developing a market orientation to strategic planning is implicit in the marketing concept.

(a) With the product concept and selling concept, an organisation produces goods or services, and then expects to sell them. The nature of the organisation's business is determined by what it has chosen to produce, and there will be a reluctance to change over to producing something different.

(b) With the marketing concept, an organisation commits itself to supplying what customers need. As those needs change, so too must the goods or services which are produced.

If the marketing concept is to be applied successfully, it must be shared by all managers and supervisors in an organisation. 'Marketing is a force which should pervade the entire firm. It must enter into the thinking and behaviour of all decision-makers regardless of their level within the organisation and their functional area' *(Boyd and Massy)*. 'Marketing' in its broader sense covers not just selling, advertising, sales promotion and pricing, but also product design and quality, after-sales service, distribution, reliability of delivery dates and in many cases (eg the retailing industry) purchasing supplies. This is because customer needs relate to these items as well as more obvious 'marketing' factors such as sales price and how products are promoted.

Another way of expressing the important point made above is: 'most firms have a marketing or sales department, but the marketing concept should be shared by managers in every department'.

It could also be suggested that marketing should aim to maximise customer satisfaction, but within the constraints that all firms have a responsibility to society as a whole and to the environment. Not only is there the idea that 'high gross national product also means high gross national pollution' but also there is a need to make efficient use of the world's scarce and dwindling natural resources:

(a) some products which consume energy (eg motor cars, houses) should perhaps make more efficient use of the energy they consume;

(b) it may be possible to extend the useful life of certain products;

(c) other products might be built smaller, so that they make use of fewer materials (eg. products made using microtechnology).

6.
> *Tutorial note.* This question is obviously difficult for anyone unfamiliar with Japanese business systems, and the solution is therefore based on the knowledge that a candidate might have been expected to show in the examination.

Since the Second World War, the Japanese economy has become one of the strongest in the world, and Japan now exports vast quantities of goods to advanced industrial countries as well as to developing countries. The success of Japanese exports has been based on good quality products sold at a competitive price, manufactured mainly by large companies in Japan - eg Hitachi, Sony, Toyota etc. Large Japanese companies have clearly been successful at producing goods that excel in terms of price/quality and some of this success appears to stem from the organisational and cultural characteristics of the employer/employee relationship in these large firms.

In recent years some Japanese companies, warned about the threat of protectionist measures by other countries against their exports, have begun to establish overseas subsidiaries, and some of the aspects of the employer/employee relationship that exists in Japan have been imitated in the subsidiaries. These characteristics are as follows.

(a) The large Japanese firms promise lifetime employment ('Nenko') to their employees, and expect employees to remain with the company throughout their careers. This guarantee of employment provides unparalleled job security. It has been made possible in Japan for two reasons:

    (i) the continuous growth of the Japanese economy;

    (ii) the industrial system in Japan, whereby each large firm uses many small firms as sub-contractors/ suppliers. If the industry goes into a short-term recession, the large firm will cut off its small firm contracts, and the small firms suffer the job losses and unemployment. Employment within the large firms remains secure.

(b) Employees of large firms, committed to working for their company for life, become 'organisation men'. Their future prospects depend on the success of the company, and they seem to identify themselves with the company. The objectives of individuals and the company tend to be complementary whereas in other countries, such as the UK, individuals may have personal objectives which are inconsistent with the objectives of the organisation they work for. Strikes in large Japanese companies would be contrary to this work culture, and the companies have benefited from years of good 'industrial relations'.

(c) Since the large Japanese companies employ individuals for life, it is essential that the companies should show some concern for the welfare of employees and their families. The company adopts a benevolent and 'paternalist' approach to employees, providing benefits for families (eg when employees are ill or injured at work) and employees themselves (eg organising their annual holidays).

(d) Large Japanese companies succeed in attracting high-calibre recruits (whereas UK industry, for example, has not always been able to do so) but promotion is based on seniority. The 'rat-race' or 'dog-eat-dog' culture of individuals competing for promotion and recognition, which is apparent in Western cultures, is not nearly as strong in Japan. The effect of this might well have been to improve co-operation between managers and departments in Japanese companies, since individuals have nothing to gain by seeking a personal advantage over other managers in discussions and negotiations.

(e) The success of Japan has also depended on the attitude of employees to their work. Japanese employees appear to show a commitment to the work ethic, and a willingness to adapt readily to new technology. Although this is not unique to Japan (in the USA and West Germany the same attitude to work is common), the Japanese display these qualities prominently.

(f) Subsidiaries of Japanese companies, in countries such as the UK, cannot adopt the culture of Japan itself, but attempts have been made to introduce some of the qualities of Japanese culture into these overseas operations - eg in the UK Japanese companies like Nissan have attempted to eliminate the traditional antagonism between management and workers, with the introduction of no-strike agreements etc.

7. (a) Factors influencing decision to delegate:

    (i) the work load of the superior. There are physical and mental limitations to what one man can do;

    (ii) any specialised or technical knowledge which the subordinate might have, making him or her better-suited to handling certain tasks;

    (iii) the nature of the decisions which are involved. Decisions have been analysed (by Drucker) as having four characteristics:

        (1) the degree of *futurity* in the consequences of the decision. Decisions which either have a short-term effect or which can be reversed quickly are more suitable for delegation. In other words, where the cost of a wrong decision is high, authority should not be delegated;

        (2) the *impact* of the decision on the work of other departments, sections or people. Decisions should not be delegated if they will seriously affect the work of another manager of equal status. These decisions should be made by their common superior, who acts as co-ordinator;

        (3) the number of qualitative factors in the decision calling for the exercise of *judgement* by the manager. More complex qualitative factors in a decision would indicate the inadvisability of delegation;

        (4) 'general rules' or 'guideline decisions' or 'policy decisions' should be made by more senior managers;

    (iv) the skill, knowledge and attitudes of the subordinates will help to determine how much delegated authority they want to have and how much responsibility they are properly capable of undertaking;

    (v) the management philosophy of the organisation may encourage or discourage delegation;

    (vi) the geographical dispersion of subordinates and the rate of change in the environment. When subordinates are not in the same office or building, and the work is not readily formalised owing to the rate of change in the business environment, greater delegation should be provided by the organisation structure. On the other hand a rigid specification of organisation tasks (job structures) will restrict the boss's options about how much to delegate;

    (vii) work involving membership of committees should be handled by a manager with the status appropriate to the committee's membership;

(viii) some work demands the attention of a senior manager (eg dealing with important customers or managers at a very senior level in the organisation).

(b) Major barriers to delegation include:

(i) the superior's lack of trust in the subordinate. He may consider the subordinate incapable of doing the work well enough;

(ii) the superior's wish to retain control over even the most straightforward tasks;

(iii) the superior's fear that the subordinate will do the work better than he could himself;

(iv) the lack of a good relationship and communication between superior and subordinate;

(v) a rigidly-defined task structure for the organisation. In association with this, concern for 'status' and 'seniority' might result in an insistence that work of a certain 'status' should be done by a manager of corresponding rank;

(vi) the reluctance of the subordinate to accept responsibility (perhaps for fear of the consequences of failure).

8. *Barriers to effective personal communication*

(a) The employees might have different attitudes and perceptions arising out of the difference in their social and family background, educational background, political opinions, or age etc.

(b) There might be inter-personal dislikes, rivalries or jealousies which prevent free and open communication between the two employees. The result might be that they tend to communicate with each other, incompletely and inefficiently, through a third person. This would be a slow, inefficient and unsatisfactory communication system.

(c) The employees, intentionally or otherwise, might either try to communicate more information than the other can use, or transmit much irrelevant information.

(d) The employees, intentionally or otherwise, might make important errors or omissions in information they provide, so that the recipient is unable to understand what he is being told.

(e) Again, intentionally or otherwise, the employee receiving the information might simply not understand what he is being told. The use of technical jargon might be one problem, but slang and poor English are equally likely to cause communication problems.

There is a tendency for people receiving information to:
(i) hear what they want to hear; and
(ii) overlook or ignore what they don't want to hear.

(f) Evaluation of the message's recipient, the use of non-verbal signs and the emotions of the giver of the message might create serious barriers to communication.

SUGGESTED SOLUTIONS

Remedies to attempt to solve the problem

(a)   The major problem might be the seemingly irreconcilable differences in background between people. The remedy to this problem lies in man-management.

    (i)   One approach might be to encourage the person who feels 'inferior' or 'aggrieved' to lessen his sense of inferiority or grievance. Similarly, a person who feels 'superior' or 'contemptuous' of the other should be encouraged to treat the other person with more respect and regard.

    (ii)   The two employees must be persuaded to recognise the problem and their own contribution towards it. When each individual in private discussion accepts his own personal failings in the matter, it might be possible to bring them into a joint discussion about their problems.

    (iii)   In the early stages of finding a remedy, it might be necessary to encourage each individual separately. This might be done by:

        (1)   trying to get each individual to convey information to the other as unevaluated data so as to give the other a chance to make up his own mind;

        (2)   try to instil some 'warmth' and spontaneity into communications.

(b)   The department manager can also take a more procedural approach to some of the difficulties. He might institute a new set of guidelines or rules for the information system within the department.

    (i)   Communications between employees must be in simple English, avoiding jargon which is unfamiliar to everyone and slang expressions.

    (ii)   The recipient of information should let the giver know what he has done or proposes to do about it, to check that he has understood the message correctly.

    (iii)   The 'principle of redundancy' should be used for certain types of communication - a message should be repeated, preferably in two or more different ways, so that if it is not properly understood the first time, it will become more clear on repetition.

9.   (a)   In the terminology of systems theory, an organisation is an 'open' system which interacts with its environment; in other words, the environment will have an influence on the way the 'system' works, and the 'system' or organisation will also in its turn affect aspects of the environment.

The economic history of the surrounding community helps to provide an understanding of the current economic, social and cultural, legal and political environment. This point may be illustrated with several examples:

    (i)   A history of growth or contraction in the community's system of education will vary the 'pool' of skilled labour available for recruitment, and the organisation's requirements for training etc.

(ii)   If there is an economic history in the community of low growth and low productivity, management will need to account for this in their forward planning. The type of products for which there will be a substantial market demand will also depend on the past and current economic situation.

(iii)   The economic history of a community will help to explain its financial systems; for example, what are the institutions which exist to provide investment capital, and how might an organisation make use of them to raise extra funds?

(iv)   The history of price inflation in a community will be relevant to explaining the current state of markets in which the organisation operates.

(v)   The community history of industrial relations may help to explain current employee attitudes within the organisation. Even within a single country, some regions may be more 'militant' in their support for trade unions than in others. Multinational organisations may prefer to invest in a country with a history of good industrial relations than in one where strikes and disruptions have been a frequent part of the economic scene.

(vi)   The development of the tax system of the community will be relevant to an understanding of consumer demand (eg resistance to indirect taxation, such as VAT or excise duty or a purchase tax), employee motivation (eg high direct taxation may mean that there is little incentive to work harder for more pay) and the organisation's profitability (eg the rate of taxation on company profits).

(vii)   The social history of the community will help to explain the strength of certain attitudes and beliefs held by the community at large, for example towards ecology, the desirability of a career in industry etc.

(b)   The nature of social responsibility will depend on the type of organisation. A commercial organisation may exist to achieve a satisfactory return on its shareholders' capital, but it is widely believed that even in commerce a social responsibility exists and that managers should accept this responsibility as their own.

The improvement of the environment is an obvious example of such social responsibility: reducing pollution, preserving the landscape, re-cultivating derelict land etc. Products should meet certain standards of comfort, safety or utility without the need for legislation.

There are practical difficulties in converting social responsibility into a practical aspect of management:

(i)   Social and ethical targets must be set by senior managers in the organisation.

(ii)   Individual managers should be given delegated authority not only to achieve operating efficiency and better profits, but also to achieve social targets.

(iii)   Managers should be held individually responsible for the achievement of social as well as commercial results.

(iv)   To hold managers accountable, performance standards need to be established by which their success in terms of social responsibility can be measured.

(v) Managers need to be motivated to accept sound responsibility, perhaps by ensuring that rewards (eg pay and promotion) are based on this aspect of their work as well as on profitability and productivity achievements.

(vi) There should be a regular review of the success and efficiency of the system of social responsibility, in a *social audit.*

(vii) An awareness of social responsibility should permeate throughout the organisation, and means of creating this awareness might include employee reports and human asset accounting. If an organisation cares for its staff, the staff may care in turn for their environment, whereas an organisation cannot be socially responsible if it does not treat its own employees with care and concern.

10. Charles Handy in his book *'Understanding Organisations'* describes a contingency approach to analysing group effectiveness. The factors involved are the 'givens', which are the group, the group's task and the group's environment, the 'intervening variables', which are group motivation, the style of leadership and processes and procedures, and the 'outcomes', which are the group's productivity and the satisfaction of group members. Characteristics of an effective work team can be identified in all of these variables.

The group itself should contain a suitable blend of the individual skills and abilities of its members, so that the group has enough personnel to do its job, it has people with sufficient experience and skill and it combines the individual members in an effective way. A project team, for example, probably needs a person of ideas, a person of drive and energy, a logical evaluator of suggestions, a person who can do the detailed, routine work and a 'conciliator' who can bring individuals to negotiate and settle their differences.

The group's task must be clearly defined, otherwise it cannot be effective in carrying it out. The group should also be given the resources to do its job properly and, if necessary, it should have the authority to carry out certain actions which it considers necessary as part of its task.

If the task is a temporary one, the work group should be a temporary project team which will be disbanded when its job is done. If the task is a continuing one, the work group should be given a defined place and role in the formal organisation structure.

The group's environment refers to conditions of work. The characteristics of an effective work group in this respect are that members of the group should have ready contact with each other. An open plan office for the group might achieve this purpose. The group must also have easy and good contacts with other groups with which they work; inter-group conflicts will reduce the efficiency of every group involved.

The motivation of the group as a whole develops as a group norm. If motivation is good and positive, the group will try to be efficient and effective. Poor motivation will result in an ineffective group. It would not be true to say that participation by group members in decision-making is necessarily a characteristic of an effective group; however, participation, when it promotes a positive group motivation, will be a means toward group effectiveness.

The style of a group's leader also plays an influential role in determining group effectiveness. This style might be autocratic, democratic or laissez-faire. Likert distinguished between exploitive authoritative, benevolent authoritative, consultative authoritative and participative group management, and suggested that the latter type will promote a more effective group.

An effective work group will use well-designed processes and procedures. A formal group structure should not necessarily be rigid, but each member of the group should be aware of his or her own individual responsibilities and tasks.

The characteristics so far described should create outcomes which 'prove' the group's effectiveness. The effective group will be efficient in its work, if the work is continuous, or it will achieve its task, as defined in its terms of reference. At the same time, it should be expected that in a group which works well and accomplishes its tasks, the individual members will show a marked amount of job satisfaction.

Training can help to create an effective work group both by building up a group identity and also by showing other members how each individual thinks and reacts in various situation. Although group learning is not common in industry, it is used by various non-industrial organisations. 'T groups' is one name given to group training, in which a series of exercises is carried out. Each exercise will involve certain members of the group, and at the end of the exercise, other group members will be asked to comment on how the exercise was performed. These exercises and discussions enable individuals to understand how they react in a given situation and how these reactions appear to other people. This helps to develop an understanding of how members of a group inter-act and to suggest ways in which these interactions can be made to work more constructively.

11. | *Tutorial note.* You might have assumed that this question concerned leadership and leadership style. However, if you re-read it you will see that the supervisor's problem is more one of inadequate planning and control: work is allocated haphazardly, information is not produced when required, the supervisor reacts to events rather than prepares for them.

The problem concerns a supervisor's failure to plan adequately, control the activities of his staff, set targets and achieve results.

Possible reasons for this situation:

(a) the supervisor has received little or no training on how to plan and control;

(b) the organisation has not adequately communicated its objectives to its employees. As a result, the supervisor does not know what is required of him and where the activities of his department fit into the overall corporate plan;

(c) the department may be short-staffed or the subordinates unable to do anything more than routine tasks;

(d) the supervisor may not be suited to leadership.

The following facts should be obtained:

(a) details of the supervisor's background and performance ratings;

(b) details of the activities of the department. One would need to know what it is required to produce and when, and the importance of its output relative to other departments;

(c) details of the level and calibre of staff under the supervisor's control.

The supervisor should be given a counselling interview and asked to give his view of why his department is under-performing. He may point out that it is under-staffed (so deadlines cannot be met) or that some staff cannot be entrusted with difficult work (so that capable staff have to be overloaded). It may even be the case that he receives little or no guidance or encouragement from his superiors so that he ends up 'firefighting'.

Depending on the reasons identified for the failure of the department, the following remedies could be suggested:

(a) the supervisor could be sent for training on the importance of planning and control and the management techniques available;

(b) more and better staff;

(c) a revision of departmental duties so that its work becomes more manageable.

(d) greater involvement from senior management, particularly as regards (i) explaining objectives and the role of the department within the overall plan and (ii) being available to give advice and encouragement;

(e) transfer of the supervisor to a less demanding job.

A review of the situation after a few months would be made to see if the department is now being run efficiently. If the same problems persist, further training or a transfer may be necessary.

12. (a) Selection is mainly but not exclusively concerned with choosing the right person for the job requirements. Selection as a process concerns a number of interrelated activities in arriving at this choice, of which tests form only one part. The process attempts to discover the capability of the applicant to perform the duties involved. Tests can help in this process where the job requires capabilities which are amenable to the conditions of testing. The results of such tests can be used to predict performance of the task and therefore aid the selection process. However, if a direct relationship between ability in the test and ability in the job does not exist, the test will have little or no value.

(b) All tests should be based on the specific requirements of job performance. It is therefore essential firstly to carry out job analysis leading to a job description to provide the information on the most appropriate tests. For a bank cashier these might include:

(i) *Manual dexterity tests*
Counting bank notes quickly and accurately is an essential feature. Tests could be devised to examine how 'nimble-fingered' the applicant was. This could in turn involve:

(ii) *Field tests*
A 'mock up' of the counter with the normal arrangement of equipment where the applicant is given a random collection of coins and notes to count and record within a certain time.

(iii) *Mathematical tests*
The ability to perform a whole range of mathematical processes is an obvious requirement for a cashier and therefore would be a useful test of capability. These may be extended into:

(iv) *General intelligence tests*

Since the cashier is in constant contact with the public it is important that he or she should have a reasonable ability to converse with them on a wide range of subjects and be capable of keeping up with and understanding developments in banking practice and world and current affairs.

Limitations of selection tests:

(i) Since they are used to predict capability to perform a particular job the tests must only examine capabilities required in the job.

(ii) They must be reliable in that they only test the capabilities required.

(iii) They must be valid so that it could be demonstrated that their use as a selection criterion does accurately predict performance.

(iv) It must be remembered that under the stress of the selection process any applicant will not perform as well as he would do in normal conditions

(v) There must be a clear link between the test and the job that will be performed by the applicant.

(c) The limitations of interviews:

(i) They fail to provide accurate predictions of how well a person will perform in the job.

(ii) The information obtained about a candidate might not be relevant to whether or not the candidate would do the job well.

(iii) The opinion of one interviewer may differ from that of another, and because of the disagreement the wrong decision may be made.

(iv) The interviewer may make errors in judgement.

(v) The interviewer may bring his personal bias into the interview situation, eg approving automatically of public school and Oxbridge candidates.

(vi) It is very difficult to assess abstract qualities such as motivation or integrity in an interview.

(vii) The interviewer may have had little or no training in interviewing techniques and end up asking leading questions or doing all the talking.

(viii) The interviewer may be restricted by the need to give grades for certain factors, thus not allowing a clear assessment to be made.

(ix) A good interview will need time to develop. A hard-pressed manager interviewing a lot of candidates will be unable to allow enough time to each applicant.

13. (a) *Job satisfaction*

Herzberg advocates that satisfaction can only arise from a job. It will require challenge, scope and interest. Herzberg did not see the working environment as a satisfier or motivator, but purely as an eliminator of dissatisfaction. This theory is substantially in agreement with 'need theories' that regard 'self actualisation' as the highest goal of human behaviour at work.

Accountants and financial controllers illustrate the scope and interest aspect of job satisfaction. Job satisfaction for such executives will come from being treated as professionals, initiated at an early stage to make a valid input to the decision-making process. However, if treated as mere bean counters, rather like plumbers' mates, then they will be frustrated and either look for ways of expanding their position or intensifying their reports. A qualified accountant earning £30,000 p.a. will derive no satisfaction from being a pure book-keeper.

Satisfaction will depend also upon ability and tolerance. Obviously, the highly qualified professional will make high demands on a job to achieve his satisfaction threshold. Equally, a research scientist, committed to some project in the electronic or pharmaceutical industry, will be satisfied that he is progressing and be prepared to wait for success.

(b) *Job descriptions*

A job description is prepared from a job analysis of the job in question, and it will list:

(i) the duties of the job;
(ii) the responsibilities of the job holder;
(iii) the limits to the holder's authority;
(iv) the relationship of the job to other positions (especially to a senior manager and to subordinate employees);
(v) major tasks to be accomplished by the job holder.

Some job descriptions include:

(vi) objectives and expected results.
(vii) terms and conditions of employment.

The advantages of job descriptions are:

(i) for job evaluation:
    (1) a standard format for analysing jobs makes it easier for evaluators to compare jobs;
    (2) job descriptions focus attention on the job, not the job holder, and so help the job evaluation process;

(ii) in the recruitment of staff. Job descriptions help advertisers and interviewers, because they give an indication of the skills and other qualities required to do the job well;

(iii) helping new employees to understand the scope and functions of their jobs;

(iv) helping the organisation's managers to recognise weaknesses in the organisation's structure (eg overlapping areas of authority);

(v) identifying training needs for the job holder.

(c) *Periodic appraisal*

As part of management development and training, many firms operate a system of periodic management appraisal whereby supervisors sit down with their superiors and are appraised to assess their recent performance (usually over six or twelve months).

Performance appraisal schedules vary, but essentially they:

(i) outline what the individual has done over the period under review;

(ii) indicate any superlative performances, satisfactory performances and any defects;

(iii) indicate any major weaknesses which require correction or further training;

(iv) provide an opportunity for exchange of views between supervisor and subordinate, possibly forming the framework for further development.

To be really satisfactory, they have to be linked with a real policy of promotion from within. Given an employee's initial personnel record, and the period updates through the appraisal system, management should be able to select for promotion the technically capable good performers. Without such an obvious demonstration of internal promotion, the credibility of appraisals is considerably weakened.

A further advantage of such appraisals are that nobody is likely to get forgotten. It provides the chance for the lowest supervisor or manager to remind his superior that he is there and to ask why he is not moving up the ladder. It will draw attention to the employee and help him identify why he is not moving.

14. *Corporate planning*

Corporate planning is the ongoing process of planning a business

(a) identifying what business an organisation is in;
(b) identifying what its objectives should be;
(c) formulating strategic plans to achieve those objectives. The strategic planning period might be 5 or 10 years, or even longer;
(d) formulating budget plans within the longer-term corporate planning strategies and objectives;
(e) formulating operating plans to carry out budget plans and day-to-day activities;
(f) establishing policies, procedures and rules for the organisation.

In other words, it is the formulation of objectives at all levels of organisational activity.

The *reasons why* corporate planning is carried out are that:

(a) the organisation needs to look at the future, to identify its current direction and to decide how it may need to change direction in order to adapt to changes in the environment - it needs a sense of purpose, which takes into account possible threats and opportunities in the future; and

(b) the organisation has to pursue its chosen objectives in an efficient manner, co-ordinating its many components and tasks into a directed effort. Planning provides a framework within which the minutiae of business resources can be integrated.

The strategic component

The strategic component of corporate planning may be divided into three basic stages:

(a) *identification of the corporate 'mission', or 'purpose':* "What business are we in?" This is deceptively simple: in fact, it may necessitate a fundamental reappraisal of the organisation;

(b) *setting objectives.* Corporate objectives are the broad targets to which the firm as a whole directs its efforts: they should be regularly refined as the environment changes, performance feedback is obtained etc. Objectives might be related to finance, market position, product development, technology, employment or public responsibility;

(c) *strategic planning* - formulation of means to reach objectives. This will involve identification of the purpose of organisational functions, the nature of the environment and the strengths and weaknesses of the organisation itself. The organisation will then be able to decide where its best options lie for fulfilling its objectives.

The tactical component

Tactical planning is the next 'stratum' of planning, at functional/departmental level. It develops strategic plans in more detail, by considering:

(a) which alternative courses of action, within the chosen strategy, the organisation should take. Detailed options will be sought, evaluated and selected, using modelling, forecasting, market research etc;

(b) how the resources of the organisation can be used effectively and efficiently in the accomplishment of strategic plans: eg how to allocate resources between different functional activities, how to price a new product etc;

(c) in the pursuit of effectiveness, what performance or budgetary targets should be set: the basic aims, criteria and standards of control systems for operational activities;

(d) formulation of policies - guidelines for response to a range of standard or recurrent eventualities. These guarantee a consistency of response, and save time on decision-making in routine situations.

The operational component

Operational planning is designed to ensure that specific tasks are carried out effectively and efficiently within the defined framework of strategic and tactical plans. Tactics 'harden' into detailed, quantified plans, including:

(a) procedures - a chronological sequence of actions required to perform a given task;

(b) rules - specific, definite courses of action that must be taken in a given situation;

(c) programmes - co-ordinated groups of plans, procedures, etc;

(d) budgets - formal statements of expected results, set out in numerical terms, and summarised in monetary values. Budgets are the 'nitty gritty' of corporate planning, used to allocate resources, set standards and timescales, and compare plan with actual performance.

INDEX

INDEX